RED INK
WHITE LIES

RED INK
WHITE LIES
The Rise and Fall of Los Angeles Newspapers 1920-1962

Rob Leicester Wagner

Dragonflyer Press
Upland, California

COVER

Daily News photographer Cliff Wesselman, standing at far right, uses a remote shutter release to photograph the night editorial crew in 1943. From left, sitting: unknown, Herbert ("Chubby") Maas, Les Leslie, Tom Higgs, W.W. Ferguson, and Milt Phinney. Standing from left: First four unknown, Jack Cravens, Sam Patrick, and John Beekman. (courtesy Jack Cravens)

Published by Dragonflyer Press
876 North Mountain Avenue, Suite 100
Upland, California 91786-4166 USA
www.dragonflyerpress.com

Library of Congress Card Number: 00-101000

Cataloging in Publication Data

Wagner, Rob, 1954-
Red ink, white lies : the rise and fall of Los Angeles newspapers 1920-1962 / Rob Leicester Wagner. -- 1st ed.
p. cm.
Includes bibliographical references and index.
ISBN: 0-944933-80-7

1. American newspapers--California--Los Angeles --History--20th century. 2. Journalism-- California--Los Angeles--History--20th century. 3. Jounalists--California--Los Angeles. 4. Newspaper publishing--California--Los Angeles-- History--20th century. I. Title.

PN4739.C2W34 2000 071.94'94
QBI00-396

Printed in the United States of America

To my parents, Jill and Howard Wagner

Contents

Acknowledgments

Six years ago I had the good fortune to strike up a friendship with Aaron Dudley, who had been an assistant city editor at the old *Daily News*. At lunch he would tell stories about newsgathering and the colorful wars between the city's daily newspapers during the 1930s and '40s. It occurred to me that these wonderful stories would be lost forever if they weren't recorded. So, from these occasional lunches, the seeds of this book were planted.

Aaron Dudley is the perfect subject to interview for this kind of book. He is kind and fair in his assessment of the men and women he competed against while covering the biggest stories in Los Angeles. He was patient with my questions and he directed me to dozens of people who spent most of their careers at newspapers in Los Angeles and its suburbs. He trusted me with the roster of the Old Farts Society, a loosely-knit organization of old newspaper, television, and publicity men who meet monthly. I owe a great deal to Aaron for his quiet instruction.

Alan Hensher, a former copy editor for the Baltimore *Sun* and the Los Angeles *Herald-Examiner*, assisted me in turning these stories into a publishable book. His line editing skills are unparalleled by any editor I know. He possesses vast knowledge of the Los Angeles newspaper industry in its heyday, and he is particularly erudite in the history of the *Daily News*. I also owe a debt of gratitude for his generous offering of notes of interviews he conducted in the 1960s and early '70s of Los Angeles newsmen who are since long gone.

My friend and colleague, Richard Gray, whom I met while I was a cop reporter on the old Ontario (California) *Daily Report*, also assisted in editing the manuscript. He kept me focused on the message I was determined to deliver.

Dace Taube, curator of the Regional History Center at the University of Southern California, allowed me free and total access to the daunting *Examiner* clip files, which also included the *Herald & Express* clips dating from 1931.

Octavio O. Olvera, with the Department of Special Collections at the University of California, Los Angeles, allowed me access to the *Daily News* clip files and assisted me in locating photographs of the *Daily News*.

Carolyn Cole, senior librarian of the photo collection at the Los Angeles Public Library, offered valuable assistance in locating photographs from the *Herald-Examiner* and the Security Pacific National Bank collections.

Assisting me with locating hard-to-find newspaper microfilm was Jean M. Griffing, project librarian for the California Newspaper Project at the University of California, Riverside.

At the Ontario City Public Library, the staff at the reference desk helped me navigate through thousands of feet of newspaper microfilm. Staff members are:

Rachel Marquez-Morales, Paul Johnson, Debbie Torrance, Linda Engelke, Joanne Boyajian, Ron Nelson, Gary Friedman, Joan Jordan, Heather Corfee, and James Augur.

Providing me with unique insight into media coverage of the African American community, particularly black officers in the Los Angeles Police Department, was police Sgt. John Thomas. John is a leading authority on the history of African Americans in the LAPD. Naturally, I owe my greatest thanks to the newsmen and women who invited me into their homes and spent considerable time on the telephone with me to make this book possible. They are:

Leo Batt (the *Mirror*), Nick Beck (United Press International), Jack Cravens (the *Daily News*), Cliff Dektar (the *Mirror*), Will Fowler (the *Examiner* and the *Herald & Express*), Nieson Himmel (the *Herald & Express* and the *Times*), Lucian Haas (the *Daily News*), Norman ("Jake") Jacoby (City News Service), Jack Jones (the *Daily News* and the *Times*), Jim Murray (the *Examiner* and the *Times*), Roy Ringer (the Huntington Park *Bulletin*, the *Daily News,* and the *Mirror-News*), Kendis Rochlen (the *Mirror*), Margaret Boutyette Scott (the *Examiner*), Rockey Spicer (the Greater Los Angeles Press Club), Coy Watson, Jr. (Acme Newspictures, the *Daily News*, and the *Herald & Express*) Delmar Watson (Acme Newspictures and the *Mirror*), Harry Watson (Acme Newspictures, the *Daily News*, and KTTV television), and Paul Weeks (the *Daily News*, the *Mirror*, and the *Times*).

Margaret ("Marne") Richardson Kaplan, granddaughter of James H. Richardson, came through at the eleventh hour to provide photographs of her grandfather.

Carolyn Hayes Uber and Tina Littell at Dragonflyer Press shepherded the manuscript through its publishing stages and demonstrated confidence in this project. Without them this book never would have been a reality.

My daughter, Selena, worked much of the time as my assistant. She took and transcribed notes during my many interviews. She also helped me scroll through newspaper microfilm. And lastly, my warm appreciation to my wife, Deniece, who read my manuscript and provided much needed support.

Rob Leicester Wagner

The Players

THE DAILY NEWS: It was originally founded in 1923 by Cornelius Vanderbilt Jr. as a clean penny paper that avoided scandal reporting. Its aim was to provide wholesome news to families. Vanderbilt bungled the operation and the ailing paper fell into the hands of E. Manchester Boddy. The new publisher embraced the New Deal after Franklin D. Roosevelt was elected president and the paper remained the city's only Democratic voice over three decades. After a series of ownership changes in the early 1950s, it folded in 1954. The plant, which still stands, is located at Pico Boulevard and Los Angeles Street.

THE EVENING EXPRESS: It was founded in 1871. During the first two decades of the 20th century it had the distinction of being the city's oldest daily newspaper. It was purchased in 1900 by Edwin Earl and earned a reputation for pursuing Progressive causes. It was sold in 1919 to F.W. Kellogg and Edward Dickson. By 1931, the paper was sold to William Randolph Hearst and merged with the *Evening Herald* to become the *Herald & Express*. Dickson retired from journalism when the paper was sold. The plant was located at 236 South Hill Street.

THE EVENING HERALD: The paper debuted in 1873 and became an instant rival to the *Evening Express*. It was home to a number of celebrated journalists including the husband and wife team of William Ivan ("Ike") St. Johns and Adela Rogers St. Johns. Its offices at 128 South Broadway were popular with the public for its massive windows that allowed passersby to view the running presses. William Randolph Hearst purchased the paper in 1922 and moved its offices to 1243 Trenton Street. It merged in 1931 with the *Evening Express.*

THE EVENING HERALD & EXPRESS: The flashy scandal sheet was a result of the 1931 merger of the *Evening Herald* and the *Evening Express*. The newspaper became the template for Hollywood film depictions of tabloid journalism. It boasted of having the city's first woman city editor, Agness Underwood. It's credited for giving sensational names for murder cases, such as the "Black Dahlia" homicide in 1947. It merged with the *Examiner* in 1962 to become the *Herald-Examiner*.

THE EVENING RECORD: It was founded in 1895 by E.W. Scripps. By the end of World War I, it shifted toward advocating Socialist causes under editor Henry B.R. Briggs and Burton Knisely. The newspaper, tucked away on Wall Street near Skid Row, was unabashed in its advocacy journalism and encouraged a literary approach to writing. LeRoy Sanders and Zack Farmer assumed ownership in 1933. It was renamed the *Post-Record*. In January 1935, a controlling interest in the paper was purchased by *Daily News* publisher E. Manchester Boddy. It eventually merged with the *Daily News* to become the *Evening News*. By 1940, the old *Record* had been completely absorbed by the *Daily News*.

THE EXAMINER: The leading morning newspaper in Los Angeles for five decades, it was founded in 1903 by Hearst as a union-friendly answer to the Los Angeles *Times*. It later abandoned its alliance with unions. It attracted from around the country the top newsmen and women of the day. It was an early pioneer in photojournalism and its Sunday reading supplements. It also was the best newspaper in covering crime and Hollywood scandals, especially under the leadership of city editor James H. Richardson. Today, it is known primarily for its fascist leanings and home front campaigns against Japanese Americans and Mexican Americans during World War II. Its offices were located on Broadway, just south of Fifth Street, and then moved to Broadway and Eleventh Street.

THE MIRROR: Founded in 1948 by Norman Chandler to attract the afternoon and commuter market, the *Mirror* was a remarkably different newspaper than its sister publication, the *Times*. It covered the ethnic minority community, conducted investigative journalism of the city's sacred cows, and provided a liberal bent in its news coverage. When the *Daily News* died, the *Mirror*, housed in the *Times* building, absorbed its masthead to become the *Mirror-News*. The newspaper was killed off in 1962 with the *Examiner* in an agreement with the Hearst Corporation to allow the *Times* the morning market and the *Herald & Express* the afternoon field.

THE TIMES: Purchased by Harrison Gray Otis in 1886, its solid Republicanism and anti-union stance prevented it from becoming a significant journalistic voice for many years. In its early years under Harry Chandler it was a booster of the Los Angeles lifestyle. Not until the late 1950s, under the helm of Otis Chandler and Nick B.Williams, did the *Times* shift from being identified as among the ten worst daily newspapers in the country to one of the best. By the early 1960s, its reputation in national and international reporting was firmly planted. Its main offices are located at First and Spring streets.

Introduction

I.

It was the best night to be liquored up. The saboteurs had been banished from the plant. The naysayers had been proven wrong. And the *Illustrated Daily News* was about to have its first scoop. The *News'* editorial, composing, and pressroom staff had put to bed the first issue of the *Daily News*. Spies, who had been hired by rival papers to plant stories to tarnish the *Daily News'* effort to publish a "clean" newspaper, had been discovered and bounced from the building. The loyalists remaining had been tapped $3 each for a case a gin. The celebration began.

Marching from the newsroom to the pressroom, the drunken lot sang, "*Daily News, Daily News*, first on the street, got the *Examiner* and *Times* beat!" The *Daily News* scooped the rest of the Los Angeles field on 3 September 1923 with stunning pictures of the Tokyo earthquake. And the moment the chorus died from the lips of the staff its refrain was never heard again. Another scoop would be a long time in coming as the newspaper pitched and weaved like a badly beaten prizefighter trying to stay on his feet. The *Daily News* managed to stand for thirty-one years. And its entry into the Los Angeles newspaper game marked the city's exposure to a new kind of journalism that had national and international news play second fiddle to intense local coverage.

Los Angeles journalists, politicians, and police were an incestuous lot from the 1920s through the early postwar era. During a period of more than forty years, the journalism field was a mixed bag of responsible, ethical newsmen and women and fascists, Communists, crooks, thugs, and opportunists. News veterans of New York's Park Row and the breezy, battle-scared Chicago newspaper wars built the foundation of local journalism. But Prohibition spawned corruption among reporters and editors, and the thinly veiled fascist agenda of William Randolph Hearst made suspect the principles of giving a voice to the voiceless in the tradition of Nellie Bly and Richard Harding Davis.

Los Angeles was a breeding ground for this eclectic collection of journalists. By 1920, Los Angeles had become a cosmopolitan metropolis. Angelenos reveled in the fact that their town had passed San Francisco that year to become California's largest city with 506,676 souls and ranking the tenth largest city in the country. Just the year before William Andrews Clark formed the Los Angeles Philharmonic. The city was only one of three in American history to boast having two orchestras. With Harry Chandler as the city's biggest booster, L.A. advertised heavily, virtually begging small-towners and big city dwellers alike to resettle in their city. And Americans were only too happy to come. During the 1920s, 2 million people arrived in the state with 1.2 million calling Los Angeles County their home and about half that number settling within the Los Angeles city limits. In the city 15,500 African Americans lived with the number climbing to nearly 20,000 in 1930. The number of Latinos living in Los Angeles that same year was 368,000.

The city couldn't issue building permits fast enough. In 1918, an estimated 6,000 new permits were issued. That number leaped to 37,000 by 1921. In 1923, new building permits peaked at 62,548. *Los Angeles Realtor* magazine reported that year that about 25,000 homes were constructed and sold to families to complement the nearly 400,000 residences already existing. The city's growth in 1920 contributed to California's stature as one of the wealthiest states in the country as state residents paid $37.2 million in income taxes, third in the country behind New York ($214.6 million) and Illinois ($83.2 million). Part of the state's wealth rested in its tremendous spurt of agricultural growth between 1910 and 1920 when 2 million acres of prime agricultural land was added to an existing 27 million acres. In 1919, the state's citrus crop brought in $75 million in revenue. Following the cultivation of oranges and lemons were rice, which brought in $73.2 million from 2.3 million acres of crops.

While the success of citrus and wheat crops was a significant factor in the state's wealth, Angelenos were more concerned about the city's burgeoning traffic system. In 1920 automobile ownership statewide hit 492,000 passenger cars and 24,437 trucks. Seven years later there were 560,136 passenger cars and 76,000 trucks just in Los Angeles County. And the county paved 130 miles of roads between 1917 and 1927 at a cost of $24 million. Along with the grading and paving came the construction of fourteen reinforced concrete bridges.

So other than sunshine, a mild climate, and the beckoning Pacific Ocean, what brought people to the West Coast, and, specifically to Los Angeles? At the dawn of the second decade of the 20th century, Los Angeles was far enough away from just about any town and city of consequence for an individual to get lost in. One's personal conduct was more often than not; say in Paterson, New Jersey, or Atlanta, Georgia, judged, even in the 1920s, by 19th century values. After all, adults in the 1920s were born either before or during the Victorian Era. Los Angeles wiped out those Victorian standards. Being 3,000 miles away from home but still in the United States with all its modern conveniences allowed individuals a certain amount of freedom not found in their native states. Decades later *Times* columnist Jim Murray observed in his autobiography: "L.A. was like a perpetual Elks convention. Everyone regarded himself as cut off from the eyeshot and earshot of people he or she cared about. It had a way of doing away with inhibitions. It also had a way of making you raise families on your own. There was no nuclear family to share the upbringing."

The motion picture industry also helped the city's growth with its emphasis on the infant, but growing star system. Douglas Fairbanks, Mary Pickford, Charlie

Chaplin, Greta Garbo, and Rudolph Valentino established a cult of personality and mores not known before.

Los Angeles County also was an innovator in municipal government. It was the first in the state to have a full-time public defender's office. In the 1920s it had the only district attorney's office with a fulltime investigation division. The city's library was the envy of every municipal-paid librarian in the state. And the city's school system was far ahead of its time, teaching immigrants in many languages. The city's school system also operated adult schools and popularized the use of junior high schools. And at the beginning of the decade alone there were 350 churches with every denomination conceivable inside the city's limits.

Wide-open plains, deserts, and mountain regions fueled land speculation. The oil boom of the 1920s brought Midwesterners by the thousands to Los Angeles, Huntington Park, Signal Hill, Long Beach, and a handful of other communities. For a modest investment, anyone with courage—or stupidity, for that matter—could become an oil entrepreneur. Money could be had. Ordinary folks were becoming rich, although it was for a very short period of time. When word reached the Midwest and the East that land in Huntington Beach could be had for the price of a set of encyclopedias, the plain folk rushed to Southern California in droves. Door-to-door salesmen would entice customers by offering a deed to a small portion of land near the beach. The land turned out to be a mere sliver and not as close to the beach as they were led to believe. These soon became known as "encyclopedia lots." While customers were misled about the proximity of the lots to the ocean, underneath lay rich pools of oil.

Lots may have been saturated with oil but it was up to the press and local businessmen to get the word out to potential investors. And oil was just a small part of the lure. There were support services and the growing job market to attract people to Southern California. As expected, Harry Chandler was in the thick of it. He, with other members of the business community and with funding from the county, formed the All-Year Club to brag about the Southland's year-round pleasant weather. Tourists were in the habit of visiting the state during the winter months but thought the summers too hot as temperatures climbed into the triple digits. The All-Year Club began an advertising campaign that guaranteed summer tourists that they could sleep under a blanket nine out of the ten days they spent in Southern California. It was a slight exaggeration before the advent of air-conditioning, but the power of the printed word couldn't be denied. The Club advertised in fifty daily and twenty Sunday newspapers during the 1920s, then in nearly eighty papers by 1930. The Club's advertising in 1926 alone had touched an estimated 12 million people. And that was strictly the Club's efforts. The *Times* complemented the drive to bring in new residents with its own advertising campaign and news stories promoting the benefits of Southern California living. It wasn't uncommon for *Times* columnists Harry Carr and Lee Shippey to join in the promoting fray.

II.

Los Angeles had been a rough-and-tumble news town long before the *Daily News* began publishing in 1923, but its entry into the field heightened the intensity of competitive local journalism. Pitted against the newcomer were two Hearst papers. The morning *Examiner*, founded in 1903 by William Randolph Hearst ostensibly to provide a voice for labor, quickly lost touch with the workingman to focus on staunchly Republican and anti-Bolshevik causes. The paper had cemented its reputation as a thorough, lively publication with Fred Eldridge as managing editor. The *Evening Herald*, purchased in 1922 by Hearst, appealed strictly to lower class blue-collar readers, serving up a steady diet of crime, sex, and scandal. Its saucy reputation was enhanced by managing editor Wes Barr and city editor James H. Richardson, two men who could have stepped off the screen from any newspaper movie featuring Lee Tracy, the prototypical Hollywood version of the tough-talking, cigar-chomping newsman.

Competing against the *Examiner* in the morning was the *Times*, which couldn't have done a better job at promoting the Southern California lifestyle if it had been on the Chamber of Commerce payroll. The *Times*, managed by Harry Chandler, who had cut his teeth on the administrative side of news papering, envisioned his role on the Southern California landscape as encouraging the winter snowbirds to abandon the likes of Chicago, Detroit, and New York for the Southland's sunny climate.

Rounding out the afternoon field was the *Evening Express*. Owned by the progressive Edward A. Dickson, it was considered a leading journalistic voice at the turn of the century and through the world war, but it grew increasingly tired and lazy by the close of the 1920s. The much smaller E.W. Scripps-Canfield-owned *Record* delighted in its rabble-rousing and attacks on the Los Angeles establishment. Depending the varying mood of any newsman or woman, the *Record* was either the only honest voice in Los Angeles or the most incompetent rag ever published.

The *Daily News* would be the city's sixth major daily newspaper. The fact that the city of a half-million inhabitants could sustain six dailies was testament to the varying backgrounds and voracious appetite of the reading community.

The *Herald*, the *Express*, the *Examiner*, the *Daily News*, and the *Record* reaped the benefits of the *Times'* boosterism with increased advertising revenue and circulation, but the papers' upper managements couldn't bear to participate in the hucksterism. Comprised of newsmen who rose through the ranks of the editorial department, the thought of championing the lifestyles of Angelenos was too commercial. Not so for Harry Chandler.

Chandler was born in 1864 in New Hampshire and came to Los Angeles in 1883 to relieve a lung condition. He briefly clerked in the *Times'* delivery room before moving up the administrative ladder. He was promoted to circulation manager and later to business manager. He and *Times* publisher Harrison Gray Otis were inseparable. It would stand to reason that he would marry the boss' daughter. He married Marian Otis, one of Otis' three daughters, in 1894. And it would stand to reason that he would one day be publisher of the *Times*. Chandler took over the *Times* publishing duties in 1917. He lived relatively simply and never drank. While tall and imposing, he possessed a baby face, but it never hindered him from bending the will of lesser men. An old guard Republican, Chandler continued his father-in-law's drive to crush organized labor and was the principal figure in developing the San Fernando Valley. He invested heavily in paper and timber mills, ranching, and water development. He also owned a huge chunk of acreage in Mexico.

A champion of the workingman was never part of Chandler's resume. And since Chandler never sullied his social and professional environment with the ink-stained wretches of the newsroom, he saw no conflict in delighting eastern residents with tales of paradise in Southern California. He demanded that water be brought from the Owens Valley to a thirsty L.A. He supported bond issues that would fund the infrastructure of the city. And he pushed for zoning that would attract business and boost tax revenues. Naturally, water, bonds, and zoning variances boosted his own holdings as well. But what was good for Harry Chandler and the *Times* was good for the city and county of Los Angeles. By the time of his death in 1944, his fortune was believed to be about $1 billion.

Chandler's hunger to bring eastern residents to Los Angeles and Hearst's insatiable appetite to sell papers in effect brought the tabloid mentality to Los Angeles. Given the varying tastes, education, and sensibilities of the city's reading public, it was inevitable that tabloid journalism would make its mark there.

The tabloid, more or less, was a natural progression of the yellow journalism founded by Joseph Pulitzer and William Randolph Hearst in the last quarter of the 19th century. The Hungarian-born Pulitzer desperately wanted to be a soldier when he was a young man but was turned down not only by his native country but England and France as well. In the United States during the Civil War, both the Northern and Southern armies had no compunction in enlisting foreign-born soldiers. Pulitzer was recruited to join the Union Army. After his discharge, he became a reporter in St. Louis, ultimately becoming owner and publisher of the St. Louis *Post-Dispatch*. In 1883 he purchased the moribund New York *World* from financier Jay Gould. He served his readers in St. Louis and New York sex and scandals using monstrous headlines and lurid photographs to illustrate the text. The transformation of these two papers under Pulitzer turned journalism on its ear.

But it was Hearst, perhaps the greatest imitator of all, who made yellow journalism a lasting standard in the industry. Born in 1863 an only child to George and Phoebe Hearst, young William was an indulged boy who had a wild streak. His father was a California prospector and U.S. Senator and his mother a woman both feared and worshipped in California society. George Hearst owned the San Francisco *Examiner*, but after his election to the senate in 1886 he turned the paper over to twenty-three-year-old William. On 4 March 1887, the masthead of the *Examiner* listed William as "Proprietor." Before William assumed control of the *Examiner* he spent a year learning the craft of journalism at Pulitzer's *World*. The *Examiner* soon became a newspaper built in the *World's* image. In 1895, Hearst purchased the New York *Journal* for a paltry $180,000. At both papers, Hearst demanded the stories be written with excitement and energy. He wanted his editorials to have a strong point of view and leave the wishy-washy approach to his competitors. He also demanded that dramatic illustrations be used to bring life to the tiny type.

Early indications that illustrations would dramatically alter news reports occurred in 1897 when the U.S. teetered on the brink of war with Spain. The *Journal* sent reporter Richard Harding Davis and western illustrator Frederick Remington to Cuba. Davis was the original Arrow collar man. He was handsome and dashing. He wrote for the Philadelphia *North American* and *Inquirer* in the 1880s before coming to New York. For the New York *Sun* and *Journal* he reveled in sensational story telling, dramatizing stories with poetic license that would become a standard for New York newspaper reporters. In 1897, he wrote a series of articles detailing the excesses of Spanish rule in Cuba. Remington left Cuba and returned to New York leaving Davis behind. In February 1897, Davis met Señorita Clemencia Arango on board the steamer *Ollivette*. During dinner she told Davis that she and two other women were being expelled from Cuba due to their sympathy for the rebels. The three women had been strip-searched at their homes before leaving for the dock, then searched again at the dock and later stripped and searched aboard the *Ollivette*. On 10 February Davis filed a report from Tampa, Florida, that was published in the 12 February editions of the *Journal*. On the front-page the headlines screamed: "Does Our Flag Shield Women?" "Indignities Practiced by Spanish Officials On Board American Vessels" and "Richard Harding Davis Describes Some Startling Phases of the Cuban Situation—Refined Young Women Stripped and Searched by Brutal Spaniards While Under Our Flag on the Ollivette."

Accompanying Davis' dispatch was a Remington illustration sketched in New York. It displayed an attractive young woman with a bared backside while her clothes were being gone through by two leering Spanish officials. Davis' story created a stir in New York and the illustration helped boost circulation for that day. When Arango arrived in New York she was startled to see her ordeal played in the manner presented by the *Journal*. She pointed out that she was strip-searched not by male Spanish soldiers or officials but by matrons. Davis noted that nowhere in his story did he report that men conducted the searches. While Hearst, Davis, and Remington later felt vindicated when several women came forward to report they were strip-searched by men, the inaccuracy of the initial report was gleefully attacked in the *World*. But it hardly mattered. Readers talked only of the *Journal* story and the 12 February editions enjoyed a huge circulation boost.

The strip-search story only served as a prelude to the power of yellow journalism. When an explosion sank the *Maine* and killed hundreds of sailors in the Havana Harbor on 15 February 1898, journalists, including those from the *Journal*, recommended caution in speculating the cause of the disaster. Hearst had other ideas. When he learned of the explosion, he called the *Journal* city desk and asked the editor on duty what other stories were to be played on the front page. When the editor replied "just the other big news," Hearst exploded that there was no other big news and the sinking of the *Maine* meant war. Two days later the *Journal* was banging the war drum with such headlines as "War? Sure!" Coverage of the Spanish-American War, soon to become the *Journal's* war, established a template for the next century of how journalists were to cover significant events.

After thirty-five years of this type of journalism, newsmen and women at competing papers were amused when Hearst issued a bulletin in 1933 that established editorial guidelines for his newsrooms across the country:

1. Make a paper for the nicest kind of people for the great middle class. Don't print a lot of dull stuff that people are supposed to like and don't.
2. Omit things that will offend nice people. Avoid coarseness and a low tone. The most sensational news can be told if told properly.
3. Make your headlines clear and concise statements of interesting acts. They should answer the question: What is the news? Don't allow copyreaders to write headlines that are too smart or clever to be intelligible.
4. The front page is your forum. Put important items and personal news about well-known people there. Sometimes condense a big story to go on the first page rather than run it longer inside the paper.
5. Nothing is more wearisome than mere words. Have our people tell stories briefly and pointedly. Let people get the facts easily. Don't make them work at it.
6. Please instruct copyreaders to rewrite long sentences into several short ones. And please try to educate the reporters to write short sentences in the first place.
7. Photographs of interesting events with explanatory diagrams are valuable. Make every picture worth its space.
8. If you cannot show conclusively your own paper's superiority, you may be sure the public will never discover it.

Hearst's guidelines are commendable but were laughable in the late 1930s, and in wartime Los Angeles. These guidelines were often pushed aside to promote a right-wing political agenda. The Hearst press, and that included the Los Angeles *Examiner* and the *Herald & Express*, demanded 100 percent Americanism from its readers. Not seventy-five percent. Not fifty percent Americanism. Hearst editors and reporters in both the news columns and editorial pages, as Japanese Americans and Mexican Americans discovered during wartime, clubbed anything less than 100 percent.

Yet Los Angeles was home to such journalism and there was an audience for such news. A six-newspaper town of the size of Los Angeles was a rare thing. No city outside of New York City could boast of such a choice for the town's inhabitants. In 1920 there were 2,061 general circulation daily newspapers operating in the United States for a combined total circulation of 27,699,140. California ranked seventh in total readers with 1.3 million people reading thirty-seven morning papers and ninety-seven evening editions. In 1920 Los Angeles, the *Evening Herald* led the daily newspaper field with a net paid circulation of 134,687. The *Examiner* followed with 92,754 daily subscribers with its Sunday edition attracting 178,807 readers. The *Times* was the No. 3 paper with a daily circulation of 86,042 and 122,269 Sunday readers. Rounding out the field were the *Evening Express* with 52,793 and the *Record* at 44,024. Even with the *Record* at the bottom rung of the ladder, it remained healthy. During the first three months of 1920 it saw its circulation increase twenty-seven percent and its advertising lineage jump forty-one percent.

When Cornelius Vanderbilt Jr. founded the *Illustrated Daily News* in 1923, the upstart publication fueled the circulation wars. In its first full year of operation in 1924, the *Daily News* had a paid daily circulation of 178,719. Vanderbilt's poor stewardship of the paper would make 1924 an anomaly as circulation would plummet by 72,000 in 1925. But 1925 circulation numbers would remain healthy for most of the other publications. The *Evening Herald* continued to lead in 1925 with 181,785 paid daily circulation with the *Examiner* following close behind with 167,935; the *Times* at 129,417; and the *Record* at 53,466. Besides the *News*, the *Evening Express* saw its circulation drop from 95,365 in 1924 to 91,565 in 1925. It would portend drastic changes for the newspaper just six years later when it merged with the *Herald* to become the *Evening Herald & Express*. By 1930, both the *Examiner* and the *Herald* would break the 200,000 mark in paid daily circulation with the latter accounting for 226,419 readers and the former at 206,089.

While Los Angeles publishers saw their daily paid circulation numbers dramatically climb, they also saw newsprint costs fall from a high in 1923 of $82.50 a ton to only $62.12 a ton in 1930. The Great Depression helped prices plunge to $40 in 1935 before a brightening economy in 1938 witnessed a rise in prices to $50 a ton. Still, high circulation and low newsprint costs didn't necessarily mean strong wages for newspaper employees. A journeyman press operator earned about a $1 an hour in 1924, but saw only fractional wage increases through 1937 when the Los Angeles Newspaper Guild was founded.

III.

If the Los Angeles population explosion and favorable newsprint prices enabled the local press to build circulation, then the advent of the tabloid in New York City after World War I kept them glued to the front page day in and day out. The picture-saturated tabloid pointed to the changing complexion of journalism throughout the country. Newspaper reading was becoming, for better or for worse, more exciting. Turgid writing gave way to a more breezy style. A Hollywood scandal in the Los Angeles *Examiner*, for example, may feature a 100-inch story with several detailed sidebars, but photos, huge headlines, and sly editorial comment made reading a delight. Major cities had their newspapers of record, but alternatives were found in the lively and sensational tabloids. The tabloid was a product of the Jazz Age. And while the true sensational tabloid never found an audience among Los Angeles readers, the local press shamelessly imitated its reporting and use of photos. It gave readers a huge dose of tabloidesque reporting without the need for tight writing. The Los Angeles *Examiner*, a broadsheet, came closest to emulating the New York tabloid in tone and spirit. It prided itself on its extensive use of photos, allowing its staff photographers a full page each day to display their work and by the mid and late 1930s, using a mix of wire and staff photos. The *Herald & Express*, which relied heavily on street sales, also believed in the tabloid approach to journalism. As the largest circulating daily in the West for three decades, it put an emphasis on large pictures and bold headlines. But its poor writing and tight newsroom budget often put it in the shadow of its sister paper, the *Examiner*.

Mimicking the New York tabloids was a bold stroke by Hearst to attract Los Angeles readers. He couldn't have chosen a better role model. Seven months after World War I ended and two days before the signing of the Versailles Treaty, the New York *Illustrated Daily News* appeared on the streets much to the consternation of traditional journalists. When the first bundles thumped on the sidewalk on 26 June 1919, curious readers probably thought they were looking at a cheap magazine. The cover was splashed with pictures and a single headline blared a tragedy across the top. Readers in England were well acquainted with the tabloid. It had been a staple of English journalism for some time. But to the traditional American journalist it was a little hard to swallow. It was small and concise. Stories were short. It could be read on the subway or standing on a street corner without elbowing passersby. Noses in the hallowed city rooms of the New York *Times* and New York *Herald* sniffed and turned upward. There was no room in their city for such garbage. "Too small, plenty of sizzle, but no steak."

There just wasn't enough news to satisfy the reader. Journalist S.T. Moore wrote that the tabloid was "an unholy blot on the fourth estate—they carry all the news that isn't fit to print." And New York publicist Aben Kandel complained the new media reduced "the highest ideals of the newspaper to the process of fastening a camera lens to every boudoir keyhole."

Almost overnight, the *Daily News* changed the face of journalism. By 1921 it had the largest readership in New York City. In 1938 its circulation had skyrocketed to more than 1.7 million daily readers with a mind-boggling Sunday circulation of more than 3.2 million. No other daily newspaper before World War II had ever achieved such circulation numbers. In a manner of a few short years after the debut of the *Daily News*, tabloids popped up across the country and were quickly accepted as a legitimate form of journalism.

Media observer Martin Weyrauch didn't see the tabloid as necessarily a threat to journalism but as "inevitable as jazz." The new journalism was as expressive as radio, motion pictures, and new concrete skyscrapers changing the landscape of big cities. It represented the dawning of a modern America in exaggerated caricature. It fit perfectly with speakeasies, jazz, the World Series, and following the daily lives of film stars.

If the followers of journalistic legends James Creelman and James Gordon Bennett lamented the passing of thoughtful journalism, they were mistaken. Bennett demanded that a newspaper's function was to startle not instruct its readers. Bennett, and any publisher worth his salt, sounded the battle cry to "raise hell and sell papers!" Tabloids just did it bolder, flashier, and naughtier.

Hearst's editorial guidelines of 1933 hold true in today's newsrooms, but the reality of a Hearst newsroom since the inception of the Los Angeles *Examiner* was quite different. Fairness and impartiality and bans on exaggeration and coarseness often took a backseat to lively coverage as evident in stories ranging from the Roscoe ("Fatty") Arbuckle scandal to General Douglas MacArthur's return to the United States in 1951 after President Harry S. Truman fired him as commander of U.S. Forces in Korea. Fairness and accuracy were all well and good, but it couldn't compete against a speculative story that spawned a compelling headline. A compelling headline meant better street sales. And to Hearst, that was the bottom line.

In a world where there is never an original idea, the New York City tabloids exploited the yellow journalism of Pulitzer and Hearst and Hearst exploited the aggressive tabloid approach of appealing to the lowest common denominator in the reader.

And in the case of the Los Angeles *Illustrated Daily News*, it looked in all respects like the East Coast tabloids with their heavy emphasis on presentation, short stories, huge art, and towering headlines, but with the decidedly unexciting slant of "clean" news. Sleazy Hollywood gossip would have to be found in the competition, but a *Daily News* exposé on downtown gambling dens would be fodder for prominent play.

Cornelius Vanderbilt, scion of the wealthy New York Vanderbilts, recognized and respected the power of the tabloid. He eschewed his family's wealth to make his bones as a reporter, earning $25 a week at the conservative New York *Herald*. He was tenacious but naive. He believed that America was ready for another tabloid, but without the sleaze factor. Choosing Los Angeles as the site for what he considered a bold experiment, he sought to provide readers with bright, crisp writing in short doses and complemented with bold headlines and compelling art. In a mixture of idealism and naiveté, Vanderbilt established "a clean newspaper ... in which vileness and sensationalism now play too great a part in the local press." He wanted an alternative to the Hearst brand of journalism. He believed readers would clamor for a newspaper that left sex and titillation for the competitors while giving fulfilling, but sanitized, reports of the day's events.

Vanderbilt's motives for launching such a tabloid in Los Angeles appeared sound enough. Los Angeles was a growing city. He also considered the Hollywood film industry a "salacious place" and he wanted to prove that placing a clean newspaper in Los Angeles to cover such an industry would be successful. While Vanderbilt's competitors may have laughed him out of their newsrooms, the entrepreneur had community support. A series of scandals had rocked the film community in 1921 and 1922, and were covered in excruciating detail in the local press, particularly the *Evening Herald* and the *Examiner*. Local community organizations held a meeting in January 1923 to determine whether anything could be done to raise the standard of Los Angeles journalism. Vanderbilt couldn't have come to the city at a better time.

Vanderbilt's vision failed to materialize, primarily through his own incompetence as a businessman. E. Manchester Boddy, who worked for Harry Chandler's Times-Mirror Company, purchased the *Daily News* in 1926. He took a more disciplined approach to managing the paper and made it a success for the next twenty-eight years, giving Los Angeles its only true Democratic voice. What Vanderbilt brought to Los Angeles journalism was an energy not previously seen by the staid *Times* and the *Express*, the frothy *Examiner* and the *Herald*, or the unreliable *Record*.

The fact that a half-dozen papers operated in Los Angeles brought much needed balance to a city that had a tendency to look inward for its diet of news of the day rather than examine what was happening in the world. The local press saw its city as the world. Home-grown economic recovery plans like Technocracy and the Townsend plan, the City Hall scandals of the George Cryer and Frank Shaw mayoral administrations, the internment of Japanese during World War II, defense work, racial problems, growth, and smog often kept national and international stories off of the front page. Attacks by U.S. servicemen on Mexican Americans in downtown Los Angeles during the so-called Zoot Suit Riots in 1943 received better front-page play than the progress made by Allied Forces in North Africa.

While local sensational stories still generated the top headlines, there were signs of a growing maturation among newspapermen and women during and immediately after World War II. Science, the military, and education became specialty beats. The reporter of the 1940s and 1950s was more educated than his predecessor. The reporting and writing became more thoughtful. Sensational murder cases such as the Black Dahlia mystery were still the staple of headline-grabbing journalism, particularly for newspapers like the *Herald & Express*, which were dependent on street sales. But in the same editions, readers could find clear, concise reports on education issues and local politics. The emphasis was always on local news.

And it was local news with a distinct agenda. Crime was daily newspaper fodder. But while sensational murders got big play, the local press allowed the Los Angeles Police Department to run amok. Local media rarely covered shakedowns, bootlegging, beatings, and even killings by rogue police officers. Authorities suspended civil liberties, from the unemployed trying to enter California in the 1930s to the incarceration of Japanese Americans during World War II. Few newspaper editors, except those at the *Evening Record*, bothered to challenge local policy.

By the mid-1950s, the Los Angeles press gained a reputation as defining the world as "the Southland." Writer Phil Kerby reported in the July 1956 edition of *Frontier* magazine: "The world of the Los Angeles press is 'the Southland'—a euphemism for California from Fresno south to the Mexican border, plus Arizona and southwest Nevada and Utah. The center of the Southland is Los Angeles, and Los Angeles as held up to view in the pages of its press, is one vast movie lot and sports arena."

"This is not to say there is a complete absence of significant national and international news in the four metropolitan papers (the *Times*, the *Examiner*, the *Herald & Express*, and the *Mirror-News*, which was founded by the *Times'* Norman Chandler in 1948 and purchased the assets of the *Daily News* in 1954 to become the *Mirror-News)* of Los Angeles, nor should it be taken to mean that important local news is omitted, but the emphasis on comparative trivia is unmistakable."

Kerby cited the 12 June 1956 editions of the four dailies as an example. The *Evening Herald & Express*, its circulation 329,347, carried about seven columns of national and international news, but also devoted two and a half columns to Hollywood gossip and thirty-one columns of sports. The *Herald & Express'* sister paper, the *Examiner* (daily circulation 342,911 and Sunday 693,999) offered nine columns of national and world reports but thirty columns of sports and two columns of Hollywood gossip. The *Times* (428,323 daily and 814,492 on Sundays), according to Kerby, ran 107 columns of national and world news from 26 May to 1 June. The St. Louis *Post-Dispatch* during the same period averaged thirty-two national and international news column each day while the Denver *Post* provided the same amount of national and international news as the Los Angeles *Times*. The *Post-Dispatc*h had a daily circulation of 388,894 and 467,021 Sunday readers and served a city less than half the size of Los Angeles. The *Post* had a weekday circulation of 248,890 with a Sunday readership of 347,768 and served a city just one-quarter the size of Los Angeles.

With the exception of the *Mirror-News*, which promoted liberal causes and was the first Los Angeles newspaper to extensively cover the Latino and African American communities, the local press was curiously myopic in its coverage. Rigidly Republican, parochial, and sensationalistic, local journalists as a whole didn't enjoy the solid reputation of their counterparts in Chicago, Detroit, New York, and Washington, D.C. But they did have more fun. And they were perhaps the most competitive newsmen and women in the country. To them a scoop meant beating the competition in street sales by getting a three-minute jump on delivering papers to the sidewalk.

Chapter One

The Birth of L.A. Celebrity Journalism

I.

For Fred Eldridge, days like these made newspapering a calling. The afternoon *Herald* and the *Express* were laid out on his desk in the *Examiner's* newsroom on Broadway, and there wasn't a word about what could be the biggest story of the decade. Young starlet Virginia Rappe had mysteriously died five days after a raucous party held by film comedian Roscoe ("Fatty") Arbuckle at the St. Francis Hotel in San Francisco.

There was nothing in the 9 September 1921 editions of the *Herald* and the *Express* about the Arbuckle affair. There was severe flooding in San Antonio, Texas; war was brewing in Spain; law authorities in Tacoma, Washington, were hunting for an elusive mail bandit. Those stories would get good play on the front page for the 10 September edition, but Virginia Rappe's death put the *Examiner* in a good spot. The paper would break the story on Saturday and since the afternoon papers didn't publish on Sunday, Eldridge had a two-day head start. He also had the resources of the *Examiner's* sister paper, the San Francisco *Examiner*, available to him. The *Times* would follow the story but wouldn't have the stomach for the details. Eldridge counted on the *Times* to be a little slow on the uptake. This story was made for the *Examiner*.

No managing editor in Los Angeles was better suited to direct the coverage of the Fatty Arbuckle scandal than Frederick William Eldridge, the elder statesman of California newsmen. Trained on Hearst's New York *Evening Journal* and the New York *American*, he had a sense to go for the jugular.

Born in Alexandria, Virginia, in 1877, Eldridge attended public schools in Baltimore and Alexandria before starting his career in 1904 as night editor on the Philadelphia *Inquirer*. William Randolph Hearst soon lured him to New York as the managing editor of the *Evening Journal*, and then to the *American*, first as city editor and later as managing editor. Though not quite thirty years old, Eldridge formed a bond with Hearst that would assure his career as a journalist. Under Hearst's supervision, Eldridge led the *American's* investigations of political corruption at the municipal and state levels of New York government. Promising to "clean house," Eldridge's reporting team wrote a series of articles detailing how private firms were subsidizing senators and congressmen. In 1908, Hearst rewarded Eldridge by appointing him to the managing editor slot at the Los Angeles *Examiner*. Hearst founded the *Examiner* in 1903 primarily to provide stiff opposition to the *Times* and support the causes of labor. In those early years the *Examiner* was particularly supportive of the International Typographical Union (ITU), the first labor organization chartered in Los Angeles. The union was aggressive and had long since earned the enmity of *Times* publisher Harrison Gray Otis. The *Examiner* would move away from such liberal agendas, but it remained a thorn in the side of the *Times,* for it was the leading morning newspaper in circulation for several decades.

At Eldridge's side was city editor Raymond T. Van Ettisch, who had joined the *Examiner* as a copy editor a year before Eldridge's arrival. Van Ettisch, a small, quiet man renowned among his staff for never losing his temper in the heat of a story, was a native of La Junta, Colorado. He had cubbed at the *Chieftain* in Pueblo, Colorado. In his first major assignment, he covered a spectacular train wreck so well that he was immediately promoted to state editor. He was just eighteen years old. After a year on the *Examiner's* copy desk he took over supervision of the city desk. Except for a year as a first lieutenant in the Chemical Warfare Service during the world war, Van Ettisch remained at the city desk. He soon moved up in management, eventually succeeding Eldridge as the managing editor. Eldridge and Van Ettisch would be the core of the *Examiner 's* strategy to cover the unfolding events. They leaped on the story that was five days old.

By the time the Arbuckle scandal was dissected in the press, the film industry had firmly been established in Southern California for more than a decade. From about 1908 through World War I, the community of Hollywood tolerated such filmmakers as Cecil B. DeMille, D.W. Griffith, and Mack Sennett as they made liberal use of the local geography for filming. Roustabouts, cowboys clinging to the 19th century, out-of-work stage actors, and young women hoping for independence arrived in Los Angeles in droves. Boardinghouse and bungalow owners shooed away potential tenants by posting "No actors" and "No film folk" signs in their windows. But it became apparent that moviemaking was beginning to inject revenue into the Los Angeles area. It was just enough for community leaders to sit up and take notice. The film community was beginning to make noises before the world war that they had the potential to be a driving force in establishing a long-lasting and healthy economy in the state.

Charlie Chaplin, who began his film career in Sennett comedies, was the first to gain international attention. By 1918, he was perhaps the most famous person in the world. His silent comedies were universally loved for their pathos. In July 1917, he signed a contract with First National Pictures for a $1,250,000.

Chaplin's Beverly Hills neighbor and friend, Douglas Fairbanks, emerged in the mid and late teens as the biggest action star of the silent era. He established a style that still carries the standard of what an action star should be. His marriage in 1920 to Mary Pickford, then the highest paid actress—earning $350,000 per film—for First National Pictures, was a sensation and cemented the Hollywood star system.

In 1919, Chaplin, Fairbanks, Pickford, and Griffith formed United Artists to give themselves more artistic control of their pictures and to provide a more solid financial gain through distribution of their own films. Subsequent mergers and acquisitions in the 1920s that created Metro-Goldwyn-Mayer, Famous Players-Lasky (later Paramount), Fox (later 20th Century Fox), and Warner Bros. further solidified the film industry as an economic powerhouse. Thousands of actors and support crews were employed, creating a need for infrastructure and housing.

While Wall Street in the early 1920s took notice of this infant industry trying to find its legs on the economic landscape, newspapers, especially the Los Angeles papers, began to clamor for its advertising as a new source of revenue. But in the editorial departments across town, a cynicism prevailed that film actors were overpaid children who got to play with expensive cars and live in spacious homes. The film industry spawned a class system that found actors and studio moguls at the top rung of the ladder. Meanwhile, newsmen earning $25 a week watched with envious upturned faces. It also appeared the local press had wearied of the dalliances of its film stars. Chaplin's penchant for teenage girls was well known. Compared to its later coverage of the Arbuckle affair, the *Examiner* was downright respectful when it published a speculative report on 25 June 1918 about rumors of Chaplin's marriage to 17-year-old Mildred Harris. The story allowed Harris' mother wide latitude in refuting the rumors, then covered without rancor the couple's marriage on 23 September 1918 when it was clear that Harris was pregnant. And hints of Arbuckle's previous sexual escapades had also surfaced. Now the gloves were off and an anything-goes approach to coverage took over.

A press-fueled scandal seemed inevitable for Arbuckle. He was already famous for his roles in Sennett comedies. Though weighing 300 pounds, Arbuckle managed to pull off agile and athletic stunts on camera. After performing in hundreds of two-reelers for Sennett, Arbuckle gained immense artistic power when with Joseph Schenk in 1917; he formed Comique, a film company. The company's films were released through Famous Players-Lasky. By 1921, Arbuckle, who was only thirty-four years old, ranked second only to Charlie Chaplin in popularity as a comedian.

After a grueling shoot of three films at a Hollywood studio, Arbuckle arrived in San Francisco over the Labor Day weekend.

Tagging along in Arbuckle's custom-made $25,000 Pierce Arrow were actor Lowell Sherman, agent Al Seminacher, and director Fred Fishbeck. They checked into the St. Francis and ordered several cases of top-notch bootleg liquor. Virginia Rappe, a pretty but marginal actress with a couple of Sennett shorts to her credit, had graduated to more substantial roles after she began dating director Harry Lehrman. She arrived at the party shortly after midnight on 5 September.

What happened next remains open to speculation. Despite detailed reporting by the Los Angeles press and three criminal trials, the exact chain of events remains murky. Arbuckle's story was straightforward. Guests were in and out of his room all night. They ate and were drinking when Rappe arrived at the room. She had a few drinks, according to Arbuckle, and inexplicably became hysterical. Arbuckle summoned the physician and the manager of the hotel. When they arrived, they saw that some of the other female guests had taken off Rappe's clothing and put her into a cold bath. The physician dismissed Rappe's condition as indigestion, suggesting that she take some bicarbonate of soda. Arbuckle went back to the party and drank and danced for the rest of the night.

Arbuckle returned to Los Angeles the next day. He told San Francisco police that he didn't even know that Rappe had died until two detectives appeared on the doorstep of his exclusive West Adams district home on Friday, 9 September—the day Rappe died—demanding that he return to San Francisco for questioning. At first, Arbuckle didn't take the incident seriously, often joking to friends about the allegation of murder.

As Arbuckle prepared to return to San Francisco Saturday morning, the *Examiner* broke the story with a screamer across the front page and two decks underneath: "Actress Dies After Hotel Film Party," "Girl Stricken in Arbuckle's Apartments," and "Death of Virginia Rappe, Well Known Here, Following S.F. Event, Being Investigated."

Under the headline, "Her Career Ended," in the center of the front page, was a photograph of the attractive Rappe, wearing a checkered dress with matching hat in her hand and her brown hair cut to just above the shoulders and combed out. She was a picture of innocent beauty.

The *Examiner's* first report of the incident was free of speculation, printing Arbuckle's denial of any knowledge of the circumstances surrounding Rappe's death. It also reported that the coroner's office determined that the cause of death was peritonitis and a police investigation was underway. On the jump page, the *Examiner* reported that Sherman, Seminacher, and Fishbeck confirmed Arbuckle's account of the party and Rappe's illness.

The *Times*, as Eldridge suspected, gave the story conservative play. The paper published a brief on the front page, teasing a more substantial story in Part II. The *Times* version was more comprehensive than the *Examiner*. It played up high partygoer Maude Delmont's version of the events. She told police she attended the party and alleged that Arbuckle violently threw Rappe on the bed. It was the first report of violence by Arbuckle that was missed by the other papers.

While the *Times* and *Examiner* reports were void of speculation, it didn't prevent different treatment from the *Evening Record*, the *Evening Herald*, and the *Evening Express*.

The night edition of the *Herald* led the front page with "Probe Cause of Girl's Death in Arbuckle Party." The deck reported that the comedian was returning to San Francisco for questioning. A smaller deck speculated that a "fall or blow" might have caused Rappe's death. The *Herald* led its story with the possible blow that may have caused Rappe's death. The paper then quoted Alice Blake, identified as a showgirl and who attended the party, as observing that Arbuckle and Rappe were sitting together on a settee before the actress became ill. Arbuckle's versions of the events were dropped deep into the jump inside the paper.

At first, the *Express* didn't take the story seriously enough to give it screamer-headline treatment. The San Antonio flood rated a headline above the masthead and in 72-point type blared under the masthead, "4 ROB L.A. POST OFFICE." The Arbuckle story occupied the third column under the modest headline " 'Fatty' Arbuckle Faces Quiz Over Film Girl's Death." There was no art of either Arbuckle or Rappe on the front page. Instead, the *Express'* main art illustrated the postal robbery story with photos of the robbed mail clerks and a crude diagram of the robbery. The *Express* down-played the story compared to the *Examiner* and *Herald*, leading with Arbuckle returning to San Francisco for questioning and giving Rappe's cause of death. It then veered into speculation that wood alcohol from a bad batch of liquor could have caused the woman's death. The *Express* ignored or was unaware of the fact that Arbuckle could afford the best liquor in town. On the jump were a photograph of Rappe and a report of Arbuckle's version of events.

The *Evening Record* high in its first-day story quoted San Francisco County District Attorney Matthew Brady promising to arrest and punish the person responsible for Rappe's death so "that young girls and women be protected from such treatment." For the remainder of its coverage, the *Record* took on an exceedingly hysterical tone as each day passed. On its second full day of coverage it noted that a "long stream of petty criminals, including numerous drug addicts," accompanied Arbuckle at his arraignment. On 16 September, it quoted anonymous sources who claimed that a Hollywood drug ring planned to kill Arbuckle because his case interrupted the flow of illegal drugs into the film community. The paper used a broad brush to report that "actors in minor capacities or employees of the studios" were members of a "Hollywood dope ring," and that Arbuckle hurt their "dope peddling" business. As if murderous dope rings were not enough to bury Arbuckle in bad press, the *Record's* San Francisco correspondent, W. Boyd Gatewood, reported that the actor "must face the wrath of ... mothers before he wins freedom." Gatewood noted that all the comedian's "money and high salaried attorneys will have to fight and scheme to clear their client."

The first-day coverage by the *Express* was clearly the most conservative of the five papers. The *Examiner* gave the story the best play and its first report was even-handed. The *Herald's* coverage hinted at a more aggressive tone but lack of facts tempered its coverage.

II.

By 1921, the *Herald* had become the leading afternoon paper in Southern California. Its circulation was approaching 140,000, and it was gaining advertising: 132,678 lines, in contrast to the *Express* and the *Record*, which would finish the year with respective losses of 81,388 and 108,478 lines. It also boasted some of the biggest stars of the local press, including Adela Rogers St. Johns, who had reported for the paper between 1914 and 1918, before becoming a widely respected correspondent for Hearst's International News Service. Also on staff was her first husband, chief copy editor William Ivan ("Ike") St. Johns.

The *Herald's* offices, at 128 South Broadway, were highly popular—at least at street level—for the public could view its running presses through massive windows. (A Los Angeles institution since 1873, when it appeared as a morning paper, the *Herald* would remain on South Broadway until 1925, when it moved to more spacious quarters at 1243 South Trenton Street.)

At the helm of the *Herald's* newsroom was the Hearst-trained Edwin R. Collins. Born an only child in Rhonerville, California, near Eureka, in 1876, Collins was educated at Walla Walla High School and later Whitman College, both in Washington state. During the Spanish-American War, he served double duty as an infantry corporal fighting against the Philippine Insurrection while at the same time sending reports to the Walla Walla (Washington) *Union*. Returning, Collins served a two-year stint at the *Union*, then moved on to the Oregon *Daily Journal* in Portland, serving as a telegraph editor; the Los Angeles *Examiner*, as a night editor; the Las Vegas (New Mexico) *Optic* and the Boston *American* (for three years); and finally, in 1912, the Los Angeles *Herald*, as its night editor. He was promoted to managing editor in 1913. Collins embraced the Hearst methods of newspapering so much that, in 1924, he was named the editorial director of the Pacific Coast Division of the chain's afternoon dailies.

To serve as his lieutenant, Collins named another Hearst-trained man to be his news editor: John B.T. Campbell, a native of San Francisco. Campbell was appointed the *Herald's* first city editor in 1911 and became its news editor in 1916. In 1933 he would become the paper's managing editor, holding that post until his retirement in 1954. He was considered by much of his staff to be the consummate newsman but a tyrant to reporters. He also displayed unusual front-page layout capabilities when he was drunk, which was often. During World War II, Gen. Jimmy Doolittle led the famous bombing raid against Tokyo that did much to raise home front morale. Campbell, who created the front page each day, finished off the screamer headline with "DOOLITTLE DOOD IT!" A rabid conservative he left his political stamp on virtually every front-page of the *Herald* and later the *Herald & Express* over four decades.

The journalistic philosophy of Eldridge, Van Ettisch, Collins, and Campbell contrasted sharply with the management of the *Evening Express*, which had carried the Progressive cause since the early 1900s.

Founded as a daily newspaper in 1871, the *Express* gained a reputation as a foil to the *Times* when it was purchased in 1900 by Edwin T. Earl, a Progressive reformer and fruit-shipping entrepreneur who earned his first million dollars at the age of forty-four in 1900. Earl teamed up with Edward A. Dickson, who would ultimately give the *Express* its personality and Progressive reputation.

Born in 1879 in Sheboygan, Wisconsin, Edward Augustus Dickson came to California as a boy and was educated at the University of California and Moravian College in Pennsylvania. He served his reporting apprenticeship at the Sacramento *Union* and the San Francisco *Chronicle* before joining the *Express* in 1907.

While covering the 1907 state Legislature, Dickson and Chester Rowell, a reporter for the Fresno *Republican* and later editor of the San Francisco *Chronicle*, became enraged when they witnessed three Southern Pacific-backed legislators directing the legislative proceedings. With Rowell and with Earl's backing, Dickson formed the Lincoln-Roosevelt League of Republican Clubs. The organization had a full agenda. It sought to break the Southern Pacific Railroad's hold on the Legislature, regulate public utility rates, and introduce workers' compensation and women's suffrage. It ultimately played a key role in a "Young Turks" rebellion within the Republican Party, which led to the election of Hiram Johnson as governor in 1911. It also made the *Express* a formidable powerbroker in state politics. Dickson served as the paper's Washington correspondent during 1911 and 1912.

After Earl's death in 1919, F.W. Kellogg bought the paper. He purchased the five-story building site on Hill Street, between First and Third, for a half-million dollars. Dickson was named publisher and editor.

III.

The *Express* covered scandals just as well as its competition, coming up with its share of lurid reports during the Arbuckle case. But it must have been something of a distraction for Dickson who saw viable issues such as water and education as the meat of his paper's coverage.

Since the afternoon papers did not publish on Sundays, the *Examiner* and the *Times* had the story to themselves. The *Examiner* went into a high gear with headlines: "Dying Girl Laid Blame on Comedian," "So Charges Woman a Bedside of Orgy Victim in Statement to S.F. Police," and "He Tried to Get me for 5 years, Virginia Rappe is Quoted as Saying Just Before Death."

The word "orgy" made its first appearance in a headline without any police officer or prosecutor ever identifying the party as such, but the word would characterize the incident forever. Arbuckle was booked on suspicion of murder soon after arriving in San Francisco on Saturday night. In the third paragraph of its lead story, the *Examiner* quoted Miller U'Ren, San Francisco County assistant district attorney, that Arbuckle was accused of taking a life during a rape or attempted rape. In a second story, under a large photograph of Rappe, was a brief sidewalk interview Arbuckle had given to an *Examiner* reporter. The comedian tried to get a room at the Palace Hotel with his attorney, Frank Dominguez, but was turned away after word had leaked out to all four-star hotels that Arbuckle would be charged with murder. As Arbuckle and Dominguez stood outside the Palace Hotel, trying to decide what to do next, police detectives arrived to take Arbuckle into custody.

The *Examiner* reporter was there to question Arbuckle about his relationship with Rappe and the events at the St. Francis. The newsman reported that Arbuckle "showed no trace of his famous screen smile" after his arrival and "appeared very serious and downcast," noting that Arbuckle "shifted his eyes" and "twiddled his thumbs and was visibly nervous" when asked whether he was alone in a locked room with Rappe. Without saying so, the *Examiner* provided its readers with all the clues of a guilty man trying to explain away his behavior.

Arbuckle's principal accusers were party guests Maude Delmont, Alice Blake, and Zay Pevron. A nurse, Jean Jameson, reportedly heard a deathbed statement from Rappe that Arbuckle had been after her for five years. Delmont gave conflicting statements to police, but reported that Arbuckle had dragged Rappe into a room, locked the door, and attacked her. Delmont told police she tried to get into the room but the door was locked. She said she heard Arbuckle and Rappe scuffling. (A coroner's report later stated that Rappe, in addition to peritonitis, had suffered a ruptured bladder and had bruises on both arms, a thigh, and on her abdomen. The initial report as to the cause of death of peritonitis suddenly became unimportant as the press focused its attention to the alleged violence to the body.)

As if statements of witnesses were not damaging enough, the *Examiner* portrayed Arbuckle as a reckless partygoer and Rappe a solid working girl. The *Examiner* published unfounded reports that Rappe had been independently wealthy as a result of astute investments in oil. She lived with her aunt and housekeeper at 504 North Wilton Place in Los Angeles. Arbuckle, in fact, had been reported saying that parties were the "keynote" of his life. He had staged parties at the slightest excuse, drove "freak" cars, and once held a "dog wedding." He had gotten in trouble in Massachusetts for staging a "wild party." The contrast between the accused killer and his alleged victim were permanently cemented in the minds of *Examiner* readers.

Right from the start, panic swept the film industry. In a single weekend, Arbuckle came to represent the sins of the motion-picture industry. Even before the *Examiner's* sensational report, two San Francisco movie theaters pulled Arbuckle's films from the bill. Sid Grauman, a close friend of Arbuckle's, pulled "Gasoline Gus" from his own theater. Studio bosses such as Adolph Zukor and Jesse Lasky, whose studio produced the comedian's films, publicly distanced themselves from Arbuckle.

The Sunday editions of the *Times* made no mention of an "orgy" and kept its reporting to the murder charge filed against the comedian and the statements by the female partygoers.

But the *Examiner* further fueled public sentiment when on 12 September it carried a Universal Services interview with Rappe's boyfriend, Henry Lehrman, who denounced the comedian. "Arbuckle is a beast," he said. "I directed him for a year and a half. I finally had to tell him if he didn't keep out of the women's dressing room I would see that he was through." Above the Lehrman interview was a photograph of Arbuckle being booked at the San Francisco Hall of Justice. On the jump page, were photos of Rappe's torn clothing and Arbuckle conferring with Dominguez.

The *Times* carried essentially the same report on Lehrman, which the afternoon papers also picked up the same day. The *Times*, however, led its front page story on an update of Arbuckle's second night in jail with the headline, "Plan to Send Arbuckle to Death on Gallows" although there was no reference to prosecutors seeking the death-penalty.

The *Herald,* though two days behind in its coverage, ignored on the front page any news breaking in San Francisco and instead had sent veteran reporter Guy Price to survey the mood of the local studios. In a off-lead treatment, Price wrote a lengthy and vague report that the Arbuckle affair was the talk of the studio staffers. Price apparently found few, if any, studio staffers willing to comment, leaving him to rehash the comedian's lifestyle and his penchant for luxury cars.

The *Evening Express'* treatment, however, on the Hollywood scene created more talk than the Price piece. The *Express* reported that Los Angeles police were conducting in investigation into " 'Fatty' Orgies." It quoted a police captain who complained that the wealth and prominence of the people involved in the sex parties were discouraging witnesses from coming forward in an effort to prosecute the offenders. The story quoted only police Captain J.H. Pelletier, who offered a vivid account of alleged sexual assaults in the film industry, although the *Express* provided no corroboration. "This rough stuff is being pulled by a small coterie, which is giving the whole profession a black eye," Pelletier said, "They have made it a practice to force themselves into the dressing rooms of new girls, and they have ruined many. Afterwards their money has kept them immune from punishment, through the buying off of witnesses, donations to the girls, threats of wide publicity for their victims, and for their families."

As movie houses across the country continued to drop Arbuckle films, the chorus to take swift action against the actor rapidly mounted. Outdoor-advertising companies peeled off his image from hundreds of billboards, and his memberships in local clubs were revoked. The *Express* was the first to editorialize against Arbuckle. In a commentary penned by Edward Dickson, the *Express* concluded that "death would be too easy and too merciful a penalty" for the person responsible for Rappe's death. The *Express* didn't identify Arbuckle or Rappe by name. And it was careful to couch its opinions on the assumption that the allegations were true. But there was no mistake about how strongly the *Express* felt. "If the statements made as to the origin, development and conclusion of this tragedy are true, or approximately true, then the horrible degeneracy that it manifests should be dealt with in such swift severity as will punish the criminal and deter other degenerates from attempting like crimes." Once the facts have been established, the *Express* argued, "then the criminal and all his works should be wiped off the face of the earth."

That same day, the *Herald* led its front page with coroner's inquest testimony by Maude Delmont, who was described as "playing the role of the avenger of beautiful Virginia Rappe" while Arbuckle was noted to be wringing his hands during the hearing. Late Tuesday, a San Francisco County criminal grand jury returned a manslaughter indictment against Arbuckle. The tide of public opinion clearly swelled against the actor.

For several dailies, Arbuckle was red meat. The *Express* assigned Colin A. Spangler to the story early in the week, but his reports were limited to sidebars published inside. The *Examiner* sent John A. Gray, a veteran newsman, to San Francisco, and the *Herald* sent a young reporter named James Richardson. When Rappe's body arrived in Los Angeles on Saturday, 17 September, two women reporters—Pauline Payne, of the *Herald*, and Lanie Haynes Martin, of the *Examiner*—were waiting at the train station. Arthur Turney covered the story for the *Express*, but Dickson had Estelle Lawton Lindsey report the scandal's effect on the film industry.

James Hugh Richardson would leave the most lasting mark, becoming the most colorful and feared city editor in Los Angeles for three decades. He was a native of Winnipeg, Canada, where he developed a love for ice-skating. In 1912 at eighteen he caught the journalism bug while in high school when he took on the job as editor of the school paper. Richardson put in such long hours at the paper that he neglected his studies and was expelled from school. When his father asked him what he planned to do, young Richardson announced that he wanted to be a reporter. His father set up an interview the next day with the city editor of the Winnipeg *Telegram*. Richardson got the job and worked there for about a year doing the police beat and general assignments. In 1913, the Richardson family moved to Los Angeles to escape the brutal Canadian winters.

Richardson made the rounds of the local newspapers but was unable to find a job. He would get his break on 24 May 1913, when he and his family attended Empire Day in Long Beach. Empire Day was staged to bring homesick Canadians and former British subjects together, just as Iowa Day brought Iowans together once each year. Richardson was following his brother to the three-story wooden Long Beach Municipal Auditorium when they saw it collapse under the weight of hundreds of people. Richardson rushed to a drugstore a block away and phoned in the details of the disaster to the city desk of the *Evening Herald*. Thirty-three people were killed and the *Herald* scored the biggest scoop of the year. Richardson landed a job there the next day at $7.50 a week. By 1921 he was a seasoned and still-rising star on the staff.

Richardson provided the *Evening Herald* with its first by-lined and locally written news account of the developing Arbuckle story. On Thursday, 15 September, Richardson reported that a death threat against Arbuckle had been mailed to Henry Kelly, the secretary of the criminal grand jury. The letter demanded that Arbuckle be convicted of murder and be given a life sentence. In the eleventh paragraph, Richardson reported that Arbuckle's defense team had given its first full interview on strategy. Richardson's story was hardly a scoop, since the *Evening Express* carried an Associated Press report on the death threat as its lead story.

Richardson's story was further deflated when on Friday the *Examiner* hit the streets with a one-on-one jailhouse interview between reporter John Gray and Arbuckle. It was Arbuckle's first comments to a reporter since his brief sidewalk interview outside the Palace Hotel the night of his arrest. Arbuckle refused to tell Gray what happened at his Labor Day party, but lamented his treatment in the press and expressed his desire to get out of jail and return to

The copy desk of the Los Angeles *Herald*, c. 1913. Ivan ("Ike") St. Johns, husband of Adela Rogers St. Johns and father of Elaine St. Johns, is third from right. (Courtesy University of Southern California on behalf of the USC Library Department of Special Collections)

The Los Angeles *Examiner* building, right, on South Broadway and Fifth Street, c. 1910. (Security Pacific Collection/Los Angeles Public Library)

Los Angeles *Daily News* copy desk, c. 1934 *(Daily News* Collection/Special Collections, UCLA)

Los Angeles. "I don't understand why some of the newspapers are rubbing it in on me this way," Arbuckle told Gray. "How are the Los Angeles papers? Are they as rough as the ones up here?" When Gray didn't answer, Arbuckle said, "but I've scarcely read the papers these past few days. Got disgusted with them."

If Gray's informal question-and-answer-style writing is any clue, the reporter lobbed a series of softballs to the actor, focusing primarily on Arbuckle's plans. At one point in the interview Arbuckle complained that the press was treating him poorly although he had allowed them to photograph him during the booking process and while conferring with his defense team.

Late in the interview, Gray appeared to be baiting Arbuckle. "Why didn't you smile in any of those pictures?" Gray asked. "How would a big smile do when you are released– if you are?"

Arbuckle shook his head. "Nothing doing on that."

"Oh, your attorneys have told you not to smile, fearing the impression you might make?"

"I can't go into that, old man, although I'd like to come through."

Richardson would come back with his own scoop on 16 September with an interview with Maude Delmont, who quickly emerged as the San Francisco County District Attorney's star witness. The *Herald's* lead story reported crowds battling for a spot to attend the actor's arraignment. On the right shoulder, Richardson's by-lined sidebar reported that Delmont acknowledged that she had given weak and conflicting testimony during the coroner's inquest earlier in the week. She also admitted that some of her testimony was wrong and blamed it on illness and medication she had taken just before taking the witness stand. But, Delmont assured Richardson that she planned to change her testimony for the manslaughter trial to shore up holes in her story.

"You mean you intend to change your testimony in certain parts?" Richardson asked.

"Yes, I do, and it will greatly benefit the prosecution's case, you can be sure of that," Delmont replied.

Delmont's credibility was severely shaken between her interview with Richardson and Arbuckle's first trial started on 14 November. Delmont also claimed, in separate interviews with Hearst reporters, that Arbuckle leered at Rappe, saying, "I've waited five years for you, and now I've got you." The story was widely circulated but never corroborated. Another un-attributed detail—also reported in the Hearst papers and never substantiated—was Arbuckle shouting to Rappe, "I'm coming, Virginia!" And perhaps the most inflammatory allegation that no partygoer ever said but was published by Hearst was that Rappe had been raped with a Coca-Cola or champagne bottle.

If Richardson had accomplished anything, it was to establish that Delmont was unreliable and a liability to the prosecution. Delmont would never testify in any of the three trials. But the specter of her early statements hung over the trial like a cloud. It virtually ended Arbuckle's future in the motion-picture industry. Although these stories were never told to the jury, deputy district attorney Miller U'Ren's closing arguments to the Superior Court jury during the first trial more than compensated for Delmont's absence. U'Ren likened Arbuckle's party to a Babylonian feast and orgy. Describing Arbuckle as a moral leper, U'Ren implied that he was a threat to all women. There was no evidence of an orgy in Arbuckle's hotel rooms or that Arbuckle preyed on young women, but U'Ren's closing arguments didn't have to be based on any facts.

Arbuckle's first trial ended in a hung jury, with a 10-2 verdict in favor of acquittal. District Attorney Matthew Brady immediately sought a second trial, which started 11 January 1922. The prosecution's case nearly collapsed when witnesses Alice Blake and Zey Prevon gave conflicting testimony from the first trial and pleaded to faulty memories on key pieces of evidence. The case went to the jury on 2 February. Two days later, it announced it was hung with a 10-2 vote in favor of conviction.

The third trial started on 6 March. This time, Arbuckle's defense team attacked Rappe's background, which included her work as a prostitute in Chicago from which she had several abortions. The defense also maintained that Rappe was known to get drunk and rip off her clothes. On 12 April the case went to the jury. Less than five minutes later a not guilty verdict was returned.

"Acquittal is not enough for Roscoe Arbuckle," the jury said in a statement. "We feel that a great injustice has been done him. We feel also that it was only our plain duty to give him this exoneration, under the evidence, for there was not the slightest proof adduced to connect him in any way with the commission of a crime."

Even so, Arbuckle was financially ruined. He mortgaged his West Adams home to repay loans made by his friends for his defense. He was fined by the government for violating the Volstead Act, and the Internal Revenue Service declared that he owed nearly $100,000 in back taxes. The exact cause and circumstances of Rappe's death were so obscured by the district attorney's office and the press that the truth never surfaced. What was clear was that Arbuckle, by hosting the party, was in the wrong place at the wrong time. He was perhaps, in retrospect, the most innocent person present at the party.

But the press coverage, particularly during the first frenzied week, had established a trend that would remain unbroken for the rest of the century. Arbuckle, whether innocent or guilty, provided sensational copy, boosted circulation, and created an intense rivalry among the local press. The Arbuckle case served as the model for the coverage of scandal: A no-holds-barred, take-no-prisoners approach to the story. Good story telling took priority over thoughtful investigative reporting. The pattern established itself quickly. On 2 February 1922, Arbuckle was suffering through his second trial when he learned that his good friend, director William Desmond Taylor, had been found dead that morning in his South Alvarado Street bungalow. Suddenly, the Arbuckle story was pushed off the lead position on the front page and the Taylor story took front-and-center stage. And in the flurry of the police investigation and press coverage, two more film careers would be ruined.

IV.

William Desmond Taylor was a Hollywood enigma long before he had been fatally shot in the chest the evening of 1 February. He was born in Carlow, Ireland, as William Cunningham Deane Tanner and came to the United States around 1890. He was handsome and affected the style of a courtly Englishman. He eventually settled in New York City, where he married and had a daughter. He earned a hefty salary of $25,000 a year at a Fifth Avenue firm dealing in art and antique furniture. About 1911, he packed his personal belongings, withdrew $500 from his office account and disappeared. Taylor worked variously as a stage actor, engineer, and gold miner in Alaska before coming to Hollywood in 1913. He acted in a string of pictures for Vitagraph and other studios before directing a series of pictures starting in 1914. After serving in the Canadian Army in France during World War I, Taylor returned to Hollywood, producing his own films for Famous Players-Lasky. He directed the leading actors of the day, including Mary Pickford, Dustin Farnum, Wallace Reid, and Mary Miles Minter.

Two women in his life occupied most of his time. The five-foot-one Mabel Normand was twenty-seven years old, dark, and considered one of the most beautiful women in the film industry. At nineteen years old, the blonde Mary Miles Minter, described in the press as a "sweet, pretty girl with an abundance of blonde curls." It had been purported that she was secretly engaged to Taylor.

Normand was considered a pioneer among women in filmmaking. The daughter of Vaudeville performers, she began acting for Biograph in New York. There, she met Mack Sennett, who was then working for D.W. Griffith. When Biograph moved to California, Normand and Sennett followed. When Sennett formed Keystone, Normand decided that working for Sennett was her best choice for her career. She enjoyed a prolific period as a comedienne in Keystone Kops pictures and later directed Charlie Chaplin and Fatty Arbuckle in one-reelers. By 1918 she left Sennett, signing a five-year contract for $3,500 a week for producer Samuel Goldwyn. But by the 1920s, Normand's star was already falling as she became addicted to alcohol and cocaine and the fast pace of all-night parties.

Minter, born in 1902 in Louisiana, was a stage child star dominated by her mother, Charlotte Shelby, whom the young Minter hated with a passion. Minter began acting in films in 1915, and by 1920, was earning a whopping $2,250 a week. Taylor directed Minter in some of her finest performances, including "Anne of Green Gables" (1919) and "Jenny Be Good" (1920).

The fact that both Normand and Minter were deeply in love with Taylor at the time of his murder was a recipe for disaster once the press got wind of it.

Though treated somewhat differently from the Arbuckle scandal, the coverage of the Taylor murder was marked by the same zeal of speculation that destroyed Arbuckle's career. The Los Angeles press vigorously pursued Taylor's missing valet, Edward F. Sands, although police showed little interest in him as a suspect. They also dug deep into the intimate relationships Normand and Minter had had with Taylor, although the women were never implicated in any wrongdoing. The case also brought the attention of the East Coast newspapers. Unlike the Arbuckle case, in which the eastern papers primarily relied on wire service reports, Eastern editors sent their own correspondents to cover the Taylor story. An instant distrust developed between the film community and East coast reporters, and out-of-town papers painting Hollywood as sex- and drug-addicted degenerates destroyed whatever tenuous relationship the city's reporters had.

Another significant difference in coverage was that women writers had received better assignments to cover the story, probably because the principal players in the story were women. The local newspapers also provided the film community with a bigger voice to balance coverage. During the Arbuckle scandal, the *Examiner* and the *Herald* wrote short sidebars in which such established stars as Tom Mix and William S. Hart defended the conduct of their colleagues. During the Taylor coverage, the press was more generous by opening up their news pages to allow such film writers as Rupert Hughes and Elinor Glyn to present another side of the motion picture colony.

The Taylor story broke on the morning of Thursday, 2 February, when Taylor's butler, Henry Peavey, arrived at his employer's residence. Taylor's South Alvarado Street bungalow typified the residence of many young married couples and single people working in the film industry. It provided a sense community with anywhere from a half-dozen to twenty small apartments spread out in a horseshoe. Many such residences became enclaves for families, relatives, and film workers employed by a single studio. Also living in the same bungalow court were comedy director Douglas MacLean and Edna Pruviance, a popular actress and co-star of dozens of Chaplin films.

Peavey discovered Taylor dead beside his desk with a gaping bullet wound to his left breast. Peavey fled screaming, alerting neighbors who called police. Before noon, the news of Taylor's murder swept through the studios and the *Herald* was publishing an extra edition. The screamer "MYSTERY GUNMAN

KILLS FILM DIRECTOR TAYLOR" pushed the Arbuckle jury deliberations to the second story on the front page and a much smaller headline, "ARBUCKLE JURORS STILL HELD UP."

The *Herald* immediately focused its attention on Edward F. Sands, Taylor's former secretary and servant. Taylor had fired Sands under mysterious circumstances and he was alleged to have robbed Taylor. Robbery, however, was not the motive in the killings. Police discovered $78 in Taylor's pockets, and the residence had not been ransacked. Police believed that Taylor had been working on income taxes. He had his checkbook at his desk when he was shot sometime after 8 p.m. The *Herald* reported that police were "confident that revenge was the motive" for the slaying. Although the story quoted no specific police officer discussing the motive, its deck above the story reported the killing as a revenge slaying.

In its home edition, the *Evening Express* provided a more detailed report and gave it a Hollywood spin in the fourth paragraph by noting that "detectives began quizzing Miss Mabel Normand, Miss Edna Purviance and Douglas MacLean all prominent in the motion picture world." The *Express* quoted extensively Normand's statement to police. Normand was told of Taylor's death the morning the body was discovered. Normand told police that she visited Taylor shortly after 7 p.m. on 1 February to talk about a book that Taylor wanted her to read. She left at about 7:45 p.m. Taylor promised her that he would call at 9 p.m., but he never did. The story also briefly detailed Purviance's attempt to summon Taylor at about midnight when she noticed the lights still burning in his bungalow.

The *Examiner* on 3 February gave considerable attention to Sands. It reported that Sands had been a former New York City police officer. In August 1921, Taylor alleged that Sands had stolen money, jewelry, and clothing from him while he was on a trip to England. The district attorney's office had issued an arrest warrant for Sands on 3 August on two counts of grand larceny. The previous January, Taylor's residence was burglarized, and police and Taylor suspected that Sands had returned. There was no evidence that Sands had committed the burglary but the *Examiner* juxtaposed the thefts with the disappearance of Sands the death of Taylor.

The *Examiner's* Lanie Haynes Martin tracked down Normand for an interview. Normand told Martin the details of her last meeting with Taylor and denied that she had a romantic relationship with him. Rather, she told Martin that Taylor was her mentor and they remained close friends.

Only the *Record* mentioned Mary Minter. On the afternoon of 2 February the *Record* reported that a distraught Minter arrived at the bungalow court demanding to see Taylor's body: "Tears streaming down her pretty face, Mary Miles Minter, famous motion picture star, hurried to the door of the Taylor bungalow at noon today and asked brokenly, 'It isn't true, is it?' Detective Sergeant (Bert) Wallis said, 'Taylor is dead.' 'Oh my God, I can't believe it,' Miss Minter cried out with a gesture of despair."

Wallis told Minter that Taylor's body had been moved to Ivy Overholtzer's mortuary at Tenth and Hill streets. Later in the day, a *Record* reporter cornered Minter, who was with her mother. When the *Record* reporter asked her about the rumors that she had been secretly engaged to Taylor, she vehemently denied it and denied that she was at Taylor's home the night he was killed.

By 3 February, the *Herald* characterized Taylor killing as a "love vengeance plot," emphasizing a "mystery woman" who may have spurred an infatuated love to commit the slaying. The Sands theory became less important to the police. The *Express'* lead story on the same day reported that two actresses were linked to the slaying, although it did not provide specifics. But Normand and Minter already had been linked to Taylor: Normand's visit to Taylor on the night of the killing and Minter's interview with the *Record*. The *Express*, too, also identified the women as possible witnesses. The inference that Normand and Minter were the two actresses linked to the case was unmistakable.

More alarming to the film community was a report deep on the jump of the lead story that Taylor had attended "hop" parties, "where drug addicts gathered." The tone established by the local press with the coverage of the Arbuckle case was repeating itself. The *Express* implied that Taylor's lifestyle had contributed to his death. It noted that Taylor apparently didn't take drugs, but morphine, opium, and marijuana had been consumed at the parties. Taylor could have attended the parties to collect information for a film scenario, the *Express* speculated.

The *Examiner's* lead story on 4 February echoed the *Express'* report, but the mystery was widened when it broke the story that Taylor was known in New York as William Deane-Tanner. Taylor, the *Examiner* reported, had a wife and child living in New York and had abandoned them. The *Examiner* also scored an interview with Taylor's former sister-in-law, who provided a detailed account of the director's life. It also published an unedited 6 November 1921 letter from Taylor's fourteen year-old daughter. And to whet the appetite of the reader, the *Examiner* also offered on its front page a $1,000 reward to anyone who could identify Taylor's killer.

The *Examiner* also contradicted its competition's report that police didn't consider Edward Sands their top suspect. Rather, the *Examiner* reported that police continued its search for Sands with "unabated intensity." And without attribution, the story stated that Sands had returned to Los Angeles on the day of the killing and announced, "I am here to get Bill Taylor." The newspaper further heightened the mystery with a sidebar interview with actress Claire Windsor. The actress claimed that Taylor had told her at a party at the Ambassador

Hotel the week before the slaying that he would "kill" Sands because he had stolen from him.

About a week into the coverage, the local press concentrated more of its attention on the relationships of Normand, Minter, and Taylor. The *Express* made much of Normand's weeping as she attempted to compose herself before her testimony at the coroner's inquest on Saturday, 4 February. Two days later, it published Estelle Lawton Lindsey's interview with Normand, who denied that she loved Taylor or that they ever discussed marriage. At one point during the interview Normand demanded that Lindsey "get it straight" so there was no misinterpretation of her feelings for the slain director. Three days later, it was announced that a batch of letters written by Normand to Taylor had been found in a boot at the Taylor residence. The contents of the letters were not disclosed. Lindsey returned to Normand's West Seventh Avenue to question the actress about the new development but Normand refused to answer the door.

Curiously, the *Examiner* appeared to have forgotten the Lindsey interview when it published reporter Walter Vogdes' "exclusive" interview with Normand on 11 February, five days after the *Express* had published its story. The Vogdes interview followed a lead story that purported that Normand gave the district attorney's office "intimate" details of her relationship with Taylor. The story offered no such details. Instead, Normand was adamant that she had nothing to do with the killing and that she had no love interest in him. She also denied published reports that a nightdress found in Taylor's apartment belonged to her. The Vogdes interview was purported to be an exclusive for the *Examiner*, but it covered much of the same ground as Lindsey's story. As with Lindsey, Normand demanded that Vogdes print the truth. This time she provided Vogdes with copies of the letters found in the Taylor home. The letters were playful, but hardly intimate or hinting at a lover's exchange. At no point did Normand consult a lawyer before talking with the press. And while each interview made it clear that her relationship with Taylor was platonic, the fact that her name appeared in headlines virtually every day during the first week of coverage, left the impression that Normand was the central figure in the case.

While Normand may have been simply suffering from guilt by association, it was entirely a different matter for Mary Miles Minter. On 7 February, the *Examiner* published love letters from Minter to Taylor that had been discovered in the director's library. Its lead art on the front page was a facsimile from Minter to Taylor that stated, "Dearest, I love you - I love you - I love you - xxxxxxxxx X! Yours always - Mary"

Disingenuously, Minter elaborated for the *Examiner* her affection for Taylor. "I did love William Taylor," she said. "I loved him deeply and tenderly, with all the admiration and respect a young girl gives to a man with the poise and culture of Mr. Taylor."

Minter later acknowledged that she and Taylor had been secretly engaged. To exacerbate Minter's involvement in the case, a dozen separate letters discovered in Taylor's boot belonged to her. They were written in personal code and signed by Minter. All professed her love for the man. The developments between 6 and 11 February tied forever Normand and Minter to the Taylor case in an unseemly way. Normand, simply because she and Taylor were close friends and she was there the night of his death, and Minter for her lack of discretion by not keeping quiet about her love for Taylor.

Not surprisingly the film community became defensive. Studio chiefs hired former U.S. postmaster Will Hays at an annual salary of $115,000 as a motion-picture czar to impose a standard of morals. Studio heads had hoped to give him minimal powers in an effort to stymie efforts by the Los Angeles City Council to establish a censorship board and to get local church groups off their backs. Hays proved to be more active. He wielded a stronger hand than the studios had envisioned, but it didn't stop the continuing tidal wave of scandal, including the morphine use by popular actor Wallace Reid in 1923.

The studio chiefs, and in particular the Hollywood literary community, felt almost powerless to deal with the press. But they learned from the Arbuckle affair that they could take the offensive to warding off meddling influences. They also were alarmed that they were being tarred with a wide brush. The conduct of Normand and Miles, if assessed independently of the Taylor murder, was not news. But their relationships with Taylor became something quite different with his death.

Writer and director Rupert Hughes warned the public against any misperception it might hold against the motion-picture industry. In an article for the *Record* on 13 February he noted, "moralists howl at the movies, but they howl without logic. Vices of every sort ran riot centuries before there were movies. Wicked people enter the movies, but they were wicked before they entered, and they would have gone on being wicked if they had stayed out of them."

English writer Elinor Glyn, who dabbled off and on writing film scenarios, also took the offensive. The *Examiner* opened its news pages to Glyn on 20 February. She observed, "The moving picture industry is, I am told, the fifth largest in America. It employs countless carpenters, electricians, painters, plumbers, artists, draftsmen, architects, designers, writers and musicians.

"Probably the smallest number of its constituents are the actors and actresses—and only a fractional percentage of these are lurid figures who delight in scandalous excesses. But the whole community is being held up to the English speaking peoples of the earth as a rotten sore on the face of America!

"Can anything be more unjust and illogical?"

The Hollywood *Citizen* published a letter on 17 February by Frances Harmer, a literary advisor to writer William DeMille. "Hollywood is not a hotbed of iniquity or a 'Sodom and Gomorrah,' nor at all worse than any other city," Harmer wrote. "In fact, its police records show a much cleaner bill than many cities twice its size."

The coverage of the Taylor murder continued to harm the innocent. Although police quickly dismissed Edward Sands as a suspect, the careers of Normand and Minter withered. The *Examiner* in 1924 tried to help Normand resurrect her film career with a serious of positive articles on her life story. Written in the first person "as told to" reporter Chandler Sprague, Normand dispensed advice on how to establish a film career and how she had achieved her fame. She never mentioned Taylor in the articles. Normand died in Monrovia, California, in 1930 from the complications of tuberculosis and pneumonia.

The Arbuckle and Taylor scandals forever changed the relationship of the local press with Hollywood. Reporters simply saw it as a good story. Editors and circulation managers saw scandal coverage as profitable. Hearst once remarked that the Arbuckle scandal sold more papers than the sinking of the *Lusitania*. Huge spurts in circulation created the model for treating sensational news: Wallace Reid's drug-related death, the unsolved death of Thelma Todd in 1935, the Charlie Chaplain paternity lawsuit in 1943, and the fatal stabbing of mobster Johnny Stompanato by Lana Turner's daughter in 1958.

Public sentiment and Los Angeles area church groups were not satisfied that the local press could contain itself to responsibly cover the motion-picture industry. In early 1923 the community sought a newsman who could cover the news in a "clean" and wholesome manner. They believed they found their answer in a wealthy East Coast scion that had the pocketbook of any member of the New York 400 but the heart and soul of the working stiff.

Chapter Two

A Clean Penny Paper

I.

If motion picture czar Will Hays and the Los Angeles clergy had hoped to find a newspaper that would cover local news in a less sensational manner and with an emphasis on positive, uplifting stories, then they couldn't have found a worse savior in Cornelius Vanderbilt Jr.

Vanderbilt, full of good intentions but woefully short in business talent and judgment, hadn't looked to Los Angeles to start a newspaper as a response to the string of scandals plaguing the film industry. And it wasn't necessarily the delegation of local clergymen who met with the newsman in January 1923 that moved him to publish a clean newspaper. Actors Douglas Fairbanks, Mary Pickford, and Charlie Chaplin encouraged him to establish an alternative daily, but Vanderbilt, while flattered, was primarily interested in his film friends as investors. Fairbanks and Pickford eventually kicked in some money, but it was hardly enough to make a significant difference in whether he started his newspaper in Los Angeles or some other city. And, at least initially, Los Angeles would reap the benefits of a new, albeit flawed, journalistic philosophy.

Vanderbilt was perhaps the most unlikely candidate to become a newspaper publisher given the robust, if not troubled history of his famous New York family. His intentions were truly altruistic, but his privileged upbringing, the lifestyle he abhorred and attempted to distance himself from, was the undoing of his fledgling newspaper publishing company. If there was a single person solely unsuited to establishing a newspaper dynasty it was Cornelius Vanderbilt Jr.

Born in New York on 30 April 1898, to railroad magnate Cornelius and Grace Graham Wilson Vanderbilt, Cornelius Jr. was heir to the family fortune. His future was secure in the palm of his hand as long as he was an obedient boy.

But even at a young age, Cornelius had a rebel streak that exhausted the patience of his parents. He chafed at being accompanied by nurses, tutors, companions, detectives, and guardians. He delighted in playing practical jokes on the family's servants and stuffy friends. With his sister, Grace, he once gathered up all the hats of the sailors on his family's yacht, the *North Star*, and threw them overboard. And when visiting government officials arrived at the Vanderbilt Fifth Avenue residence to pay homage to Cornelius Vanderbilt Sr., the son was waiting at a top floor window with a sack of flour. He let it go and struck Theodore Roosevelt square on the head. (Vanderbilt later wondered if it was the reason why, years later, Roosevelt refused to hear his mother's demands to get her son out of the Army after he enlisted during World War I.)

He traveled widely as a boy, crossing the Atlantic Ocean thirty-eight times by his sixteenth birthday. He summered at Lake Placid, New York, and spent winters in Miami. Starting at Malvern, England, his parents moved him from school to school, country to country, on a moment's notice when it appeared that he was bored or refused to be friendly with local royalty. As a young teenager, he schooled at Badnauheim, Germany, for six months before enrolling in an exclusive Russian school in St. Petersburg. His travels led him to become acquainted with Kaiser Wilhelm of Germany, King George V of England, and King Alfonso of Spain. But he was fickle in his relationships with other children and developed what would become his lifelong sensitivity to privilege. He yearned to be more common, although he preferred to be a commoner on his own terms as he continually sought loans from his parents far into adulthood.

Young Vanderbilt especially disliked Russia. There, he saw a ten-year-old grand duke pick up a riding whip and hit his servant over the head with it. His parents, however, became angry when they discovered their son didn't like any of the Russian nobility and couldn't form any lasting relationships with them. They then sent him to Austria. But the family's influence, which didn't extend as far as they thought, couldn't get him admitted. They settled for a French-run private school in Ouchy, Switzerland, which taught Cornelius to speak fluent French and provide at least a stable school record until he returned to the United States.

Journalism began to interest him while attending a military school stateside. He edited and wrote for the school newspaper, and continued writing and editing a small monthly school publication, The *Migrator*, while in Miami. While aboard the 223-foot *North Star*, he edited the yacht's newsletter, setting up a small printing press in one of the galleys and having the wireless operator obtain news for him. The ship's 70-person crew and his family were his pool of subscribers.

But for the moment, other matters were distracting the world, even the Vanderbilt family. As young Vanderbilt was about to put his school days behind him, the United States was being drawn into World War I. Well aware of the carnage, Vanderbilt's parents planned to send their son to college: the father preferred Yale, his alma mater, but the mother had in mind Harvard or Oxford.

But young Vanderbilt would have none of that. When the United States declared war in 1917, he announced his decision to join the Army. His parents didn't exactly oppose the idea—his father was a brigadier-general in the reserves—but they wanted their son to wait for a commission as an officer. But to the youth, who had just turned nineteen, that idea was elitist. He enlisted as a private.

Furious, Vanderbilt's mother used her connections with friends in the federal government to have her son declared unfit. When that ploy failed, his parents hired a private detective in an attempt to gather evidence that would make him unfit for service. That tactic failed, too.

Though he would suffer for his decision, Vanderbilt had no regrets. Years later, Vanderbilt told the San Francisco *Examiner* that being wealthy had given him more responsibility toward his fellow man. "I have felt since I was very young that we all owe a duty to humanity. That we must do something to pay for the privilege of being born into this world; that the greater our inheritance of wealth and position, the greater our individual responsibility."

For once, young Vanderbilt got what he wanted. He was assigned to the 102nd Ammunition Train. He was soon sent to France with the 27th Division as a dispatch driver. While at the front, he was severely gassed. Vanderbilt received the French *Croix de la Croix Rouge*, and then was sent to Fort Lewis, Washington, to recuperate.

When he was well enough to move around, he took a job with the 13th Division to drive a wagon to haul manure from the camp stables to a manure dump several miles from camp.

It was in Tacoma that the seeds of a newspaper empire began to take hold. Without a single day's experience as a paid newspaper reporter, Vanderbilt began to mull over the prospect of his own newspaper in a major metropolitan city. In Tacoma, he was acquainted with Hugh Wallace, who owned a home in the city and was Woodrow Wilson's minister to France. While relaxing off-duty at Wallace's home, he met a lawyer who encouraged Vanderbilt to pursue his dream. The lawyer suggested that Vanderbilt organize a stock company for the daily newspaper and start it in Los Angeles.

Without a solid foundation in journalism and no college education, Vanderbilt knew that he would meet with little success in launching such a difficult and complex project. He had already become an author by 1920, having penned two books on his war experiences, *Lines from the Front Lines* in 1918 and *The Gas Attack* in 1919. It wasn't long before he secured a reporting job with the New York *Evening Herald*. As a cub on his second assignment he managed an interview with Maurice Maeterlinck, the Belgian-French poet and dramatist. Sitting alone in a New York City hotel room on Christmas night 1919, the two men discussed art and literature. During the interview Maeterlinck turned toward the hotel window and looked out over the rooftops. He said nostalgically to his impressionable interviewer that if the chimney pots were a little longer, he could easily imagine this as his beloved Paris. The moment nearly moved Vanderbilt to tears. He was hooked on journalism and saw himself not as a wealthy New York scion but as one media observer would later call him, "The Great Commoner."

Young Cornelius' name often got in the way of his interviews. Occasionally he found himself in a position of being more famous than the subject he was interviewing. His subjects, and peers, mistakenly believed that he was wealthy in his own right. Few knew that his parents kept his money in a trust and his financial support depended almost entirely on his efforts as an author and newspaperman. And Vanderbilt seldom looked the part of the New York rich. His gassing in France made him appear even more frail than when he was a child, and put him in the hospital off and on for many years. He was tall, angular with a shock of curly hair and long, drooping jaw. He appeared hesitant, as if he was on verge of stammering, yet he was approachable and personable. He was embarrassed by his family's wealth and worked almost to the point of exhaustion to remain independent of his family and achieve a level of greatness on his own. William Boardman Knox, who served as a night city editor for the Los Angeles *Illustrated Daily News* under Vanderbilt, wrote that Vanderbilt's "whole demeanor suggested conscious inferiority shot with moments of unrestrained egocentric self-glorification."

Vanderbilt's stint with the *Herald* and later with the New York *Times* as its legislative correspondent in Albany, Washington, and Seattle, crystallized his goal to run his own newspaper. He was disturbed by the sensationalism of such rival New York papers as the *Daily Graphic*, but the compelling art and breathless tone appealed to him. He wondered if it was possible to have the best of both worlds: clean journalism told in a compelling and energetic manner.

The problem with Vanderbilt was not his motives for establishing a Los Angeles newspaper, but his background. His four years as a reporter for the New York dailies, while vital experience, was not enough to qualify him to getting in the trenches and waging a dirty newspaper war, a war that the Los Angeles press, particularly old dogs like the *Examiner*, the *Times*, and the *Herald*, were prepared to fight. The newsmen in management—city deskers, the managing editors, and executive editors—at these newspapers had spent many years at their craft. Most, if not all, were products of middle class and lower middle class families who were not afforded the opportunity to attend college. They learned their news sense from the street, most often with their fists. Beating the competition on a story meant playing dirty. And playing dirty was a fine art among Los Angeles newsmen.

Vanderbilt, by contrast, was soft and naive, believing in a code of fair play that would become painfully evident to his staff at the Los Angeles *Illustrated Daily News*.

In September 1920, Vanderbilt met in Vancouver with Lord Northcliffe, founder of the London *Daily Mail*. Vanderbilt had always admired the *Mail* for its tenacious approach to news. He was hoping to model his new venture after it. He believed that pictures being used in the New York tabloids and particularly the broadsheets across the country failed to exploit them properly as a news source. Although Vanderbilt found crime and sex news stories personally repugnant, he knew such stories couldn't be totally banned from the newspaper, but covered with modesty.

Vanderbilt was convinced Los Angeles was the perfect place for a "Penny Paper."

"The Pacific Coast," he told reporters in 1924, "will be to the coming generation what the Atlantic Coast has been to generations in the past..." He saw the *Illustrated Daily News* as the first in a chain of picture papers. Los Angeles, he believed, was the fastest-growing metropolitan city in the country that was alive and energetic.

Setting up a temporary office at the Union Bank Building, at Eighth and Hill streets, the newspaperman began in mid-1923 courting the city's movers and shakers. In a move that would signal misplaced trust in many of the people who would work for him, Vanderbilt hired E.T. Lewis, an itinerant promoter of questionable background who was originally from Pennsylvania but more recently promoting development in Palos Verdes west of downtown Los Angeles. Vanderbilt needed Lewis for his expertise in dealing with the small investor, and part of the success of the *Daily News* lay in the crux of his salesmanship.

Believing that a true voice of the people must be a democratic newspaper in ownership, Vanderbilt began a campaign that wasn't much different than the oil boom sales that Angelenos were currently witnessing in some of the suburban communities. Distributing circulars, advertising in local publications and waging a high-pressure sales campaign complete with free lunches, he offered potential subscribers a vote for a portion of the corporation's board of directors if they paid $5 for a one-year subscription. The subscription allowed the subscriber to become a trustee and the right to vote for two of the five board members. The board controlled the management and editorial content of the *Daily News*. Fifty-one percent of subscribers who held one share of stock were eligible to vote. Vanderbilt held the other forty-nine percent.

Vanderbilt and Lewis hit the luncheon circuit throughout the city, distributing a prospectus of the company. In a statement to potential investors he argued that he was "confident that there is ample room here for a morning newspaper absolutely independent and not controlled by any faction, party or interest, provided the public believes in this policy and will support it." And in a deliberate snub to his family, he noted that his great-great-grandfather Commodore Vanderbilt once stated "the public be damned." The family heir decided the keynote to his newspaper would be "The Public Be Served." The prospectus also promised the London *Times* news service, financial and market reports from London and New York, automobile and aircraft news, and comics and features. By the end of the first month of the sales campaign, 6,000 shares of stock were sold. The company was capitalized at $100,000.

Early indications through the summer of 1923 promised that the *Daily News* would boast a debut circulation anywhere from 60,000 to 200,000. Vanderbilt was free with his numbers when addressing civic groups and in interviews with the union trade newspaper, the *Los Angeles Citizen*, and an industry publication, *Fourth Estate*. Eventually he settled on the figure of 100,000 as his realistic startup circulation.

Vanderbilt resorted to other forms of publicity because rival newspapers refused to carry his advertisements, and billboard companies, under pressure from other newspaper publishers, denied him space. He hired a fleet of trucks to roar through the city unfurling huge banners touting the new publication, and he had Mack Sennett bathing beauties parade in downtown with signs and leaflets. He ignored Harry Chandler's stern warnings not to publish in Los Angeles. He also waved off William Randolph Hearst's transparent attempts to hire him to run a new picture tabloid in New York City at an annual salary of $30,000. Although probably a bit unnerved by the two newspaper giants, Vanderbilt moved forward. He hired 150 boys to paint *Daily News* messages on sidewalks much to the consternation of landlords who had to labor to clean it up.

The buzz was instant and the rumor mill churned. The *Citizen* speculated that the Los Angeles *Times* would begin publishing an illustrated daily tabloid to submarine Vanderbilt's plans. It also reported that Governor James M. Cox of Ohio, who was a Democratic candidate for president in 1920, was attempting to purchase the *Record* to offset the liberal influence of U.S. Senator William Gibbs McAdoo in Southern California. The *Citizen*, which appeared to follow the progress of Vanderbilt's venture on a weekly basis, reported in its 6 July edition that the Church Federation of Los Angeles was angling to have the Rev. Dr. E.P. Ryland run for a slot on the board of directors. And city officials in San Pedro and Wilmington had hoped to influence coverage in their cities by backing San Pedro Chamber of Commerce president Charles J. Calden as a board member. Neither man ran for a seat on the board.

What interested the *Citizen* more, however, was Vanderbilt's insistence that the *Daily News* be a union shop. This was stunning news in a predominately open shop city thanks in large part to Harry Chandler's anti-union stance. To the *Citizen*, it was "the big story of the week." Establishing a union shop also attracted business. Oilman C.C. Julian, for example, had his publication, *Truth*, printed at the *Daily News* in January 1924. Unions liked Julian because he insisted on using a union shop. And Vanderbilt, of course, liked the business.

Progress was rapid. Vanderbilt filed articles of incorporation with the California Secretary of State on 7 August to form Vanderbilt Newspapers Inc. Within two weeks, officers of the company were named. They were a virtual who's who among Vanderbilt's circle of friends. C.C. Bingham had been a captain in the same Army division as Vanderbilt during the world war. He joined the C-V Newspaper Service in 1920 as its general manager. He was a principal figure in organizing the Los Angeles venture and was named vice president and general manager. O.T. Lively, an insurance man, was named second vice president to supervise the sale of stock in the new company. Col. Joseph J. Daly, another Army buddy who had commanded the 104th field artillery and later became a chief ordinance officer, was a relative newcomer, joining the company in March. He was appointed treasurer. Edward Ralph, who served as an assistant to the secretary of war, was appointed secretary.

The board of trustees consisted of Alfred I. Dupont, Robert Goelet, J. Leslie, John W. Brodie, Ray S. Baker, William K. Vanderbilt, Jr., H.F. Alexander, and Gerard Coster.

By mid-August, the *Daily News* had a pledged circulation of 50,000 with paid-in-advance subscriptions. Vanderbilt found a three-story plant at Los Angeles Street and Pico Boulevard that had served as an Auburn auto dealership. It was originally built around 1917 by a Presbyterian hospital foundation but was never used as a hospital. In 1918, auto dealer Don Lee had bought the building. It then passed into Vanderbilt's hands. It probably was unintentional but somewhat symbolic that Vanderbilt chose a site well south of where the city's competing papers were clustered. The *Express*, the *Examiner*, the *Herald*, and the *Times* were confined in or near downtown and bordered by South Broadway to the east; Hill Street to the west; Temple Street to the north and Sixth Street to the south. The *Record* was located well outside this area, at Wall and Sixth streets near the Pacific Electric Railway terminal and adjacent to the slums. The *Daily News* took up residence eight blocks south of the *Record* in the garment district.

Vanderbilt bought the plant and property for $350,000. He immediately began remodeling, putting the press, stereotype, and mail rooms on the first floor with six showers and eighty-four lockers for the mechanical department employees. Hard maple flooring covered the department's concrete floors. Some newsprint storage areas were placed on the second floor along with the executive and editorial offices. The third floor was largely vacant. Seven modern Intertypes, two Ludlow type casters, and two Elrod casters were installed along with up-to-date lighting fixtures and a new ventilation system. A new foundation was laid to accommodate a twin Duplex tubular perfecting press equipped to print two thirty-two-page newspapers simultaneously. Since the *Daily News* carried fewer pages than its rivals, pressmen printed as many copies as they could by double plating and using two presses simultaneously or running them longer than usual.

Cornelius Vanderbilt, seated center atop truck, celebrates the first day of publication of the Los Angeles *Illustrated Daily News* in a group photograph. Vanderbilt remained editor and publisher of the *Daily News* for nearly three years before losing the newspaper due to mismanagement. (*Daily News* Collection/ Special Collections, UCLA)

Workman performs maintenance duty on a *Daily News* press in the early 1930s. (Daily News Collection/Special Collections, UCLA)

Los Angeles *Daily News* staff artists, from left: Sam Patrick, Foster Goss, and Walter Lee in 1935. (Walter Lee Collection)

Hiring editorial staff began in early August. Vanderbilt's two key men in the department were Douglas Churchill and Reed Hayes. Churchill was a hotel beat reporter for the *Times* when he was assigned to interview Vanderbilt during one of his many trips to Los Angeles. When Vanderbilt started looking for a strong leader he asked Churchill to join the new paper. Churchill signed on as the chief editorial writer and editor of the "Man in the Street" column. He would later be promoted to assistant to the publisher, then continue his journalism career as a Hollywood correspondent for the New York *Times* and *Redbook* magazine.

Named managing editor at a generous salary of $250 a week was Reed Hayes, a ruthless, forthright San Francisco newspaperman who also had been city editor of the *Record*. Vanderbilt left it to Hayes to hire the best newspaper people he could find.

With the purse strings loosened, Hayes brought in Lance Heath, former assistant city editor at the *Evening Herald*, as city editor. Ed Kelsey was hired as news editor and H. Sutherland Denlinger took on picture editor duties to supervise the paper's fourteen photographers (Staffing of photographers at rival newspapers rarely rose above ten). Fond of carrying a cane and wearing spats, he was an absent-minded man who spoke in a clipped Oxfordian accent and had a lengthy war record while serving with the French Foreign Legion during the world war. Rounding out the staff were Mort Donohue, Sunday editor; Dudley Burrows, drama editor; Bob ("Ned") Cronin, sports editor; Jack Fowler, movie editor; William Knox, the night city editor who would later write a critical profile of Vanderbilt for *The Outlook* magazine; and Martha Foley, literary editor.

The photography staff was exceptionally talented. The newspaper's top shooter was Sid Mautner. He worked for Chicago papers before coming to Los Angeles. He loved stalking his subjects with his camera concealed, moving ahead of them, then quickly turning around to shoot from the hip for an action photo. Joe Mingo specialized in aviation shots while Marvin Spafford covered dogs and animals, especially lions at Gay's Lion Farm in El Monte. Pete Rowe, the photo department's resident screwball, shot fires. He usually beat the fire department to alarms, often passing the battalion chief's red car and yelling out, "Hello, chief, see you at the fire."

The first day of publication was 3 September, and Vanderbilt was eager to beat the competition with a strong presentation of news photos. The Tokyo earthquake had struck 1 September, killing 140,000 people. Details of the disaster were sketchy and images of the devastation were nonexistent. Vanderbilt ordered photos from the scene and had them transported by ship across the Pacific. Reporter H.B.K. "Doc" Willis was assigned to charter an airplane and meet the ship off the coast of California to rush the photos to the newsroom. The plane reached the ship and the art was given to Willis. But a few miles offshore, the plane broke a connecting rod and the pilot had to ditch it into the sea. Willis jumped out onto a wing as the pilot radioed for help. Standing waist-deep in water on top of the wing, Willis held the photos over his head until a powerboat from San Pedro sidled up and rescued him. (This was a story that Vanderbilt was fond of embellishing, if not deliberately misleading interviewers. It would have been impossible in 1923 for a ship and plane to travel from Tokyo to Los Angeles in one day. More than likely, he ordered stock photos of Tokyo and then altered them to show the devastation, which was a common and accepted practice then.)

When the art found its way into the newsroom on Sunday, 2 September, the plant was jammed with hundreds of people. Vanderbilt staged a party to celebrate the debut of his newspaper and the earthquake photo scoop that would be splashed across the front page. Douglas Fairbanks, Mary Pickford, and Charlie Chaplin showed up to witness the first run. Local clergymen ended evening worshipping services early and urged their congregations to visit the new plant. Union leaders, who finally found a toehold in a newspaper plant, demanded that their members display solidarity by watching the presses roll for the first time. The first issue, to be published on Monday, 3 September, was particularly meaningful to Vanderbilt. It was his mother's birthday and it was Labor Day. (His mother, however, hated newspapers after the New York Hearst papers in the 1890s hounded her family. When her son mailed the first copies of the *Daily News* to her, she returned them without comment.)

II.

The first run was not without serious problems. Vanderbilt had underestimated just to what lengths the competition would go to crush his new venture. Shortly after 9 p.m. Sunday, the presses for the first edition began to roll. When the first copies plopped into the basket, Vanderbilt picked up a copy and quickly scanned the front and inside pages. Beside him were his guests, the Hollywood elite of Fairbanks, Pickford, and Chaplin. He looked up and quickly motioned for the presses to stop. Apparently nobody had bothered to look at page proofs. On the editorial page was a clear statement from Vanderbilt that he would publish a clean newspaper. On Page 2 was a graphic sex story about Chaplin planted by staffers. Vanderbilt quickly had the pressmen gather up the several hundred copies that already rolled off the line and had Churchill and Hayes move them to a heating plant to be burned. New plates for Page 2, with the originally planned stories, were made, and the press run started again.

Despite sabotage, outwardly the *Daily News* was brimming with hope. A week before the first issue, 80,000 subscribers with contracts for at least three months had been signed on. On its first day, Vanderbilt announced that the press run was 125,000. An estimated 1,000 delivery boys promised subscribers the newspaper at the doorstep at 6 a.m. each day with another 2,000 boys hawking the newspaper for a penny on the streets. Newsboys took the brunt of the competition's disdain for the new penny paper. Men initially used intimidation and bribery to force boys to abandon their corners. When results were slow, the boys were beaten. Up to 100 boys each week during the first month of publication were treated at local hospitals for cuts and bruises. Vanderbilt, sensing a circulation war to his benefit, began publishing photos of the injured news hawkers on his front page with the caption: "Is Los Angeles going to stand for such jungle methods of competition?" Circulation during the first four weeks began to climb slightly.

On its editorial pages, the new publisher established the paper's six-point platform: 1) Americanism. 2) California—United. 3) Adequate traffic facilities for Los Angeles. 4) More schools for Los Angeles. 5) More playfields for Los Angeles. 6) Clean press—A paper that may safely enter the home.

If circulation numbers were to be believed then the *Daily News* would rank as the city's No. 3 newspaper behind the *Evening Herald* (169,757 daily in 1923) and the morning *Examiner* (151,614). The *Times* carried a daily circulation of 120,889. But it soon would become apparent that the *Daily News'* initial numbers were inflated. Or perhaps the numbers were achieved through subscriptions sold at a substantial discount. The truth, however, was not in the circulation numbers, but the equipment possessed by each newspaper. Here, the *Daily News* ranked somewhere around the *Record*, the city's smallest paper. In 1927, for example, when the *Daily News'* circulation began to steadily climb and was under stable management, the *Examiner* owned forty Linotype composing machines, two Intertype machines, and four Ludlows. The *Daily News* possessed eight Intertype machines and one Ludlow. The *Times* in 1929, the first year reliable composing machine numbers for the newspaper became available, possessed forty Linotypes and four Monotypes. Even during World War II and the postwar boom, the *Daily News* never achieved the sheer mass of composing equipment enjoyed by the *Examiner* and the *Times*.

While the *Daily News* got off to a roaring start, the young publisher still was faced with a newsroom in disarray. In an interview published by the *Ladies' Home Journal*, Vanderbilt said his critics determined to destroy the credibility of his newspaper hatched a widespread conspiracy. "Men who were agents and cat's-paws were recommended to me in roundabout ways and from apparently good sources, and I employed them," Vanderbilt told the *Journal*. "Several of them were assigned to important executive positions in the outfit, and these bosses had enough confederates scattered through the various departments to enable them to perpetrate such an outrage as the indecent Chaplin story in the first issue."

The fallout would last for weeks and put the newsroom in turmoil. While Vanderbilt didn't identify the saboteurs and unreliable gossip failed to pinpoint the exact causes and reasons behind the planted story, nearly half the editorial staff had been expelled from the newsroom before the end of the year. But firings had less to due with the planted story than Vanderbilt's peculiar logic in dealing with the crisis. Vanderbilt hired a detective agency to ferret out the spies. One reporter acknowledged that he fabricated then planted the sex story on Chaplin without an editor or typesetter's knowledge. The reporter, who was never identified, admitted that he was paid $50 to plant the story and would have been given another $50 if the paper containing the story actually hit the streets.

Vanderbilt later said that twenty-seven news staffers were identified and fired as a result of the incident. Either Vanderbilt and Reed Hayes were the worst judges of character and hired newsmen on the competition's payroll or they were a victim of Vanderbilt's own naiveté and faulty logic. Evidence points to the latter.

Three weeks after the debacle, Hayes learned that private detectives were in his newsroom spying on his staff. A man prone to exaggerated gestures and a fierce temper, Hayes walked to the middle of the newsroom and shouted, "Ladies and gentlemen, your integrity as newspapermen has been assailed by that goddamned underhanded SOB we work for. He has insulted every one of us. The office is full of Pinkerton detectives and they've been spying on us."

Hayes demanded the staff accompany him to Vanderbilt's office for a confrontation. Between twenty-five and thirty men and women followed Hayes into the publisher's office. Vanderbilt was at his desk, leaning back in his chair and eating raw hot dogs and drinking milk. Douglas Churchill was with him.

The staff crowded into Vanderbilt's office. A copy editor defiantly sat on the publisher's desk flicking ashes at him from his cigarette. Hayes pointed his finger at his boss.

"Neil, I brought the whole staff in to learn what a dirty SOB you are!" Hayes shouted. "You've had detectives spying on us. I want you to admit it!"

"Now Mr. Hayes," Vanderbilt responded softly.

"Neil, you're a SOB!" Hayes interrupted. "Now if you're any kind of man you'll take a poke at me. I called you a SOB!"

Any attempts by Vanderbilt to reply were pointless. Hayes continued to interrupt him with insults and demands for an apology. Vanderbilt finally settled back and quietly eyed Hayes as he popped weenies in his mouth and took sips of milk.

Churchill held up his hand and stepped forward. "Really gentlemen," he said, "I think Mr. Vanderbilt has been hazed sufficiently."

Hayes' putsch ended there but the next day Vanderbilt began calling in each member of the staff who followed the managing editor into his office. The first to be summoned was Eleanor Barnes, a reporter lured away from the *Record*.

Barnes had developed a following at the *Record* as a sob sister feature writer who had run into Vanderbilt while on assignment. Vanderbilt had invited her for a job interview, but when she appeared for her appointment he didn't remember her. She was persistent, however, and finally landed a job on the *Daily News*. Now she was standing before her new boss, puzzled by his questions since she didn't participate in the office revolt.

"What did you think of this disgraceful scene?" Vanderbilt asked Barnes. "Are you on Mr. Hayes' side or on my side?"

Barnes was perplexed and attempted to convince Vanderbilt that she was not a participant. Vanderbilt had hoped she would remain loyal to him since she was so well known in the city that her participation in a revolt would demonstrate a weakness in his new staff.

Barnes replied she wasn't with the Hayes revolt and evaded questions of loyalty since she found the whole thing ludicrous. When she left the publisher's office, she told the staff she was going home sick for the day.

The remaining staff didn't handle Vanderbilt as deftly. One by one they sealed their fate by claiming loyalty to either Hayes or Vanderbilt. They were all fired on the skewed logic that it was wrong to take either side. Other than Barnes, occasional staffers gave the right answer. Artist Walt Lee told Vanderbilt that he wasn't loyal to anybody, but he was loyal to the newspaper. He survived the massacre. Others, like Hank Denlinger, "Doc" Willis, Ned Cronin, Sid Mautner, Marvin Spafford, and Sam Patrick also survived. But gone were the core editorial supervisors and many of the reporters: Reed Hayes, Lance Heath, Ed Kelsey, William Knox, and Martha Foley, among others, left by the end of the year. Whether they were identified as spies or made the mistake of pledging loyalty to a single person remains unclear

The new editorial management team gave a degree of stability to the newsroom not found under Hayes. Veteran newsman Frederick M. Shorey was named as managing editor and Douglas Turney the city editor. A year later, Lester Adams was appointed managing editor and Richard Nail the city editor. Adams was an idea man who appreciated what Vanderbilt was attempting to accomplish but understood a balance in coverage was vital to maintain the integrity of the newspaper.

For once, Vanderbilt had chosen the right editor. With Adams in charge, the *Daily News* could still uphold Vanderbilt's general philosophy while publishing an assortment of interesting news and photos. Adams had begun his career in 1913 with the Medford *Sun* in Oregon before joining the Sacramento *Union*, where he remained for six years as a telegraph editor. From the *Union* he joined the San Francisco *Chronicle* as a copy editor. He was recruited from the *Chronicle* following Vanderbilt's purge at the *Daily News*, joining the makeup desk in Los Angeles on Christmas Eve 1923.

In a sense, Adams would serve as the link that would keep the Vanderbilt chain from breaking apart. When the *Illustrated Herald* was six months old, Vanderbilt sent him to San Francisco as the paper's news editor. He would return to Los Angeles less than a year later. Adams' deftness at handling the mercurial Vanderbilt and the Vanderbilt family representative when Vanderbilt's parents later wrestled control of the newspaper from their son would become a saving grace for *Daily News'* editorial department in late 1925 and early 1926.

If the *Daily News* was competitive against the other papers it was only for subscribers and street sales, not for the content of its news pages. Veteran editors and reporters chaffed at stringent regulations that kept crime, sex, and divorce to a bare minimum while the *Examiner* and the *Herald* made hay out of every Hollywood scandal. Artists were required to touch up photos so that women's skirts fell below their knees. Wrestlers had their hairy chests covered with painted gym shirts. If fun was to be had, it wasn't to be found on the second floor of the *Daily News* building. Staffers could find some solace in covering natural disasters and train wrecks but found those events to be occasional distractions from the more numerous groundbreaking ceremonies, weddings, and tedious obituaries. It was quite a comedown for a Hearst-trained New York reporter to grab a photographer and rush to the next ribbon-cutting ceremony for a new bank building.

Editorial staff did enjoy perks that their competition did not. Reporters typically were expected to carry a roll of nickels to jump aboard a trolley to reach an assignment. Or, if there was enough loose change in their pocket, they would hail a taxicab. At the *Daily News*, Vanderbilt gave reporters and photographers access to his two low-slung Packard touring cars for transportation. The Packards came in handy when a group of U.S. destroyers hit the rocks near Santa Barbara in late 1923. Seven destroyers in all were severely damaged or sunk. The only problem the news crew saw was that Vanderbilt himself, the most inexperienced reporter on staff, would jump in his car and cover the story.

The lion's share of covering non-news events went to Eleanor Barnes and Sid Mautner. To them there was no such thing as a no news story. The pair would scour the streets of downtown accosting strangers and asking them questions about their clothes or jewelry and fashion a story out of it. Kids selling lemonade or a woman beating a rug found their way into the newspaper in the form of a fifteen-inch story and Mautner art.

Respect from reporters for Vanderbilt as a newsman was not forthcoming. Stories began to surface about his superficial approach to the profession. His news stories reeked of naiveté and his editorials were sophomoric. The editorial page often contained opinions that simply touted the newspaper's cleanliness and high moral standards. John Peere Miles, the night bureau manager for the United Press, sought an interview with Vanderbilt during the first weeks of the paper's operation. His mission was two-fold: To profile the city's newest publisher and to remind Vanderbilt that he must pay his bill to the UP on time. It had already become evident that Vanderbilt would be chronically late in meeting the demands of his creditors. Miles stopped by the publisher's office and was escorted inside by Vanderbilt's secretary. Behind the desk was the young man furiously typing on his portable Corona typewriter. Vanderbilt motioned for Miles to sit and remain silent while he finished writing. The publisher then stood up and told Miles that he would return in a moment. While Vanderbilt was out of the office, Miles moved around behind the desk to take a peek at the story. Written repeatedly was the single sentence, "Now is the time for all good men to come to the aid of their party."

His real writing added little to his growing reputation among newsmen. His columns read more like New York society columns, pieces that may have garnered a following on the East Coast, but meant little to cynical, no-nonsense Angelenos. In a column that ultimately made him a laughing stock among his own employees, Vanderbilt penned an editorial under the headline, "We're off in a Cloud of Spray."

Taking a vacation by ship, he wrote, "With our two Packards lashed to the deck of the *H.F. Alexander*, the finest and fastest vessel plying between Los Angeles and Seattle, we're off in a cloud of spray."

"We're off in a cloud of spray" became the editorial department's mantra. Rival reporters greeted each other with the phrase as they covered homicides and liquor raids together. *Daily News* sports writer Howard Langley covered the USC-Oregon football game in Portland. On the train home after the game he began drinking with competing newsmen and wired his story ahead. He wrote, "We're off in a cloud of Oregon mist with four cases of Scotch lashed to the compartments of the Sunset Limited, finest and fastest train flying between Portland and Los Angeles...." Vanderbilt never got the joke.

When the *Daily News* took on a cause, it focused on issues that most community-minded newspapers would support rather than attack. During the 1920s, Los Angeles had a powerful chamber of commerce, which had three pet projects: It sought to establish a Community Chest, build the Los Angeles Coliseum, and organize a crime commission. Heading up the projects were chamber president R.H. Pridham and Harry Chandler. Vanderbilt attacked all three projects, and the men behind them, with vigor. Circulation again boomed for a short period before the politically powerful chamber threatened to bury the paper with an advertising blacklist if Vanderbilt continued his campaign. Vanderbilt also attacked the Pacific Electric Railway, publishing photographs of smashed cars and injured motorists who collided with the rail cars. To the *Daily News*, the PE cars were the "Red Reaper." Industry gossip later attributed the newspaper's sudden loss of interest in the Red Reapers to more threats of pulled advertising.

Despite rock-bottom staff morale and heavy pressure from the Hearst papers and advertisers, Vanderbilt remained uncannily optimistic about the future of Vanderbilt Newspapers, Inc. The day after the first issue appeared on the streets he ordered a third press and announced that the *Daily News* would publish on Sundays, making it a seven-day daily.

Vanderbilt's optimism was based in the fact that when faced with extraordinary pressure, he had a tendency to look to other projects to occupy his time. He left the unpleasant tasks and day-to-day news operation to Douglas Churchill. It was only a matter of weeks, in the midst of his newsroom revolt, that he began contemplating a second newspaper.

The union trade publication, the San Francisco *Labor Clarion*, broke the story in its "Typographical Topics" column in the 28 September edition. It published a rumor that *Daily News* promoters would visit San Francisco no later than 15 October to make arrangements for a new daily. A week later, the *Fourth Estate* confirmed the story. Vanderbilt told the magazine that he was "well pleased" with the success of his Los Angeles project and its 155,000 circulation after three weeks on the streets that he wanted to begin a new daily.

By the end of October he had organized the San Francisco *Illustrated Daily Herald* and leased a building at 12th and Market streets in San Francisco. Remodeling began on the plant and twenty-five Intertype machines were ordered. The first issue appeared on 10 December with nearly 80,000 prepaid subscriptions on the books. Another Vanderbilt paper opened in January 1925, the Miami *Illustrated Tab*.

Circulation gains of the Los Angeles *Daily News'* during the first two years of its existence were due to Vanderbilt's odd crusades. It found its niche in appealing to readers weary of the sex and crime scandals. And its campaigns against the chamber and other venerable institutions won wide readership in what some newsmen in town thought of as the curiosity factor. What would Vanderbilt do next?

But the influence of the *Daily News* under the Vanderbilt regime was no more evident than the in 1925 mayoral race between incumbent George E. Cryer and federal Judge Benjamin Bledsoe. Cryer was elected mayor in 1921 on the platform of public ownership for utilities. He won the endorsement of Chandler's *Times*, which meant a virtual lock on the office. Bledsoe was a Democrat and hated Bolsheviks and labor unions. By 1925 Cryer shifted his position to municipal ownership of water and began to lose control of his police department as vice and crime ran unchecked in the city. The *Daily News* ignored the city's worsening crime problem—at least for the moment as it would later become a cause for the paper under a different publisher—and enthusiastically backed

Cryer. The paper, writing as many as four stories a day on Cryer, supported the mayor's stand on municipal ownership and his plan to fight crime, a plan that was vastly different than Chandler's own anticrime proposal. Cryer also was becoming more sympathetic to labor, which angered Chandler. The *Daily News* was joined by the *Record*, which had long waged a battle against Chandler and public ownership of utilities. The two newspapers stood alone against Chandler, who suddenly found that Bledsoe, although a Democrat, was the best choice as mayor. The *Examiner* and the *Evening Herald* remained neutral during the campaign. The *Evening Express* endorsed Bledsoe. Cryer handily beat Bledsoe to remain the city's mayor.

For a brief, shining moment the *Daily News* stood out as Southern California's leading newspaper, at least in circulation. Its weekday sales reached 178,719 in 1924, compared to the 173,548 sold by the *Herald* and the 165,026 sold by the *Examiner*. The *Times* trailed a distant fourth, with 132,105. Even after the novelty of a tabloid had worn off, in 1925, the *Daily News* remained strong, with sales of 172,409, although the *Herald* reclaimed the lead, with 177,409.

Even so, the rivals of the *Daily News* were well established. It could almost be said, for example, that the *Times* created the upper-middle class of Los Angeles. The readers of the *Daily News*, by comparison, were rarely the city's powerbrokers: perhaps some members of the film industry, residents of the African American and Latino communities, liberals, and the lower-middle class, particularly "shop girls," a group well served by the *Record*. The *Daily News* never carried more than 4.3 million lines of advertising in 1924, compared to the 23 million lines carried by the *Examiner*. The lineage at the *Daily News* would continue to slide, to a low of 2.9 million in 1926.

Unable to ignore his losses in advertising revenue and the rapid turnover in staffing throughout the paper, Vanderbilt sought financial help in 1924 from his parents. The senior Vanderbilts had been disgusted with their son's choice of profession since he returned from France and became a journalist. They finally saw an opportunity to gain control of his enterprise. His parents agreed to loan him money to keep the papers afloat, but demanded that most of the authority in the company go to their handpicked manager, Harvey Johnson.

The change in leadership was painful to Vanderbilt. He intended to endorse Wisconsin Progressive Robert LaFollette during the 1924 presidential election, but the family preferred Calvin Coolidge. Attacks on the Chamber of Commerce and big business petered out and guest columns by one-time *Daily News* enemies soon filled the editorial pages. Readers immediately caught on to the shift in editorial policy and 50,000 quit the paper.

Former night city editor William Knox later acknowledged that Vanderbilt had "held the political destinies of the city in the hollow of his hand, and there are many things in Los Angeles that for a considerable time will be different from what they would have been had there been no Cornelius Vanderbilt."

Lester Adams deserves much of the credit. Adams worked well with Harvey Johnson and put renewed energy in the paper during his short stint as the managing editor. He promised, and delivered, greater efficiency in production, as much local news as he could cram into the paper's thirty-two pages, more news appealing to women readers, and more freedom in handling crime stories.

While Adams managed to settle down the editorial department, losses continued to plague the paper in late 1925. Subscribers stopped the paper because of its shift to more moderate politics, and because it lacked substantial advertising from the city's major department stores. The editorial department had only forty-four employees and advertising revenues for October 1925 were only $22,141. In addition, both the *Illustrated Herald* and the *Tab* had difficulty collecting huge advertising bills from businesses that had failed.

Vanderbilt again went to his parents for a cash infusion, and again he gave up more control. Over a six-month period, his father had provided $1,080,000 to his son. But the hemorrhaging continued. Vanderbilt suggested to Douglas Churchill in March 1926 that he consider three options for the future of Vanderbilt Newspapers Inc. He proposed that all three dailies fold and risk criminal prosecution for stock fraud; shut down the *Illustrated Herald* and sell the building and plant equipment; or adopt a policy of yellow journalism to attract more readers. Vanderbilt then turned to Harvey Johnson and several newspaper experts for their advice. Following a survey they concluded that all three properties could survive if given another $300,000 infusion.

Vanderbilt went to his father on 23 April 1926 and asked for his third loan. His father refused. At a press conference in New York after his failed bid to his parents for a loan, Vanderbilt remained confident that he could keep the papers alive. He acknowledged for the first time, however, that he made mistakes in his leadership and had placed his trust in inexperienced executives who mismanaged the company. He appeared unable or unwilling to accept full responsibility for the failure of his business.

A desperate, eleventh-hour attempt to salvage the *Daily News* was made by eliminating the Sunday edition and cutting the street price from 2 cents to a penny (street prices were raised to 2 cents in 1925 to increase revenue). The move failed. On 3 May a petition for receivership was filed in U.S. District Court in Los Angeles to keep creditors from closing down the paper. The *Illustrated Herald* was closed and the *Tab* survived another six weeks before folding.

Vanderbilt was no longer part of the *Daily News*. His noble dream lay in ruins through his own ineptness and inability to recognize his own weaknesses and the shortcomings and strengths of the men around him.

On 3 May U.S. District Court Paul McCormick appointed Meredith P. Snyder, a former mayor of Los Angeles, as receiver for the *News*. The complaint filed in federal court listed the assets of the *Daily News* as $1,043,000 and its liabilities as $1 million. The value of the plant was estimated at $165,000 and its circulation at 92,000. The *Daily News* owed Vanderbilt Newspapers Inc. $65,000 in sixty days but would not meet the obligation.

The reaction from the newspaper industry to the failure of Vanderbilt Newspapers Inc. was swift and brutal. Five days after Snyder's appointment, *Saturday Night* magazine went on the attack. It alleged that the Vanderbilt name "hypnotized the gullible subscribers" in the company's stock-selling campaign and that $3 million was transferred from conservative investors into the coffers of the paper that ultimately a large portion inappropriately found its way to fund the *Illustrated Herald* and the *Tab*. The magazine also didn't hide its disgust that Vanderbilt traded on his family name to lure investors into the ill-fated venture. One retired investor lost $50,000 and a wealthy widow with extensive coastal land holdings lost an estimated $40,000.

The magazine also took issue with Snyder's appointment as receiver, complaining that he possessed no newspaper experience and was not qualified to run a newspaper. It noted with irony that Snyder earned a sizable article and two-column photo on the front page of the *Daily News* following his appointment. With each week the attacks by *Saturday Night* on Vanderbilt grew more vehement as it resorted to identifying Vanderbilt not as Cornelius but "Nellie."

The *Times* joined the chorus, noting that "whatever (Vanderbilt's) qualifications in other directions, he is not a newspaperman by either instinct or training. He had practically no knowledge or experience of the intricate details of the business upon which he embarked and those whom he chose as his immediate advisors were in little better case."

The newspaper industry magazine *Fourth Estate* thought otherwise, telling its readers that it refuses to "join voice with the noisy chorus which joyously proclaim the failure of Cornelius Vanderbilt Jr. as a publisher." The magazine believed that Vanderbilt's conduct was an "honest desire to give expression to an ambition, and for that we must admire him, even though we admire him alone."

The *Daily News* staff continued to crank out the paper knowing full well that a paycheck probably wasn't coming and there was no guarantee of a job in the future. But a new life for the paper was more of a reality than they imagined.

Chapter Three

Manchester Boddy's Crusades

I.

Gene Coughlin was cranky and the stranger shuffling his feet behind him while he pounded out the lead of his story wasn't helping matters any.

Coughlin, at twenty-four, had more education than most of the men and women in the *Daily News* editorial department. He had attended Medill School of Journalism then served his apprenticeship on the Chicago papers before coming to Los Angeles.

Despite his young age Coughlin had been assigned to cover the courts—a plum beat. He had spent the day covering a criminal hearing for Aimee Semple McPherson, the charismatic evangelist who had disappeared while swimming off of Venice Beach in May 1926. She resurfaced in the Mexican desert at Agua Prieta, claiming she had been kidnapped. Her clean and unscuffed shoes and new hairstyle cast some doubts on her story. It soon became apparent that Aimee wasn't abducted by money-hungry bandits but stole away for three weeks to be with her lover at Carmel-by-the-Sea. Los Angeles County law authorities didn't appreciate the holiday, since they spent thousands of dollars searching for her body in the Pacific and had lost a diver to drowning. The county insisted on prosecuting McPherson for fraud. Newspaper editors and circulation managers noted that they had sold more newspapers than they could print during her disappearance and they hoped their readers would want more.

Coughlin's job was to see that more papers would be sold. He covered every excruciating detail of the case in Los Angeles County Superior Court, spending day after day yawning through dry and vague legal arguments by the defense attorneys. During one recess he lost $2.80 playing pitch with other reporters, then discovered his favorite eatery, Thomas' restaurant, raised the price of a T-bone dinner from 60 to 65 cents.

When Coughlin returned to the newsroom at the end of the day, City Editor Joel Rickman, who wore a .38-caliber revolver as casually as some people wore neckties, demanded a lively story. Behind him was another veteran of the Chicago newspaper wars, managing editor Harry Eller. He was hoping for the same.

"Got something good and hot?" Rickman and Eller asked in unison.

"I've got seven pages of irrelevants, incompetents and immaterials," Coughlin replied sarcastically.

"Do your best to liven it up," Eller said. "It's got to be our lead story in the morning."

Coughlin sat at his typewriter, jammed a cigarette in his mouth, and banged out fifty words. He noticed that someone was looking over his shoulder. He looked up at the man and yelled, "How the hell can a man write with some Constant Reader breathing down his neck?"

Coughlin stomped off toward the composing room. Rickman caught up with him and told him to keep moving, for he had just shouted at the new publisher, E. Manchester Boddy. Believing his career was over at the *Daily News*, Coughlin returned to pick up his coat. Boddy was still standing at Coughlin's desk, laughing. Coughlin apologized but Boddy waved him off.

"My name is Boddy," he said. "And I am curious about the steps necessary in getting out the newspaper. This is the first one I've ever published."

It was surprising that Coughlin still had a boss. But Superior Court Judge Meredith Snyder officially turned over the newspaper's property to the newly formed Daily News Corporation. About 5,300 stockholders had finished negotiations to buy the publication. Named as officers were William Oliphant, president; Willis O. Lewis, vice-president; Claude B. Andrews, vice-president; and R.I. Jones, secretary-treasurer. Named to the board of directors were Boddy, R.H. Whiner, A. McDonald Kerr, J.G. DeLozier, and Joseph Mesmer. The board named Boddy editor and general manager of the *Daily News* after loaning him $116,000 for six months to purchase a controlling interest in newspaper. The ownership of the paper would revert to the board if it failed to show a profit in six months.

Assuming control on 5 August, Boddy moved quickly. Following his visit to the second floor newsroom the day he took control, he planned a treat for the employees to celebrate the purchase, boost morale, and demonstrate the paper was still alive. At the Chamber of Commerce building he put on a banquet for the paper's 200 employees. He then went on the Los Angeles luncheon circuit to drum up enthusiasm.

II.

The board had chosen Boddy because he recognized that while his talent was not in newspapering, he could make impossible tasks happen. He faced insurmountable odds to attend college and work at jobs in which he had no experience.

Boddy was born in 1891 at Lake Tapps, on the western slope of the Cascades, in Washington state, to Benjamin and Susan Dennis Morgan Boddy. One of five sons, he was named for his maternal grandfather, Elias Manchester Morgan. When he was a child, he dropped Elias to become Manchester but kept the spirit of his first name by using E. Manchester Boddy in his correspondence and schoolwork. His friends and family called him Chester and occasionally "Chet".

The Boddys flirted with poverty throughout Manchester's childhood. The Northern Pacific Railway lured Benjamin and Susan from Minnesota to Washington during an intense advertising campaign as it extended its lines from the Midwest to the Pacific Ocean. The railway had hoped to create agricultural communities in Montana, Oregon, and Washington. If farmers raised cattle and grew wheat and corn they would need to use the railroad to transport their crops. Oregon and Washington, in particular, were described as paradise where oranges could be plucked from trees, and oil fields and gold mines would provide a steady income.

The Boddys were just a single family among thousands who had taken the bait and traveled west. The railway's claims were exaggerated, and Benjamin Boddy found himself in paradise but without the means to put food on the table and a decent roof over the heads of his wife and sons. He tried working a potato crop, but when it failed, he moved his family to Black Diamond, a mining town. Benjamin found jobs as a miner, sawyer, and farmer, moving from town to town, working for day wages. The boys did odd jobs for neighbors and shot or trapped live game for dinner.

When the Boddys arrived in Pialschie, Washington, about 1905, Manchester enrolled in the local high school. There, he made perhaps his most important discovery about himself. He was articulate, for he made a sales pitch like no other student on campus. He became the consummate salesman, not through a scheme to gain wealth, but a true desire to provide an equal trade-off for each customer. The sales he made were borne from empathy for the needs of his customers and an urgent desire to achieve success in the business community.

During school, for example, he was the star attraction on the debate team. During the summers, he sold self-heating flatirons, an unpredictable contraption that was fueled with a small tank of gasoline and likely to explode unless handled carefully. On his route through farming towns, he would often roll up his sleeves to milk the cows and feed the chickens while the women of the house tested the iron. If the demonstration were successful, Boddy would usually make a sale. When he exhausted his supply of irons, he helped feed his family by clerking in a grocery story or performing janitorial work.

After graduating from high school, young Boddy continued working at odd jobs to carry him through classes at Washington State College. He was hoping to become a lawyer, but after a year at Washington and the summer off, he ran out of money. Believing that attending Kent College of Law in Chicago by day and working jobs at night would help him pass the bar, he took a friend's suggestion and stowed away in the baggage car of a passenger train. It was November, and by the time he arrived in Missoula, Montana, he was so cold and miserable that he jumped the train and headed for the nearest saloon to warm up. While in Missoula, he was told the University of Montana had a good law school. He decided to try his luck there. He paid his tuition by earning $8 a month as a janitor in the law library and serving meals in the girls' dormitory. When he learned that a local church needed a missionary for nearby Bonner, he took the job at $35 a month. Whatever work came his way, he grabbed it: Miner, bookkeeper, kitchen-appliance salesman, mining-stock salesman, English language teacher, tutor. But his work couldn't pay for his tuition at the university, and he was forced to quit again. It was 1916 and it was time to find what New York City had to offer.

The U.S. was poised to enter the war. Strangers entering New York City were often detained as suspected terrorists, undesirable labor organizers, or German sympathizers. Boddy was collared as he stepped onto the train platform in New York. He was allowed to leave when federal lawmen and police found he had only $8 and a comb. As he left the detention area, a gang boss recruited him to work for the Interborough Rapid Transit opening and closing subway car doors from the Battery to Van Cortlandt Park.

A breakthrough for Boddy came when he took a job selling the Encyclopedia Britannica. He was assigned the Bowery. The Bowery was a district of abject poverty where few spoke much English and only worked for their next meal. It was considered ridiculous to expect any family to purchase a set of encyclopedias on an installment plan much less for cash. Boddy saw, however, that the people there did want information and knowledge. They would pay what they could to buy a book, but it fell far short of the requirements of the installment plan.

So Boddy began organizing book and study clubs. During the evenings he would gather a small group of adults and children in a hot, but clean kitchen and teach them basic English and math, by using his product as a reference. At the end of each lesson, he would explain that if each family contributed a few pennies regularly, the entire group could conceivably own its own set. Eventually, many families had their own community library.

While selling for Encyclopedia Britannica, Boddy met Berenice Maud Klotz, originally from Winnetka, Illinois, who was working in the book department. On 1 January 1918, they were married. On 2 January, Boddy, who had enlisted in the U.S. Army, was shipped to Europe as a member of the 307th Infantry. By the time he landed in France, he was a first sergeant, and then was promoted to second lieutenant with the 129th Infantry in the 33rd Division, eventually winning four battle stars. Like Vanderbilt, he was seriously gassed, in the Argonne Forest, and spent several months in an army hospital before being discharged as 100 percent disabled.

When he returned to his wife in New York, he began looking for another book venture. He soon found out that the New York *Times* had a warehouse full of its weekly supplement, *Current History* magazine, gathering dust on its shelves. Boddy had the volumes bound and titled *The European War*. He sold them on a straight commission basis. The books sold so well that the *Times* bought out his contract for a hefty sum. His next job was selling both the *Current History* magazine and *Mid-Week Pictorial*—another supplement for the *Times*—at a weekly salary of $75. But the hectic pace he set for himself resulted in double pneumonia, complicated by the effects of the gas attack. His physician ordered him to return to the west.

In 1920, Boddy found himself in Los Angeles with a vague idea of continuing his book ventures. He leased desk space in the Van Nuys building in downtown at $8 month and had a letterhead made up for "E.M. Boddy Book Company." His new letterhead, the leased desk, and a new suit were the company's entire assets. A chance conversation with a man sharing his office tipped Boddy off that the Mexican government was seeking laborers to build a railroad extension from the Southwest. He began to consider the possibility of whether there was a market for information on Latin America among scholars, historians, and the general reader. At a nearby library, Boddy found the out-of-print *The Mexican Yearbook, 1914-1915*. After securing the free rights to the book from its London publishers, Boddy updated it and began selling it by subscription. He received advance payments for an order of 2,500 copies. Over several weeks he angled lower echelon employees at the Times-Mirror Company to obtain an interview with Harry Chandler, owner and president of Times-Mirror. Chandler would buy the yearbook outright, and even hired Boddy to run Time-Mirror's book publishing operation.

The company was considered a stepchild of the newspaper, but under Boddy it became a profitable and productive business. Since his early days in Los Angeles, he had been a member of the Commercial Board, a powerful clique of downtown businessmen who wielded a fair amount of power. Boddy's reputation as a resourceful businessman, coupled with early mentoring from Chandler, made him a likely candidate for bigger, more challenging projects.

Boddy's opportunity came in the spring of 1926, when the *Daily News* fell into receivership and was reorganized. A committee of the leading publishers—Harry Chandler; George Young, representing the *Examiner* and the *Herald*; and Edward Dickson, of the *Express*—began pressing Judge Paul McCormick of the

United States District Court to kill off the *Daily News*. Chicago, with 4 million residents in the city alone, could barely support four English-language dailies, whereas Los Angeles, with an estimated 900,000 people, had six dailies. Led by Chandler, the committee offered $150,000 to buy the name of the *Daily News* and pay off its creditors.

But a key figure in the future of the *Daily News* was Willis Lewis, Boddy's colleague on the Commercial Board and a member of the new board of directors for the Daily News Corporation. Lewis had an expertise in reviving sick businesses, and he had invested heavily in the *Daily News* under the Vanderbilt regime. When Lewis told Boddy that the *Daily News* was "the sickest business you ever saw," Boddy took an immediate interest. And when Boddy found out that he could take over the management of the paper without risk, he sought control of the project. Judge McCormick and Meredith Snyder agreed that Boddy had, if not the credentials, the strong desire to see the newspaper succeed. With the influential backing from Lewis, they would allow Boddy the opportunity to revive the paper.

To lure back old readers and attract new ones, Boddy recognized that he needed a crusade. But unlike Vanderbilt, he was not about to bite the hand that fed him. Battling big business was financial suicide. Besides, he liked the men in the business community and counted many of them as his friends. It would be hurtful and unnecessary to attack them. And where Vanderbilt saw many of the city's businessmen as hammering away at underdogs and enjoying a monopoly, Boddy saw them as the force behind the city's emerging influence in the country. He wanted to be part of it.

III.

The logical answer in establishing a crusade was to expose the powerful organized crime syndicate operating the city's gambling dens and whorehouses. Since 1919, the dailies had a spotty record of detailing the influence of organized crime. Part of the blame lay with Harry Chandler. In exchange for his paper's silence on the city's active vice operations, the city government maintained stringent anti labor policies and allowed Chandler to have a voice in municipal affairs.

Chandler approved of the appointment of Police Chief James E. Davis, who had a hands-off policy on vice. Hefty, broad-shouldered, tipping the scale at nearly 200 pounds, Davis was about 35 years old when he was named chief. Born in Texas, Davis had left home at fifteen to pick cotton and herd cattle. He later worked as a deliveryman, locomotive fireman, and streetcar conductor before coming to Los Angeles in 1911. A year later, he joined the Los Angeles Police Department. He lasted twenty-three days. Police chief Charlie Sabastian fired him for "conduct unbecoming an officer and a gentleman." The details were never made clear and his personnel file had been lost. But when Sabastian was eased out of office, Davis returned to the department and rose through the ranks to become the new chief.

Under Davis, Los Angeles had gained the dubious distinction of being the most crime-ridden and corrupt city in the country. The city's reputation for honesty began its slide in 1919, when *Times* city hall reporter Horace Carr was indicted by a criminal grand jury on allegations that he helped open a section of Los Angeles to gambling, prostitution, and bootlegging. Carr at the time was Mayor Frederick Woodman's closest confidante. Carr had Chandler's tacit approval for the relationship because he was an internal link in the mayor's administration. Woodman ended up being indicted on the same charges as Carr.

As vice continued to flourish, several stopgap anticrime plans were implemented. Mayor Meredith Snyder, who succeeded Woodman—and was later appointed receiver of the *Daily News*—made the first attempt. George Cryer succeeded Snyder after the 1921 mayoral election. Cryer was reelected in 1923, largely on the backing of the *Times*, and again in 1925, thanks to a campaign waged by the *Daily News* when the *Times* abandoned him. But Cryer turned out to be a dismal failure in curtailing crime.

Times editor Ralph Trueblood and Chandler set up their own anticrime commission, but Cryer rejected it. The mayor, grasping at any idea that would help stem the tide of critical public opinion, fired Police Chief Louis D. Oakes, replacing him with criminologist August Vollmer. Vollmer, a weak leader, proved ineffectual. James Davis, who allowed organized crime to flourish not through incompetence but by design, then replaced him. To compound the problem, Cryer's chief aide, Kent Parrot, described by the *Record* as the city's "*de facto* mayor," had no use for crime commissions since much of the local syndicate's activities was paying him cash to operate without interference.

There were other, more practical, reasons why the local press did a poor job of tackling vice and exposing corruption and brutal excesses of the police department against radicals. Poorly paid reporters enjoyed perks offered by police while covering a story. Free liquor, access to drugs and prostitutes, and payoffs were not uncommon.

Police officers in the Los Angeles of the 1920s genuinely liked newsmen and felt they were brethren. Cub reporters would be taken under the wing of a crusty sergeant, who would give them tours of the city and provide them with a case of gin, or, if they were so inclined, access to the evidence room for a pinch of cocaine or morphine. It wasn't considered a bribe, either by the police or reporters, but simply sharing the wealth accorded to their professions. Then, too, there was an insidious herd-like mentality of many court and police beat reporters. These men would spend all day in the pressrooms at the county courthouse or the central police station playing pitch. Reporters with the *Times*, the *Daily News*, the *Examiner*, the *Express*, and the *Herald* operated as an informal syndicate. The same news was disseminated to all five newspapers. The *Times* beat reporter would act as the *pro forma* editor, deciding which news deserved coverage. There was sameness in stories from the police and courts beats published in the five dailies. The only divergence from this practice came when major breaking crime stories required reporters to spread across the city and file their notes with the rewrite desk by telephone.

The *Record* rarely was part of this news syndicate. Its staff was too small to have full-time beat reporters at the courthouse and police stations. Instead, the *Record* relied on the other dailies for its police stories, rewriting them straight from copies off the street. The *Record* allowed its reporters to write more investigative pieces than its rivals did. The practice of the *Times* beat reporter calling the shots died in the mid-1950s when veteran newsmen from Chicago, where competitive journalism was particularly cutthroat, joined the local press corps ranks. They simply ignored the practice by filing stories without consulting the competition.

The repeated failures of the Snyder and Cryer administrations to check crime and of the press to act as a responsible watchdog between 1919 and 1922 allowed a new crime boss to join the local landscape. Emerging as the city's leading gangster in the 1920s was Albert Marco, a junior version of Chicago's Al Capone and Bugs Moran. Born Marco Albori, Marco had worked as a Tyrolean hat maker near the border between Austria and Italy before coming to America. Marco eventually found his way to Washington state, from where he would roam the Pacific Northwest as a pimp and confidence man. But in 1919, Marco was arrested in Sacramento on a charge of burglary. He fled before his trial but was picked up on a fugitive warrant and returned to Sacramento.

After a short stint in jail, Marco was recruited by a Los Angeles gangster, Charlie ("Gray Fox") Crawford, in 1922 or 1923. Crawford would help lead the rackets while running a saloon on Spring Street, about one block from the Central police station. Crawford also took control of the estimated 100 prostitution houses within the city limits. Marco's other confederates included brothers Frank and Tony Cornero and Black Tony Parmagiani. They supervised the bootlegging operation, shipping liquor from Ensenada into Los Angeles depots.

Record police reporter Johnnie Arrington was probably one of the first local newsmen to meet Marco and fail to write about it. Arrington was a cub at the *Record*. He had first trained as a copyboy and rewrite man before his editors became confident that he could handle the cop beat. Like the rest of the city's daily newspapers, the *Record* put its cubs on the police beat for instant on-the-job training. If the competition on the cop beat scooped a green reporter, the sting wasn't felt very badly. Arrington, who wore a gun on his hip and had a police badge in his pocket, through the years gained a reputation as one of the city's premiere police reporters. He later joined the *Daily News*. It was commonly understood among his colleagues that he was on the crime syndicate's payroll as he often flashed huge wads of cash and occasionally arrived to work in a chauffeur-driven luxury car.

One morning early in his career, one of Arrington's sources telephoned him in the newsroom and suggested he drive down to a warehouse on 26th Street and Long Beach Boulevard where a clandestine liquor plant had been discovered. Inside were 25,000 cases of Napa Ale and 10,000 cases of assorted liquors, whiskies, and wines. Arrington leaped into his aging Ford Model T and twenty minutes later met two police officers at the entrance. It was just the three of them and Arrington was allowed to haul away as much alcohol as his Ford could carry.

As Arrington piled the cases into his car, a Cadillac pulled up. Out stepped a fastidiously dressed heavy-set man in a straw-colored Palm Beach suit and an elegant Panama hat on the back of his head. Albert Marco identified himself, demanding to know why they were stealing his liquor. Arrington's jaw dropped in astonishment. The cub reporter was finally facing the legendary Marco while he was stealing his liquor.

"That's my booze," Marco said. "What do you guys think you're going to do with it?"

"Take it in to the police station and you with it," one of the police officers replied.

"The hell you are," Marco said.

The patrolman was unaware of Marco's connections within the city's administration. Marco's power apparently was already secure. He stepped aside with one of the patrolmen, and a moment later the officer wasn't so sure if Marco should be taken into custody after all.

Marco's power would become embarrassingly evident to the district attorney's office in 1925 when he was arrested on suspicion of assault with a deadly weapon. Marco drew a handgun on a patrolman and brutally pistol-whipped him. The district attorney's office ultimately reduced the charge to misdemeanor disturbing the peace. Marco was released with a light fine and given his gun back.

Marco then spoke to Arrington, telling him that he had no problem with the reporter taking the liquor as long as he forgot about the warehouse and what was in it. Arrington agreed, but couldn't bring himself to lie to his city editor. At the first public phone he reached, he called the city editor with the details. The editor, however, reminded Arrington that the *Record* was sympathetic to the Cryer administration and wasn't interested in a vice story that might embarrass the mayor since no arrests had been made. But the editor was interested in Arrington's cache. Arrington dropped off a case of whiskey at the *Record's* newsroom and the rest of it at the pressroom at the Central station. Five days later, federal agents raided the warehouse and all the alcohol was confiscated. Arrington never told his colleagues where he got the booty and never wrote of his experience with Marco.

Manchester Boddy was a latecomer to covering organized crime. The period between 1926 and 1928 was especially hectic. Violence, relatively absent under Marco's supervision, had stepped up when a bootleg hijacker was gunned down at a downtown warehouse. Chief Davis was forced to show the press that he had a handle on the cities vice operations. A week after the killing, the vice squad raided fifty drugstores and pool halls, confiscating slot machines. Most of the raids occurred in the African American district of Central Avenue and on West Sixth, Seventh, Eighth and Eleventh streets. But to careful readers it was clear that the raids had hit only a fraction of the thousands of slot machines throughout the city, in a way that would cause the least financial damage to the crime syndicate.

Boddy believed that Davis' philosophy of keeping vice at a static level was flawed. Crime was either going to grow and create a crisis by paralyzing the city's government or it would lead to a civil war between gangsters. The astute observer would only have to read the daily press reports from Chicago, Detroit, and New York to appreciate territorial gang wars being waged there.

Boddy consulted with Joel Rickman and Harry Eller about assigning a reporter to expose the rackets. The three chose Harry Toohill, a reporter fresh from Butte, Montana. Freckled, prematurely bald, and wearing horn rim glasses, Toohill looked more like an overworked bookkeeper than a newsman. To Boddy, he was the perfect choice.

On his first day, Toohill spent only an hour getting familiar with the gambling operations. But he had plenty to write for his first story. He discovered three businesses running slot machines within four blocks of the Georgia Street police station, which also served as the department's vice-squad headquarters. He found another seven shops on Los Angeles Street.

Rickman assigned Harrison F. ("Nick") Carter as the rewrite man for the story and Boddy and Eller shared editing duties. The first story hit the streets on a Saturday morning. Arriving for work that morning, Toohill found that most of the gambling equipment detailed in his story had already been removed. But he also found that nearly two-dozen other slot machines were operating in nearby parlors. In Toohill's estimate, 600 Chinese lottery joints were operating and about 2,000 slot machines were being used throughout downtown in drugstores and grocery stores.

At an especially seedy dive on Seventh Street, Toohill counted in four hours about 300 customers dropping hundreds of dollars into slot machines or purchasing lottery tickets. Toohill bought a single lottery ticket. The winning ticket for $10,000 would be drawn that night. Toohill took his lottery ticket to police Captain Charles E. Jackson, the commander of the vice squad at the Georgia Street station. Jackson didn't want anything to do with the ticket and refused to answer Toohill's questions as to whether his squad would raid the establishment. Jackson hurried to lunch and left Toohill speaking to a sergeant, who also left for lunch. The reporter stayed in the station until Jackson and the sergeant returned two hours later. The officers then told Toohill that detective Lieutenant Charles Hoy was in charge of gambling raids, but was unavailable.

Toohill's account of his conversations with Jackson ran in Monday's *Daily News*. That afternoon, about 100 Chinese lottery operations were shut down. They would reopen a week later. Chief Davis remained unavailable for comment, but the *Daily News* cornered Police Commissioner Rodney Webster about the open gambling den. Webster told the paper that he hadn't spoken to Davis about the operation, but voiced his confidence in Jackson: "Jackson is one of the sincerest, ablest, and willing officers ever to hold a post in the Los Angeles Police Department. If he displayed an unwillingness to knock over the place on Seventh Street, there was something back of it. If he can be entrusted personally to clean up Los Angeles, it will be thoroughly and promptly done."

The *Daily News* published Webster's remarks, which had a two-fold effect. It would later haunt Detective Jackson when Davis needed a scapegoat, and it implied that Los Angeles was in need of cleaning up. Further, the *Daily News* began compiling lengthy lists of gambling operations throughout the city. Davis went on the offensive by assuring local women's clubs that their families were safe from crime. But the gambling operations continued. The number of dens grew steadily. Though the Chinese lotteries had been hit, the slot-machine operations and bookie joints flourished.

Now Davis found himself battling a two-front war. First, City Councilman Carl I. Jacobsen began asking pointed questions of the police commission and Davis at council meetings. Jacobsen also angered Albert Marco when Jacobsen rejected a $25,000 bribe, and then informed on Marco to federal officials, who launched a tax-evasion investigation. In mid-1927 Jacobsen started his own campaign to personally pester Davis until he received a satisfactory answer about the police department's performance in handling vice. Davis was considering methods on how to deal with Manchester Boddy, but first he had to deal with Jacobsen.

The vice squad recruited police officer Frank Cox's sister-in-law, Callie Grimes, to entice Jacobsen to her modest Beagle Street cottage for a visit. The visit was arranged on 5 August on the assumption that Grimes' cottage, which was in Jacobsen's district, needed improvements. When the pair was together for some time, the vice squad raided the cottage on the pretext that Jacobsen and Grimes were committing the misdemeanor crime of "resorting." It was a misdemeanor in the city for an unclothed man and woman not married to each other to be in a room with a bed or couch. When the vice squad burst through the door, Jacobsen was wearing red flannel underwear and Grimes a negligee. Making the arrest were police Captains Bert Wallis and Frank Williams and Detectives Harry Raymond and Dick Lucas. With the police were two newspaper reporters. Critics of the police department noticed the presence of Lucas, for he was Charlie Crawford's enforcer. The *Record's* Johnnie Arrington later described Lucas as "a racketeer with a gun buttressed by the authority of a police badge." Lucas was temporarily assigned to the vice squad for the Jacobsen arrest. His usual assignment was with the department's anti-gang squad.

Lucas, a big man well over six feet tall and weighing 250 pounds, was a favorite of reporters on the cop beat. He was often seen casually carrying a Thompson submachine gun with drum clip. He provided wonderful copy for the press. He personally drove all Eastern gangsters out of the city. Typically he would drive out to West Seventh Street, just west of Figueroa Street, and park his police car to monitor a hangout where East Coast gangsters visited. Whenever he spotted a mobster, he would jump out of the car with his Thompson tucked under his arm. He suggested to the gangster that he had until 8 the next night to leave the city or find himself on a slab at the county morgue. His speech was always the same and always punctuated with the presence of the Thompson. The public would applaud these deeds, without knowing that Lucas performed the duty to protect the territory of Albert Marco and Charlie Crawford.

While the Jacobsen trial was pending, Grimes disappeared. An *Examiner* reporter found her in El Paso, Texas. He then chartered them a plane to Los Angeles. The reporter offered to pay Grimes $500 for an interview. *Daily News* reporter Gene Coughlin convinced Joel Rickman and Boddy to buy a train ticket for Grimes and have her lawyer encourage her to take the train and not speak to any reporters until she arrived at Colton in San Bernardino County. The train arrived in Colton and Coughlin and her lawyer were there to greet her. With her was the fuming *Examiner* reporter, who couldn't get a word out of her. When the competition was distracted, Coughlin bundled Grimes into a car and drove her to Los Angeles. The *Daily News* published her story of the Jacobsen setup the next day. The case against Jacobsen ended in a hung jury with a seven-to-five vote in favor of acquittal.

Grimes later told the grand jury how the vice squad had set up Jacobsen. Because of her testimony, Captains Wallis and Williams and detectives Raymond and Lucas were indicted on charges of conspiracy. Also indicted were Crawford and Marco. The indictments against the two gangsters were dropped, but the police officers went on trial. District Attorney Asa Keyes presented a lackluster

The Los Angeles *Illustrated Daily News* at the intersection of Pico Boulevard and Los Angeles Street in 1929. (*Daily News* Collection/Special Collections, UCLA)

Daily News Publisher E. Manchester Boddy, left, chats with war correspondent Ernie Pyle. Pyle passed through Los Angeles on his way to the Pacific Theater during World War II. (courtesy Alan Hensher)

case and the four men were acquitted. The grand jury, however, recommended that Lucas be dismissed from the police department and never be allowed to hold a public office again. (He was fired, only to surface briefly in 1933, when the police department rehired him. He later retired due to ill health.) Also fired was Raymond, who would play a key role in a scandal that would topple a future city administration in 1938.

IV.

Following Councilman Jacobsen's arrest, the *Daily News* stepped up its efforts, reporting, for example, that patrolmen frequented the gambling operations, enjoying free lunches, and accepting lottery tickets. Davis responded by suspending Detective Jackson, a 27-year veteran of the department, for "insubordination, inefficiency, and failure to carry out orders."

When Jackson appealed the suspension, Davis scheduled a hearing for Jackson with the Board of Police Commissioners. Davis laid out his evidence, pointedly telling the commissioners that the *Daily News* was on trial because the evidence against Jackson was based entirely on *Daily News* articles. Boddy was called to testify first. He told the board that gambling was rampant throughout the city and the police department made no genuine effort to curtail it. He also explained in detail the operation of his newsroom and how several members of his editorial staff verified reports by Toohill. City Editor Rickman testified that he personally had observed gambling dens operating in the open. And Nick Carter testified that he had visited forty to fifty gambling dens. In his defense, Jackson told the board that he had followed Toohill's tip that a gambling dive was operating on Seventh Street and detailed a surveillance team to monitor traffic in and out of the establishment. He testified that his men never saw anyone enter; after four days, in fact, detectives raided the business and found it empty.

Jackson's testimony allowed the board to save face by ruling that Jackson had performed his duty. He was reinstated without any loss of pay. The board also found in favor of Boddy and the *Daily News*. Though the board took no action against Davis, it was clear it believed that vice was running unchecked and the police department was ill-equipped to fight it.

Chief Davis remained unfazed by the outcome. Rather, he believed that Boddy needed to be silenced. Davis found an obscure municipal law that prohibited the publishing of the names of horses entered in a scheduled race. The *Daily News*, like the five other dailies in the city, had printed the entries for the Kentucky Derby. Davis rounded up a team of police officers and raided the *Daily News* editorial department on 21 May 1928. Leading the team was gambling raid supervisor Detective Lieutenant Charles Hoy. Boddy and Rickman were taken into custody and booked at the Georgia Street station. While awaiting his booking and arraignment, Boddy finished his column in longhand and had it sent to the *Daily News*.

Boddy and Rickman were arraigned before Municipal Court Judge Leonard Wilson. When Wilson asked for their pleas, Boddy stood up and suggested that he would be willing to wait for his co-defendants.

"What co-defendants?" Wilson asked.

"Why, there should be five of them—ten if you include city editors with the publishers of the other papers," Boddy said. "It appears that all six Los Angeles papers have been guilty of publishing the Kentucky Derby entries, thereby violating the city ordinance just as the *News* had done. I thought it would be more convenient if we were all tried together."

The competing papers, which hadn't participated in the investigative campaign started by the *Daily News*, rushed to Boddy's defense. The *Examiner* called the arrests an "error in zeal" and chided the police for retaliating against the *Daily News*. "The arrest of the publisher and city editor of the *Illustrated Daily News* is a piece of stupid police retaliation and an outrage," the *Examiner* commented on its 22 May editorial page. "It is the business of the police to protect life and property, not to trump up a case against their critics." A benefit of the arrest and subsequent publicity was that the *Examiner* and other papers had to give credit to the *Daily News* for its anti-vice campaign.

The case against Boddy and Rickman never got beyond the arraignment stage. No charges were ever brought by the city attorney's office, and the case was allowed to die.

For all the drum banging by the *Daily News* to stir sentiment against organized crime, particularly gambling, the other newspapers in the 1920s rarely indulged in investigative journalism, either to remain competitive with the *Daily News* or to forge their own crusade. The *Examiner*, the *Herald*, and the *Express* generally limited their coverage to breaking news such as raids and indictments. The *Record*, for example, was too understaffed provide extensive coverage. And police reporters were reluctant to anger their sources inside the department. It was an incestuous relationship that fostered silence.

The exception was the *Times*, which published a seventeen-part series in 1924 detailing corruption in the Cryer administration, dishing out a lion's share of the responsibility to Cryer's administrative aide Kent Parrot. But the motivation for series was not to expose vice, but to politically attack Cryer and Parrot. The *Times* had turned its back on Cryer after the mayor, at Parrot's urging, had begun to support the municipal ownership of utilities and had grown more tolerant of organized labor in the city. Parrot's political stock in the state had grown tremendously while he was a member of the Cryer coalition, and with his power and influence, Parrot's relationship with racketeer Charlie Crawford grew.

Crawford, Albert Marco's confederate in the Los Angeles underworld, was the antithesis of Marco. He was quiet and reserved given to wearing conservative clothes whereas Marco was given to loud clothes, exaggerated mannerisms, and unpolished speech. Crawford, a big man, looked distinguished with his silver hair, bland expression, and soft voice. With Marco he forged business relationships with the brothers, Joseph and Bob Gans, who supervised slot machines. Crawford also had former police officer Guy ("Stringbean") McAfee supervise other gambling activities. Marco remained involved in bootlegging with the Cornero brothers and helped Crawford run the whorehouses.

By allowing vice operations to flourish in the city for a share of the revenue, Parrot was firmly in Crawford's pocket. Parrot was never seen publicly with Crawford, but instead held regular meetings with the gangster in Parrot's apartment at the Biltmore Hotel. There, a steady stream of state and local public officials, gangsters, job seekers, and cronies would seek favors from Parrot behind whom Crawford pulled the strings.

Despite the sheer audacity of this relationship with Crawford and Marco, the influence of the press remained ineffective. Never operating as a single voice, the local papers were often fractionalized, depending on their individual interests and crusades. Both the *Times* and *Daily News* had flip-flopped on their support of Cryer. The *Record* supported Cryer but its influence was negligible. The *Examiner*, the *Herald*, and the *Express* continued to support the mayor. Either through negligence or corruption, the local papers often shot themselves in the foot, as shown in the Horace Carr vice operation.

As if local publishers and editors hadn't learned anything from the Carr incident, the *Examiner's* top reporter, Morris Lavine, also found himself the object of unwanted attention. Lavine was an arrogant man who enjoyed ruling the county courthouse pressroom. He was also on the payroll of stock manipulator Sheridan C. Lewis, the corrupt president of the Julian Petroleum Company, which was founded by C.C. Julian. Lavine's job was to plant positive stories about Julian oil and its sleazy stock selling operations.

Lawsuits filed by fleeced investors set off a scandal during the late 1920s. C.C. Julian was a flamboyant oil speculator who would borrow huge sums of money from investors to fund his petroleum company. Although the company did produce oil, government pressures forced Julian out of his own company. Even wilder speculators, including Lewis, took over the company. In 1927 the company collapsed, and 40,000 investors lost $150 million.

In one case, a group of stockholders filed a lawsuit in October 1929 against the Los Angeles Stock Exchange and forty-six brokers, alleging that they had continued to sell Julian Petroleum stock even though they knew it had been over-issued. The star witness in the trial was Leontine Johnson, a private secretary of Lewis. Johnson testified that one stockbroker bribed her before the lawsuit was filed to get information about Lewis and other participants in the case. She also testified that Lewis and an associate had paid $10,000 to bribe a juror in a previous trial involving Julian. In addition, Johnson said, Lewis owned fifty-one percent of the stock in the newly formed California Stock Exchange and had controlled fifty-two seats. It became increasingly apparent, primarily through the cross-examination of Johnson by the defense attorneys, that Lewis was the principal figure behind the lawsuit in an attempt to discredit the Los Angeles Stock Exchange and boost the standing of the California Stock Exchange.

In March 1930, in the middle of the trial, the *Examiner* began running the first in a series of articles under Johnson's byline. The series was a precursor of a book to be titled *My Three Years with S.C. Lewis; or, the Truth About Julian Pete* (Petroleum). Before the second article appeared, Lavine visited Charlie Crawford in the gangster's Sunset Boulevard offices. Lavine promised to keep specific names out of the stories if he and Johnson were paid $75,000. Johnson had promised a tell-all of Lewis, Crawford, Parrot, and others if the blackmail money was not paid. Rather than pay, Parrot called district attorney Buron Fitts. An arrangement was made between Crawford and Lavine for the payoff. A pair of district attorney detectives waited in an adjoining office while Lavine met with Crawford to consummate the deal. Lavine was arrested as he left Crawford's office with the cash, and Johnson was taken into custody an hour later. The *Examiner* suspended Lavine and scrapped the series. Lavine after two trials was convicted and sentenced to one year in the county jail and fined $5,000. Johnson was sentenced to nine months in jail.

Another, but more tragic, connection to Charlie Crawford emerged in 1931. Newsman Herbert Spencer, who worked for the *Evening Express* for nineteen years as a police reporter and his last seven years as the paper's city editor, suddenly quit to begin his own weekly magazine, the *Critic of Critics*. Spencer owned a half interest with Max Schindler, who served as editor. Ostensibly the magazine was to push for liberal reform in the city. The *Critic of Critics* attacked Buron Fitts, the *Times*, and organized crime. It also detailed attempts by Eastern racketeers to gain a foothold in the city.

More sinister, however, was the magazine's mysterious relationship with Crawford. The gangster had gained considerable publicity as a prominent figure in the Julian Petroleum scandal and the Lavine blackmail scheme and had to lay low. He also had lost control of his racketeering empire to his former ally, Guy McAfee. Crawford began to distance himself, at least publicly, from the rackets. He soon found religion, donating substantial sums of money to a Presbyterian church and its minister. Part of his donations helped fund the minister's radio station. While contributing money to the church, Crawford heavily advertised his insurance and real estate business in Spencer's magazine.

His advertising prompted speculation that he was subsidizing the magazine and the radio station to regain his position as Los Angeles' crime boss and to discredit McAfee. In fact, Crawford and McAfee had met several times in early 1931 to reach a peace accord but they never concluded an agreement.

On 20 May, Spencer visited Crawford at Crawford's offices. With them was David H. Clark, a former prosecutor and a candidate for municipal court judge. Clark had gained widespread support, including the *Times*, but the *Critic of Critics* endorsed his opponent. During the meeting, Clark jumped up from his chair and shot Spencer in the heart, killing him instantly, and fatally wounding Crawford in the abdomen. The exact purpose of Clark's visit to Crawford's offices remains unclear. But he testified at his trial that Crawford had been angling to wrestle control of the rackets from McAfee. Crawford wanted Clark to help him discredit the city's current police chief, Roy Steckel. Clark said he had refused and that Crawford had pulled a gun. Clark killed both men in self-defense. He was acquitted in his second trial after the first trial ended in a hung jury. While the *Express* had no longer employed Spencer at the time of his death, his relationship with Crawford continued to point to the coziness enjoyed by the underworld and the press.

To a lesser degree but still troublesome to the credibility of the press corps was the routine behavior of reporters turning a blind eye to corruption. Johnnie Arrington typified the cop reporter who may have recognized a story when he saw it, but didn't see the need to burn a source to report it. Goldie's, a gambling joint at Santa Monica Boulevard and La Brea Avenue, on the border between the city and county, was netting about $15,000 a week under police protection. Police captain S.S. Stone was the rackets squad commander based out of the Central station, and was one of the rare upper-echelon lawmen in the department untouched by graft. Westside gambling operators were well aware of Stone's unflinching honesty but believed an elaborate setup, in which Stone's movements would be observed, would reduce his effectiveness.

Arrington drove by the Central station on West First Street each day on his way to the *Record*. One day, he recognized a former Hollywood vice cop sitting in a parked car across the street from the station reading a newspaper. The ex-cop had been on the take and had earned enough money over the years to open his own bail-bonds business. Arrington stopped and chatted for a while then left. For several days, Arrington continued to see his old friend parked near the station. Arrington finally stopped again and asked why he was sitting in his car all day. The man told him that his job was to tail Stone wherever he went and if he crossed Santa Monica Boulevard and turned west, the ex-cop was to stop and use a pay telephone to warn the gambling operators. The man would then follow Stone home and watch from across the street as the captain went to bed.

One day, Arrington noticed that his friend was missing from his usual spot. He also read in a rival paper that Goldie's was raided and 300 people taken into custody. Arrington later found out that his friend had followed Stone home one night and watched him go to bed around 12:30 a.m. What the man didn't know was that Stone had called the Van Nuys division and asked its vice squad to conduct the raid on Goldie's. It had never occurred to Arrington to report the story or call the city desk for advice. It would have damaged his relationship with the men he covered.

The end of organized crime, at least temporarily, didn't result from the *Daily News* crusade or aggressive police work. Instead, Albert Marco proved to be his own worst enemy. Federal agents had arrested him on charges of illegal possession of liquor and maintaining a public nuisance for a club he operated on Spring Street. He was convicted, but remained free on bond as he awaited his appeal. The U.S. Circuit Court of Appeals upheld the conviction, and Marco was facing six months in jail and a $1,000 fine.

In a sour mood, Marco visited the Ships Cafe in Venice with Louis Bardeson, owner of a notorious nightclub in Tijuana. The pair checked into the club where a drunk who insulted Marco by calling him Irish accosted them. "I'm a wop!" Marco shouted and threw a punch at the man. A fight followed, involving Marco and several patrons. Marco then pulled out a .22-caliber handgun and started shooting. Three people were slightly wounded. He threw the gun away, but a young police officer, John Brunty, with the Venice division, found Marco and Bardeson in a restroom attempting to wash blood out of Marco's silk shirt. He took the pair into custody. Marco ultimately was found guilty in a jury trial of two counts of assault with a deadly weapon and sentenced to eighteen months in state prison. His crime empire collapsed and he never returned to restart his business. In 1938, he was spotted on a Los Angeles street and was quickly deported by the federal government.

Those who sanctioned Marco's activities found themselves without a job. John C. Porter was elected mayor in 1929 on a reform ticket. Davis was demoted to deputy chief, replaced by Roy Steckel. Organized crime did not cast its net as widely during the Porter administration but would surface in another form when Frank Shaw unseated Porter in 1933.

The *Daily News* profited handsomely from its maiden effort at crusading journalism. In addition, Manchester Boddy streamlined operations and stabilized management. In 1926 the *Daily News* saw its circulation rise from a low of 92,544 in August to 99,919 in October and 100,436 in December. Throughout the rest of the decade, the paper held on to its circulation, averaging about 100,500 readers.

Boddy's sickly child was quickly becoming a new and credible voice in Los Angeles journalism.

V.

Boddy recognized that the *Daily News* could not survive on crime and scandal alone. Other papers did the job well. Boddy saw a void to fill by covering some of the economic recovery schemes proposed throughout the country. The publisher was just as conservative as most of the leading businessmen in the city, but he saw a need to make it the city's only Democratic voice.

A staunch Republican and enthusiastic supporter of Herbert Hoover during the 1932 presidential election, Boddy could have maintained a conservative editorial posture, as he had during his six years of ownership of the *Daily News.* But conservative readers were hard to find in a city dominated by the *Times* and the *Examiner*. Boddy saw his economic future in another kind of reader. Boddy had been credited for recognizing Franklin Roosevelt's New Deal as a true cure for the country's economic ills, and, after seeing the light, abandoned his support of the Republican policies and embraced Roosevelt's policies.

But he was more pragmatic than that. During election season, Boddy had Merritt W. ("Pop") Jorz, his city editor, represent his interests at meetings of the Los Angeles Newspaper Publishers' Association. Jorz would help Boddy steer in another direction to attract fresh readers. Jorz was Boddy's trusted aide when representing the paper to civic and business organizations. He later would help the *Evening News* establish a three-page financial section and supervise a number of special projects in the editorial department. During a meeting with the publishers' association, members discussed the fact that all Los Angeles newspapers opposed Roosevelt and his proposed New Deal. To give the appearance of balance, one newspaper was needed to give editorial support to the new president. The *Daily News,* through the urging of Jorz, volunteered for the job.

The day after Roosevelt was elected, Boddy was riding with Jorz in the passenger elevator to the third floor editorial offices. Boddy turned to Jorz and said, "They (the voters) have made a terrible mistake. I helped them do it. But damn it, I had to make a living."

While Boddy's endorsement of the New Deal was borne out of his own economic necessity, he had before the election and before Roosevelt's inauguration explored radical plans to curb unemployment and rejuvenate the economy. In the spring of 1932, he toured parts of California advocating the Community Land Chest movement, a plan to relieve unemployment through the cultivation of idle lands by transforming the property into gardens.

Boddy had a hobbyist interest in the details of the engine that drove the economy, especially since it was breaking down. One program touted as a remedy for the depressed economy was Technocracy, a type of scientific management of society. The Associated Press distributed a series on Technocracy in October, which the Tacoma *News-Tribune* published. In British Columbia, the Vancouver *Sun* also gave the program prominent coverage.

A few weeks after the election, Boddy read an article by Howard Scott in *New Outlook* magazine. The article detailed how science and engineering could improve people's lives. Scott, an engineer who supervised a Columbia University study group, argued that scientific management of society, called Technocracy, would pave the way to end the Depression. The plan was vague, far-fetched, and impractical, but it captured the imagination of people who were weary of three years of financial ruin.

More importantly to Boddy, who displayed a flair for personal journalism, Technocracy meant a chance to increase circulation, especially among liberals. Though Boddy never strongly advocated Technocracy as a feasible program, he sincerely was interested in it. He first wrote about it in a 30 November 1932 column, then pulled out the stops in the 2 December editions under the huge headline, "NEW DEAL DETAILS BARED." The article didn't discuss the New Deal and didn't even mention Roosevelt, but outlined the tenants of Technocracy. In the weeks that followed, the *Daily News* banged the Technocracy drum. And it was information that readers, in a county with 300,000 unemployed workers, desperately needed. Jobless men and women, hungry for any answer to their financial condition, crowded at the press room dock of the *Daily News* building, waving dollar bills as the paper rolled off the presses with new information on the plan. Daily circulation surged to an additional 2,500 readers.

Steeped in the traditions of sensationalism, the press in Los Angeles County hardly knew how to respond to Technocracy. Several suburban editors lauded Boddy's coverage as he began stumping for the program's benefits throughout the city; a lecture in mid-December, at the Philharmonic Auditorium, drew a capacity crowd. Curiously, none of these newspapers explained exactly what Technocracy was. The *Times*, predictably, attacked the program. The *Record*, though hostile at first, soon gave the advocates of Technocracy considerable space. The editors of the *Examiner* and the *Herald & Express* remained silent, but their nationally syndicated columnists were critical.

Other radical plans also found space in the *Daily News*. The Townsend Plan, established by Dr. Francis Townsend of Long Beach in 1933, argued for the enactment of a federal law to grant $200 a month to every citizen over the age of sixty. The funding would come from a national sales tax and the money must be spent within thirty days. Radio commentator Robert Noble's "Ham 'N' Eggs" scheme to have the state treasury issue $30 checks every Thursday to the elderly, also attracted the attention of the *Daily News*. Another program that was perhaps more far-reaching than Technocracy was the Social Credit plan in which Boddy again hit the lecture circuit to advocate. Social Credit allowed "crediting" the population with the "wages" earned by automatic machines that displaced workers.

All of these plans were controversial and earned the wrath of most mainstream metropolitan newspapers. But none were more controversial than Upton Sinclair's EPIC (End Poverty in California) campaign. EPIC proposed to create a program where California authorities stepped in to run the states idle factories and abandoned farms. It also was to distribute goods produced by these factories and farms to feed and house the poor, who also were expected to work the plants and land. Sinclair, a Socialist and author of the muckraking book *The Jungle*, had lived in California since World War I. In the fall of 1933, he was living in Beverly Hills. One day he appeared at the office of the county registrar of voters to change his party affiliation from Socialist to Democrat. A few weeks later he filed papers to run governor. In the June primary, he stunned the state by knocking out George Creel for the Democratic nomination. Sinclair ran a strong campaign, and by the summer of 1934, EPIC was on the lips of hundreds of thousands of California citizens. It was a program more substantial and exciting than Technocracy. The polls were showing that Sinclair had a good chance of capturing the governor's seat. Opposing Sinclair was Republican Frank Merriam, a mediocre party choice, but strongly supported by the *Times*.

The animosity shown by the *Times* was unmatched by any other business or organization. The newspaper hated everything that Sinclair stood for: Socialism, free speech for unionists, and attacks on big business. The *Times* waged a full-scale war against Sinclair's candidacy, printing vitriol stories about his background and what EPIC would mean to California if he were to be elected. Front-page boxes appeared containing Sinclair quotes taken out of context from his novels. The stories made him appear to be a dangerous radical.

The *Daily News*, by contrast, published much of Sinclair's positions and details about EPIC without editorial comment. And when editorials did appear about Sinclair, they were generally favorable. And on 10 June 1934, Boddy opened his front page to the candidate to explain EPIC's goals. EPIC supporters had hoped that the *Daily News* would break ranks from the other major newspapers and stand up as the only daily to endorse Sinclair for governor. But shortly before the 6 November election, the *Daily News* threw its unenthusiastic support to Frank Merriam, noting that at least Merriam could be counted on to implement the New Deal.

Sinclair lost the election, but Boddy had nothing to apologize for. He said he had neither supported nor opposed many of the economic plans given considerable space in his newspaper, but believed readers were entitled to full and unbiased reports of such plans. Many years later, however, he told *The Saturday Evening Post* that Technocracy was a "crackpot" idea. "Technocracy was escape literature," Boddy said. "So were EPIC and Ham 'N' Eggs. I'll publish anybody's crackpot ideas if they're interesting, because if they're really crackpot, they'll crack up."

Whatever his motives, the strategy worked, for circulation in the mid-1930s steadily climbed. And therein lies the foundation of political philosophy of the *Daily News*, according to some of the paper's top insiders. Robert E.G. Harris, who worked for the *Daily News* as an editorial writer between 1945 and 1949, saw Boddy as a "political opportunist." Switching from a Republican paper to Democratic was made solely to attract higher circulation figures. Boddy's liberalism, according to Harris, was largely a facade. He began publishing a liberal newspaper to get the financial support of liberal readers. Harris' argument, while plausible, doesn't ring true when considering vital advertising dollars. Large advertisers, viewing Technocracy and other so-called Socialist causes as radical movements sponsored by irresponsible visionaries, threatened to pull their accounts. Circulation can grow, but if the advertising revenue doesn't follow, the paper will die. But Boddy saw that he could have it both ways, although his profit margins would never match those of the *Times*, the *Examiner* or the *Herald & Express*.

VI.

From the moment Roosevelt was elected until the day he died, the *Daily News* was an ardent supporter of the New Deal. Its journalistic embrace of economic recovery schemes, its leaning in the early 1930s toward collectivist programs, and its unabashed affection for the working Joe and the poor probably could be laid at the feet of two men who were opposites in every way, but both committed to the principle of attracting new readers.

The first prime mover was Robert L. Smith, the business manager, whom many considered a brusque, egotistical, opportunistic promoter, and a clotheshorse who could sell anything to anybody inside of five minutes. Boddy had hired the twenty-seven-year-old Smith in 1932 to be his right-hand man and the paper's general manager after his predecessor, E.G. Patterson, was shot dead in his office by a crazed janitor. Boddy recognized Smith for what he was. But, he also recognized that if anyone could boost the circulation of his ailing newspaper, it would be Smith.

At almost the same time Duncan Aikman was hired as a special writer. Aikman, though dour and colorless, was considered to be one of the top newsmen in the country. He was born in Terre Haute, Indiana, and graduated from Yale University in 1911. He worked for a variety of papers, including the New York *Evening Post* and as West Coast bureau chief for the Baltimore *Sun* before joining the *Daily News*. He later would help launch the prestigious liberal newspaper, *PM*, in New York in the 1940s. At the *Daily News* he assumed the duties of managing editor in 1934. Aikman was a leftist (although Boddy once described him as a "Communist dupe"), who had no hesitation of publicizing such Utopian movements as Technocracy, the Townsend Plan, and EPIC. But Aikman often raised the ire of advertisers. They threatened to pull out if Aikman wasn't fired. Boddy refused to capitulate. As a matter of principle, he hung on to Aikman until the furor among advertisers died down. "I could not as a decent publisher submit to that kind of pressure," Boddy told Merritt Jorz. Eventually, Aikman resigned from the paper. It was a mutual decision between the two men. Aikman thought of Boddy as a fair weather liberal. Boddy thought of Aikman as an obstacle to gaining advertising.

Smith, on the other hand, thrived in his new job. He had already proven to Boddy that he was capable of helping keep the newspaper afloat. Born in Salt Lake City, Smith was a natural at promotion and selling. While attending Los Angeles High School in the early 1920s, he landed a job as an office boy with the Union Trust & Savings Bank. He was only fifteen years old. A year later he was selling on commission subdivisions forty miles outside of Los Angeles. He promoted Wilshire Boulevard's Miracle Mile and the Los Angeles Aviation Rodeo. He later supervised the merchandising service department at the *Herald & Express* before approaching Boddy with a business-survey service.

Smith's meeting with the publisher couldn't have been better timed. After being in the black for two years, the *Daily News* slipped into the red in 1931, and recorded $42,035 in losses for 1932. It was difficult for the paper to stay alive. Boddy once lamented, "The *Daily News* was conceived in iniquity, born in bankruptcy, reared in panic, and refinanced every six months."

Taking over as general manager, Smith quickly established a plan to attract more department store advertising. In 1933, the paper had less than five percent of the total retail advertising in the Los Angeles market. Because of it meager circulation of 73,715, Smith ignored the larger retailers and focused his attention on second-tier merchants with modest budgets. These advertisers had done poorly with the larger dailies but the six-column bastard format of the *Daily News* gave them a good splash. The smaller advertisers grew with the paper and ultimately purchased more space. Advertising rates leaped from about $2 per column inch rate to about $3.30 per column inch.

Smith was a nominal Democrat at best, but he recognized that he had a product to sell. He was in it for the money, earning in later years a $75,000 annual salary and ten percent of the advertising revenue. He cajoled and browbeat advertisers to put aside their political prejudices against the paper and advertise to attract its blue-collar readers.

If Boddy was aware that Smith was universally hated by much of the editorial staff, he didn't let on. Smith was doing the job. Yet editorial staffers barely could stand him. Financial editor Herb Weinstock recalled that Smith was "very much hated. We all hated him. He had a hell of an ego. He had a hell of a presence. He ordered you around like a damn colonel." Smith dressed in the latest fashions, wrote a fashion column for the paper, and had an air about him that, in the minds of reporters and editors, reeked of the upper crust. But the criticisms paled compared to his talent in business.

Hal Lindley joined the *Daily News* in 1935 and was promoted national advertising manager in 1938. Smith, according to Lindley, built the newspaper on his personality. His influence couldn't be denied. Reporter Jack Kennett, an active member in the Los Angeles Newspaper Guild, remembered Smith, who represented management in contract negotiations, as a worthy adversary. Smith was "tricky, brilliant, and stone-eyed. He had an excellent vocabulary, was very articulate. He was a tough negotiator. He had an enormous ego. He knew he was better than anyone else—and the employees knew it, too."

Chapter Four

Mergers, Acquisitions, and Front Men

I.

Harry Chandler and Edward Dickson had been right in 1926, when they contended that Los Angeles lacked enough business to support six mainstream daily newspapers. But it wouldn't be the *Daily News* that took the first hit.

The *Daily News*, in fact, had gone into the black in 1929, just before the stock-market crash that fall. The logical victim, then, seemed to be the *Record*, which still suffered from the smallest circulation: 63,000 in 1930, thirty-five years after its founding. Even during hard times, the *Times* remained the healthiest daily, and for many years, Hearst could be counted on to pump money into any of his ventures.

It was Dickson's paper, ironically, that began to falter first. The circulation of the *Express* reached its peak at 139,438 in 1928, a year before the crash. The losses began to mount at once—5,000 readers by the end of the year—until, in 1931, the circulation had fallen to 115,527. The *Express* had also been losing advertising: 122,273 lines in 1929 alone, compared to the 12,586 lines lost by the *Herald*.

The *Express* had the distinction of being the oldest daily newspaper in Los Angeles and having one of the most respected and progressive men, Edward Dickson, at its helm. H.Z. Osborne founded the paper in March 1871. It was sold three years later to a partnership, but Osborne again assumed ownership in the mid-1890s. When Edwin Earl purchased it in 1900, it took a progressive position that lasted many years. Its focus began to change when Earl died in 1919 and ownership was sold from Earl's estate to F.W. Kellogg and Dickson. In 1925 Guy E. Earl Jr. purchased an interest and ultimately assumed eighty-five percent of the stock and Dickson owning fifteen percent. Kellogg kept $1 million in bonds and ownership of the plant at 236 South Hill Street.

At fifty-two, Dickson enjoyed a long, distinguished career. But he had already seen one of his creations—the Progressive movement—dissipate. He also was exceedingly distracted with other projects, including his activities as a regent of the University of California and his efforts to develop the UCLA Westwood campus. If the *Express* were to survive in any form, he had come to realize, it would have to be sold to a chain.

Earl and Dickson sought a new owner for the paper off and on for a couple of years, but in January 1931 the pair found a serious buyer. Earl and Dickson went to Ridder Brothers, a publishing company in New York that owned a chain of dailies, including the St. Paul *Pioneer Press*, the St. Paul *Dispatch*, and the New York *Journal of Commerce*. With Ridder, Earl and Dickson arranged to pay off the paper's debts to Kellogg and to a paper supplier the *Express* had previously refused to pay. The deal called for Kellogg to form a new company owned equally by Kellogg and the Ridders. Ninety percent of the stock belonged to Kellogg and the Ridders with the remaining ten percent going to minority stockholders Dickson and Frederick Wagner, business manager of the *Express*. Ridder Brothers then sent a management team to the *Express* plant and initiated a series of cost-saving cuts that saved the paper about $4,000 each week.

With the deal given preliminary approval by Earl and Dickson, Bernard Ridder, representing Ridder Brothers, went to publishers of the other dailies to determine whether they had any intentions of purchasing the *Express*. No executives, including Frank Barham, publisher of the Hearst-owned *Herald*, and B.P. Guild, business manager of the *Examiner*, expressed an interest in buying the paper. But when Ridder met Hearst at the Ambassador Hotel in late January he was faced with a different story. Hearst announced that he was interested in purchasing the *Express* and wanted to become a partner by paying $800,000 for forty percent interest in the new company. Hearst suddenly became a viable bidder for the company when he realized that Ridder Brothers wanted a foothold in Los Angeles. Hearst wanted no part of competing for readers against another chain. Hearst told Ridder it was worth as much as $3 million to keep Ridder Brothers out of Los Angeles.

Kellogg and Dickson wanted no part of Hearst and resumed their talks with Ridder. The chain had expected to make an announcement on a Monday that they purchased a controlling interest in the *Express*. But late Friday, Earl announced that he had a better offer. At the same time, minority stockholders Dickson and Wagner heard a rumor that Hearst had bought the paper. They were indignant and met with Ridder representatives over the weekend to hash out a strategy to withhold their stock for sale. But sometime after the weekend meeting, Dickson and Wagner changed their minds and gave up their efforts to sell the paper to Ridder. They lost their most influential ally in Earl who was interested in getting the most out of the sale. By 4 February, Ridder representatives in Los Angeles learned that Paul Block, who owned five dailies in the east, was the new owner of the *Express*. Hearst succeeded in keeping Ridder out of Los Angeles. And while Block was listed as the owner of the *Express* on paper, it was Hearst who truly owned it. He now had the largest circulating morning paper and evening paper in the city.

Not long after Hearst purchased the *Evening Herald* in 1922, he said, "I never plan extensions, but newspapers just seem naturally to keep coming to me to be taken over. I'm not as young as I once was, and the older we get the less likely we are to set out and conquer the world." His comments were prophetic for just nine years later the *Express* basically came hat in hand and asked to be taken over. As old as he was, Hearst just couldn't resist an attempt to conquer the world.

To the average reader it wasn't apparent that Hearst was the new owner of the *Express*. The *Examiner* and the *Herald*, of course, were mum, but the *Times*, the *Daily News*, and the *Record* speculated on Hearst's involvement the day after the 10 February announcement that Block had purchased the paper for an estimated $2.8 million.

The *Times* howled when it learned that Hearst was involved in the deal. When it reported the sale in its 11 February editions, it virtually ignored Block and reported that Hearst was the actual owner. It was more than sour grapes that a chain was strengthening its position both in the morning and afternoon fields. The *Times* had evidence that Hearst indeed was the real buyer and that Block had a history of acting as a figurehead for Hearst-owned properties.

On 10 February Herald employees replaced all circulation and business solicitors at the *Express*. *Express* newsboys also were directed to sell both the *Express* and the *Herald*. The *Times* reports forced Block to respond in a front page statement on 17 February. Block acknowledged that newsboys were now hawking both the *Express* and the *Herald* to cut distribution costs, but he denied that any *Herald* employees took over circulation department operations. Block stated, "Not a single employee of any other Los Angeles paper is either directly or indirectly employed by, or associated with, the *Evening Express*." Block also said the *Times* was attempting to "hurt" him and his paper because of its "policy to operate a dignified, progressive newspaper and because such a policy may eventually affect such prestige and circulation" of the *Times*.

Despite Block's indignant protestations, the *Times* was not about to let the matter die. On 26 February it ran a lengthy front-page story on Block's history with Hearst and his role as a "dummy" owner for the Hearst chain. The *Times* pointed to Block's acquisition of the Milwaukee *Sentinel* on 1 October 1929. Although Block penned a front page statement announcing the sale of the *Sentinel* to him and identified himself as the paper's owner and publisher, the *Times* asserted that it was "commonly understood" among *Sentinel* employees that Hearst was the new owner. The *Times* also noted that Hearst already owned the evening Milwaukee paper, the *News*. And although the *News* and *Sentinel* ostensibly were operated independently of each other, *Sentinel* financial statements were forwarded to Hearst's New York office. Eventually both papers were merged.

Block's advertising business, Paul Block and Associates, also handled advertising for the Hearst chain, even in cities where Block's newspapers competed against Hearst publications, according to the *Times*. And while the *Times* provided no specific evidence, it also reported that Block's acquisition of the Pittsburgh *Post-Gazette*, a morning paper and competitor against the Hearst-run Pittsburgh *Sun-Telegraph*, also was actually owned by Hearst.

Block and Hearst denied that Block posed as a front for Hearst acquisitions, but the *Times* fears about Hearst owning the *Express* and its eventual merger with the *Herald* were validated. On 9 December 1931, Block announced that he had sold his interests in the *Express* to Hearst and the paper would merge with the *Herald* to become the *Evening Herald & Express*.

In a statement, Block said he had purchased the *Express* with the intent to spend considerable time in Los Angeles, but that the country's economic condition and the conditions of his other properties forced him to spend a majority of his time in the east. He noted that under his direction the *Express* had reached a total circulation of 140,000.

Under the complete merger, most features from both newspapers continued. The *Express* plant was shut down and its equipment and employees moved from Hill Street to the *Herald* plant at 1243 Trenton Street. The new paper also contained the Associated Press, the Hearst-owned International News Services, the Pacific Coast News Service, and the United Press. It also featured an expanded sports staff, including writers Sid Ziff, George Davis, Jack James, Darsie L. Darsie, Ed Krauch, and Harry Culver. Special contributors and columnists included Edwin C. Hill, Walter Winchell, Mark Hellinger, Elsie Robinson, Helen Rowland, Fay King, and Hazel Blair Dodd. Frank Barham, who owned an interest in the new paper, was named editor and publisher, and John B.T. Campbell took over managing editor duties.

The *Times* was resigned to the merger, noting that the afternoon field was now reduced to two newspapers, the *Herald & Express* and the *Record*. The *Times*, the *Examiner*, and the *Daily News* published in the morning.

The *Times* couldn't resist taking a stab at Hearst on its editorial pages. On 11 December, it said although it was common knowledge that Hearst had been the owner of the *Express* since February, "it will still occasion some regret to see this, the city's oldest daily, now completely lose its identity through the merger with Hearst's *Evening Herald* ... the merger is, in fact, a submerging and that the last trace of the old *Express* has been sunk in an open and characteristic Hearst product."

The *Times* added that although the *Express* had been losing heavily throughout 1931, it would have been better "to have admitted his purchase in the first place and to have conducted the *Express* as an openly Hearst property..."

The new *Herald & Express* became the largest circulating evening newspaper west of the Mississippi, with an initial circulation of 268,402. Initially, circulation dropped off by 5,000 in 1933, but had soon exceeded Heart's expectations of hitting 280,682 in 1936 and 288,365 the following year. It showed a considerable drop-off in circulation in the late 1930s as the Depression deepened (242,138 in 1939) but the war years would see a dramatic climb in circulation starting in 1943 when it reached nearly 300,000.

II.

Though the *Times* lamented the passing of the *Express*, the demise of the *Record* was a greater loss to newspapermen and women. It was the very nature of the *Record* to take on impossible crusades in a David-versus-Goliath fashion that reminded journalists that they were in a profession to afflict the comfortable and comfort the afflicted.

The *Record*, one of thirteen West Coast properties operated by the Scripps-Canfield chain, was staffed mostly by a group of men and women who were committed Socialists and who saw nothing wrong with advocacy journalism. Perhaps best known was Reuben W. Borough, an excitable man, devout Socialist, and the self-appointed keeper of the flame of investigative journalism. He served as reporter and political editor from 1917 to 1932. He mentored under editor Burton Knisely, a Socialist with Marxist leanings, who scrapped the newspaper's anti-intellectual and anti-cultural bent in favor of a more progressive and humanist approach.

To Borough, born in 1883 in Ohio and the son of Populists, the members of the editorial staff of the *Record* believed they were incorruptible. Reporters and editors didn't necessarily wear their Socialism on their sleeves in the news columns of the paper but fought causes popular with Socialists of the day. It took on causes embraced by the American Civil Liberties Union, and attacked Ku Klux Klan activities when other papers ignored them. A more practical reason for its aggressive journalism was the fact that it carried no large advertisers. The *Record*, in fact, prided itself on appealing to small business for advertising. It also was a favorite for Jewish-owned businesses, which often were denied space in the larger papers by anti-Semitic advertising directors.

The *Record*, especially Borough, entertained its readers with a "rough sort of humor" or sarcasm. Borough once identified a lobbying group the "Sizzle 'em Boys" because they obtained a patent to heat asphalt material to a certain point until it sizzled. The patent was for expensive street-paving material that really wasn't any better than the cheaper material used by other cities. Long after Borough wrote stories about the paving patent, a county grand jury issued a report that estimated the city spent more than $246,600 for the higher priced material.

Money for salaries was always minimal but it was secondary to the job. "We didn't get as much money on the *Record,* as much as some of the others on other newspapers, but we didn't care about that because we had a freedom that some of these reporters never had," Borough once told an interviewer. "We were serving a purpose in the community, and when any of our reporters left the *Record* to go on the *Herald* or the *Examiner* or the *Times,* we said, 'that fellow is good riddance. He isn't worthy of us or he wouldn't leave us.' "

There was a good deal of loyalty on the *Record.* Borough and Gilbert Brown, a features writer who would later become the paper's editor, and Gertrude Price, the woman's editor, had been with the paper for years. But Borough's memory was probably more wistful. Coy Watson, a photographer at the *Record,* never considered himself the elite of Los Angeles journalists. Rather, he thought of himself as overworked and underpaid, rushing from one assignment to another to shoot art *and* report the story for the rewrite desk. The *Record* newsroom was in a perpetual state of chaos because many newsmen and women were pulling double and triple duty. Thus, turnover in the editorial department was constant with reporters starting pay ranging from $15 to $25 a week in the 1920s while other newspapers paid as much as $32.50 a week.

Perhaps sensing that his staff needed freedom and a morale boost, Burton Knisely, who had worked on the Cleveland newspapers, insisted that reporters practice literary journalism and employ a narrative style in their writing. It was a noble experiment among Los Angeles journalists who generally practiced straightforward writing spiced with inflammatory adjectives. To Borough, the news ranks were filled with reporters solely interested in writing "a good scoop story" and "getting drunk maybe on Saturday night and drawing a paycheck." The professional standard of a news reporter up until the mid-1930s was inferior to later journalists who became members of the American Newspaper Guild and the local Los Angeles Newspaper Guild.

To set high standards for his reporters, which numbered perhaps a half-dozen at best at any given time, Knisely founded the Pomegranates and Pemmican Club. The informal group consisted of five or six reporters who, according to Borough, aspired to be intellectuals and discuss at length literature and art. The work of Socialist author Upton Sinclair was a popular topic. Knisely hoped by fostering a literary air in his newsroom, his reporters would approach their stories different from the standard journalism of the day. Borough covered the Aimee Semple McPherson case and attempted to abandon the formula writing of the day-to-day coverage. In one story he attempted to "paint a human picture of her and of her love affair and weep a little bit over it." While his competitors went for the salacious details of her affair with her church organist, Borough pictured her as a "tragedy—a servant of God surrendering in love to this carnal man."

When illness forced Knisely to retire in February 1925, Henry B.R. Briggs was brought in as editor and publisher. Briggs was born in 1881 in Kalamazoo, Michigan, where he had served his reporting apprenticeship on the *Gazette*. At the outbreak of the Spanish-American War he joined the 33rd Michigan Volunteer Infantry as a private and participated in the invasion of Cuba. Between 1899 and 1908 he reported for the *Gazette*, the Saginaw *News*, the Kalamazoo *Telegraph*, the Cleveland *News*, the New York *Journal*, and the Detroit papers. In 1909 he served as the European correspondent for the Newspaper Enterprise Association and later became its managing editor. Briggs continued the Knisely tradition of literary journalism much to the delight of the *Record* staff.

The newspaper's proudest moment under Briggs's management occurred as a result of the Julian Petroleum scandal case. The *Record* initially opposed the way Julian had attracted investors and his wild claims of potential oil strikes, but later wrote favorable stories about his operation and ran a series of positive profiles about his life. When the company faltered, the *Record*, like the rest of the local press, attacked Julian managers and demanded swift justice. It heightened its criticism in 1930 by attacking Superior Court Judge Frank C. Collier and the county grand jury for delaying the case. It also accused Collier of bias. On its editorial pages, Briggs demanded that Collier disqualify himself.

On 17 May 1930, Frederic I. Morris, grand jury foreman, responded by filing thirteen counts of contempt of court against Briggs, editor Gilbert Brown, and managing editor Rodney Brink. The charges were based on editorials and cartoons published by the newspaper. In April 1932 the California Supreme Court finally heard a portion of the case. It ruled that Collier should be disqualified from the Julian case. The following month, Superior Court Judge Harry Archibald dismissed the contempt charges against the three newsmen following a motion from the Los Angeles County Bar Association. The Bar Association was planning to try the journalists in an independent tribunal. But after the Supreme Court's ruling against Collier, the association decided that the Julian case was "no longer of public interest" and "no good would be served" by reminding the community of the unpunished perpetrators of the oil fraud.

The events of the spring of 1932 proved to be the *Record's* swan song. The Depression wreaked havoc on the paper's finances and small businesses cut back on their advertising budgets. A seasoned reporter like Agness Underwood, who later would become the city's first woman city editor at the *Herald & Express*, saw her salary slashed from $20 a week to $10. Though desperate for a change, Scripps-Canfield was at a loss how to effect changes that would translate into

The Los Angeles *Evening Express* building on Hill Street. Photograph was taken in May 1932 (courtesy Alan Hensher)

The Los Angeles *Evening Record* building on Wall Street, at the edge of the city's infamous Skid Row. Photo was taken about 1935. The building still stands. (courtesy Alan Hensher)

Newsroom of the Los Angeles *Evening Record*, c. 1935. (courtesy Alan Hensher)

Composing room of the Los Angeles *Evening Record*, c. 1935. (courtesy Alan Hensher)

Ad-makeup area of the Los Angeles *Evening Record*, c. 1935. (courtesy Alan Hensher)

Pressmen make a final check of an edition of the Los Angeles *Evening Record*, c. 1935. (courtesy Alan Hensher)

Mail room of the *Evening Record* in 1935. (courtesy Alan Hensher)

Daily News columnist E.V. Durling wore a different hat every day while he wrote his column. When he was gone one day, the editorial staff decided to use them for clowning around. From left: Gene Coughlin, Ned Cronin, Matt Weinstock, Sam Patrick, J.W. Ward, Walter Lee, Todd Moss, Hal Rorke, and Nick Carter, c. 1935 (Walter Lee Collection)

The *Daily News'* Manchester Boddy believed that Los Angeles County District Attorney Buron Fitts was corrupt and hired James Richardson specifically to ferret out any wrongdoing by the prosecutor. Fitts, thanks in large part to coverage by the *Daily News*, was charged with perjury stemming from a real estate deal. Here, Fitts, third from right, appears in court on 17 December 1934 to quash his perjury inictment. In additon to Fitts, from left are: Attorney Roland G. Swaffield, Mrs. Gregory, attorney Harold Judson, and Fitts' attorney, Jerry Giesler. (*Herald Examiner* Collection/Los Angeles Public Library)

Matt Weinstock became the prewar voice of Los Angeles while a *Daily News* columnist, c. 1934. (*Daily News* Collection/Special Collections, UCLA)

revenue. The change would manifest itself during the November national and state elections. Yet instead of providing the boost the faltering *Record* needed, it signaled its death knell.

As the Noverber 1932 election approached Edward W. Scripps, son of James G. Scripps and grandson of E.W. Scripps, drove down from his Seattle offices, where he supervised Scripps-Canfield's thirteen Western newspapers, to Los Angeles to visit the *Record*. Meeting him there were Jim Marshall, an editorial and feature writer for the Seattle *Star*, and Neal Jones, a former managing editor of the Seattle *Post-Intelligencer* serving as assistant to Edward Scripps.

On 7 November, the day before the election, the 6 a.m. edition of the *Record* hit the streets. Briggs, leading the paper's editorial board, had endorsed Franklin D. Roosevelt for president and the reelection of liberal California Senator William Gibbs McAdoo. By 8:20 a.m., Marshall and Jones walked out of the Alexandria Hotel at 210 West Fifth Street and dropped down 2 cents for the *Record*. As Marshall scanned the paper and read the McAdoo endorsement, Jones held several sheets of copy paper pasted together that measured about thirty inches. It was a new editorial for the paper's third edition. The editorial was an endorsement for McAdoo's opponent, the Rev. Bob Shuler, fifty-two, a fundamentalist preacher with the Methodist Episcopal Church South, a rabid anti-Semite and segregationist who used his radio broadcast to attack Jews, Catholics, anti-prohibitionists, and his rival across town, Aimee Semple McPherson. His single-tone platform during the election was to clean up the city's vice and demand a clean municipal and state government. The *Record* had a long history of attacking Shuler, describing him to readers as a "snooper" and a "meddler."

As the two newspapermen stood outside the hotel, Marshall warned Jones about changing endorsements between editions, "Oh yes we can—and it'll make people talk," Jones replied. Jones tore off the front page of the *Record* and scrawled "KILL" across the top, then threw the rest of the paper in a garbage can. They drove down to the newspaper plant, on Wall Street near Sixth. In the newsroom were Gertrude Price, Relman ("Pat") Morin, Agness Underwood, Charles Dagget, and Llewellyn Miller. Inside the conference room were Briggs and Gilbert Brown.

Jones sent Marshall into the composing room with the new copy. Marshall wrote a head, "The *Record* is for Bob Shuler for Senator" and handed it to foreman Elmer Cobb. Jones, meanwhile, met with Briggs and Brown. When Marshall joined the trio, Jones was explaining to Briggs and Brown that Edward Scripps wanted to "pep up" the paper and had sent him and Brown south to supervise it. "I have already done something to lift the sheet out of the rut," Jones said.

Briggs and Brown sat silently for a moment before a copyboy came into the office with the 11 a.m. edition. Briggs read the headline and lead of the pro-

Shuler story and looked up at Jones. "Jones, you have wrecked the *Record*." He grabbed his hat and walked out of the office and never returned.

Reuben Borough was on his "North-of-First-Street" beat at the courthouse when he caught the first edition. He was pleased to see the FDR endorsement since Roosevelt was about as close as the country would get to elect a Socialist. He had less enthusiasm for McAdoo, but anybody was better than Shuler. When the second edition hit the streets, the endorsements were identical. But during his noon break, he stopped at the newsstand for a peek at the 11 a.m. edition and was startled to see the Shuler endorsement. To Borough, half a century's work by his beloved paper had been crushed in a single blow. He rushed down to the plant's office and spotted Jones in the middle of the newsroom talking with the editorial employees. Borough thrust the editorial in Jones's face. Jones asked him his name.

"I am Rube Borough. I have been called The Soul of the *Record*!" He quit on the spot.

"I am sorry that the *Record* is to lose its soul, but perhaps in losing it we may gain some circulation," Jones said.

In a single afternoon, the paper lost the two remaining men who held together the Socialist leanings of the paper that made it a champion of the unemployed and working class.

The *Evening Herald & Express* couldn't resist taking a poke at the *Record* and advancing a conspiracy theory as to the motives behind the abrupt switch. In its 1 p.m. edition, just two hours after the Shuler endorsement was published, the *Herald & Express* reproduced the *Record's* two front pages of the McAdoo and Shuler stories over four columns on its own front pages. It reported that the *Record* had been sold to the Atchison, Topeka & Santa Fe Railway. It offered no sources or evidence, but it didn't matter. Its presentation of the Shuler debacle made the *Record* the laughing stock of the local press corps. Under a picture of a huge hand pointing toward to the McAdoo endorsement, the *Record* defiantly identified Shuler as a "blatherskite." To the right, next to another hand and pointed finger was the huge headline, "At 10:30 a.m. today," with a reproduction of the *Record's* McAdoo front page. Below it was the same hand and the headline "at 11:45 a.m. today" with the Shuler editorial with a *Herald & Express* sarcastic headline that small afternoon daily performed "the flops of flops."

The next day the *Record* felt a need to explain itself in a front-page editorial accompanied by a statement from Edward W. Scripps that the Shuler endorsement signaled no fundamental change in the paper's policy. Scripps urged readers to continue as subscribers and judge for themselves in a few months whether the paper had changed direction. The editorial, however, presumably penned by Jones and Marshall, was hardly a ringing endorsement of Shuler. "We expect Dr. Shuler to disappoint us—whether or not he is elected—in many things he does, and says, in (the) future," the editorial stated. "It is highly probable he will disagree with us—but he has always been extremely capable of carrying on a disagreement, and we feel no qualms about hurting his feelings. They have been hurt by better hurters than we."

The *Record* slipped into conservatism virtually overnight, leaving only the *Daily News* to champion liberal causes. In 1933 it saw its daily circulation drop to 40,803 from 61,864 the previous year. Scripps-Canfield was ready to cut its losses.

On 31 October 1933, LeRoy Sanders, of Pasadena, a former editor of the *Record*, and Zack Farmer, once a business reporter for the *Herald* and the general secretary and manager of the Tenth Olympiad Committee, which had brought the 1932 Olympics to Los Angeles, formed the Post Newspaper Co. The company was formed to purchase a controlling interest in the *Record*. Sanders and Farmer owned 69 1/2 percent of the Post Newspaper Company's stock, and the Scripps family held 16 1/2 percent. The remaining stock was distributed among several minor stockholders, including editor Gilbert Brown.

Sanders, who had been a stockholder of the *Record* since January 1931, now would have complete supervision of the operation. In the weeks preceding the sale he increased the personnel in all of the newspapers' departments and infused fresh cash to upgrade its equipment. On 2 November, the paper appeared on the streets as the *Post-Record* to reflect the name of the new company. Art Ritchie, a former managing editor for eight years at the Seattle *Star*, assumed the post of editor.

The circulation of *Post-Record* began to climb, reaching 63,188 readers in 1934 and an impressive 74,252 in 1935. But some internal problems still plagued the paper and its advertising revenue never came close to keeping the paper healthy. In March, Zack Farmer suddenly left the paper. And efforts to attract larger advertisers failed. Sanders was ready to give up.

Quietly, Sanders began negotiating with Manchester Boddy to buy the *Record* in exchange for the Huntington Park *Signal* that Boddy had bought in 1930. Negotiations appeared to have progressed well for both men. During the summer of 1934 the United Press and its photo affiliate, Acme Newspictures, moved its operations from the *Record* building at 612 Wall Street to the *Daily News* building. The move was somewhat of a boon for the *Daily News* as it gave reporters easier access to Acme photographers. And it was probably a relief to UP staffers, who had had to contend with the noisy Pacific Electric streetcar terminal next door to the *Record* plant and the rats that had run of the place.

The United Press staff would occupy the second floor of the *Daily News* building (later moved the third floor when the building was remodeled to accommodate the *Evening News* operation) and was placed in the back of the newsroom in the southeast corner on a raised platform and separated from the partitioned composing room. Staffing the UP were reporters John D. Lowry,

George Beale, Duane Hennessey, Hal Swisher, Leon Baron, Ron Wagoner, Theon Wright, Allen McWelwaine, Jack Guenther, Jim Wickizer, Bill Gordon, Alex Kahn, Bill Payette, Bob Miller, Lisle Shoemaker, Freddie Othman, and Leicester ("Les") Wagner. It was only a matter of months before other operations were consolidated.

If Reuben Borough was the soul of the *Record,* then Henry Briggs was its intelligence, and his peers in the city were perhaps more upset about his quick departure from the field than any journalistic transgressions by his former paper and Scripps. In February 1934, Briggs was named postmaster of Los Angeles, putting an end to his distinctive journalism career. In September 1936, he fell ill from pneumonia in Washington, D.C., while on government business and died on the 27th. He was 55 years old.

III.

On 7 January 1935, Boddy announced that he had acquired seventy-six percent of the stock of the Post Publishing Company. He would continue purchasing stock until he acquired ninety percent by 1940. On Saturday 6 January the last issue of the *Post-Record* under Sanders was published. The day Boddy made his announcement, he changed the nameplate back to the *Post-Record.* In July Sanders had dropped "*Record*" to a 14-point line under the larger nameplate *Evening Post.* Boddy's intent was to return the *Post-Record* to its liberal voice.

He named joint managers for both operations: Robert L. Smith, business manager; William Powell, advertising director; William A. Robare, circulation manager; Thayer Ridgeway, national manager; and John A. Conway, classified advertising manager. While personnel between the *Daily News* and the new property would be combined in many departments, the two papers would remain, at least for the next year, separate entities.

The new publisher also planned to gradually change the typography of his new acquisition to be similar to the *Daily News.* The new nameplate would be made more simple and plain with blacker type and headlines would be moved flush left.

The paper was instantly revitalized. As Boddy brought over *Daily News* managers and editorial employees, it gained more news managing experience, which translated into a new energy not seen since the days of Burton Knisely and Henry Briggs. A lion's share of the credit belonged to two veteran competitive newsmen, Steve O'Donnell and James H. Richardson.

O'Donnell, a brash young editor hired by Boddy to act as publisher of the Huntington Park *Signal,* was named editor of both the *Daily News* and the *Post-Record.* Boddy purchased the *Signal* in May 1930 from J.A. Bowen for $225,000. Richardson took over managing editor duties of the *Post-Record* while Matt

Weinstock, who was appointed managing editor of the *Daily News* in 1934, remained at that spot for the morning paper.

O'Donnell was an old hand at the *Post-Record*. He was hired by Briggs in 1925 as a reporter, and then later joined the *Daily News*. He moved up fast through the ranks, and Boddy gave him new duties at the *Signal*, first as editor then publisher.

It was Hearst-trained Richardson, though, who helped the *Post-Record* become competitive again, at least briefly, in the afternoon field. He had become somewhat a legend among newspapermen in the 1920s for his aggressive newsgathering and heavy drinking. Balding, with a lazy eye and mean temper, he scored scoop after scoop working the City Hall beat for the *Evening Herald*. He counted former police chief Charlie Sabastian, mayor George Cryer, and district attorney Thomas Woolwine among his friends. He gained a reputation for playing fair on stories that had the potential of making or breaking political careers. *Herald* publisher Frank Barham and his managing editor, Wes Barr, thought so highly of Richardson's news skills that they named him city editor in 1924. Richardson, who adopted Hearst's penchant for sensational, scandalous news stories, wielded his power on the city desk with an iron fist. He was fiercely competitive with a cruel streak toward lazy and inattentive reporters. His standards for a story were so high that many reporters wilted under the pressure. He was truly simultaneously hated and admired by his staff, but he still engendered a loyalty not enjoyed by other city editors.

Richardson was younger than most editors when he became city editor at the *Evening Herald*. He was only thirty, but he had an uncanny ability to work a story himself, often even usurping a reporter's story and making it his own. The result more often than not was a scoop for his newspaper. When the last edition of the paper was put out he often would simulate ice-skating around the newsroom with his hands behind his back, displaying moves he had learned as a championship ice skater in Canada. He could display a wonderful sense of humor after deadline. Before deadlines, reporters quaked at the thought of speaking to him. He lasted at the job four years. His drinking became steadily worse, especially after the death of his wife, Edna. Hateful, mean, and ultimately ineffective as a leader, he was fired in 1928. He knocked about a while as a press agent in films before returning to the *Herald* as a rewrite man. But again, drinking got him in trouble and he was asked to leave.

Manchester Boddy brought Richardson back to the newspaper business at the *Daily News*. In his autobiography, *For the Life of Me: Memoirs of a City Editor*, Richardson claimed that he was hired ostensibly as a reporter, but was secretly employed to help work up a case against the city's current district attorney, Buron Fitts. During his newspaper's crusades against vice operations, Boddy developed a keen interest in Fitts, whose office failed to competently prosecute vice and corruption cases at trial. Richardson's job was to find corruption within the district attorney's office.

Richardson uncovered an incident in which millionaire real estate playboy John P. Mills was arrested on suspicion of seducing a 16-year-old girl. Fitts dismissed the case due to lack of evidence, primarily because Fitts kept the girl locked in a hotel room so she couldn't be interviewed. Fitts was then summoned by the county grand jury to testify about the purchase of a seven-acre orange grove by his parents for $18,000. The property was sold to Lucien Wheeler, who had been employed by Mills. The county grand jury alleged that Fitts lied about the transaction and indicted him on a charge of perjury.

The rest of the local press corps followed with the story, but it was Richardson and the *Daily News* that covered it more intensely and demanded swift action against Fitts. Richardson stood alone in his aggressive coverage while the other papers gave it light treatment. The *Times*, in particular, supported Fitts. When the indictment was returned against Fitts, Richardson's rival reporters were in the courtroom. Al Nathan, a reporter with the *Times*, threatened to beat up Richardson for his coverage of Fitts. Several district attorney investigators encircled Richardson in an effort to intimidate him. Carl Greenberg, a reporter for the *Examiner*, was certain that Richardson was about to be attacked. When Richardson left the courtroom a D.A. investigator wielding a .45-caliber revolver stuck the gun in the newsman's stomach and threatened to kill him. The investigator was drunk and eventually walked away, but Richardson's relationship with the office was destroyed. Fitts was acquitted of the charge after arguing that overwork had caused him to forget about the purchase.

The *Post-Record* staff was a little more than nervous when Richardson was named managing editor in 1935. Photographers in particular had little use for his autocratic behavior. Photographer Coy Watson was one of six Watson brothers —Harry, Bobs, Billy, Delmar and Garry—who enjoyed a prolific journalism and film career in Los Angeles over four decades. His uncle, George Watson, who became the *Times* first photographer in 1917, taught him his craft while working for Acme Newspictures. While at Acme Coy Watson met Richardson while Richardson was at the *Daily News*. Their first assignment was less than successful for Watson. The two men were assigned to cover a story at the Glendale airfield. They drove Watson's 1929 Ford Model A to the airport. On the way back to the newsroom, the car had a flat tire in Griffith Park. Watson jacked up the car, retrieved the spare tire and was putting the tire on the car. He asked Richardson for help, but Richardson just sat on the ground and laughed and heckled him.

Richardson's lack of sensitivity and teamwork infuriated Watson who preferred never to have to work with him again. But a few months later, he wanted a job at the *Post-Record* and found himself in the newsroom face to face with his nemesis.

"What the hell do you want?" Richardson asked Watson.

"I understand you're looking for a photographer."

"Know a good one?" Richardson asked.

"Yeah, I know one," Watson said.

"Can you change a tire?"

"Yeah."

Watson got the job at $35 a week and 5 cents a mile for gasoline, but it was a tenuous relationship at best with Richardson.

Brother Harry Watson would have a less successful job interview with Richardson ten years later when Watson wanted to work for the *Examiner*. Harry Watson asked Richardson for a job.

"Your uncle's George?" Richardson asked.

"Yes," replied Harry.

"Your brother's Coy?"

"Yes."

"Okay, you're hired. Now you're fired. I always wanted to fire a Watson."

The employees of the *Post-Record* during Boddy's early tenure as publisher were a mix of staffers from the *Signal, Daily News,* and holdovers from the old *Record*. City editor Lee Payne came with Richardson from the *Daily News*. He sat in the middle of the newsroom with Richardson but always attempted to keep Richardson an arm's-length away. Charlie Judson was an original *Record* staffer and acted as assistant city editor for Payne. The copy desk also included many old *Record* men: Topham ("Grim") Grimshaw, Ray Smith, Hugh Murdock, Herb Allen and Herb ("Chubby") Maas. Gertrude Price ran the women's page and Virginia Wright helmed the drama department. Both women were veterans of the *Record*. Gene Coughlin, now sports editor and Ned Cronin, also on the sports desk, were from the *Daily News* from the very early days. Other staffers included Jerry Ramlow, Phil Garrison, Tom O'Conner, Dolph Winebrenner, Tom Austin, Betty Bennet, and Herb Weinstock, brother of Matt Weinstock.

Although not directly supervising the *Post-Record* operation, *Daily News* Managing Editor Matt Weinstock still had a great influence on the afternoon paper. His liberalism, sensitivity to the anonymous person, and sense of place in crowded Los Angeles were instilled in the *Daily News* staffers who were assigned to put out the *Post-Record*. He was a perfect balance, a foil, for the sometimes-reactionary Jim Richardson.

Born to Russian parents Frank and Sarah Mantel Weinstock in Pittsburgh, Pennsylvania, on 12 December 1903, Matt Weinstock came to Los Angeles with his family at the age of eight. He was attending UCLA and writing sports copy for space rates at the *Examiner* when he landed a job at the *Daily News* in February 1924. He rose through the ranks taking assignments as the night city editor, city editor, picture editor, and ultimately managing editor. He began toying with a column but found his managing editor duties too much to maintain a column and perform administrative duties.

He found his true métier in 1936 when E.V. Durling, a longtime *Daily News* columnist of "Town Talk," jumped ship and joined the *Times* to replace columnist Harry Carr, who had died. Weinstock couldn't find a reporter to take on a column, so he began writing his own. When it proved too much, Manchester Boddy offered him a choice between the two jobs. Weinstock chose the column. He soon eclipsed Durling as the premier Los Angeles newspaper columnist with "My L.A." and set the standard for future columnists Jack Smith and Jim Murray. Jack Smith later wrote of Weinstock: "Hundreds of thousands of nobody people, who could not find their likenesses in the newspapers or on television or in the other mass outpourings of the modern media read Matt Weinstock and knew they were still alive.

"He was more than a person. He was a place; a meeting place, a part of Los Angeles, where those who were bruised, baffled or merely ignored could find grace."

Weinstock would provide the foundation for how reporters covered a story and interact with their sources and contacts. He provided lessons that livened the young crew of the *Post-Record* and later the *Evening News*.

But there were few people like Jim Richardson who could break a story, ensure the newspaper had full possession of it, and reduce the competition to "Johnny-come-latelys." He demanded that copyboys race down to Sixth and Main streets, with watch in hand; to buy the *Herald & Express* to see how far ahead or late the *Post-Record* was with the last screamer story. And he implemented Hearstian touches never seen at the Wall Street newsroom. When Franklin D. Roosevelt was scheduled to arrive in Los Angeles, Richardson had the first edition that day run an eight-column mug shot of the President. It covered the entire front page save for a column on the right for copy. It was dramatic in an era when photos were not used to sell broadsheet newspapers. "When you're for somebody you're for him," Richardson said as the front page was being dummied. No one dared to contradict him. Richardson wasn't necessarily for Roosevelt, but the paper was, and Richardson was a loyal soldier. Under Richardson, the circulation of what had been the puniest paper in town nearly doubled to 80,000.

For Boddy, the next natural step was to combine the operations. In late January 1936, nearly a year after his purchase, Boddy announced that the *Post-Record* would become the *Evening News* on 3 February. The departments of the *Post-Record* were moved to the plant of the *Daily News*, where newly installed presses would print both papers. (The old *Record* building was soon sold to a lighting-fixture company.) Robert L. Smith remained the general manager of the combined operation. In charge of the newsrooms were O'Donnell, as editor, and Weinstock, as managing editor before starting his column.

When the *Post-Record* issued its last edition, the competing newspapers and industry publications lamented its passing as a champion of social causes, but many couldn't resist raising the notorious Shuler/McAdoo mess. It is regrettable that its passing was not judged by its Don Quixote quests but the insensitivity of out-of-town journalists and a petulant Scripps grandson.

During these days of the Great Depression, the consolidation offered heaven-sent opportunities. Advertising could be sold in the morning editions alone, with circulation approaching 101,000 (up from 73,715 in 1933); the evening editions alone, with a circulation of 80,163; or, with only a small increase in cost for production, advertising could be sold in all editions, at 183,211 copies.

Such savings in production could be achieved best by consolidation. Compared to the old *Record* building, which contained only 5,400 square feet, the *Daily News* plant contained about 40,000 square feet, of which only 30,186 square feet were being occupied. All newsgathering operations were moved to the third floor, the front of which housed the United Press staff. In the rear were the newsrooms of the *Daily News* and the *Evening News*, separated by a glass partition. The composing room occupied the rear half of the second floor, where four Linotypes were added. The front half contained all the business offices, where seven-foot-high glass replaced wood partitions. The public lobby occupied the first floor.

The papers also were to have a distinctive appearance. Both were printed on peach-colored newsprint, in a "bastard tab" format: six columns wide and eighteen inches deep. The papers continue using flush-left heads but published more photos than before.

As was customary, the editions of the evening papers came out between 9 a.m. and 4 p.m. and morning editions usually appeared at 9 p.m. for delivery in the country or rural areas. City delivery started at 12:30 a.m. for morning papers and 3 a.m. for street sales. The *Daily News* issued three editions each day and the old *Post-Record* put out five editions. In the consolidated plant, more than 200,000 papers a day were printed.

This system demanded that the staff, through staggered hours, write for all editions. The morning edition required a "yesterday" lead for stories, but the p.m. papers were required to have stories containing the "today" time element. It remained an ironclad rule for years, which the news staff found impossibly confining. Reporter and rewrite man Chris Clausen, who joined the editorial department shortly after World War II, demolished the rule in a single sitting at the typewriter. He wrote, "John J. Doe, prominent Los Angeles businessman, was still dead today." City Editor Charlie Judson found it accurate but not particularly sensitive. The rule was never applied again.

With the afternoon and morning versions of the *Daily News* securely in place, and its ultimate merger into a single entity in 1940, Boddy's growing empire was becoming the city's only Democratic voice that provided a voice for the voiceless in a sea of conservative journalism.

Chapter Five

Spies, Vice, and Bombs

I.

On a rainswept January night in 1938, the *Examiner's* city editor Jim Richardson hurried to the Georgia Street Receiving Hospital with reporter Carl Greenberg in tow. Private detective Harry Raymond was fading in and out of consciousness after a bomb had exploded under the hood of his car at his Boyle Heights home, critically injuring him.

After Raymond dismissed a nurse watching over him, he summoned Richardson to his bedside. Greenberg stood by with a notepad.

"Who did it, Harry?" Richardson asked.

"That son of a bitch Earl Kynette," he whispered.

Across town at the spacious law offices of attorney Arthur Brigham Rose, Los Angeles police homicide detectives Warren Hudson and Aldo Corsini had asked Rose the same question earlier in the day.

"I not only have an *idea* who tried to kill Raymond, I *know who* tried to kill Raymond," said Rose, who was serving as counsel for a number of political reform groups in the city.

"Who?" Asked the detectives.

"Captain Earl E. Kynette. Just go out and pick up Earl Kynette and you will have the criminal."

The attempted murder of Harry Raymond and the subsequent arrest of Earl Kynette, chief of the police department's infamous intelligence-gathering unit, the Spy Squad, was a crime that would play out in the city's press and courtrooms with remarkable drama. It would end nearly twenty years of vice and political corruption and launch a reform movement for the next fifteen years under a new mayoral administration.

Raymond and Kynette were the two unlikeliest men to spark the end of organized crime. Both men, while Los Angeles police officers, shared a penchant for shakedowns, frame-ups, beatings, and bribes that many police officers and newsmen thought was the normal course of law-enforcement business.

It was almost happenstance that on the day of the blast, Raymond was working for the reformers on an anti-vice crusade. Under a slight twist of circumstances Kynette could have been on the payroll of the reformers. Both men had a price. In this case, it was Kynette who was the principal figure in planting the bomb. And in this case it was with the tacit approval of Mayor Frank Shaw's administration and police chief James Davis.

Raymond had joined the Los Angeles Police Department in 1907 at the age of twenty-five. He was fired once for reasons never made clear, then returned to the department as a vice detective. The press celebrated him as a hero when he played a key role in capturing William Edward Hickman, who had murdered a young girl. He also was credited for arresting two men who had threatened to kidnap actress Mary Pickford. During the height of Marco-Crawford crime regime Raymond became a celebrated lawman between both the underworld and colleagues. With Crawford's strongman, police Detective Dick Lucas, Raymond secreted himself in a garage of a known bootlegger who had hijacked a supply of Marco's illegal liquor cache. Raymond and Lucas opened fire with machine guns and instantly killed the bootlegger when he opened the garage door. Critics later suggested that Marco and Crawford had hired the detectives to kill the man. After being fired for trying to frame Councilman Carl Jacobsen, Raymond found work as chief of detectives for the district attorney's office. And while serving as police chief of Venice, before its merger with Los Angeles, he was indicted by the grand jury for extortion and then fired. He also was fired as police chief of San Diego before taking a job to supervise the theft bureau of the Automobile Club of Southern California. His career was so checkered that it was once suggested that Raymond Chandler used it as the model of a corrupt policeman.

Earl Kynette's police service was only slightly better. He had joined the police department as a patrolman on 1 September 1925 and was promoted to sergeant two years later. But he was soon caught shaking down a prostitute for $25 and was suspended from the department. He was exonerated and returned to active duty six weeks later without any loss of pay. In October 1933, newly elected Mayor Frank Shaw re-named James Davis as the city's police chief after a four-year absence. Kynette joined the chief's office after serving a stint at the Hollenbeck Heights division. In 1936 he was named captain of detectives, then was assigned to the intelligence-gathering squad answerable directly to the chief.

The Raymond bombing, and Kynette's involvement in it, ended a vice trade in Los Angeles that flourished under two underworld regimes with the approval of two mayoral administrations. Marco and Crawford under the Cryer administration gave way to Guy McAfee and Bob Gans under Mayor Frank Shaw and his brother, Joseph, who acted as the mayor's personal secretary. Organized crime under Marco and Crawford was no cheap-change operation. It raked in hundreds of thousands of dollars annually. But under McAfee and Gans, illegal gambling, prostitution, and drug revenue amounted to as much as $50 million a year.

The city of Los Angeles under Mayor John C. Porter between 1929 and 1933 enjoyed a brief respite from this type of organized crime. Born in 1871 in Iowa, Porter came to California at the age of eleven and worked as a railroad agent for fifteen years. He became a used car dealer before running for mayor in late 1928 on a reform platform. His four years in office amounted to little as he struggled with the onset of the Depression. And he was hardly a smooth politician. He managed to insult Franklin D. Roosevelt on a visit to Los Angeles, and had the poor taste to lecture the French. An avowed dry, Porter was in France on city business when he refused to drink champagne during a toast. He complained to his startled hosts that it was Prohibition.

Never popular with his constituents, Porter still survived a recall attempt in 1932, but the field for the 1933 election was wide open. Porter's primary opponent was Shaw, then a county supervisor who had been elected to the board in 1928, serving a rather undistinguished term.

Born in Canada in 1877, Shaw had been a grocery wholesaler in Los Angeles before entering politics. A small, stocky man with wire-rim glasses and a mustache that looked better on Adolf Hitler, the supervisor drew snickers from city and county reporters for his mangling of the King's English. He knew his shortcomings as a speaker and used to write notes on small cards, which he would keep in his pocket whenever called upon to make some off-the-cuff remarks.

The *Times* was Porter's most vocal supporter, asserting that he had kept the city in relatively good financial condition despite the Depression and had helped to keep taxes low. The paper attacked Shaw for failing to reduce taxes at the county level, although the supervisor had earned the paper's praise the previous year. The *Times* also alleged that Shaw was misusing federal relief money by bribing the unemployed for votes. The *Herald & Express* and the *Examiner* threw their weight behind Shaw, mainly to attack Porter for his failing administration. Shaw, like nearly every mayoral candidate since the end of the world war, was running on a reform platform, promising "a clean, honest government, free from graft and private exploitation." He was a liberal answer to Porter's oppressive moral and religious conservatism.

By election day, Shaw had the city sewn up. He swept into City Hall with fifty-four percent of the vote. His first act as mayor was to bring in his younger brother, Joe, to manage his political organization. Essentially Joe Shaw assumed the duties of Kent Parrot, granting favors and doling out jobs to friends. The extent of his political machinations would become increasingly apparent over the next five years. Political insiders noted that Frank Shaw was a man of good intentions, but his brother was one bad apple.

Joe Shaw was twelve years younger than his brother, and had joined the Navy at the age of sixteen, eventually gaining a promotion to lieutenant—a rare feat for one without a background from Annapolis. He served in the Navy for twenty-eight years, and then took a leave of absence to work in his brother's campaign. After the election, he quit the Navy to work for his brother full time. Nicknamed "the Sailor" or "the Lieutenant," Joe Shaw assumed a corner office on the ground floor of City Hall. He took over Frank Shaw's appointment calendar, supervised the mayor's office staff, monitored city correspondence, and became involved in policy decisions. It was unfortunate for Frank that whatever the press or public thought of the mayor they also thought of Joe. It was Joe Shaw's personality that identified his brother's administration.

Joe Shaw demanded loyalty from the City Hall staff in a peculiar way. He would sell civil service promotions to city employees by having them donate funds to his brother's election campaign. Friends in the press also won jobs. James Bolger, a city hall reporter for the *Examiner* during the 1920s, was a field secretary for Frank Shaw while he was serving as supervisor. After his election, Shaw tried to have Governor James Rolph appoint Bolger to the vacant supervisor's seat. When Rolph refused, Bolger landed a job as confidential secretary to police chief Davis. In 1935 he was named to the Board of Public Works. And Steve O'Donnell of the *Daily News* was named publicity director of Shaw's reelection campaign while still employed by the newspaper. O'Donnell's prominent presence in Shaw's camp was believed to be one reason why the *Daily News* remained neutral and refused to endorse any candidate during the election. O'Donnell also was on the payroll when the police department's intelligence unit provided reports to Shaw that identified Manchester Boddy as a silent backer on the successful recall movement against the mayor in 1938.

Frank Shaw also was responsible for the resurrection of James Davis, who had been on the sidelines since his demotion in 1929. Shaw forced Roy Steckel out as chief to make way for Davis. The appointment of Davis as chief was a signal that organized labor and leftist movements would be strictly curtailed in deference to the city's big businesses. Harry Chandler sent emissaries to Shaw shortly after the election offering the *Times'* support in exchange for the appointment of Davis. It was a perfect deal for Shaw since Davis was a personal friend and Shaw wanted to keep the city's subversive elements under control. Now with the solid backing of the *Times* and his continuing support from the *Examiner* and the *Herald & Express*, the lone holdout was the *Daily News*. The *Daily News* didn't have the courage to endorse a candidate during the election, but would later raise its voice for the recall movement.

II.

To understand how Los Angeles police officers could be involved in a conspiracy to bomb a political rival of Frank Shaw, the history of the department's renegade Red Squad, also known as the Spy Squad, under Kynette, must be examined. The Red Squad was operated virtually unchecked over two decades both by Davis and the press. The local media first embraced the actions of the squad during the 1920s, and then saw it simply as good copy during much of the next decade. It was perhaps Davis' most lasting and questionable contribution to the city.

The squad broke up potential strikes and ran labor organizers out of town. It also ferreted out Bolsheviks, and beat them, then drove them to remote areas outside the city and abandoned them. The Red Squad emerged in 1921 after the City Council approved funding for the intelligence unit at the behest of the Better America Federation (BAF), an organization of prominent business leaders opposed to radical labor causes. Among BAF's members were railway executive Eli Clark and Henry Robinson of First National Bank. Harry Chandler was not a member, but was closely aligned with BAF and its mission to protect the open shop status of business and crush communism and organized labor. And Chandler wasn't above using his influence with the BAF to have the Red Squad perform work for him. Occasionally, the *Times*, specifically the newspaper's ace troubleshooter Al Nathan, solicited intelligence on opponents and enemies from the Red Squad.

Seven years after the unit was formed, Davis appointed Captain William ("Red") F. Hynes to supervise the squad. A native of St. Louis and a World War I Army veteran, Hynes was twenty-five years old when he joined the Los Angeles Police Department in 1922. His supervisors immediately recognized his fervent anti-Bolshevik feelings and assigned him to undercover work. A year after he joined the department he infiltrated the International Workers of the World (IWW) during its paralyzing strike at San Pedro Harbor. He became secretary of the union's strike committee and editor of its strike bulletin. After the strike, the leaders were tried on a number of charges and Hynes took the witness stand to testify against them. The U.S. Department of Justice credited him for almost single-handedly breaking their West Coast operations. When Communists tried to wrestle local control of the American Federation of Labor, Hynes helped its leaders expel the Communist organizers.

The press didn't know what to make of Hynes. He was good copy, and most Los Angeles journalists during the 1920s were wary of Communist activities. It wasn't until the Depression that newsmen and women were attracted to radical causes. Hynes, however, had an almost evangelical approach to his work. To anyone willing to listen, whether to a reporter or city councilmen, Hynes preached the evils of Communism. And he preferred violence in an effort to curb it.

In February 1931, his men broke a Communist gathering of 4,000 people who tried to enter Walker Auditorium at Seventh and Grand streets to hear Communist leader William Z. Foster. Hynes and his men, claiming no permit was issued for the meeting, barred entry, leaving the crowd milling in the street. When word spread that Foster moved the meeting to the Cooperative Auditorium on Brooklyn Avenue, the crowd began marching toward the new venue. Hynes' men met the crowd there and dispersed them with tear gas and clubs. Hynes employed the same tactics the following November when he used tear gas bombs to rout 500 Communists who attempted to meet at a hall on South Spring Street. This time the squad was lying in wait in a nearby alley as the crowd gathered at the Plaza after another group of lawmen blocked their entry at the hall. The incident at the Plaza occurred two days after Hynes met with suburban city leaders and neighboring county officials in an effort to broaden the scope of the squad to their communities. His efforts only succeeded in alarming neighboring mayors and council members who feared violence may be brought to their cities.

Rioting at the Plaza raised the hackles of the Los Angeles Bar Association. The Bar argued that Angelenos had a legal right to assemble at the Plaza without being jailed. It passed a resolution condemning Hynes' actions as a violation of the Constitution. The Bar also cited a 30 October melee at Pershing Square when union radical Tom Mooney attempted to speak at the Philharmonic Auditorium.

The *Evening Record* led the chorus among the city's newspapers demanding that Hynes curtail his methods in dealing with Communists. In a 30 November 1931 editorial, it noted the squad indiscriminately clubbed people it only believed were Communists. The editorial argued that Mooney's meeting was a legal gathering. But Hynes, in a lengthy letter to *Record* editors, claimed the rioting that occurred at Pershing Square was instigated by the "Communist Party and its Red Defense Squads, which were organized to fight and combat the police, and who did attack the police...."

Hynes further alleged Communists influenced the *Record* and that it had hampered police in suppressing their activities. The *Record* editorial infuriated Hynes so much that he spoke publicly at every opportunity to denounce the newspaper.

The *Record* only reveled in the fight with Hynes. It responded in a 2 December editorial:

"One real test of an American is his willingness to let the other fellow enjoy the rights guaranteed by the federal constitution.

"All real Americans come to realize, sooner or later, that when Cossacks trample on the constitutional rights of the furthest under-dog or the meanest Communist, the civil rights of every American are in danger."

The *Record* also noted that whenever someone "dared to criticize" Hynes and the Red Squad, they were labeled a Communist.

Still, the strong-arm tactics of the Red Squad continued. Norman ("Jake") Jacoby, who would later become the dean of police reporters while working for City News Service, recalled that when he was a student at Los Angeles Junior College in 1932, Red Hynes' squad had been summoned to the campus to keep order during a peace demonstration. A young woman standing at the top of the steps of the library began to address a crowd of several hundred demonstrators when Hynes' right-hand man, Luke Lane, walked up to her and bashed her on the head with a sap. She fell to the ground like a sack of potatoes. *Daily News* photographer Harry Spang shot a picture of Lane's sap crashing into the girl's head. When asked to comment, Hynes denied the incident ever happened. The *Daily News* ran the photo across six columns in the afternoon edition, but only the *Daily News* expressed concern about the beating.

Not much had changed for the squad since its round of running battles with Communists and other leftist organizations throughout the 1920s and up until Kynette's unit began gathering intelligence on Harry Raymond. The *Record*, often taking on Hynes and the Red Squad alone, failed to influence Porter or the new mayor. Leftists and Communist organizers continued to find themselves under tight surveillance and their meetings were violently broken up. It appeared the mayoral administrations'—whether it was Porter or Shaw—tacit endorsement of the Red Squad's activities emboldened Hynes' mission against radicals. Some incidents, however, were not necessarily limited to radicals. In December 1931, Hynes and four members of his squad confronted sheriff's deputies who were observing a meeting of radicals at 233 South Broadway. Although the meeting was held within the city limits, the Los Angeles County Sheriff's Department's policy was to have at least one deputy attend such meetings as an observer. Hynes complained they were infringing on his territory. The issue was resolved during a meeting among sheriff William L. Traeger, police chief Steckel and members of the county counsel's office and the district attorney's office. The incident, however, caused a rift between the two law-enforcement agencies.

The confrontation with sheriff's deputies was only a minor irritant to Hynes compared to a rather bold move he took on 12 February 1933 to break up a suspected Communist meeting of 400 Japanese, blacks, and whites at the John Reed Club on North New Hampshire Avenue in Hollywood. The crowd had gathered to celebrate "Japan Night," but Hynes claimed it was Communist inspired. Police officers ripped through the meeting hall wielding blackjacks. The *Examiner* reported that police stormed "through a riotous crowd" although it failed to mention the crowd was orderly before police arrived. Police seized several rifles, bayonets, and clubs. Arresting officers alleged the organization had kept an "arsenal." Police officers then destroyed several murals in the hall before taking people into custody.

But the debacle at the John Reed Club was only a precursor to a more public event three days later when about sixty men and women tried to stage a protest against the raid at the City Council Chambers at City Hall. Fighting erupted when city councilmen demanded that police remove several disruptive members of the audience who were heckling the council. Hynes and several plainclothes officers grabbed the hecklers. Other protesters didn't recognize the police in plainclothes and attacked the officers. Women began hurling heavy cuspidors at the police, who responded with nightsticks and blackjacks. Dozens of people sustained minor cuts and bruises as fighting moved from the council chambers into the hallway and ultimately out onto Spring Street where most of the protesters had fled.

In June 1933, the Red Squad went after striking women, this time at a South Broadway millinery factory where strikes were held to protest sweatshop conditions. Several women were taken into custody. Six months later, milkers hit Adohr Dairy with a strike. An estimated 300 strikers fought with police.

And if the City Council believed it was immune to Hynes' red-baiting, they were mistaken. In early 1936, the council approved a request by the Public Works Unemployment Unit to hold a rally. Davis reacted angrily against the "weak-kneed politicians," and threatened to bring in a force of American Legion members to disrupt and scatter the "Reds."

The squad began to commit itself to spying on the Shaw administration's enemies. Newspapermen, political opponents, and civic reformers all were targets of the squad. Shaw directed about $100,000 in funding toward the intelligence unit each fiscal year. After the Raymond bombing, the arrest of Earl Kynette, and the continuing Depression, the unit came under increasing pressure to disband. Councilman James M. Hyde likened it to a "goon squad" while some residents, opposed to its funding, described the police department's reliance on the unit as being confined in a "parliamentary strait jacket."

To compound the rogue activities of the squad was Davis' flagrant disregard for the Constitution and preference to street justice. He once boasted that forty-three people had been gunned down by police officers in 1933 alone. The Wickersham Commission, formed at the request of President Herbert Hoover, described the police department as still using "the old-fashioned methods in dealing with crimes," such as beatings during interrogations and running gun battles initiated by police. Harassment, not only of radicals, but of the poor, also ran rampant. In one year under Davis, police arrested an estimated 15,000 jobless people.

Encouraged by Harry Chandler and big business operators, Davis, with the approval of Frank Shaw and the city attorney's office, sent 100 police officers to border counties where they were deputized to turn back anyone who looked poor. At the height of the "bum blockade" in February 1936, nearly 150 police officers patrolled the borders to try to keep in check the thousands of mid-westerners migrating to California. In less than a month, thousands of men and women looking for work in California were turned back and more than 500 people were arrested as suspected criminals.

The *Times* praised the action in a lead story published on 14 February, noting that the police department had "turned back at the state lines more than 1,000 penniless transients with a resultant decrease in crime, begging and pilfering in the city." At the Arizona border 662 men and women were turned away; 312 at the Oregon border; and fifty-one at the Nevada stateline. In all, 1,031 people were denied entry into California in one week. Police also arrested 1,470 people in one month on charges of evading railroad fare and vagrancy and begging. More than 300 of them had felony records. Davis asserted that crime in the city dropped by twenty-five percent.

While the *Times'* stories read like victory songs, the *Daily News* reacted differently. Manchester Boddy questioned in his daily column whether the effort by the police could stand up under the Constitution. "We have an idea that a man without even so much as a plugged nickel in his pocket has a right to walk from here to there and back again in the United States even if a state line intervenes," Boddy wrote. "And it seems to me that the *constitutionality* of this new, even though badly needed measure, should be tested as promptly as possible!"

The border checks began to unravel by the end of March when Modoc County demanded that the police officers leave because they were harassing local residents. After the state attorney general determined that it was unlawful for local police to conduct operations outside their county, the American Civil Liberties Union obtained a restraining order. The blockade ended in April. And while Davis attempted to revive it from time to time, it was essentially dead by the end of the year.

As he did during the 1920s, Davis considered organized crime a low priority. Frank Shaw ignored his earlier promises to combat racketeering and endorsed Davis' policy of harassing radicals and the indigent. Davis and Shaw emphasized that hard crimes instead of gambling, drugs, and prostitution should be targeted. Shaw did try to curb gambling. In 1937 he proposed to the city council that all bookmaking within the city limits be banned or that bookmakers be licensed and required to pay an annual fee. The council rejected the plans. But other than these half-hearted attempts, vice ran unchecked.

Bob Gans became the principal figure in gambling operations. He manufactured his own slot machines and placed them in clubs, bars, and grocery stores. These machines preyed on working class patrons. Police did little to control it since it was considered a poor man's sport. Another reason for lack of interest by police was Joe Shaw's promise to Gans that vice operations would remain untouched as long as Frank Shaw remained in power. By the time Frank Shaw was up for reelection in May 1937, 23,000 slot machines, 600 whorehouses, 300 gambling dens, and 1,800 bookie joints were operating without interference. To Joe Shaw, vice was a legitimate business subject to the same demands for contributions to the mayor's campaign coffers as City Hall employees and friends and acquaintances seeking city jobs. Joe Shaw received funding for election campaigns in exchange for free rein on vice. *Daily News* reporter Johnnie Arrington recalled that the syndicate spent $400,000 on a district attorney election and $250,000 for a mayoral election. The underworld also routinely financed advertising, radio time, pamphlets, and press agents for various political causes.

Typically, the city's newspapers were useless, if not harmful. As late as the spring of 1937, the *Examiner*, the *Herald & Express,* and the *Times* printed volumes of positive stories of Frank Shaw. And in April 1937, in the final days of the election campaign, the three newspapers made it clear they were behind Shaw who was seeking a second term against challenger John Anson Ford, a county supervisor and rising star in local politics. The *Times* endorsed Shaw not with the expected zeal of a newspaper behind the best man for the job, but more against Ford for his friendly attitude toward labor and economic issues. The *Examiner* and the *Herald & Express* invoked their policy not to endorse candidates in local elections, but their favorable stories about Shaw left no doubt who their choice was for mayor.

As it would for years, the *Daily News* also remained neutral probably not to risk offending advertisers. *Daily News* reporter Sara Boynoff would recall that over the years, the *Daily News* became increasingly erratic in its liberal causes, prompting angry Democrats such as Carey McWilliams to lament that "Manchester Boddy leads every liberal movement—up a blind alley where he clubs it to death."

III.

With the city's newspapers refusing to pick up the crusade, the battle against organized crime was left to a handful of people who had very little to gain and much to lose. The solution came down to just four men: Restaurateur Clifford E. Clinton, attorney A. Brigham Rose, Superior Court Judge Fletcher Bowron, and county Supervisor John Anson Ford.

Clinton had impeccable credentials as a crusader against vice and corruption. Clinton was born in Berkeley in 1900 to Salvation Army missionaries, spending part of his childhood in China. His parents returned to set up a restaurant in San Francisco after the 1906 earthquake. Handsome and conservatively dressed with wire-rim glasses, Clinton could pass as Clark Kent's double. He had a square jaw, an unwavering stare, and a forceful demeanor.

In 1931, the young Clinton came to Los Angeles to open his own restaurant. He opened Clifton's Brookdale Cafeteria at 648 South Broadway with its plush and exotic decor of faux redwood trees and running streams. He operated the eatery under the principle that patrons pay what they wished or even dine free. The strategy worked and he opened second cafeteria. Liberals, reformers, Communists, Technocrats, Utopians, and others made Clifton's their meeting place. Slowly, Clinton absorbed the talk and came to know the city's ills.

In late 1935, Ford came to Clinton with a proposal to investigate the food services at Los Angeles County General Hospital. Ford believed there were instances of graft at the facility. Clinton conducted a probe and documented a trail of corruption that led back to Frank Shaw's tenure as a county supervisor. Clinton also made a series of recommendations that could save the county as much as $120,000. Shaw supporters alleged that Ford had Clinton conduct the investigation to embarrass the mayor. But it was a minor squabble compared to the chain of events that would soon occur.

Almost immediately his restaurant became unsafe for patrons. City inspectors for health and safety code violations cited Clinton. Slip and fall complaints were filed and cases of food poisoning were reported. Clinton also alleged that the Shaw administration was responsible for raising his taxes and that the mayor's operative encouraged African Americans to patronize the restaurant to drive whites away. Some of these allegations by Clinton couldn't be substantiated. Tax issues came under county authority and there was no evidence that a larger percentage of blacks began eating at the restaurant. Still, the message was clear: Clinton, back off.

The intimidation tactics only strengthened Clinton's resolve. When Ford asked Judge Fletcher Bowron to name Clinton to the 1937 county grand jury, Clinton leaped at the opportunity. He was on the grand jury only a week when he asked the presiding judge for permission to have the grand jury conduct an investigation into vice operations within the city. His request was denied. Rather than accept the decision, Clinton began conducting a private investigation into the Shaw machine but much too late to affect the outcome of the April election, which saw Shaw win his second term. However, Clinton gathered evidence that Guy McAfee and Bob Gans were the kingpins of the city's vice operations and that Joe Shaw was peddling civil service appointments for cash and taking in revenue to keep gambling interests alive. He also found that district attorney Buron Fitts used the grand jury system to settle old scores and ensure that gambling operations remain untouched by investigators. When Clinton turned over a list of locations of gambling dens, brothel, and bookie joints to Frank Shaw's office, no investigation by police was conducted. Clinton employed gangsters and other underworld operatives through Harry Raymond to gather evidence. When his minority report was published (the grand jury, Clinton alleged, was tainted by underworld connections, Fitts, and the Shaw administration) it contained some information not supported by evidence and probably could not have passed muster in a courtroom. Still, there was enough evidence to demand a full investigation into organized crime. The *Times*, never to buck the status quo, lambasted Clinton and continued to back Shaw and Fitts.

Curiously, the idea of a separate investigative body formed by Clinton came from Frank Shaw. Socialite Louise Blatherwick rallied several churchwomen to accompany her to the mayor's office to question Shaw about vice. Shaw asserted the claims of vice were exaggerated and offered to appoint civilians to a vice investigating committee. Shaw attempted to withdraw the offer when Chief Davis reminded him the committee could easily look into the mayor's administration and become a political tool for Clinton and his allies. It was too late. The Citizens Independent Vice Investigation Committee (CIVIC) was founded on 19 July 1937.

Attorney A. Brigham Rose joined Clinton in his attempts to ferret out corruption by giving him legal advice. A brilliant trial lawyer, Rose was known for his courtroom histrionics. His technique was extremely effective and his acquittal rate for clients was unparalleled by fellow lawyers. Like Clinton, Rose became a target for harassment and death threats. His telephone rang continually and his mail contained threats. Rose's colleagues began to distance themselves from him. Rose remained behind the scenes, allowing Clinton to become the public face in the crusade.

The standoff between Clinton and organized crime set the stage for an escalation of intimidation. Shortly after midnight on 28 October a bomb exploded next to a wall at the Clinton residence at 5470 Los Feliz Boulevard near the western entrance of Griffith Park. Clinton wasn't at home and his wife and three children were sleeping on the opposite end of the house. The bomb wasn't big enough to seriously intend to kill anyone but if the message sent in the form of health code violations at his restaurant was not clear, then the bomb left no mistake that Clinton should end his investigation. Chief Davis speculated that Clinton himself planted the bomb as a publicity stunt. While it's unlikely that Clinton would put his family in jeopardy, it was odd that he wasn't at home at the time of the bombing. But newspaper photos published the next day showed him in his pajamas, implying that he was at home and had been awakened by the blast.

Pressure against the Shaw administration and the vice-lords began to mount. And while investigative reports by private citizens and the occasional outbursts from the press could be ignored, it was a much different matter when the courts became involved. The beginning of the end of organized crime in Los Angeles didn't start with Clinton's one-man crusade, but with the simple collection of a $2,900 debt.

Harry Munson in 1933 was Frank Shaw's first campaign manager who also acted as a bagman for local gangsters. His job was to collect thousands of dollars from Guy McAfee and Bob Gans to fund the Shaw election campaign. Shaw as the city's police commissioner rewarded Munson for his efforts with an appointment. During the campaign Ralph Grey was hired by Munson to handle some routine work for the campaign. Munson agreed to pay Grey $2,900 but then changed his mind and refused to pay. Grey hired Rose, who was prepared to subpoena McAfee and Gans and expose the entire racket. Rose hired Raymond because of his extensive underworld connections to conduct an investigation and serve subpoenas on McAfee and Gans. Munson countered by filing bankruptcy. The move backfired because Munson's finances, including payoffs from McAfee and Gans, would be explored in court.

Before the case reached a hearing, an explosion shattered a modest wooden garage at 955 Orme Avenue; a quiet residential mix of Mexican American and Jewish families nestled between Whittier Boulevard and East Seventh Street. It was an explosion that promised to "blow the lid off Los Angeles."

IV.

Shortly before 10 a.m. Raymond went to his garage behind his bungalow-style single-story home and got into his new sedan. He stepped on the starter, which ignited a bomb encased in a 10-inch steel pipe. The blast blew apart the four wooden walls of the garage and sent a piece of the engine through the roof as the roof collapsed onto the car. The left portion of the engine compartment and left fender were blown away. Shards of metal tore through the interior of the car. Raymond sustained two puncture wounds to the left side of his chest, a fractured right ankle, fractured left elbow and more than 100 lacerations.

The *Evening Herald & Express* broke the story that afternoon. Managing editor John B.T. Campbell chose to run a huge two-column photograph of Raymond that was probably more than a decade old, taken while he was a member of the police department. The paper immediately seized the angle that Raymond was working for Clifford Clinton and CIVIC. It got an interview with Rose who said that he to investigate the Munson bankruptcy case and to serve subpoenas on Gans and McAfee employed Raymond. Since Rose served as counsel to Clinton and CIVIC, the *Herald & Express* drew the erroneous conclusion that Raymond was working for CIVIC at the time of the bombing. The Munson case was only peripheral to CIVIC.

The *Times* danced around the issue of any underworld connection to the bombing by reporting the CIVIC angle in a sidebar on the inside pages and dropping toward the end of the main story the Munson case as a possible motive. Up high in the story on the front page, however, was a curious statement by police detective Joe Taylor, who told a *Times* reporter that "this bombing and the one at Clifford E. Clinton's home several months ago are undoubtedly connected." The *Times* didn't make mention of it again in the story.

Coverage by the press was either profoundly inept during the first five days of the story or reporters and editors were simply unwilling to examine possible connections between CIVIC's campaign to expose organized crime, which obviously included McAfee and Gans, and Raymond's small role in it. The papers also refused to examine the obvious links between the bombings at the Clinton and Raymond homes. Apparently inside links to ex-newsman James Bolger in Chief Davis' office and Steve O'Donnell's relationship with Frank Shaw were useless. And if *Examiner* city editor Jim Richardson's boast in his autobiography was true, that Raymond identified his attacker shortly after the bombing, then Richardson kept it to himself until the district attorney's office was ready to announce that arrests were made.

The *Daily News* was more thorough than the *Times* in its first-day coverage. It reported the rift between Raymond and district attorney Fitts, observing that Raymond demanded that Fitts leave his hospital room, shouting, "I don't want you around." It also reported that Raymond discovered that Munson received a fistful of $100 bills from McAfee to finance Shaw's 1933 mayoral campaign and Gans paid his $200 a month salary while on Shaw's staff.

As usual, the *Examiner* pulled out all the stops in its first-day coverage, running photos of all the principal players: Fitts, Munson, Raymond, Clinton, and Rose. It also featured a picture page of the bombing scene. Its front-page art of the injured Raymond was less staged than the competitors' art with Fitts, Rose, Clinton, and others walking next to Raymond's gurney down a hospital hall.

The *Times* and the *Daily News* ran nearly identical art of a stern-looking Clinton staring directly into the camera while detective Warren Hudson, pencil in hand, examined Raymond. The photo had been taken during the evening of the 14th. While Raymond looked unconscious or nearly unconscious, he had a cigarette between his fingers. Later press photos always showed Raymond smoking in bed. Given the number of visitors Raymond had the first night and his ability to apparently have a cigarette at will, one had to wonder how seriously he was injured.

Although the *Daily News* and the *Herald & Express* made no link to the Clinton bombing, the *Examiner*, like the *Times*, thought it worthy of mention. But instead of presuming that the same bombers may have been responsible for both attacks, the *Examiner* noted that a publicity man in the CIVIC camp once suggested to Clinton that a "good bombing would bring him notoriety." Clinton acknowledged that he had received such a suggestion, but thought it was "crazy." But it also gave credence to chief Davis' suggestion in October that Clinton may have been responsible for his own bombing.

By Monday, the 17th, the story was beginning to lose steam. The *Examiner*, the *Daily News*, and the *Herald & Express* noted low in their updates that "officials" in "high places" were linked to the attack. Only the *Times* was mum about that angle.

On Tuesday, the story was dropped from the lead front-page position. All papers but the *Daily News* were running the stories inside. The *Times* and the *Examiner* carried interviews with Raymond for the first time with the *Examiner* giving Raymond a byline "as told to" reporter Walter Naughton. The interviews yielded little except Raymond's playful apology to Jerry Giesler, celebrated defense attorney, for knocking the Paul Wright murder trial off the front pages.

Late Wednesday, the morning papers scrambled to put the story back on the front page. The *Examiner's* Jim Richardson was apparently caught unaware that the district attorney's office had arrested Earl Kynette, among others. None of the papers, in fact, had realized, or were willing to publish, that Rose had identified Kynette as the bomber shortly after the attack. On Wednesday night, Fitts took Kynette into custody, not on attempted murder charges but on suspicion of illegal wiretapping.

For most of Wednesday and through the night, Fitts and police detective Joe Taylor interviewed Kynette and sixteen members of the intelligence unit. At the end of the session, Kynette and Detective Lieutenant Dan M. Draper were taken into "technical" custody on the wiretapping charges. D.A. investigators and police had discovered dictographs at Raymond's home and wiring leading from the Raymond residence to another bungalow around the corner 2711 West Seventh Street. The squad to observe Raymond's movements rented the Seventh Street residence. Investigators also found out that several residents of Orme Avenue and Seventh Street knew that strange men were occupying the Seventh Street bungalow. The men cleaned up the residence and quickly left immediately after the bombing. No reporters interviewed the residents until after Kynette and Draper were taken into custody.

Despite rumors circulating for days that city officials may have know, something about the bombing, no paper seemed to notice that chief Davis, mayor Shaw, and his brother, Joe, were all out of town at the time of the attack and the crucial first days of the probe. Joe Shaw accompanied Davis to a marksman contest in Mexico City where the police department would be a star attraction. Frank Shaw was in Washington, D.C. on business. Six days after the bombing, the *Examiner* reached Davis in Mexico City for comment. Davis denied any knowledge of Kynette's activities and stood behind his officers. Davis and Shaw were expected to arrive at the Grand Central Air Terminal on the afternoon of the 19th, but only Joe Shaw stepped off the plane. Shaw refused comment to waiting reporters.

On the 20th, the *Daily News* linked a series of incidents together that might have been the handiwork of the Red Squad. In addition to the Clinton bombing in October, the newspaper outlined three other incidents involving people battling the city vice operations. The home of Lyndon R. ("Fearless Red") Foster, a political pamphleteer, was bombed in 1936 after he publicly accused the Shaw administration of participating in the prostitution racket. It also noted that Jack Diamond, a former investigator for the district attorney's office, had disappeared in 1935 and was presumed dead during the height of a anti-vice crusade movement. The *Daily News* also reported that the squad in late 1936 had framed Orville Forrester on drug charges during another campaign against organized crime and the gambling racket. Forrester was never convicted of the charges.

Despite the lack of evidence against the squad, it was a bold move by the *Daily News* to address previous alleged conduct by the unit and showed, albeit briefly, that at least one newspaper was willing to break away from the herd. The *Times* predictably gave the Kynette arrest light treatment and never mentioned Clinton, CIVIC or previous conduct of the squad in its 20 January editions. The *Herald & Express*, always endeavoring to come up with a new angle, provided little insight into the Kynette arrest. It did offer an interesting piece of information deep inside the paper that a man had reported to police that he was offered $1,500 to place a package in the restroom at Clifton's Cafeteria. The man was to collect the money and pick up the package at Gilmore Stadium in Hollywood. Detective Bert Wallis accompanied him to the location, but the person offering the money never showed up.

The papers had scant little to report as the investigation wore on. Speculation was rampant as to why Davis remained in Mexico. And Joe Shaw shed little light on any city-sanctioned operation against Raymond. But he attacked the investigation as borne out of hysteria created by CIVIC. When Davis arrived in Los Angeles late in the evening of the 19th, he kept a low profile until he squared off against Fitts a few days later. Fitts demanded that Davis suspend Kynette and Draper during the investigation. Davis refused. "It is self-evident that there has been already too much injustice done to the police department by malicious, unfounded accusations, as well as criticism based on suppositions and rumors," Davis said in a prepared statement to reporters.

Late on the 24th, the *Herald & Express* published statements by Davis implying that his officers did indeed spy on reform groups. Without mentioning either Raymond or CIVIC, Davis told the *Herald & Express*, "It is an age-old practice of criminal elements to attempt to destroy public confidence in law enforcement agencies. This is done by disseminating insidious propaganda and innuendoes through the medium of individuals who wear the cloak of crusaders or reformers.

"Naturally, operations of this nature are conducted with the greatest secrecy, and it is only through an intelligence unit that the police department can keep informed as to the real identity of persons involved in such activities and their motives and operations."

The other dailies picked up the statement the next day, but none asked Davis to elaborate.

At 5 p.m. on 25 January, Fitts called a press conference and announced that Kynette would be charged with attempted murder. The move infuriated Davis, who complained that Fitts, just the day before, dropped the wiretapping charges to make way for a grand jury investigation. Without warning, Kynette faced new charges. "If Buron Fitts will make up his mind as to how he wishes to proceed we are perfectly willing to cooperate with him to the limit," Davis told the *Examiner*. This time, however, Davis agreed to suspend Kynette once he was taken into custody. Shortly after the announcement, Fitts had fellow squad members Roy J. Allen and Fred E. Browne also taken into custody on the same charges.

The trial began on 14 April and would last nine weeks. The press corps was content to allow the details of the bombing conspiracy to play out in court rather than conduct any independent investigations. Court reporters and photographers were more concerned about getting dramatic art during the opening days of the trial, when Judge Thomas L. Ambrose ordered that pretrial photographs be shot only in his chambers and not in the courtroom. Agness Underwood, who had left the *Post-Record* to join the *Herald & Express* in January 1935, was assigned to cover the Kynette trial. She had sought the aid of criminal lawyer Bill Conners to argue for the press to allow cameras in the courtroom. Conners prevailed, much to the consternation of the defense attorneys who were dogged endlessly by camera-toting photographers through the corridors of the Hall of Justice at Temple and Broadway.

Defense attorney Joe Oliver gave up, hoping to use the photographers' conduct as a motion for appeal if Kynette was convicted. Trapped in an elevator with a persistent reporter, Oliver showed the reporter a copy of the front page of the *Herald & Express* which displayed a photo of Kynette under the overline: "Kynette Spies Again." The photo showed Kynette peering through a window in the door between the prisoner's room and the courtroom. It was routine during the trial that photographers Albert ("Smitty") Smith of the *Herald & Express*, Irvin ("Buck") Forbes of the *Examiner*, and Tommy Thompson of the *Daily News* would find any opportunity to obtain a photo of Kynette then have an editor run a sarcastic overline over the top of the photo. Oliver abandoned his plans for an outright ban on photos.

By now the news was making national headlines and the *Times* lamented that the city had spent much money attempting to maintain its good name. "When we permit it to be thus publicly inferred to the world that conditions here are so incredibly rotten ... what is it going to do to that reputation?" The Hollywood *Citizen-News* responded incredulously: "Are we to consider ourselves good citizens when, knowing the facts, we would seek to condone corruption in order to maintain a reputation to which we are not entitled?"

As the trial progressed, chief Davis defended the activities of the squad, but prosecutors had Raymond testify that Kynette had been responsible for the bombing and took his orders from Joe Shaw. Kynette's defense strategy was that he was framed. There was no evidence to corroborate Raymond's allegation that Joe Shaw had ordered the bombing. But evidence did show that Kynette had purchased materials for the bomb and had at one point discussed it with a police stenographer two days before the blast of spying on Raymond. On 16 June, Kynette and Allen were convicted of attempted murder. No evidence was uncovered that city officials knew of the bombing although Joe Shaw was aware of the spying. Allen died in prison while Kynette served ten years of a two-to-life sentence at San Quentin state prison. Browne also was sentenced to prison.

Seven years after the bombing, details of the incident surfaced that pointed to Buron Fitts as supervising the surveillance on Raymond, not Joe Shaw or chief Davis. From 1940 through 1948, Raymond fought against Kynette's parole from prison with an extensive letter-writing campaign to Governor Earl Warren. In a letter dated 29 November 1945, Raymond revealed the contents of a letter purportedly written to him from Kynette while in prison. In Kynette's letter dated 13 October 1940, the former intelligence unit chief wrote that D.A. investigator Jack Southard had first approached Kynette about investigating Raymond. "That Fitts and Southard, and in fact all the rest of Fitts' confidential investigators, knew that you carried a lot of incriminating material against Fitts and that they were trying in every way possible to get the originals of that material," the letter stated.

Fitts also called Kynette after the bombing and asked where Raymond's briefcase could be found since it carried information about the district attorney. Most of the men around the Raymond home before the bombing were district attorney investigators, Kynette wrote in his letter.

Kynette also acknowledged to Raymond that he supplied information to Fitts about notary Frank Angelillo, who gave damaging testimony to the grand jury that foreman John Bauer had cornered all of the city's paint contracts. Fitts took a squad of investigators to Angelillo's home and severely beat Angelillo's wife.

After Kynette's trial Clinton convinced Judge Fletcher Bowron to step down from the bench and run against Frank Shaw in a recall election in September.

Bowron served as Clinton's mentor during the now three-year-old vice crusade by the restaurateur. Ultimately Clinton would spend $100,000 of his own money to finance the recall. Under the umbrella of CIVIC, a new organization, Federation for Civic Betterment (FCB) was organized to spearhead the recall. Exploiting the fresh outrage of Los Angeles residents over the bombing, Clinton's group gathered 120,000 signatures for the recall. The *Daily News* and the Hollywood *Citizen-News*, owned by liberal Harlan Palmer, led the press campaign in favor of the recall, publishing scores of anti-Shaw editorials and articles and praising the courage of Bowron. The *Daily News* took this position, too, although the paper's editor, Steve O'Donnell, helped Shaw mount a campaign against the recall movement. Typically, the *Examiner* and the *Herald-Express* refused to endorse a candidate but its coverage of the Bowron/Shaw issue clearly favored Bowron. Only the *Times* stood behind Shaw, although its support was lukewarm. Given the paper's track record of viciously baiting opponents of Shaw, its criticism of Bowron was mild.

In September, Shaw was defeated with Bowron obtaining 233,427 votes to Shaw's 122,692.

Driving organized crime from Los Angeles didn't occur overnight, but Bowron issued sweeping changes throughout City Hall and the police department. His tenure as mayor (until 1953) was considered somewhat of a golden age for city government as corruption and vice was cleaned up. His appointees to the police commission promptly abolished the infamous Red Squad, or Spy Squad. The City Council slashed funding for the Spy Squad, rendering it ineffective. Chief Davis was forced into early retirement and twenty-three other high-ranking police officers were deemed uncooperative by the Bowron administration or too cozy with organized crime. They were forced to retire or were fired. By 1951, the Kefauver Crime Commission ruled that Los Angeles was one of the cleanest cities of its size in the United States.

In his autobiography, *Examiner* City Editor Jim Richardson claimed that the press was responsible for exposing the squad and igniting the events that led to the downfall of the Shaw administration. The newspaperman pointed to Manchester Boddy's *Daily News* column, "Views of the News" on 15 February 1938 which went to extraordinary lengths to congratulate the *Examiner* for publishing the "inside" story of the "Earl Kynette-Harry Raymond-Bob Gans-Mayor Shaw-Harry Munson-Police Commission 'invisible government' mess." What Richardson failed to point out was that although he implied that Raymond had identified to him the bomber almost immediately after the attack, the *Examiner* didn't publish Kynette's name until an announcement of his arrest was made by the district attorney's office. And the *Examiner's* expose appeared almost a month after the bombing when much of the information was already available.

The press conducted itself more like bystanders than participants. It was not the press exposing the corruption of the Shaw machine through its own probe but by the administration's failed attempt to silence Raymond that ignited the downfall of the mayor and police chief. Unlike the period of 1926-28 when the *Daily News* tackled vice by sending a reporter into gambling dens and scattered efforts by other newspapers to perform undercover work during the 1920s, the press in the mid and late 1930s was satisfied to sit back and allow police and prosecutors to dole out information on an incremental basis. The press effected change not through investigation but through its sometimes-overwrought sensationalism.

Chapter Six

The Los Angeles Newspaper Guild

I.

While Agness Underwood was scooping the competition by interviewing the widow of an ex-newspaperman slain alongside gangster Charlie Crawford, her editors at the *Evening Record* decided she could live on half her wages. The Great Depression reached Los Angeles a little late in 1931, but when it did reach the *Record* newsroom she was one of the first employees targeted.

Across town at the new City Hall at Spring and Temple streets veteran *Herald* reporter William teGroen was having his daily chat with Mayor John Porter. The topic more often than not in 1931 was enlarging the Los Angeles Memorial Coliseum to accommodate 105,000 people for the 1932 Tenth Olympiad. A hard-drinking man who carried shrapnel in his leg after a tour of combat in the world war, teGroen had been with the *Herald* since 1920. When he returned from his beat to the newsroom one day he learned his salary was cut ten percent. Between 1930 and 1933, the *Herald*—and after 1931, the *Herald & Express*—management cut editorial employees' pay four more times in increments ranging from five to ten percent. The *Times* also was making economy moves. It slashed its staff plantwide by ten percent, then cut payroll by ten percent on three separate occasions.

Artist Sam Patrick was with the *Illustrated Daily News* since the Vanderbilt days and could remember getting all the dirty work while the more seasoned artists drew comics. He also was there in August 1926 when no one in the plant got paid two weeks wages because the paper was in receivership and Manchester Boddy had to reorganize the entire operation before anyone received their salary. Patrick started at the paper when there were fourteen photographers and fourteen artists. By the early 1930s there were three photographers and two artists carrying the same load. He was lucky to get $30 a week for his efforts.

The newspapermen and women in the 1930s were a clannish lot. The veterans snubbed the cubs and demanded that a hierarchy be observed. Only veterans sat at the press table or the front row in a crowded courtroom. Only veterans played pitch in the pressroom at the police station, courthouse or City Hall—that is unless they saw a sucker cub they could fleece. Mentoring youngsters was not on the agenda.

There were exceptions, of course. Aggie Underwood had A.M. Rochlen, the legendary *Examiner* reporter, who demonstrated patience, understanding, and kindness when the all-male reporting corps wouldn't allow Underwood any slack. William teGroen would help out a green Jake Jacoby when he was hired by City News Service to cover City Hall and the district attorney's office. And Charlie Saxton, managing art director of the *Daily News*, took Sam Patrick under his wing.

Usually though, the going was tough for the rookie or out-of-town reporters new on the job. The character and personality of the Los Angeles newspaper staffer would change dramatically after World War II, but small changes began to show in the typical beat reporter in the early and mid-1930s. Many of the top editors of the day had been trained on the big-city newspapers of New York, Philadelphia, Detroit, and Chicago. While young and making their reporting bones, they lived in the city. They drank. They caroused. They gambled. Prohibition exacerbated the drinking and drew reporters closer to police officers as they spent long nights on liquor and vice raids. The image of the hard-bitten, hard-drinking reporter, which had some basis of fact in the late 19th century and early 20th century, was a common reality in the profession by the 1920s.

The ranks began to diversify after Prohibition with the entry of young news people such as Aggie Underwood, who got a job on the *Record* switchboard in 1926 to earn extra cash for her struggling family.

Underwood in many ways typified the new generation of reporters, but at the same time, she was perhaps an anomaly. She was a rare female cityside reporter who moved to the police and courts beat when other women were not afforded the opportunities. It spoke volumes for the *Record*, which, despite its sometimes sloppy editing and advocacy journalism, encouraged experimentation in the newsroom and gave young women a chance to report hard news. Underwood pioneered the role of the female hard news reporter.

Born in San Francisco in 1902, Underwood was on her own at a young age. Her mother died when she was six years old. Her father was an itinerant glassblower who left Underwood and her younger sister in the care of relatives or foster parents. The two girls knocked around in Illinois and Indiana during their childhood. Underwood then went to live with a relative in San Francisco, but the woman abandoned her. She joined another relative in Los Angeles, but the woman kicked her out of the house, and then threatened to call the juvenile authorities that she was a destitute teenager living on the streets. Underwood had been working as a waitress in downtown then. A soda jerk suggested they marry to prevent her from being sent to Juvenile Hall. They were married in April 1920. She was seventeen years old. By 1926, the couple had two children and Underwood's sister was living with them. To make ends meet and to provide her with some minor luxuries, such as silk stockings, Underwood took a job with the *Record*. While working the switchboard, she often assisted Gertrude Price with the Cynthia Grey column and the annual Christmas gift program the *Record* sponsored each year. Two years later she was working as a cityside reporter.

Although Underwood moved from Ocean Park to live downtown, many of the reporters employed by the metropolitan dailies chose to live in the suburbs. Gertrude Price, who wrote the Cynthia Grey column for the *Record*, cared for her aging mother in the San Fernando Valley. The *Examiner's* Jimmy Richardson lived with his son and second wife first in Glendale, then in Arcadia. Jake Jacoby would start his family in Montrose, in the hills above Glendale. Coy Watson, who shot pictures for Acme Newspictures, the *Post-Record*, and the *Herald & Express* during the 1930s, grew up in Edendale. Other newsmen, who would become the core of the reporting ranks after World War II, such as Aaron Dudley, grew up in Pomona.

In small steps, then, the city-bred, hard-drinking single male reporter gave way to the newsman and woman who lived outside downtown. In the 1930s, their ranks were small, but they would make a difference.

When the management of the *Record* decided to cut Underwood's salary by half, she was already paying $5 a week—one-quarter of her weekly salary—for a woman to babysit her two children. Half her salary would now have to pay for childcare. She decided to take what management gave her.

When the *Herald* began cutting salaries, William teGroen, however, set out to protect himself and his fellow reporters. And the protection would come in the form of a union designed specifically to give news people like Underwood some influence.

Like the rest of the country, Los Angeles was experiencing an increase in union organizing. The National Industrial Recovery Act (NIRA) and the Wagner Act gave labor leaders the right of collective bargaining and boosted attempts by local workers to organize. Before the Wagner Act was passed, workers had been faced with firings, threats, violence, and other forms of intimidation if they attempted to organize.

Newspapers were no different. The climate against union organizing in Los Angeles was particularly hostile because of Harry Chandler's vehement opposition to organized labor since the bombing of the *Times* building on 1 October 1910. Radical unionist brothers John J. and James B. McNamara were tried and convicted of the bombing. The blast killed twenty people and injured seventeen. The incident set back the cause of union organizing for a generation.

Even so, the existence of printing-trades locals at the other newspapers in Los Angeles provided a base for the organization of a local of newsroom workers. On the Eastern dailies, after all, strong printing-trades unions were enjoying favorable contracts. In 1923, at the end of a severe recession, the reporters who covered the courts and city hall in Los Angeles decided that the time was ripe to affiliate themselves with the main local of the printers' union, a traditional member of the American Federation of Labor (AFL). Late that year, Al Phillips of the *Examiner* and Leslie Powell of the *Daily News*, joined teGroen to meet with John Horn, president of the Los Angeles Central Labor Council, and J.W. Buzzell, the council's secretary. The reporters and union men met at the old City Hall, a massive fortress-like stone and mason structure built in 1889 on Broadway between Second and Third streets.

The effort by teGroen was doomed from the start. The printers, bound by traditional ways of thinking, were reluctant to include editorial employees in their local, and the parent union, the International Typographical Union (ITU) had consistently neglected to organize news people. These prejudices hindered any serious negotiations between the three newsmen and the Labor Council. In addition, newspaper management learned of the meetings and leaked word that organizing editorial departments would be strongly resisted.

Another effort, in the 1920s amounted to little more than a fraternity among newsmen. Organized under the title of the Los Angeles Press Club, it bore no relation to the Greater Los Angeles Press Club founded in 1946. The group met in the basement of a downtown building primarily as an excuse to drink bootleg booze. It moved to a warehouse in Hollywood so the club's still could operate unmolested by federal agents and local police. It was never a true bargaining organization for reporters as the group appeared to more preoccupied with drinking and furnishing its headquarters with such items as a coffin complete with skeleton, skull ash trays and portable beer tanks.

Despite the early failures in Los Angeles, the seeds of newsroom unionism took root elsewhere. The catalyst seemed to be a series of setbacks in New York City in 1923, when the New York *Globe* folded; a pressmen's strike turned out to be especially bitter; and a labor daily, the *Leader*, shut down. Altogether, more than 1,000 men and women lost their jobs. The AFL that year began chartering news writers' unions—nine of them by 1935—of which five would survive and form part of the American Newspaper Guild in 1936. These events would help Los Angeles reporters summon the courage to try again.

But it wasn't until Heywood Broun, a columnist for the New York *World*, threw down the gauntlet in 1933. Broun was a popular sports writer, columnist, and essayist. He had garnered a liberal following in the 1920s after his series of articles defending Nicola Sacco and Bartolomeo Vanzetti. The two Italian immigrants had been charged with murder and robbery in 1921 and were convicted and executed despite dubious evidence. Sacco and Vanzetti proclaimed their innocence and alleged they were being tried because they were immigrants and held radical beliefs. The case had a dramatic effect on Broun's politics. Not long after this series, Brown was fired for "disloyalty to the New York *World*."

His discharge didn't hurt his career, as he became a syndicated columnist, enjoying a wide readership in other publications. In 1933, he wrote in a column appearing in the New York *World-Telegram* that he intended to organize a union for editorial employees. In October 1933 the Guild of Newspapermen and Women of New York was founded. It became an early local of the American Newspaper Guild and helped establish the *Guild Reporter.* Copies of the *Guild Reporter,* a two-page broadsheet, were distributed in newsrooms throughout the country. By the end of the year, newsroom workers in every major city, including Los Angeles, began efforts to unionize their ranks.

By the time the New York Guild was established, the editorial staffers of the Los Angeles *Evening Herald & Express* had just suffered their last round of salary cuts for a workweek that remained sixty hours spread out over six days. The salaries on the larger dailies—the *Examiner*, the *Herald & Express*, and the *Times*—averaged about $30 a week; even veterans earned no more than $32.50. At the *Daily News* and the *Record*, most newsroom salaries ranged from $20 to $30 a week. Cub reporters had it even worse. In 1935, Jimmy Richardson offered Charles ("Chuck") Chappell a job on the *Record* at $17.50 a week and a weekly streetcar pass worth $1. On Chappell's first day on the job, Richardson took Chappell aside, put his arm, around him and told the young cub that the *Record* really could only pay him $15 a week. Chappell shrugged and accepted the cut in pay without comment. He had no recourse until a year later when he took a job at the Compton *News-Tribune* at $22.50 a week.

Spurred by the successes of unions in the East and the reality of a protracted Depression, court reporters in Los Angeles decided in 1934 to attempt to organize again. The reporters obtained permission from the city Board of Public Works to meet at the old City Hall (vacated in 1928) so they could do their business in privacy. About 100 newsmen and women attended the meeting, which included a representative from the American Newspaper Guild. Other organizational meetings were held at the San Fernando Valley ranch of actor Edward Everett Horton. As was expected, informants at the meetings reported the details to the management at the five dailies. Management, however, failed to react quickly, and plans to establish a local to proceed relatively unmolested. In September 1936, editorial staffers from the *Daily News* and the Hollywood *Citizen-News* formed the Newspaper Guild of Los Angeles (later called the Los Angeles Newspaper Guild). In all, the roster included sixty members from the newsrooms of the *Daily News*, the *Evening News*, the *Citizen-News*, the *Progressive News*, the Los Angeles office of the United Press and City News Service. The key members of the infant local were teGroen, Roger C. Johnson, a columnist at *Citizen-News*, who was named president; Phillip ("Slim") Connelly with the *Herald & Express*; newsman Morgan Hull; and Jake Jacoby of the City News Service.

Though all were dedicated unionists, the membership showed a great diversity of ideology. Johnson, for example, was a progressive liberal whose political philosophy reflected the prolabor editorial position of the *Citizen-News*. Connelly, a big and blustery man, was a committed Communist; he had once been an executive with the *Herald & Express*, but a falling out with other supervisors there made him rabidly anti-management. His adversarial attitude toward management, especially during contract negotiations and strikes, seemed to characterize the personality of the Los Angeles Newspaper Guild as a whole.

Charles Ellis wrote in the Guild newsletter in 1946 that Connelly "probably has more friends and more enemies than anyone else in town, (and) runs his office as secretary-treasurer of the Los Angeles CIO council almost as if it were a city desk. In Los Angeles Connelly is Mr. CIO and largely responsible for labor's permanency and prestige here."

Herald & Express reporter Nieson Himmel recalled that Connelly earned the enmity of the Los Angeles Police Department so much that the union man couldn't drive down a street more than a few blocks before he was pulled over by patrolmen and harassed.

The antithesis of Connelly was Jake Jacoby, who would play a critical role in attempting to oust suspected Communists from the Guild in the late 1940s. He was as ardently conservative as Connelly was radical, but he was quiet and reserved.

Jacoby was born in Vancouver, Canada, in 1915. The son of a jeweler and auctioneer, he moved with his family to California when he was seven years old. He worked on the school newspaper at Fairfax High then joined City News Service when he was nineteen. With teGroen he became active in forming the Guild, during the early period of the Guild's formation.

During the formative years of the local, Jacoby found that a very active Communist contingent was making decisions about Guild business. After repeatedly voting no on many issues, Jacob came to realize that the Guild's agenda was Communist inspired. Jacoby rejected the blandishments of Communist members, who tried to recruit him, but the experience would eventually lead him on a campaign to drive the Communists from the Guild.

But for the moment, Jacoby recognized that the local needed Communist leaders because of their aggressive approach to dealing with newspaper management and their finely tuned organizational skills. Who exactly were Communist Party members in LANG was never clear. Slim Connelly certainly was. Charlie Judson, city editor of the *Evening News*, also was an acknowledged Communist. Judson actively recruited members for the Communist Party as would become painfully evident to *Daily News* staffers during the postwar anti-Communist purge. Connelly was more circumspect in his recruiting methods; he was best at organizing strikes and conducting contract negotiations. There is scant evidence that the Communist leaders influenced other Guild members, but they employed the tactics and strategy of Communist organizers.

The Communist influences inside the Los Angeles local simply reflected the same issues facing the parent union, the American Newspaper Guild. The first indication occurred in 1937, when the *Guild Reporter* began publishing arguments in support of the Russian-backed Loyalists in the Spanish Civil War. Loyalist supporters in the late 1930s were often branded as Communists. The newsletter also relentlessly attacked the Nazi Party in Germany, but suddenly stopped when the Soviet Union signed its Nonaggression Pact with Adolf Hitler. In Los Angeles in 1940, John Cohee, a reporter with the *Daily News*, LANG member, and a Communist, proposed a resolution that suggested that military reservations eliminate armed guards and refrain from arming specific islands off the Atlantic Coast. Cohee argued that the resolution would help restrain the U.S. from entering into an "imperialist war." The resolution could have reflected isolationist leanings that prevailed in prewar United States, but it also employed language used by the Communist Party.

For the most part the beliefs of news reporters in Los Angeles mirrored the rest of the working professionals across the country. They had little knowledge of Communist ideology either before or after the war, but they were aware in varying degrees that it was a threat—or at least a perceived threat—to democracy. To *Herald & Express* reporters a Communist cell operating within the infant LANG was probably not relevant. The lost jobs brought about by the merger of the *Herald* and the *Express* had already made reporters eager for LANG representation. In fact, as the largest-circulating afternoon paper west of the Mississippi, the *Herald & Express* made an appealing target in the local's first battle to secure a contract. The union quickly organized the paper's 101 editorial employees. When word reached management they wasted no time in seeking legal help to fend off union efforts. But in a period of rapidly changing labor laws and a judicial and legislative system that were becoming increasingly sympathetic to organized labor, the lawyers hired by management to face the aggressive LANG were woefully ill-prepared.

On the advice of legal counsel, *Herald & Express* publisher Frank Barham offered a "yellow dog" contract that was already deemed illegal. The contract called for a one-year agreement that would give editorial employees a pay increase within $8 a week of pre-1929 levels. Management, however, blundered on the next step by having its own printing department run copies of the contracts. The proofs didn't go directly to Barham's office. They went to Guild organizers in the *Herald & Express* newsroom. When editorial employees were brought in individually to sign the contract they already knew its contents and refused to sign. Their resolve was further strengthened when management began posting notices on bulletin boards and conducting lectures in small groups to dissuade employees from unionizing. Not only did the efforts fail, LANG leaders brought these efforts into the open by sending a letter to Barham on 17 April 1937 seeking a meeting to discuss their proposed contract. Barham agreed to a meeting.

On 19 April, Barham and his negotiating team met with Guild representatives V.M. Gillette of the Musicians' Union; Ralph Lund of the Glendale *News-Press;* Milt Phinney of the *Evening News;* Anson Reeder of the *Examiner;* and Roger Johnson, president of LANG. Negotiations dragged through May then suspended when the local took a break in June to attend the ANG convention in St. Louis. They wanted to determine if ANG's policies would affect LANG's negotiations with local papers. The parent organization was apparently so impressed with LANG's initial efforts to unionize the *Herald & Express* that it formally adopted it as Local 69 and backdated its membership to October 1936. But internal struggles within the national organization continued to delay the negotiations. On 6 August, the national convention followed Heywood Broun's lead and switched its affiliation from the AFL to become affiliated with the renegade Congress of Industrial Organizations (CIO), led by John L. Lewis. Under the CIO the union was opened to all newspaper employees, skilled or unskilled.

When negotiations resumed in late summer, local Guild leaders went for the jugular under a new strategy. They demanded a minimum weekly salary of $30 a week for inexperienced reporters and a salary of $65 a week for reporters with more than five years experience. Rookie copyboys, librarians, and clerks would earn a minimum of $20 weekly while those workers with three years or more experience would be paid $30 each week. Employees dismissed from the paper would receive severance pay equal to two weeks pay for every year of service. Employees also would be paid for syndication rights and be reimbursed for supplies and expenses. Equally important was a new effort, under the CIO's open-door policy, to organize the paper's circulation department. The circulation department was especially critical, for in case of a strike, deliveries would be difficult, if not impossible.

Negotiations continued through October. The sticking point was the union's insistence that the *Herald & Express* be a closed shop. The parent union pressured the local to accept a compromise by establishing a preferential shop, which allowed a union/non-union employee ratio of 9 to 1. Non-union employees had the option of joining the Guild. Following the approval by the national organization, the contract became effective 8 November. The weekly pay scale for reporters with five years' experience was $42.50; district managers with five years' experience, $40; mechanics, $36; library clerks with three years' experience, $27.50; and copyboys with three years' experience, $20.

Although negotiations remained unfinished, officials of the local became confident to take on another newspaper: the *Examiner.* A small group of reporters was soon organized. But the management of the *Examiner* was determined to learn from the mistakes made by its sister paper and decided early that it would use no intimidation or strong-arm tactics.

The *Examiner* moved quickly. It took advantage of the fact that in mid and late 1937 the American Newspaper Guild and its Los Angeles local were unproven organizations. The negotiations with the *Herald & Express* were still underway. Instead of resisting unionization, the *Examiner* management encouraged the founding of the AFL-affiliated American Federation of Newspaper Writers and Reporters, Local No. 1. In the fall of 1937, J.W. Buzzell, secretary of the Central Labor Commission, which was operating for the AFL, walked into the *Examiner* newsroom, sat behind a desk, and started gathering signatures to organize the local. The first to sign the petition was City Editor Warden Woolard, who would have been ineligible for membership in LANG. Buzzell collected signatures from every editorial employee, then forwarded the petition to the National Labor Relations Board (NLRB) for certification. On 3 November, five days before *Herald & Express* news staffers signed their LANG contract, *Examiner* employees had their own agreement. The contract called for a pay increase of $7.50 a week, overtime, and a five-day, forty-hour workweek. It was the quickest and cleanest organizing effort seen by any news employee.

Despite the Guild's failure to gain a position in the *Examiner* newsroom, organizing and negotiating contracts for Los Angeles news staffers were remarkably trouble free. Already in December 1936, 100 Guild members at four Los Angeles newspapers had received blanket raises providing a minimum of $60 a month for copyboys and $180 a month for experienced editorial workers.

In the Guild's contract with the *Daily News* and the *Evening News,* effective 31 July 1939 through 30 July 1940, employees were guaranteed a forty-hour week. Reporters, rewrite men, copy editors, full-time correspondents, artists, and photographers received a minimum weekly salary ranging from $25 to $55. The head librarian received $50 a week. Editors in sports, drama, society, and business received a minimum of $60 a week, and display-advertising salesman obtained minimum scales of $35 to $60 a week.

While the Guild local in 1937 was flush with success, it would never gain a foothold in the open shop at the *Times*. A handful of *Times* reporters joined the Guild, but there was never enough to organize the editorial department much less negotiate a contract. Jake Jacoby recalled once pigeonholing a *Times* reporter in front of the federal courthouse and convincing him to join the Guild. As he was signing up the man, a *Times* photographer drove by and playfully shot a picture of the two men. The pained look on the face of the *Times* man with the Guild application in his hand was priceless.

II.

The local's biggest stumbling block to true success came in late 1937 when union leaders squared off against Judge Harlan G. Palmer, owner and publisher of the *Citizen-News* and a friend of labor. Slim Connelly and Roger Johnson had hoped that Palmer would readily accept a contract given the Guild's professional approach to the *Herald & Express* issues. They were surprised that Palmer was anything but cooperative.

At first, all the conditions seemed to favor the union. For one thing, the *Citizen-News* was the sole daily in a prosperous district with an unusually strong identity. The paper was the result of a merger between two small afternoon dailies on 2 November 1931: the *Citizen*, owned by Palmer, and the *News*, published by Ira Copley (who had bought the paper from F.W. Kellogg in 1928). Palmer's purchase, for $600,000, also included Associated Press service, which was then considered a valuable franchise, to complement the *Citizen's* other sources of news: United Press, City News Service, and Central Press.

Under Palmer, the *Citizen-News* shared the liberal voice in the Los Angeles area with the *Daily News*. Palmer had a reputation among news staffers for insisting on strictly observing responsible journalism. An unpretentious man who was considered among his employees as fair-minded and compassionate, Palmer never shirked from controversy when it might raise the ire of advertisers. Editorial staffer Haig Keropian once turned down a news assignment that involved a major advertiser of the paper. The advertiser's wife was furious and complained bitterly about Keropian's decision not to send a photographer and reporter to the event. After the woman left Palmer's office, the publisher visited Keropian's desk and asked him for his side of the story. After Keropian finished, Palmer silently puffed on his cigar for a moment then said the right decision was made. "If only these people would learn. Thank you," said Palmer as he turned on his heels and walked away. Palmer's loyalty to his news staff was warmly appreciated.

Hope for an early resolution for a contract for *Citizen-News* employees were dashed in the negotiation process when Palmer unexpectedly refused to yield to the local's demands. The union negotiators comprised of Slim Connelly, Charlie Wathey, C.H. ("Brick") Carrigues, Tom O'Connor, and Bill Oliver, a reporter with Communist leanings who had joined the drama department at the *Herald & Express* in 1936. The group met with Palmer and T. Harwood Young, business manager, on 22 December 1937. Negotiations with Palmer and Harwood would serve a model for future meetings. Accompanying the five Guild members were eleven "observers," a number that grew with each succeeding meeting. Meetings were often scheduled after working hours to allow as many observers as possible to attend. Sometimes meetings grew so large that auditoriums were rented to accommodate overflow crowds. These negotiating sessions were often rambunctious and crude, for Guild leaders encouraged rank-and-file members to voice their opinions, which often degenerated into heckling. These types of meetings were ostensibly staged to stimulate interest in contract negotiations among union members, but they also applied considerable pressure to management.

Whether Palmer balked at Guild demands because he truly believed they were unreasonable or because of the manner of how the meetings were conducted is unclear. But he wasn't about to cave in without a fight. (It's interesting to note that the *Daily News's* Manchester Boddy, who was not as committed to his liberal principles as Palmer, could enjoy friendly relations with LANG throughout most of his tenure as publisher.)

Negotiations stretched through early 1938 with Palmer asserting that demands by the Guild would require layoffs and cost his newspaper an additional $500,000 annually. In May, just as the local appeared to win out, Palmer submitted a proposal, which had been tentatively approved by the local. The snag was that Palmer immediately announced that three newsroom staffers and two commercial department employees would be laid off to pay for the increased costs required by the new contract. The Guild rejected the contract offer and, at a 14 May meeting held at Jacoby's home, authorized a strike.

Fewer than twenty employees went on strike, but it generated enough publicity to make any Hollywood starlet envious. Connelly blustered, promising a loud and noisy picket line outside the *Citizen-News* offices. He established a plan to discourage merchants from advertising and organized a boycott of those advertisers still buying space in the paper. Pickets also were organized in front of stores that continued to advertise. Celebrity journalists Dorothy Parker and Ring Lardner Jr. participated in demonstrations in front of the newspaper's offices. Screenwriters and directors also marched alongside of sympathizing typographers, longshoremen, and teachers. Cocktail parties and costume parades were held in the street. At one point Connelly and Johnson were taken into custody for refusing to obey police orders to stop distributing handbills. They were released three hours later on $25 bail, but the Guild made the most of their arrests by elevating them to martyr status.

The *Citizen-News* was badly hurt by the strike. Although the paper never missed a day of publication, it lost as much as fifty percent of its display advertising and more than a quarter of its circulation.

The strike dragged on for ten-and-a-half weeks. Strikers were beginning to weary of the demonstrations and dwindling funds. Their morale was beginning to ebb. Palmer, meanwhile, was incurring the wrath of his advertisers who were losing customers because of the boycott.

In the end, little was achieved. When LANG leaders revisited the negotiating table with Palmer, they were presented with a contract that wasn't much different from the one they were given in May. The union won a clause in the agreement that allowed temporary reinstatement of laid off employees. As for the contract, it called for salary increases to $45 a week for newsroom employees, two weeks' vacation, a standard work week, reinstatement of striking workers, and a dismissal indemnity of up to twenty-five weeks pay.

As if LANG and newspaper publishers didn't learn anything from the *Citizen-News* strike, a new job action loomed at the Huntington Park *Bulletin* with near identical strike tactics employed with virtually the same results. As in the case of Harlan Palmer, Guild leaders didn't enjoy a good relationship with *Bulletin* publisher Max Ward, described by news staffer Aaron Dudley as a "flag-waving, Lions Club conservative who hung tough and was ready to go down fighting" against the Guild. When Ward fired several card-carrying Guild members, a strike was called on 9 September 1939.

The *Bulletin* was a twice-a-week throwaway headquartered originally in Southeast Los Angeles, near the neighborhood of Hyde Park at Florence and Western avenues. It later moved to Pacific Avenue in Huntington Park, a workingman's community that strongly supported its local newspaper.

With the *Bulletin* strike, LANG couldn't prevent the publication of the paper as AFL mechanical trade workers refused to honor Guild picket lines. But strikers did manage to bring economic pressure on Ward by staging secondary boycotts of the newspaper's advertisers. Intense picketing, public demonstrations in front of stores that advertised in the *Bulletin,* and petitions circulated by non-union sympathizers contributed to a drop in circulation.

The strike also tested the loyalties of *Bulletin* coworkers. Roy Ringer, who would later enjoy a distinguished career at the *Daily News* and the *Mirror,* joined the *Bulletin* in 1938, when he was nineteen years old. Born in Pittsburgh, Roy was the son of traveling manager for Florsheim shoes. He attended eight elementary schools before going to high school. At the age of twelve, the Ringer family moved to California and young Roy attended Huntington Park High School. Politically, the Ringer family was progressive. His mother was an Irish Catholic and his father was an organizer for Upton Sinclair's End Poverty in California (EPIC) movement in Huntington Park.

In 1936, while still in high school, Ringer was hired at $20 a week by Les Adams, who was then editor of the Huntington Park *Signal*. For the *Signal*, Ringer pulled United Press copy or wrote sports in the morning before going to school, then returned in the afternoon to cover city hall and the police and fire beats. After graduating in 1938, he quit the *Signal* to work for Aaron Dudley at $30 a week at the *Bulletin*. Working at the *Bulletin* afforded Ringer the opportunity to write for outside trade journals published by the newspaper. The *Bulletin* published the *Retail Liquor Bulletin* and *American Police Patrol*. Both Dudley and Ringer were paid an additional $50 a month for putting copy together.

As editor, Dudley remained loyal to management when the strike hit. Ringer walked out. Ringer edited the strike newspaper and participated in picketing local businesses that still advertised with the *Bulletin*. To keep the *Bulletin* alive, Ward slashed salaries of those employees remaining on the job. Dudley saw his $55 a week salary cut to $35 a week. Some paydays his pay envelope was empty. Ward was determined to wait out the strikers and refused to give any concessions at the negotiating table. But the secondary boycotts were hurting businesses still advertising. Huntington Park Mayor Howard Seybold had enough and stepped in. Virtually pushing Ward aside, Seybold negotiated an end to the strike that resulted in minimal, if any, pay raises for newsroom employees.

Eleven months and eleven days later the strike, in what Dudley described as an "excruciating, painful, and expensive" experience, ended with both Ringer and Dudley out of a job. According to Ringer, a new Guild unit consisting mostly of scabs was installed at the newspaper and agreed to some layoffs. The terminations were based on marital status and not seniority. Older, married employees kept their jobs and single workers were fired. Ringer was especially bitter since he believed his financial obligations were at least equal to many of the married employees. He also resented that the Guild did nothing for him despite his strong union loyalty and activity during the strike. Dudley, however, insisted to Ward that Ringer be rehired. But it took two more months after the end of the strike before he got his job back. By then, Ringer felt uncomfortable working with scab colleagues and took a newspaper job in 1940 in Santa Barbara.

Dudley was dumbstruck when he discovered that he also was fired. A new newsroom staffer joining the *Bulletin* from the *Signal* complained that Dudley could never get along with Guild members. As far as Dudley was concerned, nothing could be further from the truth. While on opposing sides, Dudley enjoyed a close relationship with many Guild members and often had beers with Ringer after hours during the strike. But Seybold, who now ran the *Bulletin* operation, authorized the termination. Dudley immediately staked out Seybold's home and refused to leave the mayor's back porch until he had a confrontation with him. When Seybold finally agreed to hear the young editor out, Dudley told him he was loyal to the paper and expected his job back with a weekly paycheck. Seybold acquiesced and Dudley returned to work. He left several months later on his own terms.

While Ringer's union activity didn't garner him any benefits after the strike, there were indications that other Guild members were rewarded for their strike activity. Don Kirby was an advertising salesman for the *Bulletin* and Guild member who had a strong relationship with the city's markets. During the strike some of the markets suddenly stopped advertising with the *Bulletin*. After the strike was settled, Kirby was given a job just a few weeks later on the plum court beat for the *Daily News*. During his tenure as court reporter, Kirby enjoyed the support of

Aaron Dudley, right, sided with management in 1939 when members of the Los Angeles Newspaper Guild went on strike at the Hungtington Park *Bulletin*. He later joined the *Daily News* (courtesy Aaron Dudley)

Agness Underwood in a 1983 photograph outside her home in Colorado. She was the first woman city editor of a Los Angeles metropolitan daily. She began her newspaper career as a switchboard operator on the *Evening Record*. (courtesy Will Fowler)

The Los Angeles Newspaper Guild picket line in front of the Los Angeles *Herald & Express* building in September 1946. More than 500 *Herald & Express* employees staged a strike for three months before returning to work. Their gains at the negotiating table were negligible. *(Daily News* Collection/Special Collections, UCLA)

Vern Partlow of the *Daily News* in 1950. He was fired by management for refusing to deny that he was a Communist. (*Daily News* Collection/Special Collections, UCLA)

Darr Smith of the *Daily News* in 1948. He was identified in a federal committee hearing as being a Communist. Although he was laid off from the *Daily News* before the accusation, his name was stricken from the rehire list because he refused to deny that he was a member of the Communist party. (*Daily News* Collection/Special Collections, UCLA)

fellow reporters and Guildsman on the beat to see that he succeeded in a job he had no qualifications for.

Strikes at City News Service and the *Herald & Express* in 1946 also proved particularly troublesome and ended with little for Guild members to celebrate.

City News Service had gone through ownership changes during the war and management had become increasingly uncooperative during its six-year relationship with LANG. When it was clear that new owner Marvin Willard was not enforcing provisions of the Guild contract, fifteen CNS employees walked off the job on 14 May 1946. The strike completely shut down the operation and the striking employees established a strike news service to provide local news to fifty weekly newspapers, eight dailies, and eight radio stations. CNS management never wavered from its position that it was under no obligation to honor a contract signed by previous owners. By August, CNS was dead and all news employees were out of a job.

The strike against the *Herald & Express* in the fall of the same year was particularly brutal for 525 Guild members. It had become the most protracted strike against a Los Angeles newspaper and involved the most Guild members until the *Herald-Examiner* was struck in 1967. The *Herald & Express* strike carried what observers at the time considered Communist overtones. Particularly since the two leading Guild negotiators had, or were accused of having, Communist ties. Negotiating a contract due to expire at midnight 3 September were Milton Murray, past ANG vice-president, William Brodie, a LANG administrative officer, and Slim Connelly. Murray would later be accused under oath during the House Un-American Activities Committee (HUAC) hearings of being a Communist. Connelly rarely disguised his Communist affiliation and would become editor of the Communist Party newspaper, *People's World*. Again, ideology mattered little to strike leaders, but tactics were employed that would bring the most attention to their cause, which would bring more support.

As now customary, Guild negotiators organized large numbers of rank-and-file union members to attend meetings between their representatives and newspaper management. An auditorium with a large stage was rented with all the principal negotiators sitting at a table on stage while LANG members heckled management. To conservative Guild members the display was unseemly, rude, and embarrassing. To leftists, it provided a forum to attack the policies of William Randolph Hearst for his strident attacks on the Communist Party and Socialist causes. Strip away the rhetoric and LANG members discovered that thirty-three of the forty-two issues on the table were agreed upon. The heart of the disagreement between the two parties was demands by LANG for minimum weekly wage scales of $100 per week for reporters. Management countered with a weekly wage increase of ten percent or $5, whichever was greater. At the last moment, management upped the ante to twelve-and-a-half percent. The offer was rejected.

Initially, a dispute arose between the Guild and management of whether the Guild called a strike first or declared a strike only after management had locked employees out of the building. The Guild claimed that *Herald & Express* management locked employees out and the strike was in retaliation. The *Herald & Express'* sister paper, the *Examiner*, reported in its 5 September editions that employees walked off first. It reported that at 12:01 a.m. on 4 September, the Guild invoked a "no contract, no work" declaration and Guild members, mostly janitors, walked off the job. The *Herald & Express* then suspended publication. While the job action was characterized as a lockout strike, the state Department of Employment ruled on 26 September that the newspaper employees were on strike and were not locked out by management. The ruling made employees ineligible for unemployment insurance.

By dawn on 4 September, Norma Barrigan, chairwoman of the Guild's auxiliary committee, already established a picket and 24-hour commissary in front of the Trenton Street plant.

Committees were established to generate publicity, organize volunteer workers, and monitor strike expenses. Despite broad support from Guild members from other papers, there was dissension among some longtime members. William teGroen, police reporter Jimmy Shambra, and staffer Fred Arnelled voted against the strike. teGroen was severely beaten after the vote. In addition, Connelly opposed cooperating with the police over picketing and demonstration issues, hoping to incite violence among strikers, thus creating a social cause for unionists. But Guild members detailed to act as liaisons to the police department and the district attorney's office refused to allow emotions carry them away, and worked out a cooperative relationship that resulted in peaceful demonstrations.

Pickets were placed around the main *Herald & Express* plant, the paper's offices in the Broadway Arcade and the Southwest branch on Figueroa Street, the City News office, and railroad yards where truckloads of newsprint destined for the newspaper were diverted to other cities. In addition to the strikers, members of the Newsboys Union, the *Daily News*, the *Labor Herald*, CIO Longshoremen, Marine Cooks and Stewards, CIO office workers, and representative of other union locals have joined the picket lines. At the beginning, about 360 pickets appeared daily from 7 to 8 a.m., followed by a 24-hour shift of 188 regularly assigned pickets.

Strikers also published their own newspaper. A city room was set up at Guild headquarters, then moved to a larger office at 823 West Pico. Named the *Guild Striker*, the tabloid was published once a week. Limited by the shortage of paper, the four-page newspaper rounded up strike activities and carried photos and paid advertising. In addition, a mimeographed daily bulletin was put out to the members.

LANG members received about $25 per week in strike pay but as negotiations dragged on it became apparent that striking employees could not last long on so little money. By the first week in November, an "Adopt a Striker" plan was launched that established "adoption" papers for strikers complete with biographical sketch of the employee and his or her family and accompanying photograph. The papers were then sold for $5 down and $5 a week to the public and union sympathizers until the employee returned to work.

By the seventh week of the strike, the parent ANG spent $30,000 on the strike and its newspaper. Management hadn't appeared in any hurry to resolve their differences, probably because it had strike insurance. All Guild members from competing newspapers were tapped two days pay, on average about $27 per Local 69 member, as contributions to the strike fund. While the contributions were deemed "voluntary," union leaders made it clear the contributions were a must. Strike pay was cut to $20 per week while management indicated to unionists it was willing to hunker down for the long haul.

LANG also held a "Meet the Strikers" party that attracted 250 people. Mixed drinks were served for 25 cents. The party netted $81.60 for the strike kitty from admissions and a nylon hose raffle, but little money was raised from the bar because volunteer bartenders had been giving away sample cocktails.

Hope for employees to return to work surfaced on 11 November when management and Guild leaders announced that the LANG accepted an offer of a fourteen percent wage increase. "There is now no barrier from the Guild side which would block immediate reopening of this plant," said Milton Murray. "The sole question is whether management wants to reopen the plant."

Murray was either too optimistic or he wanted to stir the emotions of the strikers. Less than forty-eight hours later, the Guild announced that an impasse had occurred over retroactive pay to 21 October. LANG already revised its demand from a $100 weekly minimum to $90 and wasn't about to budge now on retroactive pay. Vic Dunsmore, business manager of the *Herald & Express*, said management had no intention of granting retroactive pay. Management expertly played the waiting game. Strike pay was poor and the grind of walking the picket line was beginning to wear. Employees were ready to return to work.

On 26 November, LANG and management reached a final agreement that allowed workers to return to their positions on company payroll "without prejudice on the part of either of the disputants." They also settled for much less than originally demanded. Journeymen editorial workers were not to receive the $100 weekly minimum or even the $90 weekly minimum under their own revision, but raises boosting the minimum from $70 to $80 per week. The increases amounted to a fourteen percent raise. The new contract also called for three weeks vacation after five years of service, added holidays, and increased mileage rates for employees using their own cars.

"It is the best that we can wring out of management at this time or for a foreseeable future," William Brodie told the *Herald & Express* unit members at the Musart Theater. "It enables us to seal off the gains we have won in this long struggle. It enables our union to return to the plant in strength and with the ability to protect our members come what may."

Guild members from other newspapers were disappointed. Roy Ringer, who joined the *Daily News* after a stint in the U.S. Coast Guard during the war, served as editor of the *Guildsman* and had walked the picket line in front of the *Herald & Express* plant. Ringer recognized that strikers "got tired of the whole damn thing and wanted to go back to work," but he and other sympathizers felt "sold out" after working so hard to keep the strike alive.

The union had little to celebrate, but it couldn't resist staging a dramatic contract signing on the stage of the Musart with the more than 500 strike participants and other LANG members looking on. On 2 December the newspaper resumed publication with amazingly little bitterness displayed by employees, many of whom worked for as long as thirty years for the company and had invested much of their lives in the paper. And unlike the damage done to the circulation of the *Citizen-News*, the *Herald & Express* suffered no such losses, and, in fact, its circulation increased 4,000 for a total of 410,248.

Despite the modest gains by the union following the strike, LANG members remained fiercely loyal to their local. Four months before the *Herald & Express* strike was called, *Daily News* staffer Les Claypool wrote of his affection for his union in the 3 May edition of the *Guildsman*: "After I had been kicked around a few years it dawned on me one day that the people who always seemed to want newspaper reporters to be neutral and objective were the owners of the newspapers or their stooge editors . . . I found I was working nine hours a day every day but Saturday. On Saturdays I worked from 7 a.m. until 3 a.m. In other words, I worked 65 hours a week and got not a penny for any such thing as overtime . . . Then the Guild came along and put an end to all that. It wasn't easy and to this day there are short sighted and narrow minded newspapermen who do not realize that their 5-day, 40-hour week and overtime are all due to the pioneering of the Guild."

Still, LANG's toughest test was ahead, and it had nothing to do with contracts and strikes.

III.

Much had changed in postwar newsrooms. Tolerance, if not the embrace, of the Communist Party agenda during the 1930s was absent in the late 1940s. The House Un-American Activities Committee created a chilling effect in how individuals expressed themselves politically. But in the *Daily News* editorial department in the late 1940s, reporters had a tendency to wear their political beliefs on their sleeves. Always careful to keep their political opinions out of the news columns, *Daily News* staffers loved the good fight of the underdog.

City editor Charlie Judson and managing editor Phil Garrison in their early years as journalists were extremely liberal. Judson later would acknowledge having Communist sympathies while Garrison considered himself a "flaming liberal" who became increasingly conservative and disenchanted with liberal causes after the war. Judson was twenty-four years old when he began his career with the *Evening Record* in 1933 as a copyboy at $10 a week. Garrison joined the *Daily News* in May 1935 as a copyboy, earning $7 for a forty-eight-hour workweek. Just a year later Garrison was promoted to assistant financial editor at $15 a week. Judson and Garrison formed the core of the newsroom management with both men occasionally switching positions of city editor and managing editor.

Opinions of Judson among staffers were divided. Many of the cityside reporters thought well of him, but other staffers like reporter Paul Weeks found him to be an editor who was "sort of a guy playing the movie role of a editor." He also was hardheaded, preferring to run a newsroom to his liking with little room for compromise. To others he was a "son-of-a-bitch" who routinely made poor decisions and then blamed subordinates the next day when accountability was demanded. He could be cruel and seemed to resent staffers who were happy with their jobs and their personal lives. Still, *Daily News* management was attracted to hiring thinking, unconventional reporters who were a breed apart from the Hearst crowd. Over the years, the paper had garnered a reputation as being a newspaperman's newspaper, allowing reporters more freedom to write and express themselves. Sports writers particularly enjoyed wide latitude in their writing. Discussions among beat reporters—sports writers and copy deskers rarely participated—about liberalism and conservatism were frequent. Many reporters voiced their concern over freedom of speech and freedom of thought as the power of the HUAC continued to grow. They also found it difficult to have open discussions in the newsroom about politics, as they had enjoyed before the war, because of the prevailing anti-Communist climate in the country.

Debates of abstract ideologies shifted dramatically to practicality in 1951 when jobs were on the line over political affiliations. In September, drama reporter Darr Smith, a staffer with the *Daily News* since 1936, was laid off in an economic move by management, but was placed on a rehiring list and expected to resume his position within a few months. In June 1952, the United Press sent a dispatch reporting that Judson testified before the HUAC and had given general assignment reporter Vern Partlow's name as a suspected Communist. He also named Smith as a Communist before the congressional committee. By then, Judson was working as a senior editor of *Fortnight* magazine. When he was summoned to testify, his employers told him that if he invoked the Fifth Amendment there would be no job waiting for him when he returned from Washington, D.C. Judson needed his job and named Partlow and Smith. Lee

Payne, executive editor, and William R. Powell, plant assistant manager, immediately quizzed Partlow about his alleged affiliation with the Communist Party. Partlow refused to confirm or deny his membership. Partlow was fired on 7 June. The *Daily News* struck Smith from its rehiring list.

Editorial employees were perplexed about Smith's treatment by management. His leftist leanings were common knowledge in the newsroom, but he was considered a "classy" guy who rarely engaged in political debates with co-workers. Quiet and introspective, he had at one time worked in the script departments at film studios before turning to journalism.

Partlow was another matter. The kind of trouble he was in at the *Daily News* was a pattern that had established itself when he worked on the Milwaukee *Sentinel* in the early 1930s. Born in Harris, Illinois, in 1910 to a farming family, Partlow grew up in Bloomington. He cubbed at the *Pantagraph* as a high school campus correspondent for space rates. He did well at the morning paper and had more work than he could handle, writing about films, road shows, and sports. His weekly rate averaged around $20. While his experience at the *Pantagraph* was important to his career, he quit high school and went to Chicago to work in a public relations office. He returned a year later to finish his senior year and resume his work at the *Pantagraph*. After high school he moved around a bit, working for a traveling theater stock company and returning to Chicago to work another brief stint as a press agent.

In the fall of 1931, he joined the *Sentinel*, and was given the plum assignment of covering the 1932 presidential campaign. In 1935 he joined the American Newspaper Guild and began organizing a local at the newspaper. It was a period when the Hearst chain periodically fired its news staffs, hired new employees, then rehired the old news staffers back at a lower rate. Partlow was part of a dozen or so journalists from the Milwaukee *Journal*, the *Sentinel*, the *News* and the *Socialist Daily Leader* who met and eventually founded the Milwaukee Newspaper Guild. Partlow was fired from the *Sentinel* when his city editor discovered he was the organizer and accused him of being a Communist. The editor demanded that Partlow give him membership cards of Guild members, but he refused and was fired and blacklisted. Oddly, though, the *Sentinel* asked Partlow to return to work but wanted to know if he had "learned his lesson." Partlow reaffirmed his loyalty to the Guild but assured his editors that he was "no troublemaker." The Guild, however, went on strike just two weeks after Partlow returned to work. When the strike was over six months later, management agreed to all of the Guild's demands. The only exception was that it refused to take back Partlow.

Out of work, Partlow moved to California where he struck up a friendship with Matt Weinstock and Charlie Judson. He didn't immediately take a job at the *Daily News*, but instead moved to San Francisco where he joined the *Examiner* as a reporter. He was promoted to night city editor four months later. His past Guild activities haunted him. When the *Guildsman* published his name as an organizer, he was fired again. After kicking around at several writing jobs, including a job with the WPA writers project in Wisconsin, Partlow landed a part-time job at the *Daily News* in 1940. He became administrative officer in 1942 for the Guild, where he was considered a middle-of-the-road member. Partlow agreed to the post because, he said, "dissenting factions couldn't agree on anybody else. I was a compromise."

In April 1944, he joined the *Daily News* full-time as a copy editor. Lanky and talkative, Partlow was popular among staff. He authored several folk songs, writing in the tradition of Woody Guthrie and occasionally singing for staff members and at Guild meetings. The *Guildsman* once said of Partlow: "With his long fingers on his guitar and his vocal chords throbbing, he goes through a transformation which suggests that, even for a newspaper reporter, he has found his way to the present by a strange, unbelievable route. He has been called 'a singing newspaper,' which is as good a way as any to define him when he's operating before a group with his guitar. Of the atom bomb, he sings: 'We hold this truth to be self-evident, that all men are cremated equal. . . . The atom bomb is here to stay but are we?' " The song, titled "Old Man Atom," received extensive radio airplay until it was banned during the height of the McCarthy hearings.

Paul Weeks saw Partlow as "very much an intellectual liberal" or perhaps a Parlor Bolshevik, but one who never put his political views in his stories.

The firings of Partlow and Darr Smith, and Charlie Judson's role as informant, put LANG in an awkward position. It was a tumultuous time for the CIO as it expelled nine leftist unions after its 1950 convention. One such union, the International Longshoremen's & Warehousemen's Union, had a strong base in Los Angeles and was particularly friendly to LANG. The local Guild was sharply divided over whether they wanted to defend the two newsmen or revoke their memberships. Conservative members demanded their ouster from the union. The Guild meetings were emotional as members debated the fate of the pair. Jake Jacoby, who by then was editing *Alert*, a *Red Channels*-type anti-Communist newsletter, was part of the conservative contingent. Jacoby founded *Alert* with Ed Gibbons, who was associated with *Variety*. The newsletter was published from 1947 to 1952.

Editorial employee Lucian Haas was accustomed to red-baiting when he became the LANG shop steward at the *Daily News*. He saw a newsroom virtually polarized over the issue. His argument before the Guild was to invoke the union contract that allowed employees freedom of association and freedom of speech. It didn't matter that Partlow and Smith were Communists. They were entitled to their Constitutional rights and were protected by the Guild contract. Lee Payne asked Partlow to sign a loyalty oath shortly before his termination. Partlow had signed such documents before, but on this occasion he believed that signing a loyalty oath violated the Guild contract and established a dangerous precedent. Since the Guild would not allow Partlow to sign the document and the local challenged the firings, the issue went before a panel of the National Labor Relations Board in July 1952. Its members were arbitrator Paul A. Dodd, a one-time liberal and the dean of Letters and Science at UCLA; Phil Garrison and Arthur G. Pollock, *Daily News* business manager, to represent management; and makeup editor Larry Fowler and Jack Rarick, an *Herald & Express* editorial employee, to represent the Guild.

Before the panel, LANG members argued that Communist Party membership was not relevant and that the Communist Party was just another political party. The fact that Partlow and Smith didn't deny an affiliation to the party was not reason enough for their firings. Partlow and Smith were then summoned separately to testify before the panel. They were asked if they had been members of the Communist Party. Both men refused to answer, "on the grounds of personal conscience, on the basis of immateriality and other grounds outlined by Guild counsel."

Daily News management readily acknowledged that neither Partlow nor Smith slanted stories or in any way failed to perform their job. While the case was still in arbitration, Payne told *Editor & Publisher*, "Our position is that the employment of these two men would be detrimental to the best interest of the *Daily News*. It has been held in court that it is libelous to call a man a Communist. We feel that it is equally damaging for a newspaper to employ men who have been identified as party members."

Robert L. Smith, *Daily News* president, asserted that the paper was a quasi-public institution that was "peculiarly sensitive to public reaction and to public opinion." In fact, the newspaper argued that it was more sensitive to public opinion than other metropolitan dailies because of its reputation as a liberal newspaper, "Having espoused numerous controversial liberal causes, even at the risk of less (sic) subscriptions and a decline in its circulation."

It was peculiar logic for the *Daily News*. By arguing that it advocated liberal causes, it still refused to defend the rights of two employees innocent by the newspaper's own admission of writing slanted copy, and of exercising their rights of freedom of speech and freedom of association. The decision from the panel came in August. Predictably, Garrison and Pollock threw their votes for dismissal while Fowler and Rarick sided with the fired newsmen. Dodd cast the deciding vote in favor of management. Dodd ruled that the publisher, "in self-defense against anticipated serious financial repercussions brought on by unfavorable public opinion, has the right under the terms of the working agreement to ask and expect those accused to clear themselves of the serious charges made under oath against them, if they were to continue their employment with the publisher." Dodd determined there was sufficient cause to uphold the firing of Partlow and not rehire Smith.

Time magazine was gleeful over the ruling, going so far as to needle LANG for adhering to its contract and the American Newspaper Guild's constitution that bans discrimination. "In spite of the obvious fairness of Dodd's decision, the Los Angeles Guild stuck to its anachronistic view that because the national Guild's constitution (written in 1933) specifically forbids any discrimination for political beliefs in admitting members, the Guild must therefore defend members fired for political reasons." *Time* also couldn't help but take a swipe at Smith for making the terminations a business issue. "President Smith might have done better to stand on a clear-cut principle, rather than the argument that Communist damage the paper 'business wise,' " the magazine reported.

Manchester Boddy had retired from newspaper publishing in 1952, leaving the paper to Smith, whose only interest in the paper was its moneymaking, potential. The paper's editorial staff considered Smith to be Boddy's hatchet man, with little or no journalistic principles. Whether the case of Partlow and Smith would have been handled differently under Boddy will never be known. But under Smith it was certain that their fate would be decided on the financial welfare of the newspaper and not a constitutional issue.

Partlow rebounded from the incident, finding work in public relations. He would later express disappointment for Darr Smith whom he considered "completely innocent" of the Communist accusations. Smith, who worked for the *Daily News* for sixteen years, was hit hard with the blacklist. He moved from job to job after his firing, and often found his movements reported in *Variety*. He never worked on a metropolitan daily again. Liberals like Lucian Haas and even Partlow were understanding toward Judson for his testimony before HUAC. Partlow said years after the incident that he held no grudges against Judson while Haas described him as a "professional." Other liberal newsmen, however, did hold grudges. Jake Jacoby was an early signer of the petition to start the Greater Los Angeles Press Club, but he was denied membership largely because of his anti-Communist activities. It also cost him his friendship with *Daily News* columnist Matt Weinstock, who wrote strident columns condemning the McCarthy hearings and HUAC investigations and was a staunch supporter of Partlow and Smith. He never spoke to Jacoby again.

Partlow, too, continued to be viewed as a threat by anti- Communists. While working for a public relations firm a few years after his firing from the *Daily News*, Partlow briefly visited Jack Jones in the city room of the *Times*. Jones had been a colleague of Partlow's at the *Daily News*, and then joined the *Times* when the *News* folded in 1954. Partlow chatted with Jones at Jones' desk then left. The moment Partlow was gone, Kerby Ramsdell, a *Times* editor, rushed to Jones' desk. "What in the hell was that damn Communist doing in the *Times'* city room," Ramsdell demanded.

Jones looked at Ramsdell blankly and said, "He's my friend."

But the message was clear: There was no room for leftists at the *Times*.

Chapter Seven

Newspaper Terrorism

I.

The United Press bulletin clanged four bells in the *Daily News* city room late Monday night on 24 February 1942. A Japanese submarine had shelled an oil field at Goleta nine miles north of Santa Barbara. City editor Charlie Judson ripped the bulletin from the UP Teletype and handed it to Jack Cravens, a young reporter on the city side staff.

Cravens, who worked as a singing waiter at the Cocoanut Grove at the Ambassador Hotel before studying journalism at Los Angeles City College, would later help found the Greater Los Angeles Press Club. Later in his career he distinguished himself as one of the city's leading reporters covering the Los Angeles County District Attorney's office. But late on that brisk, clear night, barely twenty-five years old, he was asked to grab photographer Gib Brush and cover the first enemy attack on U.S. soil since German U-boats lobbed shells on Cape Cod, Massachusetts, during the World War I.

Early Wednesday morning, while Cravens and Brush were covering the Goleta story, anti-aircraft fire rocked Los Angeles, waking thousands of residents as a blackout was ordered and searchlights stabbed the sky looking for enemy planes. Shrapnel from falling anti-aircraft shells fell in the southwest portion of the city.

The city's air raid and the Goleta incident coincided with the FBI's pending roundup of Japanese aliens and Japanese Americans after the bombing of Pearl Harbor on 7 December 1941. Judson had assigned photographer Coy Watson, a veteran of Acme, the *Post-Record,* and the *Herald & Express,* and now working for the *Daily News,* to accompany federal authorities. Watson covered with photographers and reporters from competing papers the arrests and detention of hundreds of Japanese Americans from Terminal Island to the canneries to the farms overlooking the Los Angeles Harbor. On a trip to Japanese American farms near the harbor, FBI and immigration agents uncovered what they alleged were signal-making devices for the enemy.

To Watson his assignment to cover the internment of the Japanese Americans was simply another job. He was detached from the trauma of their forced removal from their homes and had hoped he wouldn't come across anybody he knew. Any sympathy Watson had for the Japanese quickly diminished when he learned that his friends in the military had suffered casualties during the fighting in the Pacific.

Los Angeles residents in 1942 were jittery. Six blackouts were called between December 1941 and April 1943. Tolerance for the Japanese was ebbing with each passing air raid and with each bulletin reporting the enormous setbacks American forces were dealt in the Pacific. Los Angeles newsmen and women, particularly in 1942, reflected the varied mood of the city. Some were anti-Japanese. Others were indifferent while a handful expressed sympathy for Japanese Americans' loss of their civil liberties. The events immediately following Pearl Harbor also established the press' preoccupation with the racial issues first involving the Japanese and later with Mexican Americans when the so-called Zoot Suit riots erupted in June 1943. It was a period of adjustment in attitude toward the Japanese American and Mexican American communities. Some newspapers and their reporters matured while others, notably the *Examiner* and the *Herald & Express*, lapsed into overt racism that would remain strong through the decade, either through shrill editorials and sensational news accounts or neglect of the minority community's wants and needs.

Historians have a tendency of painting the Los Angeles press with a broad brush in the coverage of the internment of Japanese Americans and the Zoot Suit riots. The *Examiner*, the *Herald & Express*, the *Daily News,* and the *Times* were guilty of excess in dealing with these two minority groups. None of the newspapers can be commended for balanced coverage. Balanced presentation of the Japanese American internment issue throughout 1942-43 often was almost nonexistent. And at least in the news columns of all four papers, very little space was devoted to the Mexican American community during the wave of violence between sailors and soldiers and young Latinos. Newsmen were virtually slavish in their attention to the authority figures of the U.S. military and the Los Angeles Police Department. Yet there were distinct differences in how the four newspapers treated the Japanese and Mexican communities. Often after the initial rush to judge these two minorities with heavy-handed coverage, the *Daily News* and the *Times* would pull back and offer relatively racism-free coverage, although the editorial pages were still guilty of excesses.

The *Daily News* prided itself on its liberal approach to reporting and editing. But its liberalism rarely extended to such minorities as the city's Japanese, Latino, and African American residents, at least in an even-handed and positive manner. Instead, the liberalism of the *Daily News,* was more general: the advocacy of the U.S. Constitution and the Bill of Rights, as shown when liberal reporters tried to prevent the unions from expelling Communist members. This liberalism-with-blinders attitude left untouched the usual ethnic stereotypes—the zoot suiters as hoodlums, the Japanese Americans as having questionable loyalties, and the African Americans as prone to immoral acts.

By contrast, the *Herald & Express* reflected the political leanings of its managing editor, John B.T. Campbell. Although many liberal staffers at the *Daily News* considered Campbell a reactionary, he was more concerned about telling a good story. This story-telling attitude resulted in simplistic, sensational coverage of issues. In fact, the *Herald & Express* relished using military and warlike metaphors while covering the Japanese American internment and the clashes between Latinos and American servicemen. The *Herald & Express* perhaps can be dismissed as almost comic in much of its coverage of volatile issues in wartime Los Angeles (although it remained the largest circulating newspaper in the city in 1942 with 265,087 readers).

The same can't be said for the *Examiner*, which led the morning field with 235,530 readers. The paper carried considerable heft with its readers. More importantly, however, the paper wielded influence with federal authorities that were unwilling to challenge the powerful William Randolph Hearst. In what had emerged over the years as a pattern for the *Examiner*, the newspaper worked itself into a slow burn about perceived threats to loyal Americans. In 1942 and 1943 that would be principally the Japanese American. It was also during this period that the Hearst philosophy that all citizens must be "100 percent American" was drummed daily into *Examiner* readers. It blurred the line between fascism and patriotism. The call for 100 percent Americanism was pushed to the limit during the war, and soon patriotism was overshadowed by a strong fascist dogma among Hearst papers. It was especially evident when perceived threats to democracy surfaced and Hearst editors demanded state or federal intervention to protect the city.

In its 8 December 1941 editions, the day after the surprise bombing of Pearl Harbor, the *Examiner* already drew the distinction between the Japanese and "Occidentals." In the hours after the news of the bombing spread through the city, residents, mostly Anglos, converged on Little Tokyo, more out of curiosity than malice. The *Examiner* noted that several drunken "Occidentals" were arrested for verbally abusing Japanese Americans but "the conduct of the Japanese was exemplary." While it dutifully reported the arrests of dozens of Japanese throughout Southern California, it did report on the same day an interview with Togo Tanaka, editor of the Los Angeles *Japanese Daily News*. Tanaka told the *Examiner* that Japanese residents who felt a greater loyalty to Japan had already left for that country. He said the Japanese who remained in Los Angeles can't "go for" the ideas advocated by the Empire of Japan. "If we are treated as Americans—which is the way we want to be treated—we will respond as Americans. We can be extremely useful in any war between this country and

Japan, and we want to be useful. We welcome this opportunity to demonstrate that no other group is more loyal," Tanaka said.

Any pretense of balanced coverage vanished on 19 December, when the *Examiner* published a charge by Senator Guy M. Gillette that a local Japanese group was part of a "fifth column plot."

The newspaper reported that Rikita Honda, a forty-eight-year-old Japanese physician, had committed suicide in his Terminal Island cell after being taken into custody in a sweep. Honda was president of the Imperial Comradeship Society that Gillette identified—with marginal evidence—as a group planning sabotage and subversive activity. The article was entirely based on information supplied by Gillette, who claimed the FBI was probing the organization. There was no comment from the FBI. Gillette also alleged that Honda's organization was linked to the Black Dragon Society and the Japanese Military Service Men's League. In a hint of what could be expected of the *Examiner's* future coverage, the paper reported in racially tinged detail the suicide of Honda, who "had slashed arteries in his left wrist and left arm in a modified version of hara-kiri."

The paper continued its one-two punch the next day when it reported that "leaders of Nippon" had established secret Japanese language schools in the state. Without attribution, the article stated the language schools were part of a master plan of espionage and attacks against American unity. In what would have appeared ordinary during peacetime, the *Examiner* gave the curriculum of the schools a sinister tone. Citing a survey, but providing no details of its origins, the paper reported that 248 Japanese language schools were operating in California, with 454 teachers and 19,310 pupils attending classes after public school hours. It reported that forty such schools were operating secretly. Taking the contents of a textbook out of context, the story noted that the schools teach "loyalty to the Emperor is next to godliness" and to "become a good Japanese" one must set Japan and its rulers above all else in the world. The paper also failed to mention that before the war the schools were never considered secret.

In April 1942, the *Examiner's* editorial policy was clear. All Japanese should be removed from California. In a six-part series by Joseph Timmons on the "Japanese problem," the *Examiner* painted a portrait of a culture determined to gobble up precious agricultural land in the state. Amplifying most Hearst editorials on Japanese Americans, Timmons asserted that the presence of the Japanese in California was a "race problem." In his first article on 14 April, Timmons concluded that if it hadn't been for vigilante justice during the first two decades of the century, "possibly a million or more Japanese would now be spread over the Pacific Coast states in a deadly blanket" instead of the 93,000 Japanese residents then living on the coast. Timmons argued that the Japanese were a two-fold threat to California because Japanese immigrants were unable to assimilate into American culture through intermarriage, and that by being virtual outsiders they could as a group undercut wages in labor.

The next day Timmons hammered again at the race issue. He suggested that Japanese Americans plans to destroy American institutions were a decades-old plot. He also suggested they were not entitled to their civil rights. "(Japanese) picture brides came on every ship, frightened, simpering, every one with the capacity for bearing six or eight or 10 little 'dual citizens'—every one of the children to have claimed for it all the civil rights that Attorney General Francis Biddle recently was so determined should be accorded them, while every one of them was registered in those days with the nearest Japanese consul as a subject of the Son of Heaven, the Japanese Emperor."

The Hearst press elaborated on its racial stance throughout 1943. On 25 January, the San Francisco *Examiner* offered a skewed, but consistent Hearstian logic: "Bad as the situation is in Europe," the *Examiner* editorial opined, "the war there is between European Occidental nations, between white races. Antagonisms, hatreds and jealousies, no matter how violent, cannot obscure the fact that the warring nations of Europe stem from a common racial, cultural, linguistic and social roots. It is a family affair...." On 23 March, the Los Angeles *Examiner* gave its opinion on the Pacific Theater. "The war in the Pacific is the World War, the War of Oriental Races against Occidental Races for the Domination of the World."

In his 1944 book, *Prejudice—Japanese-Americans: Symbol of Racial Intolerance*, Carey McWilliams examined the relationship between the press, particularly the Hearst papers, and the anti-Japanese forces determined to block the return of internees to California during and after the war. Those forces were principally led by members of the Dies Committee, which launched an investigation into the War Relocation Authority management of internment camps. Also staging an anti-Japanese campaign was Albert B. Chandler, Democratic Kentucky senator, who asserted that the Japanese army was poised to invade the West Coast through Siberia and Alaska.

The *Examiner's* Washington correspondent Ray Richards picked up the ball from Timmons in 1943 with a series of anti-Japanese reports based on documents and interviews given to him by Chandler. Richards also wrote thinly disguised editorials in the *Examiner's* news columns—appearing as exposes on the front page—that were extremely critical of the WRA. According to McWilliams, Richards worked with Warren Francis of the Los Angeles *Times* to manipulate the anti-Japanese movement. Richards would report in lengthy feature stories the movements of Chandler on his inspection tours of internment camps in Arizona and Arkansas. The stories would whip up state residents living in the vicinity of the camps with the state legislatures in both states ultimately introducing bills to curtail the authority of the WRA.

The coverage by the *Examiner* was especially inaccurate. *Examiner* city editor Jim Richardson sent reporter James E. Lewis to Parker, Arizona, and to the Poston Internment Camp to survey the mood of Parker residents. Lewis also was to confirm information that internees staged a "riot" in November and had hoarded food and stolen dynamite that threatened the safety of Parker Dam.

Lewis couldn't confirm allegations of hoarding food. He obtained a food ration report dated 13 January 1943 that proved to the contrary that 18,004 internees at Poston were receiving the minimum in rations. Internees, over the age of twelve, received 2 1/2 pounds of beef and a half-pound of sugar each week. One pound of coffee was distributed to adult internees every five weeks. In late May, the Washington newspapers reported that internees in California camps were given "food and wine" and that they were so well fed that they were sending "butter, coffee and other rationed foods to friends outside the centers." The allegations were patently untrue but the Los Angeles *Examiner* didn't refute them, even though they had the Poston evidence of severe rationing.

A 1 May 1943 memo from Lewis to Richardson provides some explanation for the *Examiner's* rectitude to present a true picture of camp life at Poston. First, it had been suggested to Lewis by the Office of War Information not to publish specific incidents involving Japanese internees either inside the camp or at Parker. Second, Lewis also saw the Japanese American's interaction with Parker residents as a racial issue. And third, an interview between Lewis and camp information officer Norris E. James about the alleged riot at Poston in November was off the record. If Lewis attempted to confirm James' information that Japanese Americans virtually took over the camp in a protest, it was not mentioned in his memo to Richardson. His virulent anti-Japanese remarks, however, indicate that he was less than willing to explore the controversies inside the camp unless it came from military or police sources or white residents in Parker.

Lewis noted that "scores of Japs previously had been allowed to run loose in Parker, crowding white women off the sidewalk, eating up the town's meager supply of meat in cafes, buying things in the stores to deprive the whites.... "

The reporter also addressed the stolen dynamite story in a superficial manner, writing that the Japanese "could float some dynamite bombs down the Colorado River on a long raft, and blow a hole in the (Parker) dam." Lewis said that 350 pounds of dynamite had been stolen but failed to mention the theft had occurred three years earlier. Lewis' memo did not reflect any interviews with Japanese Americans or WRA authorities that supervised Norris James.

Lewis' memo only strengthened the *Examiner's* resolve to continue its litany of anti-Japanese coverage to arouse the public's ire in time for the June subcommittee hearings.

The stories, coupled with the Dies Committee's announcement in December 1942 to probe the WRA, would set the stage for the Los Angeles press corps' local effort to keep Japanese Americans out of the state. Ostensibly, the Dies Committee, headed by Congressman Martin Dies of Texas, was to conduct an impartial investigation of all relocation areas in California. Hearings were conducted in the state throughout 1943, with a subcommittee arriving in Los Angeles in June. Congressmen John M. Costello of Hollywood with the aid of Congressmen Herman P. Eberharter of Pennsylvania and Karl E. Mundt of South Dakota headed the subcommittee. The publicity-hungry group sent its point man, New Jersey Congressman J. Parnell Thomas, to Los Angeles in May to soften the press by spoon-feeding them stories. Ensconced in the Biltmore Hotel, Thomas began issuing press releases to drum up anti-Japanese support. Local newsmen took the bait with the *Herald & Express* particularly apt to give Thomas considerable space. On 13 May, the *Herald & Express* shouted, "Dies Probe Charges Whole Relocation Plan is Farce" and "Rep. J.P. Thomas Reveals Jap Army in L.A." On 19 May another headline, "Stop Freeing Japs," played up allegations that the WRA were freeing hundreds of internees back into the state. The paper ignored the common knowledge that there were three classifications of Japanese permitted to return to specific areas in California: Soldiers on leave; Japanese in public institutions; and Japanese women married to Caucasians.

When Costello's subcommittee opened its hearings on 8 June in the Federal Building, it was ready to heap more bad press on the WRA. Unfortunately it found itself in the position of having to compete for headlines with the Zoot Suit riots. With some exceptions, the *Daily News* and the *Times* relegated Costello's hearings to the inside pages while they gave front page lead positions to the street brawls. The *Examiner* and the *Herald & Express* gave the committee front-page status virtually every day it was in town, often juggling its lead position on the front page between the racial fighting and committee testimony. Even when testimony didn't justify front-page coverage, the Hearst papers were unwilling to give up the story's prominent play.

The subcommittee focused its attention on Poston, the site of the alleged internment camp riot. It also was to hear testimony by current and former WRA employees who alleged hundreds of Japanese Americans had voiced open disloyalty to the United States and openly conducted military training exercises. Costello set the tone of the hearings by stating at the onset that the hearings were designed to "substantiate evidence uncovered by Dies investigators of unsatisfactory conditions at the various relocation camps."

The *Herald & Express* opened its coverage by leading with a story of opening day of the hearings of whether the WRA was "coddling" the Japanese. It reported that Ralph M. Gelvin, associate project director at Poston, was grilled by committee members whether the WRA was lax in its control of "Japanese gangsters" dominating the camp operations and that trained spies and saboteurs may be among some internees released from the camps. The story virtually assured the reader that the allegations were true by stating them as fact and giving Gelvin little space to respond.

The *Times'* version of the same hearing was decidedly different from the *Herald & Express*. It led with testimony from Gelvin that about 630 American-born Japanese were openly disloyal to the U.S. Gelvin testified that 450 Nisei responded "no" to the question, "Will you swear allegiance to the United States and forswear allegiance to the Emperor of Japan or to any other foreign power?" The remaining 180 Nisei responded, "I'm neutral."

The *Herald & Express* used inflammatory words as "gangsters" and "coddling." By contrast, the *Daily News* tried to clarify the issue. The *Daily News* instead reported that the Japanese language was being taught to 200 American-born Japanese in preparation for a military intelligence course in Minnesota. Gelvin, according to the *Daily News* account, denied that there was any subversive activity in the courses. The *Daily News*, in fact, gave most of its space in its first-day coverage to Gelvin's explanations about activities at Poston, including his denial that internees raised the Japanese flag to protest the jailing of one of its members.

But the subcommittee's methods made it unlikely for the press to present balanced coverage. Witnesses making strong anti-Japanese allegations were called first, whereas WRA officials were placed last on the witness list to give testimony—often too late to include in the afternoon editions.

Less than a week into the hearings, the *Examiner* began a series of articles lambasting the WRA. Most of the stories were based on spoon-fed reports from the Dies Committee to the Washington-based *Examiner* reporter Ray Richards. The stories reported that the WRA were releasing internees into sensitive areas and that thirty-five internees were released to high-ranking government officials to be employed as servants. Many of the reports by Richards were based on a single source. On 12 June Dies Committee investigators raided the Japanese American Citizens League in Washington, seizing documents relating to the League's collaboration with the WRA. The *Examiner* reported allegations "of a suspected movement to install Japanese servants in the homes of high Government officials." Subsequent information gleaned from the files was parceled out on an almost daily basis to Richards. On 15 June, Richards reported more data from the files, which alleged that a "scheme by high Government officials" to "dump" 107,000 internees back into the West Coast combat zone. The move, according to Richards' report, was initiated at the advice of Carey McWilliams, a frequent critic of the Hearst chain and supporter of Japanese American rights. Richards identified McWilliams as serving as an officer in thirteen Communist organizations.

Five days later, another Richards report, again using the seized documents as a source, claimed that 70,000 Japanese American votes would be offered as a block to the governors of New Mexico, Colorado, and Idaho in exchange for the right of mass settlement in those states. The story was based on a single letter from a Los Angeles promoter to the Japanese American Citizens League, but never acted on. The letter was typical of much of the documents seized by the Dies Committee, which on its face appeared to be routine correspondence, if not benign. But under the large headline, "Dies Bares Offer of Jap Votes for Mass Settlement" with the deck declaring, "Letter Reveals Amazing Plan to Trade Ballots," the reader is left with the impression that the Japanese offered the block of votes that hints at an attack on democracy. This coverage certainly helped marginalize the Japanese American after the war as Hearst readers were given a diet of racist reporting. The influence of Hearst reporting not so much made the reader hate Japanese Americans, but to view them suspiciously. As the war continued, the average reader—a majority of them women during the war—were more concerned about their loved ones overseas, rationing, and working to support their families. Perceived threats of Japanese Americans sabotaging military installations were a low priority. If anything, the Hearst press continually threw obstacles in the way to better relations between the white and Asian communities.

Such editors and reporters as Joseph Timmons and Ray Richards parroted the Hearst editorial policy, as did San Francisco *Examiner* columnist Elsie Robinson, who wrote that she would "cut the throats" of Japanese Americans who returned to the West Coast after the war.

But what did the columnist and rank-and-file reporter employed by competing newspapers believe? Hedda Hopper, the Los Angeles *Times'* movie gossip columnist, had no sympathy for the Japanese American. She implied that "explosions, train wrecks and serious accidents" have increased since some Japanese Americans had been released from internment camps. Yet for every Hopper, Timmons, and Richards, there were other newsmen and women who felt little anti-Japanese sentiment, an opinion that reflected the general attitude of most Angelenos as the war progressed. This was especially true after residents began to realize after 1942 that the Japanese in reality posed little threat to the safety of the city. As far back as the early and mid-1930s, Los Angeles *Times* columnist Harry Carr had said there was little anti-Japanese feelings in the city. And *Times* reporter Chester Hanson and *Times* columnists Lee Shippey and Bill Henry were critical of anti-Japanese movements. Also sympathizing with the plight of the Japanese American were Chester Rowell, San Francisco *Chronicle* columnist, and the *Daily News'* Matt Weinstock. The Hollywood *Citizen-News*, the Santa Barbara *News-Press,* and the Catholic publication *Tidings* also editorialized against the continuing attacks made by some papers and state and federal lawmakers against the Japanese.

Other rank-and-file staffers such as Jack Cravens and Coy Watson saw their role as newsmen not cheerleaders for either side but simply to report the story. Les Wagner, a *Daily News* reporter, attacked the coverage of the Hearst press and the anti-Japanese hysteria, not in his own newspaper but in his own column published in his father's magazine, *Rob Wagner's Script*.

Born in 1904 in Detroit, Wagner had moved with his parents, Rob and Jessie Brodhead Wagner, to Santa Barbara while he was still a toddler. A Socialist, Rob Wagner was active in many liberal causes in the state while earning a living as a portrait artist and writer. After his mother died of tuberculosis in 1906, Les Wagner was left in the care of his paternal grandmother and later attended boarding school in Santa Barbara. Meanwhile, his father abandoned his painting to pursue a career in magazine journalism and later directing and writing motion pictures. When he became a teenager, Les Wagner and a brother, Thornton, joined his father in Los Angeles, where Les attended Franklin High School. After graduating in 1922, he joined the Santa Barbara *Morning Press* as a reporter, covering several major breaking news stories, including the grounding of seven destroyers in 1923; the destruction of much of the city by an earthquake in 1925; and the collapse of the San Francisquito Dam in 1928.

When Rob Wagner founded *Rob Wagner's Script*, a literary magazine for the film industry, in 1929, Les joined him briefly to help launch it. The same year, the *Daily News* hired Les. He remained at the *Daily News* until 1933 when he joined the United Press, housed in the *Daily News* building. He transferred to the San Francisco bureau in 1938. When his father died in 1942, Les Wagner returned to Southern California to help his stepmother, Florence, manage *Script* and to rejoin the *Daily News*. Wagner was the kind of independent, liberal thinker that caught the attention of *Daily News* management. But unlike his colleagues, *Script* provided him with a forum to express his views on local issues.

Wagner complained in his column that the Dies Committee was strongly under the influence of the Hearst papers and had already made a determination on the conduct of interned Japanese Americans long before testimony was given. As the hearings unfolded, Wagner was alarmed at how witnesses were handled. "Anyone who could speak a damning word about the Japs was welcomed with open arms; those who sought to give the Japs an even break were refused a hearing. Such is the working of democracy in A.D. 1943," Wagner wrote. He recounted the *Examiner's* allegations against interned Japanese, who were said to be conducting military tactical training at Poston, where Japanese gangs supposedly had "instituted a reign of terror" against other Japanese. But Wagner noted, "When representatives of the War Relocation Authority protested admission of this unsubstantiated evidence, they were told their testimony was not wanted. The committee had heard exactly what it wanted to hear; if there was another side of the story, it wasn't interested."

Wagner took issue over a stinging *Examiner* front-page editorial on 20 June that stated, "Americans are naturally soft-headed and stupid," that they were allowing the enemy to be coddled and to run loose to operate a fifth column.

Wagner reminded his readers that the U.S. government attempted to treat the Japanese well "because most of them *are* American citizens" and that the government has "temporarily robbed them of a livelihood."

"After the war we shall have to do one of two things with the Japanese in this country," Wagner opined. "We can either amend the Constitution to permit statutory expression of racial intolerance and ship every person of Japanese blood to Japan, or we can give them the protection of the Bill of Rights."

Though not alone in his support of Japanese Americans, Wagner was one of the few Los Angeles newsmen who had the opportunity to attack the Hearst mindset in a publication outside of his own newspaper. Still, it was a voice lost in a sea of biased front-page reporting by larger circulating newspapers.

II.

Did the Hearst papers conspire to stage a campaign to deprive Japanese Americans of their constitutional rights and prevent them from returning to California after the war? Clearly James Lewis' memo reveals the *Examiner's* propensity at best to put the Japanese American, "question" on an emotional and racial level. At worst it showed a pattern of hate-mongering that could lead to the deprivation of the internees' constitutional rights. Ray Richards' promiscuous use of data gathered by the Dies Committee and Senator Albert Chandler also illustrate an organized effort to keep the Japanese out of the state.

The pattern of anti-minority coverage by the Hearst press continued throughout 1942 and 1943. As the anti-Japanese coverage began to get old, the press began to focus on the Mexican American communities, particularly young men and women who dressed in over-sized stylish zoot suits and frequented downtown night clubs and theaters. Although the press could rationalize that the Japanese posed a threat to the national security, the attacks on Mexican American youths was strictly a racial issue. The catalysts for the attacks were the August 1942 death of Jose Diaz, whose body was found near Sleepy Lagoon, and the so-called Zoot Suit riots ten months later.

Once again, the Hearst papers fanned the fears of an alien conspiracy. If any conspiracy existed, however, it was directed against Latinos. Guy Endore, a member of the Sleepy Lagoon Defense Committee and the author of *The Sleepy Lagoon Mystery*, published in 1944, argued that Hearst's dailies in Los Angeles had conspired to create a "crime wave" perpetrated by young Mexican Americans. Although Endore didn't mention a motive for such a conspiracy, by the 1940s, it was perhaps the worst-kept secret among the press corps in Los Angeles that the Hearst papers would pick on some underdog or a motion-picture celebrity to increase sales.

Until 1942, the Los Angeles *Examiner* and the *Herald & Express* had paid little attention to the Mexican American community. Anti-Latino sentiment had ebbed and risen with the tides of national and world events. During the boom of the 1920s, Mexicans had been tolerated because they filled vital low-end jobs. But when the Depression hit Los Angeles in 1931, the Mexican was the target of local law-enforcement authorities. Claiming that the welfare department could no longer afford to keep Latinos—supposedly seventy-five percent of the caseload—on relief, the county authorities evicted thousands of Latinos from their homes between August 1931 and March 1932.

Although the city's papers did not whip up anti-Mexican sentiment, they misreported the situation. The press, for example, did little to find out the true number of Latinos on relief. A survey conducted by then-Supervisor Frank Shaw, however, revealed that only twelve percent of the recipients were Latinos. The press also failed to report that hundreds of those evicted were American citizens. Further, the *Times*, the *Examiner*, and the *Herald & Express* reported that Latinos were being "deported"—a term implying the use of due process. To add further insult, the press reported that Mexicans were eager to return to Mexico.

In a 30 October 1931 story by the *Examiner*, a reporter wrote, " 'In Mexico everything will be all right.

"Smiling and appearing undismayed at their inability to make a living here, more than 1200 Mexican residents of Los Angeles County yesterday voiced this hope as they boarded three special Southern Pacific trains to return to their own country." The fact was that many families were torn apart by their removal and in some cases they were separated for many months or years before they could be reunited. Unlike the sensational coverage during the Zoot Suit riots, the local press gave marginal attention to the events of 1931-32. Coverage of the removal process over a six month period amounted to barely a few inches on the inside pages. The press was guilty of neglect and disinterest.

In 1942, with a war on, the press began looking for enemies on the home front. Suddenly, after years of indifference by the media, the Mexican now posed a threat. The conspiracy was real: The conspiracy was the Hearst press looking for scapegoats.

Guy Endore claimed he had found such evidence when he interviewed a Hearst reporter for his book. The unidentified reporter told Endore the "Mexican crime business" had originated with a Teletype message from William Randolph Hearst's San Simeon mansion. The message stated, "Chief suggests L.A. editors make survey of crime reports—all types—with particular emphasis on numbers of police bookings of Mexican and Negro citizens—and or aliens. Chief suggests L.A. editors transmit findings to all other Hearst editors."

The reporter acknowledged that there was nothing significant about the number of crimes committed by Mexican and African American residents, but reports of such crimes instantly grew "by leaps and bounds" after the message was dispatched. A few days later the Hearst papers were blaring that a "crime wave" was rampant throughout the city. The crime wave was followed a series of reports quoting law-enforcement authorities and judicial experts on the causes of the outbreak.

The city and county officials quoted in the Hearst papers were part of a "stooge" list kept by Jim Richardson, the city editor of the *Examiner*, and Cappy Marek, the city editor of the *Herald & Express* and a longtime Hearst loyalist. The list contained the names and phone numbers of men and women who enjoyed having their names published. They were quite willing, on a moment's notice, to provide a quote on any subject. If a source on the list turned out to be unavailable, a reporter would sometimes make up a quote. No one on the list ever complained.

It came as no surprise that the law-enforcement authorities overreacted when the body of Jose Diaz was found on a south-central city road near the Delgadillo Ranch. There was considerable evidence that he may have died from an automobile accident. There were no witnesses, and no weapon was recovered. But his death occurred near the Delgadillo Ranch where Mexican American teenagers had been in a fight the previous night. It also occurred near Sleepy Lagoon, a pond not much better than a muddy pit where Mexican American kids swam because city- and county-run swimming pools were segregated.

As many as 600 Latino youths, were rounded up. Brutal interrogations by police followed over several days before the Los Angeles County Grand Jury settled on indicting twenty-four young men on first-degree murder charges. The trial was little more than a state-sanctioned lynching. The defendants were not allowed to shower or have haircuts, wear clean clothes or consult with their lawyers except during adjournment. To the public primed on press coverage, the trial was a perfect tool to get tough on the Mexican American hoodlum element portrayed by the Hearst papers. However, to the veteran court reporter experienced in observing measured justice it must have smacked of a system gone awry. Superior Court Judge Charles W. Fricke ridiculed and battered the defense attorneys. Some witnesses such as Ed Duran Ayres, the chief of the sheriff's department's Bureau of Foreign Relations, provided detailed testimony that extreme violence committed by Mexicans was inherited from their ancestors. The press reported these events throughout the trial as fact and essentially confirmed the phony Hearst reports of a "Mexican crime wave."

Unlike the plight of the Japanese American, the Sleepy Lagoon defendants had a network of supporters, including some of the most visible Anglo residents of Los Angeles. This group, called the Sleepy Lagoon Defense Committee, consisted of many union locals, including the liberal or leftist locals of the International Longshoremen's and Warehousemen's Union, the American

Newspaper Guild, the Screen Actors Guild, and the Congress of Industrial Organizations. Prominent Anglos such as Carey McWilliams, Alice Greenfield, Orson Welles, Mrs. Will Rogers, and Endore, joined Latinos Anthony Quinn, Rita Hayworth, and Bert Corona on the committee.

As the trial progressed, the committee, especially Endore, became convinced that the Hearst-inspired "persecution" of Mexican Americans was not only a conspiracy to spread hate, but also was working with the Nazis. Endore claimed that the Hearst papers—exercising "newspaper terrorism"—exaggerated Americanism, found daily in its editorials and news columns, and was orchestrated by the Axis to hurt American morale. Adolf Hitler once boasted, "It will be a simple matter for me to produce unrest and revolt in the United States, so that these gentry will have their hands full with their own troubles." According to Endore, Hitler's goals were being realized as the Hearst papers encouraged a lynch-mob mentality against Mexican Americans within the judicial system.

In turn, city and county officials believed the defense committee was a Communist front. It was difficult for the committee to dodge such accusations. The *Examiner* was already alleging that McWilliams belonged to what it said were Communist organizations while he conducted work on behalf of interned Japanese Americans. And though the Hearst papers didn't acknowledge it on the news pages, *Herald & Express* staffer Phil Connelly, who also acted as state chief for the CIO, was a well-known Communist. Mayor Fletcher Bowron told a joint committee, headed by state Senator Jack B. Tenney, who investigating un-American activities, that Connelly demanded that deputy district attorney Clyde C. Shoemaker be removed as prosecutor in the Sleepy Lagoon trial. Connelly objected to the racist way in which Shoemaker was conducting the trial

In January 1944, seventeen defendants were found guilty of first- and second-degree murder and of lesser charges. Coverage of the case created another unfounded negative image of the zoot suiter. Where there had been no previous press investigation, and certainly no police probe, into zoot-suit related criminal activity, it suddenly was a regional menace in late 1942 and through 1943.

The *Eastside Journal*, a weekly that served the predominately Mexican American community in East Los Angeles, put some of the blame on the press. "The real crime in this trial was the way these boys were handled at the bar of justice," wrote *Journal* staffer Al S. Waxman. "Long before their case came to court the boys were tried and convicted in the metropolitan press."

The appellate court overturned the convictions two years later, but the damage to the community had been done. The Mexican American was viewed as un-American.

Wartime Los Angeles was unique among major metropolitan areas. It attracted thousands of defense workers, including many African Americans from the South. The region also was home to thousands of servicemen, the largest concentration of military personnel of any American city. As many as 50,000 uniformed men and women would spend their weekends on liberty in the beach cities, San Diego, and Los Angeles, and especially Hollywood where the film community sponsored the wildly popular Hollywood Canteen.

Los Angeles was exotic in another way. The largest military posts were bordered by barrios, where, for the first time, many servicemen encountered Mexican and Mexican American civilians. There was no effort by military brass to acclimate servicemen to their new environs. The prejudices and poor education of many enlisted men, the continuing hostile coverage of the Sleepy Lagoon case, and frequent press reports of Mexican juvenile delinquency were ingredients for an explosion.

Frequent violent outbreaks between uniformed personnel and civilians had brought little attention in the press beyond the standard brief notices on the inside pages. In his book, *The Zoot-Suit Riots: The Psychology of Symbolic Annihilation* (1984), Mauricio Mazon noted that there were eighteen major clashes involving servicemen which had taken place between 1 May and 6 June 1943. Seven of these confrontations resulted in death. On 20 May, for example, a soldier killed a civilian and a day later a civilian shot and killed a soldier. On 25 May, two deaths occurred in similar incidents.

Not surprisingly, the *Examiner* was the first paper to target the zoot-suiter as a threat to American servicemen. It reported on Saturday 5 June on Page 3: "Sailors Hunt Zoot-Suiters, 2 in Hospital." It reported that twenty carloads of sailors sought revenge against the Mexican Americans for attacking the wives of two seamen and knifing two others during the previous nights. The sailors had spent much of the night unsuccessfully finding victims, but finally cornered two *pachucos*—or zoot-suiters—at First and Rowan streets and manhandled them. The *Examiner* identified zoot-suiters as gangs of thirty to forty without attribution or providing specific details of the gangs. Employing language by identifying the marauding sailors as a "convoy" and on a "punitive expedition" gave the report a warlike theme. The paper also reported that zoot-suiters had been involved in "riots" at Venice Pier and in San Fernando, Duarte, Monrovia, and Azusa, although the incidents didn't warrant much previous press attention and certainly were not identified as "riots."

By contrast, the coverage in the *Herald & Express* was unrestrained over a one-week period. Because it depended heavily on street sales, sensationalism was a priority. The newspaper treated the clashes as if they were a wholesale invasion by enemy forces. "Sailor 'Task Force' Hits L.A. Zooters" cried the lead story. It read: "Two hundred Navy men sailed up the Los Angeles River early today, and in a task force of taxicabs launched a reprisal attack on 'zoot suit' gangsters in the East Los Angeles area. The fleet men, who went methodically about applying fists and rope's ends to the gang terror problem, reported 'all's well,' following a night of wild rioting which sent the hoodlums under cover."

The story left no doubt that U.S. servicemen had rescued the public from "gangsters" and "hoodlums" by using efficient tactics learned in military training. The paper's own reporting, if the reader took the time to pay attention, contradicted the alarming report of "wild rioting." Rather, a handful of Mexican Americans were treated and released from Georgia Street Receiving Hospital for minor injuries and nine sailors were cited for disturbing the peace.

The *Daily News* also slipped into military jargon in its coverage of the clashes, describing the assaults by sailors as a "landing" and the beatings as obtaining "their objectives." The *Daily News* also implied that *pachucos* were cowards as they fled the beatings of the servicemen or attacking sailors when they numbered thirty to one. The paper also ridiculed their clothing as "silly pants" and "circus coats."

By 8 June, the *Daily News* toned down much of its reporting, but its objectivity was hampered by companion stories written by John Upton Terrell. Terrell's interpretation of the events often rivaled the straight news reports coming from the *Examiner* and the *Herald & Express*. Characterizing zoot-suiters as hoodlums and marauders armed with deadly weapons, Terrell made little distinction between Mexican Americans victimized in unprovoked attacks by servicemen and true gang members. In fact, his stories said that zoot-suiters were conspiring to assault sailors. "And last night they gathered their broken bottlenecks, their tire irons, their wrenches, guns and fish knives for the battles they expect to be staged at any moment," Terrell had no evidence that zoot-suiters were armed with guns or even defending themselves from attacks with broken bottles and knives. Manchester Boddy, *Daily News* publisher, added weight to Terrell's stories by echoing allegations that Mexican Americans were harassing the wives of servicemen and deliberately provoking fights. In one column, Boddy used the disturbances as an opportunity to argue for the construction of a state prison in Chino in San Bernardino County.

The *Herald & Express* took an almost gleeful tone, which appeared to encourage servicemen to continue the assaults. The best story telling lies in reporting the conflicts as between heroes and villains. But the *Herald & Express* ignored a basic journalistic rule of allowing the events of the story to hold the reader's attention. Instead, by embellishing the facts, the paper elevated what amounted to street bawls into a full-blown military action.

In an upbeat, if not giddy, tone, the *Herald & Express* reported on 7 June "Flying squadrons of soldiers, sailors and marines in a new outbreak of battle with zoot suit gangs today chalked up six more zooters on the casualty list while a score of other hoodlums were arrested." Under a subhead of 'THREE BIG BATTLES," the paper reported that "invasion operations in the zoot gang territory can be roughly classified as 'the Battle of Firestone' the 'Battle of the Skid Row' and the 'Battle of North Broadway.' "

The next day's coverage on 8 June, the paper reported "wild rioting" in the streets and again characterized the fights as the "Battle of Gangland." On its second front page, the *Herald & Express* published seven photos of the previous night's melee, depicting young men stripped of their clothing and one photo of spectators clearly in a festive mood. Nowhere were photos of the actual "rioting." Only the *Daily News* published a photograph of actual violence in which Los Angeles police wrestled with a soldier resisting arrest.

That same day, the *Herald & Express* almost incited vigilante actions. In an editorial presumably penned by John Campbell, the *Herald & Express* stated that servicemen "promise to rid the community of its newest evils—those zoot-suited miscreants who have committed many crimes and have added a very serious side to juvenile delinquency problems. Zoot-Suiters don't relish falling into the clutches of servicemen. It isn't healthy. Maybe we'll be rid of such budding gangsters as some of them have turned out to be very soon."

By then Los Angeles press coverage of the incidents was attracting attention in the East. *Time* magazine noted the way the local press played fast and loose with the facts. "The Hearst newspapers, the Los Angeles *Examiner* and the *Herald & Express*, and Harry Chandler's Los Angeles *Times* began to blaze. Late-afternoon editions printed black-faced leads about a purported anonymous call to headquarters: 'We're meeting 500 strong tonight and we're going to kill every cop we see.' The Hearst *Herald & Express* bannered: ZOOTERS THREATEN L.A. POLICE."

In the *Examiner*, a headline blared, "Police Must Clean Up L.A. Hoodlumism." The first paragraph of an *Examiner* editorial stated, "Riotous disturbances of the past week in Los Angeles by zoot-suit hoodlums have inflicted a deep and humiliating wound on the reputation of this city."

The *Herald & Express* took a more temperate view on its editorial pages on 10 June, condemning both "hoodlums" and "vigilantes" for bringing disgrace to the city. It was careful, though, not to identify vigilantes as servicemen. And it still reserved its harshest criticism for *pachucos*, describing them as an "irresponsible generation." As it was often wont to do during a crisis, the paper recommended invoking the power of the state to enforce the law. (It wasn't the first time a Hearst-owned paper suggested resorting to martial law or a state police action. The *Examiner* had made the same recommendation during the Harry Raymond bombing when the police department appeared paralyzed in solving the case.)

To show that zoot-suiters were part of a dangerous hoodlum element, both the *Examiner* and the *Herald & Express* used selective language to imply that zoot suit clothing was a narcotic. On 15 June, for example, the *Herald & Express* reported

Byron Raddon, right, checks a front page proof with two other printers at the *Daily News*. The edition announces the surrender of Japan during World War II in August 1945 (Byron Raddon Collection)

that the county grand jury was investigating whether alcohol and marijuana use contributed to the alleged delinquency of teenage zoot-suiters. In the same article it suggested that young men were "addicted" to zoot suits. In a 12 June report, the *Examiner* carried a brief item that the alleged leader of a *pachuco* gang had been "cured" of being a zoot-suiter.

Daily News reporter Terrell, who reported that Axis agents had "been active in fermenting gang warfare in Los Angeles," raised the influence of Nazi fifth columnists on 9 June. Terrell's article was lengthy and he led with the fifth columnist angle, but most of the report concentrated on the Navy's banning all its personnel from the city. Only toward the end of the article did Terrell return to the Nazi angle. But he only reported that some Axis agents had been taken into custody and their identities were not disclosed. No follow-up stories were published to identify the enemy agents or their influence on Mexican American gangs.

Two days later, the *Times* published an interview with the Rev. Francisco Quintanilla of the Mexican Methodist Church in Watts. Described by the *Times* as a "two-fisted man" who once had served as a captain in Pancho Villa's revolutionary army, Quintanilla said he believed that "vicious propaganda" being spread by "enemy agents" was responsible for several attacks made by Mexican American youths upon servicemen. He pointed to an instance in which a white man had approached him and asked in broken English if he could address the young men in his congregation. Quintanilla refused the request but later spotted the man haranguing the boys on a nearby street corner. Quintanilla could provide no specific evidence that the man was a fifth columnist, but the report added credence that the rioting had been the work of foreign agents.

The *Times* coverage of the violence had been fair compared to its competitors. The *Daily News*, after a few days of sensational coverage, shifted gears dramatically. In a rare gesture the paper provided front page space to the Mexican American voice, although undoubtedly from pressure exerted by Mexican American organizations.

In his 11 June column, Manchester Boddy published a letter from a Mexican American mother: "This racial discrimination they have in schools is where the youngsters' pride is hurt and hatred is started—always being called Mexicans. In schools there are all nationalities, but only Mexicans are called by their ancestors' blood. There are Irish, Jews, English, French, Swedes, etc., but as long as they are born in this country they are Americans. Why not those of Mexican descent? They are treated as rare specimens."

Les Wagner, in his *Script* column, acknowledged, "our minority groups in Los Angeles have been very shabbily treated." He noted that there have been an "alarming" number of cases of rape and assault perpetrated against Mexicans, reminding his readers that the jails were crowded with servicemen charged with violent crimes against Mexicans. Wagner wrote that a young girl had called, complaining about the press coverage and the lack of attention on the causes of the violence. She told Wagner that a sailor had raped her thirteen-year-old friend and that she and her friends would not stand idle as they were attacked.

But as with the Japanese American issues, the support of the Mexican American community had been barely heard amid the din created by the *Examiner* and the *Herald & Express*. In fact, years would pass before enterprising reporters began to portray the Mexican American in a positive light. Paul Weeks, *Daily News* reporter, would begin exploring minority issues in the late 1940s and through the 1950s. Jack Jones of the *Daily News* revisited the zoot suit issues with articles in the early 1950s on the fates of the Sleepy Lagoon defendants.

But it took the upstart *Mirror*, founded in October 1948 by Norman Chandler, to establish a pattern of balanced reporting of Mexican American issues. Led by such reporters as Elaine St. Johns, daughter of popular Hearst journalist Adela Rogers St. Johns, and Charlie Erickson, the *Mirror* ran a series of articles that promoted the understanding of Mexicans.

In early 1949, the *Mirror* ran its first series of articles on Mexican American gangs. Elaine St. Johns wrote the series. Accompanied by photographer Roger Bath, St. Johns tagged along on the swing shift with members of the Los Angeles Police Department's juvenile gang squad. St. Johns and Bath trailed Fred Benavidez as he gave the *Mirror* staffers an inside view of the gang squad's daily routine of dealing with Latino gangsters through the Hollenbeck, Central, and Highland Park divisions. St. Johns centered the series on the squad's work and kept the stereotypes and inflammatory language to a minimum. Bath's pictures illustrated an upbeat and smiling Benavidez talking with suspected gang members. St. Johns' contact with gang members was superficial at best, but her angle was to show that the police department's approach to solving gang violence appeared to be working. The two-part series, published 27-28 March 1949, served as a foundation for future reporters over the next five decades as metropolitan and suburban daily reporters and photographers participated in ride-along programs with local police departments to study gang issues.

By 1954, *Mirror* editors recognized the growing influence of the Mexican American in Los Angeles, noting that 300,000 of the state's 775,000 Latinos were living in Los Angeles. In December, in what was groundbreaking work for its time, reporter Erickson, who had joined the *Mirror* in 1948 as a copyboy, wrote a three-part series that detailed the influence of the Mexican American in the community and the discrimination they faced in housing and employment. Erickson reported that Anglos living in restricted neighborhoods complained that their property values could drop by as much as fifteen percent if Latinos moved in. He also interviewed one job placement coordinator who complained that Mexican workers were "undependable, poor workers." However, other interviews revealed that many employers found Latinos to be excellent workers. According to a *Mirror* poll, ten out of twelve employment agencies were reluctant to send Mexican American applicants to fill jobs involving public contact. However, every employer polled by newspaper said Latinos were satisfactory workers.

Erickson's series provided an early example of which direction the press of Los Angeles was headed, especially in covering the Latino community. Carey McWilliams singled out the *Mirror* in a 10 June 1950 article in *The Nation* as the only Los Angeles newspaper to refuse to participate in a "wolf-pack" mentality of attacking Mexican American youths as hoodlums. But McWilliams chided the rest of the press for failing to learn lessons from its role in the Zoot Suit riots. Although by then the press no longer referred to Mexican Americans as gangsters, it usually published their Spanish surnames and made a point in editorials that "hoodlumism is not a racial problem." McWilliams argued that by "elaborately disclaiming any bias, these editorials have clearly implied that hoodlumism was identical with Mexican American status."

McWilliams pointed to a 6 May 1950 story in the *Daily News* that typified the manipulation of the news to imply that Mexican Americans were ruthless criminals if not subhuman. The article was headlined "12 Jailed in New Attacks of L.A. Rat Pack." The names published in the story were Latino. McWilliams acknowledged there was nothing improper in publishing the names. But in the same edition another story, "Beverly Hills Boys held in Vandalism," was given lesser play. The story reported that youths drove through the streets of Beverly Hills in a station wagon, shooting out the windows of sixteen store buildings with an air gun. The *Daily News* identified the young men as "vandals," but in the report of Mexican Americans committing a similar crime they were identified as "wolves," "mad dogs," and "rats."

Despite these instances of biased reporting, the Los Angeles press slowly began to change its coverage. The instances of double standard reporting, like that in the *Daily News*, began to diminish as the 1950s dawned.

In 1950 there were some early signs that the Hearst press began to soften its view of the minority communities. Veteran *Examiner* reporter Marjorie Driscoll reported on 22 October that the Latino community organized the Mexican Civil Defense Corps during the Korean War to sponsor trips for Latino celebrities to entertain soldiers at Southern California military bases. The corps also sponsored blood drives and nursing training. However, Driscoll's report was an exception rather than the rule to the *Examiner's* approach to the minority community.

But, generally, it took much longer for the *Examiner* and the *Herald & Express* to abandon the "wolf-pack" mentality. The *Herald & Express* never embraced the concept that the Mexican American and African American communities were part of the city landscape and history. The *Examiner* did catch on in the late

1950s, but credit went to its reporter, former *Daily News* staffer Sara Boynoff, who enterprised a series of articles on the city's minority communities that helped pave the way for the *Examiner* to take a more moderate approach to minority coverage.

III.

Given the treatment of the Japanese American and the Latino by the press it might have been some relief to African Americans that they had been almost ignored through most of the first half of the century. The black community, unlike other minorities, had a distinct and separate relationship with the city's mainstream papers. That relationship, while showing promise in the mid-1920s of regular, unbiased coverage, vanished in the late 1920s, when only crime stories mentioned African Americans.

Though ignored by the mainstream white press, the black community was well represented by its own press. From the turn of the century through the 1950s the community's news was covered by the Califo*rnia Eagle*, the *Criterian*, the *Neighborhood News*, the *Los Angeles Record* (unrelated to the Scripps-Canfield paper), the *Sepia Hollywood*, the *Los Angeles Tribune*, the *Teller*, and the *Herald-Dispatch*. While the Los Angeles media focused any attention on blacks by publishing crime stories, the Negro press paid relatively little attention to crime. And whereas white papers often played up stories in which crimes were committed by blacks against Anglos, the opposite was true in the black papers where crimes against African Americans frequently made the front pages. By the same token the Negro press routinely devoted two-thirds of its front-page coverage to black-white race relations and often just a third of its front page to strictly African American news.

Until World War II, the editors in the mainstream press could, with some truthfulness, argue that the African American population was too small to seriously cover. The migration of African Americans to California had been small during the 19th century. But by 1910, Los Angeles County with 9,424 African Americans, which accounted for forty-three percent of the state's black population, had emerged as the leading center of African Americans in the West.

Untouched by the race riots that became commonplace in the East, Los Angeles began to experience an increasingly heavy migration, mainly from Mississippi, South Carolina, Georgia, and Alabama. By 1920 the African American population grew to 18,738 in Los Angeles with 15,579 living in the city. That number more than doubled in 1930 with 46,425 blacks living in the county limits and 38,894 living in the city.

Up until the World War, blacks enjoyed a freedom in Los Angeles not enjoyed in other major metropolitan cities. They lived along First and Second streets in downtown, West Temple, the West Adams district, Boyle Heights, along Welles, the Furlong tract in the southeast portion of the city, and Jefferson Boulevard between Normandie and Western. After 1912, however, the black ghetto was shaped largely by the construction of a hotel on Central Avenue. It accepted African American guests and became the demarcation line between white and black residents. As the Ku Klux Klan gained influence after World War I and through the 1920s, black neighborhoods throughout Los Angeles began to dry up as blacks moved toward the Central Avenue area. This enclave was strengthened in 1928 by the construction, with black financing, of the Hotel Sommerville, which would become the venue for the convention for National Association for the Advancement of Colored People.

Times columnist Harry Carr typified the attitude of the white mainstream journalist toward the African American community. In his 1935 book, *Los Angeles: City of Dreams*, Carr observed, "Central Avenue has jazz night clubs, tough Negroes with razors, joints as rough as Beal Street, Memphis; but it also has Negro banks, a Negro trust company, an insurance company, two handsome theaters, as clean as a New England kitchen ... two excellent Negro newspapers which live largely on anti-kink hair advertisements. Negro beauty shops, strange to say, flourish. The black flappers taken anti-kink remedies; then permanent waves."

Maddened, patronizing, even mean-spirited, Carr nevertheless couldn't be described as an overt racist in his time. Yet he found the black community a mystery, a contradiction that couldn't be adequately explained. He also pointed out correctly that the African American didn't know his status in pre-World War II Los Angeles. Interviewing his "bootblack," Carr noted that the man knew his "place" while living in Mississippi, but he had no idea about what the social rules were for blacks in Southern California. Can a black man stand in front of a soda fountain in a white neighborhood and expect to receive service or not? One never knew until he asked for service. A negative response could be painful.

But for a brief moment, before the Klan gained influence in Southern California, the mainstream press appeared to consider giving blacks relative equal treatment in its coverage. The *Evening Express* stood out among the mainstream papers. Whenever a black police officer was honored for his work or retired, the *Express* cheerfully reported the details on its inside pages. When the Los Angeles Police Department's first black detective, W.L. Stevens, retired in August 1926, the *Express* printed an article and his photograph. Headlined "Negro Detective Presented Badge Upon Retirement" with the deck reading "Capable Officer Retires Today After 21 Years of Service," the article was remarkably free of patronizing language and stereotyping. The paper described Stevens as a "capable and fearless" officer who had risen through the ranks to lieutenant. It also chronicled Stevens' bravery and accomplishments.

During the same week, the *Express* interviewed Dr. Beverly H. Shaw, president of Haven Teachers' College, a black institution in Meridian, Mississippi. Shaw was vacationing in Los Angeles where the *Express* sought him out for an interview to discuss education for blacks. A photograph of Shaw and Dr. M.S. Davage, president of Clark Negro University of Atlanta, Georgia, accompanied the brief article.

In June 1926, the *Express* also reported on its front page that the Rev. James Edward Lewis, a black pastor and promoter living in San Pedro, planned to purchase a freight steamer and move his congregation to Liberia.

Though this type of coverage was encouraging, the *Express* still couldn't free itself from stereotypical coverage. A knife-fight between two African American men resulted in this lead on 7 June 1926: "Ending an argument with the time-honored weapon of his race, a razor, H. Dennison, a Negro, is alleged to have cut and probably fatally wounded Freeman Hughes, 28, both of whom lived at 511 Ceres avenue."

Other newspapers were reluctant to give more than scant attention to African Americans. On 14 January 1923, the Los Angeles *Times* tied three separate shootings, one involving the murder of a black police officer, into a single report. Apparently not considering the slaying of Patrolman George Williams newsworthy on its own, the *Times* reported that Williams had been slain in a "pistol duel" by "another negro." The story, played in the lead position on the left shoulder of the front page, provided details of the other shootings before returning in the fourth paragraph to state that Williams had been married and "had been on the police force for a number of years." It gave no further details. The next day, the *Times* reported that Williams' killer had been arrested. Again the newspaper devoted most of the follow-up story to the other shootings, giving the Williams' incident only cursory attention. The reporting was neither patronizing nor hostile but incomplete.

By contrast, the California *Eagle* bannered the slaying in its 18 January edition. Headlined, "City Pays Great Tribute to Slain Police Officer," the story occupied the far left column and was accompanied by a photograph of Williams in uniform. The *Eagle* report made no mention of the race of Williams or of his killer. It reported in detail the circumstances of the shooting. Williams had arrived at Eighth Street and Stanford Avenue to quell a dispute between John Pryor, a landlord, and Pryor's tenants. When Williams arrived at the street corner, Pryor shot Williams twice before Williams returned fire. The *Eagle* also reported details of the inquest that had followed the killing and identified virtually every African American and white police officer involved in the investigation. It also stated that Police Chief Louis D. Oaks was personally involved in the investigation. Details of Williams' family also were given.

The difference in coverage of the Williams slaying by the *Eagle* and the *Times* was typical of the way the two newspapers viewed the profession of law enforcement, and, of course, the black community. The *Times* and other white establishment newspapers accorded police officers rarely more than blue-collar worker status. The *Eagle*, however, reflected the attitude of its readers. Being a police officer in the African American community was a high honor, a heroic way of life. Every promotion or commendation was listed in the *Eagle*.

Given the indifference by most white-owned newspapers toward the triumphs and tragedies of black police officers, it was easy for them to turn a blind eye to the injustices heaped on blacks. The *Express'* coverage of the black community, as modest as it was in the mid-1920s, was still an important step toward fair treatment. But it was short-lived and typified the drying up of balanced coverage in the second half of the 1920s when the Ku Klux Klan gained influence. In the early 1920s, membership in the Klan surged. Southern and Midwest businessmen joined the huge influx of migrants to Los Angeles bringing their Klan memberships with them. Increasing numbers of neighborhoods began to sanction the use of restrictive covenants in sale of housing and public facilities.

The Klan enjoyed particularly strong support within the Los Angeles Police Department. Jesse Kimbrough, an African American police detective who joined the department in 1916, recalled that a white police officer showed him a Klan poster in the locker room in the Newton Street Division. The poster read, "It is our dedicated aim and duty to save White America from the sacrilegious Jews, the Rome-directed Catholics, and the subhuman Niggers. White Protestant Americans join now!" The white officer, a Catholic, warned Kimbrough that "several paid up" Klan members were his co-workers. White detectives would talk with Kimbrough inside the station but would ignore him on the street. Black police officers were not allowed to arrest and handcuff white suspects. These prejudices became so entrenched in law-enforcement culture that not a single African American would be hired in the police department between 1929 and 1934 and not a single black already employed as a police officer would receive a promotion between 1925 and 1936.

The Klan's influence reached high levels. Police chief Oaks, sheriff William Traeger, and city councilman Ralph L. Criswell were card-carrying members. Sanctioned racism inside the police department mirrored racial biases elsewhere. White merchants would refuse to serve black customers or hire them. Advertisers would pressure white editors to keep African American news out of the papers.

Daily News reporter Roy Ringer recalled that his newspaper refused to support the Fair Employment Practices Commission (FEPC) because management feared it would alienate advertisers. Merchants didn't want to employ African Americans and Mexicans and didn't want them as customers.

Coverage of the black community remained virtually nonexistent from about 1927 until the end of World War II, when the NAACP had become more active and the Klan lost its influence in California. Newspaper editors and reporters were slow to respond to the changing tide of race relations after the war, but there were signs in the late 1940s that the barriers were beginning to give way. Editors had little or no interest in coverage unless it was black-on-white crime. Black-on-black crime resulted in no coverage. Reporters often frequented black jazz clubs on Central Avenue in the evening, but thought little during the day of covering any black-related news.

The single exception was the Ted LeBerthon, who had been writing his "Night Court" column for the *Daily News* since the 1930s. LeBerthon literally wrote about the misdemeanants coming and going through the night hours at the Lincoln Heights Municipal Court. He specialized in coverage of the downtrodden and consequently wrote extensively about religious issues and about African Americans. The column was never patronizing or melodramatic, instead the column highlighted the injustices faced by the poor and minorities.

A native of San Francisco, LeBerthon had worked for many years at the New York and Chicago newspapers. By the time he joined the *Daily News*, about 1938, he was in his mid-forties and a veteran of the newspaper wars of the East. Manchester Boddy described LeBerthon as speaking "for the untold thousands who would say what he says if given the opportunity. Truly, he *is* the 'Voice of the People.' " A personable, if even eccentric, fellow, LeBerthon often played his coveted set of jazz records on a phonograph at his desk much to the amusement of some staffers and to the annoyance of others. His column, according to fellow *Daily News* staffer Sara Boynoff, later "became a platform for LeBerthon's involvement in the Catholic religion, and he began to see the face of Christ in every bum he encountered at night in that dreary court." When editors couldn't control LeBerthon, he was fired. Later he wrote for such Catholic publications as the Los Angeles *Tidings* and the *Catholic Digest* in St. Paul, Minnesota. He also was a contributing writer for the *Negro Digest*. But his absence from the *Daily News* silenced the only voice the black community had in a white newspaper.

On its news pages in the late 1940s, the *Daily News* performed marginally better than its competitors on some racial issues. Much of this type of coverage was limited to confrontations between whites and blacks, but was generally free of bias. When 500 Fremont High School students staged a noisy demonstration against the enrollment of seven African Americans on 16 March 1947, the *Daily News* wrote a sympathetic front-page story about the black students. The demonstrators were suspended from school and the newspaper identified the organizers as "hotheads" who had browbeat and threatened other students. The story also noted that Principal Herbert Wood demanded that "offensive" signs be taken from the demonstrators and that each student could return to school only after a private meeting with him and the white student's parents. Though the story didn't quote any black students, it clearly portrayed them as victims of harassment by whites.

In 1953, the *Mirror* took dramatic steps to increasing its African American coverage. In an unprecedented decision, *Mirror* editors assigned Wayne Lockwood to write a five-part series of articles to celebrate the 28th annual Negro History Week. Starting on 9 February Lockwood presented a lengthy narrative detailing the achievements of California's African Americans in the 19th century. His series covered such leaders as William Leidesdorff, a San Francisco city councilman and city treasurer, and Biddy Mason, who opened her home to the destitute and had a long history of organizing Los Angeles charity drives. Each historical piece was accompanied by a sidebar highlighting the community contributions of such blacks as baseball great Jackie Robinson, L.A. police commissioner Dr. J.A. Sommerville, hat designer Mildred Blount, and financier George A. Beavers. The series, for perhaps the first time, exposed white Los Angeles readers to the varied and lively history of their black neighbors. Even by then, other dailies were already used to the *Mirror* giving above-average coverage to Mexican American and African American issues. Still, the amount of space devoted to the project must have startled editors in the Hearst newsrooms (although they didn't follow the *Mirror's* example, *Examiner* editors thought enough of the series to preserve it in their own library).

The *Mirror's* competitors in the late 1940s and early '50s were timid about reporting on minority issues. Margaret Boutyette Scott, who joined the *Examiner* in March 1945 as a copygirl and later promoted to reporter, recalled city editor Jim Richardson as gingerly handling African American affairs. Richardson, a stickler for journalism style in the copy of his reporters, ordered in the late 1940s that Negro be capitalized "out of deference" to the community. But minority reporting then was meager at best. Scott, for example, had once been assigned to cover an NAACP convention but the story received poor play. It appeared that Richardson had not given serious consideration to the convention as a news event and was simply checking out her politics. On another occasion, Scott witnessed a court proceeding in which a Mexican American fisherman who didn't speak English was having the full weight of the law thrown at him for fishing commercially without a license. Scott was horrified at the treatment of the defendant. But when she pitched the story to her editors they expressed no interest.

There were attempts by the minority community to educate white mainstream reporters about racial prejudice. In 1946, the black community was hit by a series of apparent Ku Klux Klan attacks. The Rev. George E. Dunne complained to white reporters at a Los Angeles Newspaper Guild meeting during the summer. He said that the city's "recent wave of racial terrorism as evidenced by burning crosses and threats of violence may have been brushed aside by the mayor and the police department as 'just pranks,' but the fact remains that these incidents are nothing more than examples of the ever rising tide of racism."

Though LANG members were sympathetic, such stories rarely made the front page for fear of offending advertisers.

Blacks and other minorities had even less success in obtaining jobs at newspapers, especially in the editorial department. In the 1 June 1946 *Guildsman,* Ed Marciniak, a Chicago newspaperman and a member of the Chicago Newspaper Guild, urged U.S. metropolitan newsmen and women to appreciate their roles in race relations. Marciniak wrote, "What a Guildsman says about Negroes or Mexicans in the columns of the daily press makes an impact on the conduct of race relations throughout the city." He suggested that Chicago papers: "1) End the practice of labeling Negroes in crime stories. If individuals are not identified as 'white' in crime news, why should 'Negroes' be so labeled? 2) Write news stories about the positive contributions Negroes are making in the city. 3) Work to have Negroes hired as reporters on the Chicago dailies. It's a major crime that not a single Negro is employed in the editorial departments of any of the Chicago papers. 4) Use Guild meetings, the Guild News and the ANG's mailing list to bring this problem before working newspaper men and women. 5) Eventually work up to a point where we can have "no discrimination" clauses inserted in Guild contracts with newspaper managements."

At its sixteenth annual convention in Columbus, Ohio, in 1952, the American Newspaper Guild's race relations committee adopted a resolution to help blacks obtain jobs in the industry, particularly with the trade press. The Los Angeles local attempted to implement the resolution by calling on Los Angeles newspaper publishers to hire blacks where none were previously employed. The program met with little success. At the *Herald & Express*, an African American was hired as a reporter, but he sat in the newsroom every day for nearly two weeks without receiving an assignment and no other reporters spoke to him. He eventually became disgusted and walked out.

The *Daily News*, however, prided itself on having hired minority staffers long before the Guild or NAACP made demands. It employed a black copyboy, and Mary Katano, a Japanese American, was the newsroom librarian. Another Asian, Mamie Leung, had been a writer at the paper since the 1930s. Though it had set the stage in minority coverage, the *Mirror* struggled to employ minorities on its staff. It hired a black reporter schooled in the Negro press, but he had difficulty adjusting to white mainstream journalism. His white peers considered him subpar, but no older reporters were willing to become his mentor to allow him to improve his skills.

White reporters performing enterprise reporting in the black and Mexican American communities were often met with hostility from their colleagues. Reporter Paul Weeks, who first worked on the *Daily News* then the *Mirror*, considered himself a student of the U.S. Constitution and the Bills of Rights. Firmly believing in equality for all people under the Constitution, Weeks embraced coverage of the black community. It was a difficult job, for he was met with skepticism from African American leaders who doubted his sincerity. *Mirror* Managing Editor J. Edward Murray assigned him stories about black issues and he dived in enthusiastically. He soon began writing in-depth pieces on community leaders and the issues. It wasn't long before he gained their trust and ultimately built a strong network of sources. Many of his colleagues at the *Mirror* believed Weeks was wasting his time, occasionally accosting him in the hallway demanding that he justify his coverage. One *Mirror* staffer once told Weeks, "Paul, the way you were writing those stories, you would think you were part nigger." Weeks replied, "I don't often have occasion to talk about it, but I am eighth black. The reporter's face reddened, and he walked away without comment. Weeks found the outrageous statement worked as fewer staffers confronted him about his stories. While some reporters simply couldn't even look at Weeks after his stories were published, his editors were immensely proud of the coverage. It didn't impress publisher Norman Chandler, who complained to city editor Hank Osborne about the coverage. "We don't sell newspapers down there (in the black community)," Chandler said.

The lure of advertising dollars in the African American community made little impression on the city's white daily newspapers. By 1956, blacks on the West Coast were spending an estimated $25 million a year in cosmetics, beauty salon treatment, and beauty-preparation products. About $55 million was spent on savings and War Bonds. An estimated 417,000 blacks lived in the communities of Watts, Willowbrook, Compton, south and central Los Angeles, the eastside, Temple, Boyle Heights, Santa Monica, and Pacoima. They had a buying power of more than $600 million annually. Eighty percent of those residents owned a television and at least two cars per family. Sixty-three percent owned a home and thirty-nine percent had a college education. Even in this competitive market advertising directors of white papers saw no need to attract black business.

The *Times* had an unofficial policy of virtual non-coverage of the black community. Reporter Jack Jones recalled that *Times* editors refused to send reporters into African American communities. In the late 1950s, some black families began moving into white neighborhoods. It didn't take long before white families began posting "for sale" signs in their front yards, abandoning their neighborhoods as more and more African Americans moved in. During this transition, *Times* editors would send a reporter and photographer in a radio car to the scene of a news event, not knowing whether the neighborhood was white or black. When the crew arrived on the scene and saw that the neighborhood was African American, they would use code over the radio to notify the city desk there was no story. "N.G." meant "no good," and when reporters identified themselves over the radio as "Mike Fox," it meant "motherfucker," as in "There are only motherfuckers down here." It took the Watts riots in August 1965 to get the *Times* to respond to black issues. After the riots, Jones was assigned to write a series of articles on the causes of the riots. He discovered that Watts had no transportation services, for bus lines stopped running early, poor schools and no colleges, and few grocery stores. Blacks also were offended by the construction of freeways. Although freeways were the pride of Los Angeles' movers and shakers, they represented nothing to African Americans in Watts. Many didn't have cars. The findings published in Jones' series in October 1965 came as a shock to the white community.

The coverage of black issues, however, became more balanced and less sensational after the 1954 U.S. Supreme Court decision to desegregate schools. But even then, reporting was limited to African American issues that also touched on the city's white population as with the desegregation of the Los Angeles Fire Department between 1954 and 1956. The transfer of black firefighters from an all-black station to white stations created tensions not only within the firehouses but also between the city's fire commission and Fire Chief John H. Alderson.

The *Examiner's* coverage of the struggle was a far cry from its attitude toward the minority community just ten years before. The newspaper covered two separate issues involving African American firefighters. In October 1953, the NAACP filed formal complaints that black firefighters faced discrimination in the oral portions of promotion exams. In December the city received a second complaint about the department's segregationist policies. Deputy Mayor John J. Irwin, an attorney, determined that the Fire Department's policy of assigning firefighters to specific stations based on race alone was illegal. Alderson was ordered by the fire commission to implement desegregation of the stations. When Alderson balked at integrating the stations in a timely manner, Irwin resigned his post as deputy mayor. The NAACP criticized Alderson for delaying integration. The program also was marred by a campaign by rank-and-file firefighters to give newly transferred African Americans "the cold shoulder." Hazing of blacks also occurred at Company 10, based at the 1335 Olive Street station. Some fire department supervisors also resigned rather than face integration.

With the tensions among Alderson, the NAACP, and a fire commission that supported the program mounting, the Fire Department faced heightened scrutiny from the press. The *Examiner's* coverage lacked the usual sensational racial language and presented a balanced picture of the issues, quoting both Alderson and NAACP attorneys equally. In fact, the pendulum of coverage swung slightly toward the NAACP's position as the revelations of hazing and harassment of black firefighters appeared. The *Herald & Express* also was considerably less frothy in its coverage, although in some stories on integration, the reporting gave its predominately white readership a distinct feeling of us versus them. The *Herald & Express*, in its continuing quest to spice up even the most straightforward report, identified in its 2 February 1956 editions that Engine Company 7 at 29th and Main streets was a "guinea-pig" station for the integration of eight blacks and eight whites under one roof.

Though the *Examiner* and the *Herald & Express* displayed considerable maturity compared to the previous decade, their editors were far from enlightened. No white Los Angeles daily newspaper, with the possible exception of the *Mirror*, championed the causes of the minority communities. Rather, newspaper editors and reporters reacted to the events surrounding them: the U.S. Supreme Court ruling to desegregate schools; the burgeoning civil rights movement in the South; and the progress African Americans had made in the military, particularly President Harry S. Truman's move to desegregate the armed forces. The role of the local press was being defined by the emergence of the minority communities and a changing view of society after World War II. War-weary men were returning to the newsroom with a clearer view of social injustices. Many women, who replaced them during the war, stayed on the job. And the cub reporters, although they had their own prejudices, came up through the ranks with a college education, and, generally, tended to lack the stronger prejudices of the previous generation.

Chapter Eight

"Noblesse in a Rat Pack"

I.

For a newspaper reporter, Los Angeles after the war was a world turned upside down. The Depression was over and with it had gone the Utopian schemes of promoters and social reformers. Labor organizations had overcome the hurdles of the prevailing open shop to become recognized in key industries throughout the county. Labor's power increased, leading to strikes both in the newspaper and film industries.

Second-generation Mexican Americans demanded equity in both the workplace and in housing. They became less isolated from the mainstream and had begun to urbanize. African Americans continued to migrate from the South. Influences from the Ku Klux Klan had waned while the voice of the NAACP became more powerful. Women, who secured well-paying jobs in factory work during the war, were fired and told to go home as servicemen returned to work.

Major shifts in approaching new markets, like any industry, must come from the top down. The war—with its vast influx of workers into the city, rising newsprint prices, and newsprint shortages—brought a creativity in journalism not seen since William Randolph Hearst perfected yellow journalism and the New York press brought the world the penny tabloid.

Some publishers were quick to capture much of this promising market, which Clinton D. McKinnon, the founder of the San Fernando *Valley Times*, estimated at $10 million in 1942. McKinnon, who would serve as the last publisher of the *Daily News*, established two weekly shopping guides for war workers: the *Aircraft Times*, published in Los Angeles, and the *Shipyard Times*, published in Long Beach. Distributed at eight assembly plants and a handful of small factories around the city, the *Aircraft Times* soon boasted of a free circulation of 80,000. Averaging about sixteen pages, the paper carried news about the plants and war-related events. It also had its shares of scoops. When the government announced draft deferments in the aircraft industry, Los Angeles metropolitan papers published general lists. The *Aircraft Times*, using a Washington news service, published complete lists of the deferments. The two publications also featured a women's page for its large female readership.

Mainstream newspapers also adjusted to their new audience. The *Herald & Express* published its daily "Herald-Express Page for War Workers" and usually featured the byline of Don Ryan, a veteran *Herald & Express* reporter. Typical in Ryan's feature stories was this lead: "Katherine Eldridge is a riveter on the nose of the Douglas A-20. When they had an alert in Santa Monica last April she dropped her gun and slid to the air shelter. Katherine is a good healthy armful and at the bottom of the chute the catcher muffed her. She hit the concrete and broke her right ankle."

By 1943, thirty percent of the county's 450,000 factory workers changed shifts between 10 p.m. and 1 a.m. The *Daily News* seized the opportunity, eliminating one afternoon edition and offering another edition catering strictly to night workers. The first copies of this "22.00 o'clock" edition rolled off the press on Sunday night on 20 June. Newsboys hawked papers along workers' routes of travel, and at the factory gates. Street sales leaped, eventually hitting 10,000 copies daily.

The circulation of all the downtown dailies, in fact, ballooned during the war. From 1941 to 1944, the sales of the *Herald & Express*—the leader—rose by 124,000. The *Examiner* jumped by 145,000, while the *Times* leaped another 155,000. And the *Daily News* saw its circulation climb another 45,000. All the dailies were selling for 5 cents a copy, which was increased to 7 cents in 1948.

But such prosperity also exacted a toll. The price of newsprint shot up from $50 a ton in 1942 to $58 in 1944 and $72.14 in 1946. Wages rose even faster. Unionized pressmen, for example, enjoyed a hefty increase: from an average of $43 (for a 40-hour workweek) in 1941 to about $60 (for 37 1/2 hours) in 1946. Meanwhile, the minimum and maximum scales for Guild-affiliated reporters, rewrite men, copy editors, photographers, and artists rose from $28.75 to $57.75 a week to $40 and $73.43 a week.

Despite these increased expenses, newspapers were making money. During the war, the *Daily News*, for example, saw its profits double in a single year. In 1943, it earned a profit of $439,992 over 1942, and then saw it jump again slightly to $458,618 in 1944. Profits for 1945 fell to $314,807, but ad lineage for that year amounted to 6,535,444, up several hundred thousand lines since the early days of the war.

II.

Newspapers after the war were flush with eager young men and women mixing it up with veterans. Both the young and the middle-aged served in the Pacific and European theaters and had a sense of what the world was about.

One such young man was Paul Weeks, who found himself on 9 September 1946 standing in front of an elevator on the third floor of the *Daily News* building on his first day at a big-city paper. It was a warm day that reminded one that the end of Los Angeles summers were still weeks away. Across the city room, traffic could be heard below at the intersection of Los Angeles Street and Pico Boulevard.

To Weeks' right was the horseshoe-shaped copy desk. In front of the copy desk was the city desk, a revolving door for city editors in the mid- and late-1940s. When Weeks was hired it was James Felton, but Milt Phinney and Charles Chappell also found themselves directing the news traffic. Opposite the city desk was the rewrite battery, which included John Clarke, Sara Boynoff, and Herb Maas. Beyond the rewrite desk in the corner was sports, society, the artists' office, and the wire machines. Directly to Weeks' left was Manchester Boddy's office, the library, the managing editor's office, and executive editor Lee Payne's office.

The city room was a beehive of activity, and Weeks stood there for a moment very green and very scared. It was his first exposure to a metropolitan newspaper.

Born in 1920 in North Dakota, Weeks grew up in Albuquerque, New Mexico, to working class parents. He was editing his high school newspaper when he got his first paying newspaper work collecting basketball box scores for the Albuquerque *Journal*. He worked the 7 to 11 p.m. shift for $1 a night, five nights a week. He got the job in June 1937. A month later the sports editor was fired and Weeks moved into the position. After graduating from the University of New Mexico, he enlisted in the U.S. Coast Guard in September 1942. There, he met Phil Garrison, who would serve as the *Daily News'* managing editor from 1948-52. Garrison was working public relations for the Coast Guard and the two men would often spend their days spinning newspaper stories. Weeks was discharged in September 1945 and eight months later the *Daily News* offered him a job.

When Weeks arrived in Los Angeles, Jim Murray had been on the job for a year at the *Examiner*. Previously a police reporter for the New Haven (Connecticut) *Register*, Murray was eager to live in California. Born in 1919, Murray was the antithesis of the prewar newspaperman. Poised, reserved, and strikingly handsome, Murray wore wire-rimmed glasses that gave him a bookish quality. And he loved to write, much more so than working a beat.

While at the *Register*, Murray covered a homicide and had obtained detailed police reports. He wrote a story, but the *Register* refused to run it so Murray offered it to the Associated Press. The AP grabbed the story and its editors immediately developed a strong relationship with the young reporter. When Murray expressed an interest in living in California, the AP had no openings there, but did set up an interview with the Los Angeles *Times*. When Murray arrived in Los Angeles, he found he would have to wait a week for a job to open, but he needed money right away. He drove down Broadway toward 11th Street and wrangled an interview with the *Examiner's* James Richardson. Murray was confronted with a "one-eyed" tyrant who had a propensity to take over crime stories from his reporters. But Murray wasn't about to be intimidated.

Richardson began to pepper the young man with questions.

"Do you know where the FBI headquarters is?" Richardson asked.

"No," said Murray.

"Do you know where the police headquarters is?"

"No."

Murray didn't know where a damn thing was, but the first question he asked Richardson was for an advance on his salary if he was hired. Richardson instantly knew he had a newspaperman in front of him and hired him on the spot.

Joining Murray at the *Examiner* in 1944 was Will Fowler, the son of Gene Fowler, the legendary Hearst newspaperman and author. The elder Fowler between 1918 and 1928 was the prototypical colorful if not jaded newsman of New York's Park Row. At the age of thirty-three, he had been the youngest managing editor of a New York daily, directing the massive newsroom of the *American*. He named his youngest child Will, after his boss, William Randolph Hearst. When Will Fowler was thirteen years old in 1935, the family moved to Southern California where Gene Fowler wrote screenplays for 20th Century Fox. While attending Beverly Hills High School, Will Fowler hung around with Hollywood's elite, including John Barrymore, W.C. Fields, and Ben Hecht.

Fowler graduated from Beverly Hills High School in 1940 and joined the Coast Guard two years later, serving as a seaman on convoy duty to the South Pacific. Will was discharged a year later. He was just twenty-two years old when he joined the *Examiner*.

Also arriving in 1944 and joining the local press corps was Nieson Himmel, a short, squat man who would come to represent the most tenacious and competitive cop reporters ever to hold down a beat. The son of a merchant, Himmel, who was Fowler's age, had been born in Faribault, Minnesota, about forty miles south of Minneapolis. As a young man the Foreign Service intrigued him. Hoping to become a diplomat, he attended Georgetown University. But it became apparent that he was not suited for the conservative nature of diplomatic service. He returned to Minnesota to attend college. He majored in journalism and found work as a copyboy, and later as a reporter, on the Minneapolis *Star*. When the war broke out he enlisted in the Army, serving on the Aleutian Islands before his discharge in 1944. He worked for nine months at City News Service before briefly joining the *Daily News*. The *Herald & Express* then took him on as a reporter.

Weeks, Murray, Fowler, and Himmel typified the postwar newspaperman. Though trained in prewar journalism by newsmen who had been in the business since the turn of the century, this new generation of news hounds was shaped by the events of war and their childhood during the Depression. Weeks (and later Jack Jones, Charlie Erickson, Elaine St. Johns, and Kendis Rochlen) had forged a new attitude among newspapermen and women that crusading journalism—long absent during much of the 1930s—would not only sell papers but also have a positive effect in the community. Reporters cut from the same cloth as Jim Murray, would greatly improve writing and presentation in local journalism (many reporters such as Jimmy Shambra of the *Herald & Express* and Johnnie Arrington of the *Daily News* actually wrote very little). Fowler and Himmel provided the foundation of local newspapering by excelling in crime coverage that even today in many dailies remain the bread and butter of big city coverage.

The contrast between the prewar and postwar reporter was no more apparent than the two newsmen who best reflected much of Los Angeles: Matt Weinstock and Jack Smith.

Moving to Los Angeles as a child, Weinstock embraced the city as his adopted home and never left. He was grounded in a journalism that offered a voice for the common man. His writing was simple, unadorned. *Times* columnist Jack Smith wrote of his colleague: "Matt Weinstock was Los Angeles in a sense that no other man had been. He lived in and observed and wrote about a Los Angeles that existed only through him." His wry observations of Angelenos slowly crept up on the reader. During the war Weinstock wrote, "Experienced shoppers can tell if the butcher has meat by the number of cars in his parking lot." And when a new drink made the rounds in 1952, he observed, "L.A. drinkers are discovering martini-on-the-rocks –a martini over two cubes of ice in an Old Fashioned glass."

Smith succeeded Weinstock. Born Jack Clifford Smith in 1916 in Long Beach, he had witnessed the world from a foxhole and tramp ships before finding a spot in a newsroom. Joining the Marine Corps during World War II, he served as a combat correspondent and participated in the battle of Iwo Jima. He traveled around the world, paying his way by working aboard dirty cattle boats. After the war, Smith served briefly at the *Daily News* before joining the Los Angeles *Independent*, a zoned throwaway that died shortly after it was launched. He worked at the *Herald & Express* as a reporter and rewrite man, but then returned again to the *Daily News* to write for its Sunday editions before permanently signing on at the *Times*. He was a hard drinker, prone to three-day binges that not only jeopardized his health but his job.

When the *Times* gave him a column it probably saved his life. It also gave Los Angeles a voice and gave *him* a voice. Witty, literate, and urbane, he saw his city quite differently than Weinstock. Weinstock's city was young, if not immature; certainly not like Chicago and New York. Los Angeles after the war had become a thriving metropolitan center that Smith saw directly competing with New York to attract entertainment (it wrestled television, for example, from New York in the 1950s) jobs and big business. Smith's column was autobiographical, a skill not many columnists could pull off.

There were other subtle signs that the Los Angeles newspaper person was changing. Paul Weeks recalled early in his tenure at the *Daily News* being assigned to question a man charged with murdering a young girl. When Weeks arrived at the police station he found fellow *Daily News* reporter Jerry Ramlow roughing up the suspected killer alone in the interrogation room. Weeks was stunned. "God, that's no way to get a story. You must treat him like a human being," he told Ramlow. On another occasion, Weeks had been on the job nine months when he was sent to cover the assassination of gangster Benjamin ("Bugsy") Siegel. Weeks arrived at the Beverly Hills home where the victim was found dead in the living room. Inexperienced and perhaps nervous over covering one of his first major stories, Weeks was sickened to see the *Examiner* and the *Herald & Express* reporters "swaggering around" the home, pawing through the gangster's belongings.

Some young reporters refused to use subterfuge to obtain a story, a common practice in the prewar days. A typical clash involved relative newcomer John Beckler and veteran newsman Sparky Saldana.

Daily News assistant city editor Sparky Saldana joined the newspaper in late 1926 and served his cop reporting apprenticeship starting in 1932 under such tough newsmen as Pat Sheppard, Smoky Hale, Lynn Spencer, and Otto Winkler. Born in Mexico, he was one of the first Latinos to work for a mainstream white newspaper as a reporter and editor (The Los Angeles *Star* in 1851, hired Latinos to translate articles for the Spanish-language page). Saldana later graduated to the harbor and district attorney beats, and then supervised the Spanish-language division of the Office of War Information. One Sunday, the city attorney of Culver City was shot dead by his teenage son during an argument. Saldana sent Beckler down to the widow's home to get a photo of the dead man. Most of the reporters had been chased away by the woman. Saldana was expecting Beckler to walk into the home and pocket a photograph from the coffee table or bureau, a job made easier since most police reporters since the 1920s had carried handguns and a police badge (Saldana carried detective lieutenant's badge No. 745). They often deliberately misidentified themselves as a police officer to gain access to a home. Beckler would have none of that. He returned to the city room empty-handed. Saldana was furious.

"John, you go back and grab a picture," Saldana said. "Get a picture off the piano."

"I'm not going to go there and force myself on this poor wife," Beckler said.

"John, maybe you are in the wrong business."

"Maybe I am but I'm not going back."

"Go home then."

Saldana turned to Aaron Dudley, who been with the *Daily News* since the war, and sent him to Culver City.

Dudley pulled up to the home in an old pickup truck and knocked on the door. Inside, the mother was trying to clean her husband's blood from the carpet. Dudley pulled out his press badge and said, "I'm from the police press room." Dudley hadn't lied but he was vague enough not to alarm the woman. He told the distraught woman that the newspapers would use crime-scene photos of her husband, and he thought it would be more appropriate if a studio portrait would be more tasteful. After gently talking with the woman for some time, she handed him every photograph in the house. He returned to the city room with family albums and a full set of studio proofs of the family.

The competition was left with nothing. A fuming Aggie Underwood called the *Daily News* city room and threatened to have Dudley arrested for theft. "If you don't let us have those pictures, I will have charges pressed against you," Underwood seethed.

Dudley promised Underwood a photo and dropped it in the mail. It arrived a day later but was completely useless to the *Herald & Express* since the story was too old by then.

The postwar newsman thought of himself as a professional, but some traditions died hard. One such tradition was receiving gifts, a prewar practice, when reporters and editors often accepted bribes, dope, and bootleg liquor from gangsters and the police. Leo Batt, a veteran Chicago newspaperman, joined the *Mirror* in 1951. In Chicago, reporters received a turkey and a bottle of wine at Christmas. Those were crumbs compared to the fringe benefits that Los Angeles newsmen collected. Batt noted "there was blatant, horrible gift-giving whenever a reporter did a story." Hugh ("Bud") Lewis, a *Times* editor, temporarily assigned to help manage the *Mirror*, ordered that his gifts be sent directly to his home. Roy Ringer of the *Daily News* recalled that theater press agents gave out elaborate gift baskets every Christmas. The day the *Daily News* folded, a week before Christmas in 1954, Ringer drove down to the plant to collect his booty. A security guard seated at a desk greeted him. "Yeah, I have it for you," the guard said. Ringer was handed a single bottle of Scotch. Ringer knew exactly what he was supposed to receive. Thieves had made off with almost all of it. Elaborate gift giving, mostly from film studio and theater publicists, didn't tarnish the professionalism of the news reporter.

Nor did the issue of accuracy tarnish the reputations of reporters. Although Paul Weeks would later bristle at the suggestion that some reporters would embellish their stories, as Don Dwiggins had contended in 1974, some fakery was a well-established practice. Many reporters, in fact, prided themselves on writing with a swashbuckling flair. A homely girl became a comely girl. A reporter could score an interview with a man on the street and turn it into a lively piece while maintaining the integrity of the story.

But Dwiggins never let the facts get in the way of a good story. An avid aviator, Dwiggins had authored more than two-dozen books, mostly on aerospace subjects. He joined the *Daily News* after the war, then moved to the *Mirror-News,* and later he worked in television. Dwiggins spent much of his spare time—and company time occasionally—freelancing magazine stories. When assigned to the rewrite desk, he would drive his fellow deskmen to distraction by writing his magazine stories in between telephone calls from the beatmen. His reputation among *Daily News* staffers for writing fake stories was legendary. He once had a photograph of an armless and legless man, that he would build elaborate stories around and would sell them to special interest and national magazines.

When an electroplating plant exploded near the *Daily News* building, causing extensive damage to a city block and killing seventeen people, Dwiggins was assigned to run exposed plates between the scene and the city room for chief photographer Dick Farrell. On the way back to the city room, Dwiggins stopped to help a man laying flat in the gutter. Dwiggins got the man's name and gave the information to rewrite man Chris Clausen. Clausen fashioned a sidebar out of the information. But for the rest of the day and into the evening, the sidebar by Clausen and Dwiggins grew elaborately with each edition until the man came to be identified as an unsung hero of the disaster. When the Red Cross saw the story, they wanted to recognize the man for his heroic achievements, but he couldn't be found.

Dwiggins became so notorious that his editors and fellow reporters stopped believing anything he wrote. It was that attitude among editors that would come back and haunt them. In late 1960, Dwiggins took a press junket to the Retalhuleu Province in Guatemala. There, he found a large jet airstrip under construction in the jungles. Since Guatemala had no jets, Dwiggins investigated the source behind the construction. He discovered that a Texas construction firm building the Pan American highway had been approached to build the airstrip. He also found out that the CIA might have been involved in funding the project. When Dwiggins returned to Los Angeles, he interviewed an ex-U.S. Air Force bombardier who said he had been hired for $25,000 to fly a war surplus B-25 in a mission against Cuba's oil refineries. Dwiggins learned that CIA-backed soldiers were prepared to overthrow the Fidel Castro's fledgling Communist government.

Unimpressed, *Mirror-News* editors chose not to run the story. Dwiggins then fed his report to Carey McWilliams, then editor of *The Nation,* which ran the story. The New York *Times* then picked it up. The Bay of Pigs invasion had to be postponed four months. The *Mirror-News'* greatest triumph in investigative reporting had been ruined by Dwiggins' reputation for fabricating news.

III.

In 1946, some newsmen were ready to improve their image as professionals. While vacationing in Denver with his wife, Bevo Means, a popular and colorful reporter for the *Herald & Express*, went for a walk and found a bar that catered to Denver newsmen. After a few drinks, he found the club was part of a professional organization for newsmen: the Denver Press Club. Means brought the idea back to Los Angeles. He enlisted two men from each paper to meet at the Mayfair Hotel and discuss the possibility. Joining Means to outline the beginnings of the Greater Los Angeles Press Club were Jack Cravens and Sparky Saldana of the *Daily News*; Gus Newman and Sid Hughes of the *Examiner*, Marvin Miles and Gene Sherman of the *Times*; and Bill Kennedy of the *Herald & Express*.

Kennedy quit after the first meeting when the founding members decided to pattern themselves after the Denver organization and bar women from membership. "If Aggie Underwood isn't as good or better a newspaperman than us, I'm getting out," he said. Newsman Jud Smith replaced him and Robert A. Neeb, a lawyer, served as legal counsel. Gene Sherman of the *Times* was named president; Newman was elected first vice president; Smith was treasurer; and Saldana was secretary. The press club was formally founded on 24 September 1946.

In what Will Fowler described as "brawling, young, brash and still in swaddling clothes," the Press Club quickly brought a professional tone to local journalism. At a meeting at the Cabrillo Hotel to celebrate its first anniversary in late 1947, the club members discussed ways to generate national attention to the organization. Means suggested inviting President Harry Truman to speak during his cross-country whistle stop tour, scheduled in the spring of 1948. An election year, Truman would be focusing his attention on the West Coast where the Democratic Party was particularly weak. Means' suggestion was met with dead silence at first, but by the end of the meeting, board members had warmed to the idea and drafted an invitation to Truman the next day. The four newspapers knew of the invitation but remained silent until the club received Truman's reply. When word was received that Truman would speak on 14 June, city and county politicians, including Mayor Bowron, were taken by surprise. City and council officials had hoped Truman would include Los Angeles on his agenda, but none realized that the relatively unknown Greater Los Angeles Press Club would scoop them. Within days, every leading politician was scrambling for a ticket to the speech.

The speech and luncheon were held at the Ambassador Hotel. Truman's motorcade to the hotel attracted an estimated 1 million people. More than 1,000 guests attended the event, far exceeding the Club's goals of bringing itself national attention to their efforts.

The decision to bar women, however, certainly didn't make the press club a leader in gender equity. For well before the war, women had been proving themselves equal to any journalistic task.

The role of queen of the newspaperwoman in 1940s Los Angeles, if a single woman could lay claim to such a title, probably belonged to Florabel Muir. A lumbering, heavyset woman with a face that had been through a million wars, Muir already was a legend with the New York *Daily News*. In her colorful career she once secretly snapped a photograph of Ruth Snyder as she was being executed in the electric chair at Sing Sing prison. Muir briefly owned City News Service and covered Hollywood for the New York *Daily News* through most of the 1940s, and afterward she became a columnist for the Los Angeles *Mirror*. Respect among her male peers was never an issue. She was aggressive in news gathering, often leaving male reporters chasing after her stories. Almost every evening Muir would cruise Sunset Strip and Hollywood Boulevard in her blue Cadillac, looking for stories. She frequented Ciro's, Musso and Frank's and the Macambo, sitting at her own table. On a warm summer night in 1949, while driving along Sunset just after midnight, she spotted one of her favorite sources: Mickey Cohen. Cohen was standing outside Sherry's nightclub following a late dinner, accompanied by henchmen Johnny Stompanato and Neddie Herbert. Muir stopped to chat with Cohen on the sidewalk. Moment's later members from a rival gang sprayed the group with gunfire. Herbert was mortally wounded and Cohen was clipped in the shoulder. Muir received a load of buckshot in the buttocks. Though bleeding, she rushed to a telephone, and reported the story to the *Mirror's* city desk.

No less colorful was Eleanor ("Pony") Garner, a rollicking, hard-drinking reporter for the *Times*. Garner was inventive in her reporting skills and out-of-control in her personal life. When a depression-haunted politician leaped from a high window at, Garner and a *Times* photographer were sent out. They arrived late and the competition had already left with pictures of the body under a blanket, which police had removed. Rather than face her editors empty-handed, she grabbed a hospital attendant to help her fill in her story and had him show her exactly how the body had been positioned. She then stole a hospital blanket, and waited for emergency room personnel to thin out a bit. She then lay down on the driveway and had the photographer shoot her under the blanket. Feeling guilty, Garner confessed to the staff artist at the paper that it was she under the blanket. "I know," the artist replied. "I had to airbrush out your high heels."

Garner was equally enthusiastic with her peers and the people on her beat. Armed with a pint of whisky, she once threw Will Fowler into her car and demanded sex. Fowler knocked her flat, dumped her at a streetcar stand and drove away in her own car. By then, Fowler was well acquainted with her reputation. In a brawl with a police officer, she had bit off his nipple.

For every Florabel Muir and Pony Garner, there were women staffers who served a steady diet of hard news, never flamboyant and always temperate in both reporting and writing. One of them was Marjorie Driscoll. A senior reporter at the *Examiner* since the 1920s, she quietly trained two generations of young men and women.

A graduate of Stanford University, Driscoll first worked for the San Francisco *Chronicle* on the rewrite desk. When President Warren G. Harding died suddenly in San Francisco, she assembled reporters' notes into a brilliant story. When William Randolph Hearst read the unsigned piece, he demanded that the publisher of the San Francisco *Examiner* hire the author on the spot. She signed on as a Hearst reporter and never left the company.

Slightly heavy, Driscoll liked to wear sensible shoes, nondescript cotton print dresses, and hats given to her each year by Louella Parsons. With her thick gray hair, her motherly appearance fit in well with her kind and gentle demeanor that made her a favorite of such hard-boiled newsmen as Jim Richardson and cubs such as Margaret Scott. She took care of her ailing mother in a modest home in Pasadena and rented extra rooms to young college men. She sold poetry regularly to the *Ladies' Home Journal*. Newsroom gossip had it that she never cashed her *Examiner* checks because she made an adequate living off her poetry earnings.

Driscoll shared the rewrite desk with Jim Murray, Joe Santley, Julian Hartt, and Hank Sutherland. "She was simply an oasis of serenity everywhere she went," recalled colleague Margaret Scott. "She was treated with the utmost respect by everybody on the desk. They spoke about her in reverential tones."

Scott recalled an assignment in August 1949 to accompany a baby being taken from Los Angeles to San Francisco to see its dying father. It was a gut-wrenching sob piece. Scott dictated the story to Driscoll on the rewrite desk. Driscoll wrote the story the way Scott *should* have written it. When Scott asked her how she had been able to convey such empathy and warmth, Driscoll simply said, "I've been there, I've seen it."

Scott benefited from the low-key mentoring from Driscoll, learning to compete against other aggressive newswomen. Born in Pennsylvania and adopted when a baby, Margaret Boutyette Scott was not yet twenty-one years old when she took a job at the *Examiner* in March 1945, at $18.50 a week. Unknown to Scott, her father, Stewart Cole, had arranged the job for her, although he disliked Hearst and yellow journalism. When she was promoted to apprentice reporter, Jim Richardson was merciless in needling her about her father, while giving her dull stories and obituaries. Scott endured the treatment for a couple of weeks. Richardson one day confronted Scott, kicked over a brass spittoon, and lashed into her about her father. Finally, he moved up close to her and said, "You didn't know did you? Your dad got you a job here!"

The young reporter weathered the hazing, excelling in writing breaking news stories from "the women's angle." Perhaps her biggest challenge was taking dictation from Louella Parsons, who often telephoned in her movie gossip column while rip-roaring drunk. The upper management policy was that Parsons' copy was never to be changed. Before her assignment, Scott would watch deskmen literally sweat as they took almost incoherent dictation from Parsons, knowing that not a single word could be changed. When Scott took a crack at the assignment, she was appalled with the poor quality of the copy. Finally managing editor Ray Van Ettisch wound up editing the column.

Scott had little confidence as a writer and was leery of other women reporters such as Pony Garner and Kendis Rochlen, who often bulldozed their way to get a story. Richardson, as demanding as he was, took a liking to Scott. He recognized a strong writer buried under her reserved demeanor. Once, when Scott had lost nearly all confidence, Richardson wrote a lengthy letter to her, detailing her strengths. Richardson prodded and cajoled her into recognizing that self-doubts among good writers were common, a sign that she had arrived as a competent scribe. Richardson's letter, however, wound up revealing that under the tough exterior of a city editor, he had the same insecurities as she.

"I seem sure of myself to others because in my job I must let others think I'm sure of myself," Richardson wrote. "If I didn't, where in the hell would I be? But Margaret, I'm really not sure of myself, away down within myself, either. I hate to use this trite phrasing but no one knows my faults and my insecurity more than I do." In Richardson's view, it was Scott's own doubts that made her a candidate to be an exceptional writer. And it was the recognition of those insecurities that gave him the strength to make nearly impossible demands on his reporters, many of whom performed well under the pressure.

Richardson's letter, written in December 1951, illustrates the changing relationship between city editor and reporter. Senior reporters on her beat had snubbed Agness Underwood, who had started her newspaper career in the 1920s. She came to learn her craft from Gertrude Price and a handful of other journalists. A generation later, Scott and other young reporters—male or female—benefited from the mentoring of a veteran editor who had been in the business for four decades.

Some women, though, rejected male mentors and excelled at their craft without their help. One of these mavericks was Kendis Rochlen who was hired at the *Mirror* as a reporter. She was bright, hard-edged, and tenacious, both in obtaining a story and in newsroom politics. Upon her arrival, editor Bud Lewis took an instant interest in her. He often sidled up to her desk while she was working, asking her about her boyfriends, especially whether she had sex with her dates. He peppered her with personal, if not lewd questions, leering at her all the while. Rochlen remained frozen during these encounters, hoping Lewis would lose interest in the conversation and move away.

Her timid reaction to Lewis—she tolerated the encounters because she feared losing her job—belied her journalistic achievements on a story. When she arrived on the scene of a public suicide, she found Tom Caton, a *Herald & Express* reporter with a ruthless attitude toward women, syndicating his story to other reporters. When Rochlen walked up to the group of newsmen, Caton, who was first on the scene, turned on his heels and asked everyone to follow him into a men's restroom for a debriefing. Rochlen stood outside the restroom for a brief moment, burst into the room to get her story. Caton looked at her angrily but continued to read his notes to his colleagues, including Rochlen. Fellow *Mirror* reporter Leo Batt recalled that *Mirror* city editor Hank Osborne had "complete and utter disrespect for her." But she was so deft in office politics that she angled for the best assignments for herself and ultimately obtained more power in the newsroom than Osborne.

To Batt, Rochlen was "the most ambitious reporter on staff. She wanted to be better than any man and woman. She had balls. Very thorough, wrote a good story. She thought everyone was the enemy. I learned to like her." Although she was competitive, her male counterparts appreciated her warm-hearted nature while she wasn't pursuing a story. On Saturdays, Will Fowler, who had left the *Examiner* to work for the *Herald & Express*, covered the sheriff's beat with Rochlen. They'd go on their rounds together, then Fowler would catch a nap on the pressroom couch while Rochlen made breakfast across the hall in the coroner's office. When he woke up they'd share a meal standing up at an embalming table.

Until the 1960s many women reporters were saddled with "women's angle" or sob stories. Others managed to secure coveted beats and assignments by simply turning down lesser stories. Sara Boynoff was perhaps the most popular reporter—man or woman—in the *Daily News* newsroom. Joining the paper in 1937, when she was twenty-three years old, Boynoff proved an able beat reporter and writer, earning a spot on the rewrite desk. She could be demanding, if not curt, with colleagues while handling their copy. She rarely allowed anyone to take advantage of her, much to the consternation of fellow rewrite man John Clarke. Boynoff shared the same shift with Clarke, who often complained about "the girl" under his breath. With a cigarette dangling from the corner of her mouth, Boynoff would fly through copy, plop it in the basket, and yell "boy!" to have a copyboy move it less than five feet to another desk. Clarke would watch this exercise throughout the day while muttering to himself about "the girl." If Boynoff heard his insults, she never let on. She joined KNX Radio when the *Daily News* died, then moved to the *Examiner*. Her career spanned fifty-two years before her retirement from the *Herald-Examiner* in 1989.

When the *Daily News* developed a science beat during the war, its most experienced candidate was Carol Phinney, who, by the time she joined the paper in 1942 was a journeyman reporter. Phinney was born Carol Tiegs in 1918 in Crystal Falls, Michigan. After graduating from the University of Southern California School of Journalism, she landed a job on a weekly. She soon moved to the San Francisco *Call-Bulletin*, where she reported for four years. When the *Daily News* sought reporters to take the place of men being drafted, Phinney was hired. She soon became the science editor and a member of the National Association of Science Writers. In August 1946, she married *Daily News* staffer Milt Phinney. Even after the births of three children, she stayed on the job and was considered one of the top science editors and writers in the state. Many of her stories dealt with the elderly. When the *Daily News* folded, she moved with Boynoff to the *Examiner*. Management there, however, didn't appreciate her science background (former *Daily News* staffer Chris Clausen won the job) and demanded that she write a series of articles on "working wives." It was a difficult, immensely unhappy experience. She died of cancer in August 1956.

IV.

This group of newsmen and women in late 1940s and early 1950s Los Angeles mirrored the mood of the city. The battle-scarred and competitive journalist was fodder for *film noir*. Reporters thrived on their romantic reputation built by Lee Tracy, icon of many Hollywood newspaper films, and by Hildy Johnson in "The Front Page." The thrill of a story excited them, often seeing themselves as a loose confederation of musketeers. While the postwar journalist was more sophisticated, the bloodlust of pursuing crime stories provided thrills not found in specialty or topical beats. Perhaps the single most telling event that would best represent the postwar Los Angeles newspaper reporter in both image and substance was the Black Dahlia murder case. The 1947 murder of twenty-two-year-old Elizabeth Short had all the ingredients of a mystery that would go down in the annals of Los Angeles history as its most sensational slaying ever. It featured a hard-bitten city editor who often played reporter; the mother of the victim who was fed lies so she would tell her daughter's life story; fistfights between competing newsmen; newspaper investigations that were more thorough than police work; stealing copy from a rival newspaper; and even a fair amount of drug abuse by some newsmen to stay awake during long hours.

It was a cool morning on 15 January, but the day promised to be muggy by the afternoon as *Examiner* reporter Will Fowler and photographer Felix Paegel were driving east on Venice Boulevard on the way back to the paper after an assignment. They had been complaining about their interview subject's being stingy with his booze. As Fowler and Paegel approached Crenshaw Boulevard, a police radio dispatcher crackled that a naked and drunk woman was laying in an empty lot one block east of Crenshaw, between 39th and Coliseum streets. The newsmen were only a few blocks away. They swung south on Crenshaw. The neighborhood was Leimert Park, where homes cost an average of $11,000, not a bad price in a city with an acute housing shortage. Each passing vacant lot along Crenshaw was marked off at thirty feet intervals for construction of retail stores. The body was found on Norton Avenue, east of Crenshaw between Coliseum and 39th Street.

Fowler and Paegel arrived before the police. The body of Elizabeth Short, who had been five feet, five inches tall and weighed 115 pounds when she was alive, had been sliced neatly in half. The body had been bisected and scrubbed clean elsewhere and dumped in the lot just a few feet from the sidewalk, probably during the early morning. The victim's right breast had been excised and the left breast had been sliced to the left of the nipple, exposing muscle tissue. Her mouth had been slashed. Fowler also noticed bruising around her neck, arms, and wrists, as if she had been bound then tortured. With no one at the scene except Paegel, Fowler had closed the young woman's half-opened eyes.

Right after Paegel had snapped two photos with his Speed Graphic, two patrolmen pulled up to the lot. After a tense moment when Fowler had to take a minute to convince the officers that he and Paegel were newsmen, the two were allowed to leave the scene. Fowler rushed to a nearby pay telephone and called Jim Richardson in the city room. As soon as Fowler said the victim had been cut in half, Richardson ordered him to bring in the photos to the newsroom without delay.

Richardson remembered the chain of events differently. In his autobiography, he recalled that police reporter Bill Zelinsky tipped him about the body. He then sent out "every" available reporter and photographer to the scene. Sid Hughes then called in. "It's a pip," Hughes said.

"Who is she?" Richardson asked.

"Don't know. Can't find a thing to identify her. Nothing on the body. Good looking gal."

"Pictures?"

"Plenty, but you can't print them. She's all cut up. Face and everything."

Richardson might very well have learned first from Zelinsky and Hughes the details of the homicide. But Fowler, recognizing he was on a big story, insisted to police investigators that the report reflect that he and Paegel arrived first. He also had Paegel shoot a photograph of him with the body before officers arrived to provide documentary evidence of his exclusive.

The *Examiner* had a phenomenal jump on the story, remaining far ahead of any of its rivals. Fowler and Paegel rushed into the newsroom. Paegel made a beeline for the photo lab, emerging a short while later with an 11X14-inch print of the body. Richardson then walked into managing editor Ray Van Ettisch's office. When he returned, he announced they would put out an extra to beat the afternoon editions of the *Herald & Express* and the *Daily News*. The afternoon shift was called in early and the race was on.

Fowler and Paegel returned to the empty lot to find bedlam. Dozens of uniformed and plainclothes policemen hovered around, as did the competition Dwiggins with the *Daily News*; Hughes and Zelinsky; and several *Times* men. Underwood chided Fowler for allowing the *Times* to beat him to the scene. When Fowler told Dwiggins that he had already seen the body and had left with photos, then returned, Dwiggins didn't believe him. An argument followed, then the two men traded a few punches. Fowler later described the incident as "noblesse in a rat pack." It was the press at its worst and perhaps at its most colorful best.

When the *Examiner's* extra hit the streets, two hours before the afternoon papers, it quickly sold out. The Black Dahlia story proved to be the second largest run in the newspaper's history, outsold only by the V-J Day extra in 1945.

Fowler, Hughes, Zelinsky, and county sheriff's beat reporter Howard Hertel fed their notes to rewrite man Wain Sutton. His lead in the 16 January editions had a staccato quality, which gave a brutally vivid picture of the killing:

"Slain by a fiend, the body of a teen-age girl was found in a vacant lot here yesterday.

"The nude body was severed at the waist.

"The girl had been killed elsewhere and her body taken to the lot and left in plain view, not three feet from the sidewalk.

Death came to the girl, police scientists said, after hours of torture."

Accompanying the story was Paegel's photo of the bisected body with a blanket airbrushed over it. The *Examiner* also had its artist, Howard Burke, draw a live likeness of the woman by using Paegel's photos of the corpse's face.

By late afternoon, the autopsy had been completed and the victim's fingerprints were sent airmail to the FBI, in Washington, D.C. Assistant managing editor Warden Woolard thought that perhaps the fingerprints could be transmitted by the *Examiner's* new Soundphoto machine. He had Richardson call Los Angeles police Captain Jack Donahoe, chief of the department's homicide bureau, who agreed it was worth a try since planes back east were grounded due to blizzard. At 4 a.m. on 16 January, the International News Photo wires opened, and the fingerprints were immediately transmitted. Washington bureau chief Ray Richards was waiting to scoop them up and give them to FBI agents. The prints, however, couldn't be read because they were blurred by the transmission. *Examiner* photographer Ray Lapp suggested the photos be reversed as negatives and then enlarged. Within minutes after the second transmission the FBI made identification. Elizabeth Short, originally from Massachusetts and whom most recently of Santa Barbara, once had once been employed as a PX operator at Camp Cooke near Lompoc and at the Naval Hospital in San Diego.

The competition was limping badly after the first day of coverage. On the afternoon of the 15th, the *Herald & Express* was already beaten by the *Examiner's* extra. It was too late for the paper to replate its afternoon and night editions. The murder story ran under a head about Water and Power commission salaries in the far left column. Underwood phoned in eight paragraphs of slim details. The *Daily News* in its ten-star night final edition did slightly better than the *Herald & Express* Under the headline, "YOUNG L.A. GIRL SLAIN; BODY SLASHED IN TWO, the *Daily News* ran a four-column photo of the crime scene with an arrow pointing to the body. On the right shoulder was a one-column story that provided a clear and sober account of the homicide.

Jack Smith was working the rewrite desk when Dwiggins called in his notes. Within a minute he was banging away on the typewriter: "The nude body of a young woman, neatly cut in two at the waist, was found early today on a vacant lot near Crenshaw and Exposition boulevards.' " When the first edition came out, Smith found that city editor Milt Phinney had put the word "beautiful" between "a" and "young." Phinney knew no more than Smith whether Elizabeth Short was beautiful, but all dead naked women were beautiful according to the journalistic standards of the day.

The *Times* didn't have the bloodlust of the *Examiner* or even the *Daily News* or the *Herald & Express*. Nor did it care to engage in an active investigation of the Black Dahlia murder. The *Times* remained a stuffy, conservative sheet under managing editor L.D. Hotchkiss, who himself was as strait-laced as any Iowa-born man could be. Loyal Durant Hotchkiss had served a stint as a deskman on the *Examiner* before joining the *Times* in 1922. He assumed the M.E. post in 1934 when Ralph Trueblood died. He exhibited little, if any, imagination or desire for sensational news coverage. He best personified the *Times'* tired and gray pages of the 1940s and well into the 1950s.

By the afternoon of the 16th, *Examiner* staffers were relieved when the afternoon papers hit the streets and the woman had not been identified. It gave them clear sailing to gather information for a full portrait. Fowler was sent to Santa Barbara to retrieve a booking photo of Short. In 1943, she had been sent home to Medford, Massachusetts, as a delinquent. Sid Hughes drove up to Camp Cooke and found some personal information about her in camp records, along with her mother's name, Phoebe May Short. Richardson then had rewrite man Wain Sutton find her mother. When Sutton found Phoebe Short's Medford telephone number, Richardson demanded that he get her on the phone and obtain as much information as possible about her daughter without telling her she was dead.

Jack Smith, left, Ruth Harvey, and Paul Weeks, all of the *Daily News*, in 1946 represented the new generation of postwar Los Angeles journalists. Smith would later become a columnist for the *Times*. Weeks was noted for his early civil rights reporting, most with the *Mirror* and the *Times*. (*Daily News* Collection/Special Collections, UCLA)

Sara Boynoff with the *Daily News* in 1948. She was a rare female news reporter in prewar Los Angeles and strong rewrite desker after the war. She later joined the *Examiner*. (*Daily News* Collection/Special Collections, UCLA)

Two pioneering journalists during the 1930s and '40s were Sparky Saldana and Carol Tiegs Phinney. Saldana was the first Mexican American to become an editor of a modern Los Angeles metropolitan daily. Phinney covered the science beat. (*Daily News* Collection/Special Collections, UCLA)

Roy Ringer of the *Daily News* in 1947. He was one of many *Daily News* reporters to exemplify the liberal leanings of the newspaper. (*Daily News* Collection/Special Collections, UCLA)

Pat O'Hara of the *Daily News* in 1946. He worked on the Chicago and New York papers before coming to Los Angeles. (*Daily News* Collection/Special Collections, UCLA)

Will Fowler in 1991. While working for the *Examiner* in January 1947, he was the first reporter on the scene of the Black Dahlia murder case. (courtesy Will Fowler)

The Black Dahlia murder case captivated Angelenos for months. Here, four people in a diner scan the front page of the *Herald & Express* for more news. (*Herald Examiner* Collection/Los Angeles Public Library)

Sutton was concerned the mother would start asking questions about why he was calling. Richardson suggested Sutton tell her that her daughter had won a beauty contest. The rewrite man got the woman on the phone and interviewed her about Elizabeth Short's childhood. Sitting across the rewrite desk was Jim Murray, wide-eyed at Sutton as he fired questions at the mother. In a moment Sutton was silent, then said, "Well, Mrs. Short, your daughter has won a beauty contest and we want to know all about her." Phoebe Short gave more details. After a lengthy interview, Sutton ran out of questions. He looked up at Richardson. "Do I have to tell her? She's so damn happy about the beauty contest."

"Tell her," Richardson said.

Sutton told her.

Incredibly, Mrs. Short remained on the line and gave further details. She also was desperate to hear details of the murder from Sutton.

It was a major scoop for the *Examiner*; not only leading with the identity of Elizabeth Short, but with a in-depth interview with the mother. The *Examiner* made the most of its role in the case, noting that it helped the FBI with the fingerprints. The editors even ran a photo of an FBI agent examining a set of fingerprints with Hearst Washington bureau staffer Jerome Butler.

Using information provided by Phoebe Short, *Examiner* reporters and photographers fanned out along the coast. Fowler in Santa Barbara; others to San Diego where it was learned that Short had left the city with a man named 'Red." Meanwhile, Richardson was tipped by an anonymous caller that Short had several personal albums that contained photos of herself and friends in a trunk. Reporters began checking bus and railway stations. Reporter Baker Conrad found her luggage at the Greyhound bus station in downtown Los Angeles.

At the station was not a trunk but a suitcase and some bags. Richardson called Detective Donahoe and offered the bags to him if he was willing to give the *Examiner* an exclusive as long as the luggage was opened in the newsroom. Donahoe agreed and police and reporters found a cache of photographs that depicted an Elizabeth Short in a fashion only found in a Raymond Chandler novel. On the front page of the 18 January editions, the *Examiner* ran a one-column photograph of Short in a two-piece bathing suit. Inside, was a striking photo of her seated at a table. Other photos included a friend who allowed Short to live with her for a short period and a photo of Elizabeth and her mother.

The other scoop, broken the day before the *Examiner* published its photos, had been made by the *Herald & Express*. Bevo Means scoured nightclubs and low-rent bars in Long Beach. He found several friends of Short's, who said the young woman had been dubbed "The Black Dahlia" because she favored black sheer dresses to complement her dark hair. The *Herald & Express* had a penchant for naming murder cases, including "The White Orchid" case or the "White

Flame Murder." It stood to reason it would claim rights to naming Short "The Black Dahlia." Before Means named the case, however, the *Herald & Express* already had struggled to give the case a name to make it sexy and attract readers. It initially named the murderer of Short the "werewolf" killer because the victim had been mutilated. Even after "Black Dahlia" proved a better name and was later picked up by the other papers, the *Herald & Express* awkwardly clung to both the "Black Dahlia" and "werewolf" monikers until it finally dropped "werewolf" altogether.

Most reporters from the downtown dailies stayed up a straight seventy-two hours tracking down leads. Don Dwiggins piloted his own plane to Victorville in San Bernardino County in search of a witness that ended up a wild goose chase. Fowler drove up and down the coast while Hughes, Gus Newman, and other *Examiner* reporters tracked down every lead in Los Angeles and the coastal cities in San Diego, Orange and Los Angeles counties. Fowler recalled fortifying himself with healthy doses of whisky. Nieson Himmel, with the *Herald & Express*, was more pragmatic. He chewed on Benzedrine for three days to stay awake.

Benzedrine, the 1940s version of amphetamine, was a standard pick-me-up for *Herald & Express* reporters on hot stories. The newspaper was hampered, especially during the Black Dahlia case, without a night shift. Himmel and other reporters were required to cover their own beats, and then resume their coverage of the Black Dahlia case after regular hours. By the time the story broke, many *Herald & Express* reporters already were freely using Benzedrine because they were required to be in the office early after near nightly drinking bouts that ran into the early morning hours. Benzedrine kept them on top of their game. Himmel's use of Benzedrine would later get him in trouble. Aggie Underwood once assigned him in January 1961 to buy some narcotics in Mexico to see if it could be done easily. Himmel purchased a quantity of Benzedrine, but federal customs agents arrested him when he tried to re-enter the U.S. from Mexicali. Himmel had spent a brief stint in jail and had to pay a fine.

The *Daily News*, meanwhile, was getting hammered. Compared to the dozen reporters dispatched by the *Examiner*, the *Daily News* could field only two. Roy Ringer was new on the job at the *Daily News* and had performed mostly office work. He wasn't known well by the police or rival reporters. The city desk decided to send Ringer over to the *Examiner* offices to steal their copy. At about 2:30 p.m. for three consecutive days, Ringer drove west on Pico from the *Daily News* offices, then north on Broadway past 12th Street to the *Examiner*. He got out of his car and casually walked up to the paper's composing room where he found several of the day's proofs of the Dahlia stories on spikes. He filched one copy each day and returned to the *Daily News* where they were rewritten. On the fourth day, Ringer walked up to the *Examiner* composing room and reached for a set of the day's proofs. Just as he was about to make his grab, a hand clamped down on his shoulder. "Nice try," a voice said from behind. Ringer turned around to face a smiling Richardson. "Don't do it again," said the city editor. Richardson then slapped Ringer on the back and sent him on his way.

It was no wonder that the competition gave in to such tactics, for the *Examiner* not only set the pace for day-to-day coverage, but it remained one step ahead of the police most of the time. Baker Conrad remembered a telegram in Short's luggage that had been sent to a Pacific Beach address, outside of San Diego on 7 January. Tommy Devlin, a seasoned hard-news reporter with striking snow-white hair and black, bushy eyebrows, found the recipients. The telegram was signed "Red," of Huntington Park, who had asked to pick her up at Pacific Beach and return her to Los Angeles on 8 January. Devlin found that Elvera French and her daughter, Dorothy, had taken in Short for a brief period. Dorothy, a cashier at an all-night movie theater, felt sorry for Short who had bought a movie ticket in order to spend the night there. On the 9th, Red had picked up Short and her luggage and took her away. The French women knew only that Red had stayed at a nearby motel before picking up Short. They gave Devlin a good description of the man. Devlin scoured nearly all of the motels in San Diego and Pacific Beach; finally finding a manager who said a man matching the description of Red had stayed at his motel. He had signed the register "Robert Manley" of Huntington Park. Devlin also obtained a license number of Manley's car.

Richardson had the police run the license plate and it came back with an Mountain View Avenue address in Huntington Park. Richardson sent Fowler out to the address. There, he flashed his sheriff's badge to Manley's wife, Harriet, and entered the house. While Fowler was interviewing Harriet Manley, Red called and told her that he was arriving at a fellow salesman's home in Eagle Rock the next night to pick up his own car before driving back to Huntington Park. A few minutes later Fowler left the Manley home with recently shot studio portraits of Manley, his wife and toddler son. Manley was unaware the press was on to him.

Manley, it turned out, was a twenty-five-year-old pipe and clamp salesman, married just fifteen months. The couple had a one-year-old son and owned a modest home in Huntington Park. *Examiner* reporters later found out that Manley had delivered Short to Los Angeles and was home the evening of the 9th. Later in the week he left for San Francisco on business with a fellow salesman.

Late on the 19 January, Fowler and photographer Ferde Olmo staked out the Eagle Rock home with police. At 10 p.m., Manley drove up. Police appeared just as he stepped out of the car. As he raised his arms, Olmo flashed photos. "I know why you're here," Manley told police, "but I didn't do it." While Manley was being handcuffed, Olmo shot a photograph that was published in the home editions on the front page. Wain Sutton took Fowler's notes and wrote the details of Manley's arrest. He also wrote of the details of the suspect's relationship to Short and his willingness to take a lie detector test. On the inside pages was a studio shot of Manley in uniform as an Army Air Force corporal and another glamour shot of Short. Typical of the *Examiner's* boasting, the newspaper carried a short sidebar chronicling its scoops of helping the FBI identify Short through fingerprints, interviewing Phoebe Short, and locating the dead woman's luggage. The story ran under a three-column photo of a police detective examining photos found in Short's luggage. The paper had a propensity of injecting itself in its stories by routinely running sidebars of its successes. One sidebar reported that Phoebe Short thanked the *Examiner* for helping the FBI identify her daughter. It was accompanied with a photo of Mrs. Short interviewed by Fowler.

Aggie Underwood followed in the afternoon *Herald & Express* with an interview with Manley, who gave a blow-by-blow account of his relationship with Short. Manley acknowledged that he had met Short in December, while on a business trip to San Diego where he picked her up on a street corner. He had a few chaste kisses with Short, but described the relationship as a "test" to "see if I loved my wife." Accompanying the Underwood interview were a series of photos of Manley. The lead photo featured Manley with detectives F.A. Brown and Ray Pinker, then a series of three mug shots of Manley during the interview. All were lighted harshly from a low angle with dark shadows in the background, giving the impression that the suspect was featured in a B movie.

Manley had the misfortune to be the last man to see Short alive before she met her killer. But he was only the story of the day. Police quickly dismissed him as a suspect when they verified that he had been home and later in San Francisco between 9 and 19 January. Not to be denied a good story, readers had to search the papers' inside pages to find that Manley was absolved of the killing. Only the *Daily News* led its front page with Manley's innocence. "Robert (Red) Manley was released 'with a clean bill of health' late today after police disproved the story of a witness that he had been seen with Elizabeth Short the day before her murder," the *Daily News* told its readers.

The Black Dahlia case became a rare story based on the victim's own records. Elizabeth Short's luggage contained dozens of photos, most of which were published over several days. A stack of letters, tied together with red ribbons, was given to Marjorie Driscoll, who fashioned a sob story. Published excerpts of the letters painted a portrait of a woman looking for love, but usually ended only with hurt. The most emotional letters had been written by Short to an army lieutenant but never mailed. She professed her devotion to him, but letters from him revealed he was less interested. Another army officer also rejected her despite her hopes for marriage. The letters were intimate and all the more poignant given the circumstances of her death. The *Examiner* published these details and the public's appetite was whetted for more.

By 25 January readers probably learned about all they could of the Black Dahlia. After Robert Manley was released from custody, the story began to lose steam. On 22 January, Richardson received a call at the city desk. A man on the phone first congratulated Richardson on the *Examiner's* coverage of the case, then observed that the paper had run out of fresh material. Richardson agreed, and the man suggested that he had new documents that would spice up the story: more photographs, an address book, and birth certificate. Before Richardson could think fast enough to keep the man on the phone, the caller hung up. Richardson was convinced that he had spoken to the Black Dahlia killer.

Two days later, Harry Morgan, the *Examiner*'s night city editor, called Richardson at home. The post office had intercepted a parcel addressed "To the Los Angeles *Examiner* and other papers." The parcel had been soaked in gasoline to make a fingerprint check impossible and it was addressed with lettering clipped from newspapers. In the parcel contained Short's address book, a newspaper clipping of the marriage of an Army Air Force officer to a woman whose name was scratched out, Short's birth certificate and more photos. *Examiner* editors and police believed the killer had mailed the parcel. Other than the manner in which the parcel was addressed, there was no new evidence or strong news value to the contents of the parcel. The phone book yielded few leads for the police.

The *Examiner*, of course, went full bore on the story, publishing photos of the parcel addressed in letters cut from newspaper clippings on the front page. Inside were more photographs of Short and a photo of her birth certificate. The *Herald & Express* published additional photos of men in uniform and one of Short accompanied by an unidentified man in civilian clothes. But within days the story again began to lose momentum and soon faded on from the front pages. Richardson, so convinced the killer had spoken to him, waited in vain for further contact. Although the police lifted partial fingerprints from the parcel, they were of little use.

Up until the Black Dahlia case no other Los Angeles homicide had so enraptured the public. Elizabeth Short had left a trail of heartbroken romances with a number of military officers. Her habit of wearing black clothing and dyeing her hair black had captured the imagination of readers who consumed every detail of her life until her disappearance. The media's role in the case had left the public with the indelible impression of the hard news reporter. Clearly, as evident on the inside pages of the *Examiner,* with its sidebars lauding its own journalistic performances, the image of the crusading, romantic news reporter dressed in a suit and wide-brimmed fedora became cemented in the minds of the city's residents. For better or worse, these jaded reporters had bent the rules, toyed with the emotions of the players involved in the story, and outright lied to get a scoop. It was their performance during a hectic single week in January 1947 that had polished their hard-bitten image. And generations of young reporters would follow their footsteps, many with the single image of Will Fowler, wearing a porkpie hat and a copy of the *Examiner* shoved in his jacket pocket, kneeling next to the body of a naked beautiful woman cut surgically in half.

Even the shelf life of the Black Dahlia case was limited. Two months after her death, another equally sensational case took over the front pages.

V.

George ("Bud") Rector Gollum was a twenty-one-year-old Navy veteran and pre-med student who desperately wanted to marry his girlfriend, Beulah Louise Overell, daughter of Walter and Beulah Overell of Flintridge. Walter Overell, sixty-two, had founded Overell Furniture Company before selling the business to establish the Washington Finance Company in Los Angeles. The mother, Beulah Overell, fifty-seven, had a blueblood background and was active in charities. Their seventeen-year-old daughter stood to inherit an estimated $600,000 if her parents should die.

Gollum and young Beulah were deeply in love. The son of an ex-police commissioner, Gollum was cocky and arrogant. He had served in the Navy during the war and won the Bronze Star for gallantry during the Leyte landings. Beulah Louise, however, could hardly be described as beautiful. Her full face matched her plump figure. She lived a pampered life of private lessons.

Just before midnight on 15 March 1947, Mr. and Mrs. Overell were killed when their yacht, the *Mary E*, exploded at its slip off B Street between Balboa peninsula and Balboa Island and sank in sixteen feet of water. Gollum and Beulah Louise had just stepped away from the boat to go out to eat. It was later determined the young lovers rigged the yacht with dynamite and set if off with a timer after beating to death the Overells with a ball peen hammer.

True to form, the *Examiner* was the first newspaper on the scene. Ben Reddick, a former *Examiner* staffer, was editor and publisher of the Newport-Balboa *Press* and remained as a correspondent for the *Examiner* while putting out his own newspaper. Reddick arrived first and shot pictures of the destroyed craft and fed his notes to the *Examiner* rewrite desk. Reddick's art ran on the front page of the 17 March editions with an eleven-paragraph story and another picture of the Overells taken during their twenty-fifth wedding anniversary celebration. On the same day, the *Times* ran its photos taken on Sunday morning and a more thorough report of the incident. The *Herald & Express* buried the story on page A-6, with a six-paragraph story while the *Daily News* ran its story on the front page. Neither of the afternoon papers carried art.

On Monday morning, the first day of coverage, Richardson called Will Fowler by radio, a new piece of equipment installed in the newspaper's cars and trucks. By then, all of the dailies were using two-way radios in their vehicles to co-ordinate coverage. On this morning, the radio would not serve Fowler well.

Richardson had asked him if he knew about the Overell case. Fowler, who hadn't looked at the morning edition, said "no." Richardson let loose a string of expletives before cutting himself off the air. He turned to Jim Murray sitting at the rewrite desk. Asking Murray the same question and Murray said "yes." Murray hadn't read the article either, but he knew that Richardson demanded that his reporters read the paper and he assumed the Overell story would be there. Richardson sent Murray and photographer Al Monteverde to Santa Ana to cover the story. Fowler would lose out on one of the biggest stories of the year because he failed to read the day's paper. But if Murray had his way he would have wanted Fowler on the story. Murray was a rewrite man and liked it fine on the desk. As it were, he spent 17 March through 6 October living in a hotel while covering one of the biggest murder cases of the decade.

Orange County law-enforcement authorities had released Gollum and Overell after a preliminary investigation. But just a day after the press set up camp in Newport Beach, police found thirty-one sticks of dynamite in the yacht's galley. It appeared to be the second set of dynamite that was supposed to explode in tandem with the first bundle. The dynamite had been wired to a clock and battery, but it failed to ignite because the bulkhead had separated the two sets of explosives.

Four days after the explosion, Gollum and Overell were arrested on suspicion of murder. For the next seven months nearly two-dozen newsmen and women made their home in Santa Ana as they covered the trial. The murder case had all the elements that made perfect newspaper fodder. Two young lovers—one a decorated war veteran and the other a young socialite—accused of plotting then carrying out a vicious murder of the young girl's parents because they didn't approve of their daughter's pending marriage. The parents had threatened to withhold Overell's inheritance.

The *Examiner* put the full weight of its considerable resources in their coverage of the trial, staffing it with six people. Maurice Mitchell, Buck Forbes, Hank Sutherland, and Dave Cicero soon joined Murray and photographer Monteverde. The *Times* sent five men to cover the story: Gene Sherman, Ray Graham, Frank Brown, Maury Godchaux, and Phil Bath. The Associated Press rotated five staffers during the trial with Charlie DeSoriac, George Lewin, Clete Roberts, Frank Frawley, and Harry Matosian. The afternoon papers could afford to send only a few reporters. Pat O'Hara and Dan Hoster represented the *Daily News*. The *Herald & Express* sent Bill Pigue and Ed Phillips, although Agness Underwood would cover the trial briefly, and ultimately scoop the morning papers with an exclusive jailhouse interview with Overell. The Hearst-owned International News Service sent Adela Rogers St. Johns to write lengthy observation pieces. The United Press received news reports from the *Daily News*.

As with any big story, stars would emerge from the reporting ranks for either cunning in getting a story or for being a city editor dupe. Jim Richardson who was notorious for stealing stories from his reporters, found an opportunity to upstage his staff covering the case. It would come at the expense of Murray, who really didn't seem to mind that his own editor had scooped him. He would later express amusement over it. While attending a court proceeding Murray had run into George Gallagher, who had been an assistant for state Attorney General Fred Howser. The Attorney General's office had stepped in to prosecute Gollum and Overell in Orange County Superior Court. Gallagher, a cigar-smoking Irishman never seen without his trademark derby, made friends easily and was always passing tips to reporters. In the hallway at the Santa Ana courthouse, Gallagher told Murray that the two lovers were passing notes to each other in jail. Although Murray had no clue of the contents of the letters, he understood them to be sexually explicit. "The letters from the boy were right out of the Marquis de Sade," Murray recalled later. Overell's letters were more reluctant, if not a little more embarrassed. Gollum had asked one of the jailers if he would pass a note to his girlfriend. The jailer agreed, but tipped off Orange County Sheriff Jim Musick, who had the letter photo stated then passed on to Overell. Soon the pair was passing letters almost daily with the jailer copying each one. Two boxes of letters ended up in Howser's office under lock and key.

But Murray suffered from a malady that many young reporters experience on a big story: a lapse in judgment. He did nothing with Gallagher's tip and he didn't pass it along to Richardson. Pat O'Hara was a little more enterprising. He told his city editor of the letters only to be advised to sit tight on it. O'Hara promptly forgot about it. Ben Reddick, however, wasn't sitting tight. The Gollum-Overell letters soon became the worst kept secret among the press corps. When Reddick got wind of it, he telephoned his old boss. Unaware that Murray already knew of the letters, Richardson decided to act on Reddick's information himself without telling any of the *Examiner* staffers covering the case. He telephoned Howser, who promised Richardson the letters but managed to put him off for three weeks. Finally, when Richardson was convinced the contents of the letters would be leaked to the competition, he pressured Howser into slipping him the material.

Virtually unheard of today, newspaper editors and reporters enjoyed an almost incestuous relationship with law-enforcement and politicians from the turn of the century well into the 1950s. Favors were routinely exchanged. Information was bargained. Secrets were kept. But few California politicians underestimated the power of the Los Angeles press, particularly the *Examiner* and its Hearst influences. And Jim Richardson was an extension of that influence. To anger Richardson was to anger Hearst. And to anger Hearst could mean a swift end to a political career. There is no evidence that Richardson strong-armed

Howser for the letters, but Richardson didn't have to employ such crude tactics. The *Examiner* was the only leverage the city editor really needed.

Howser agreed to leave a motel key at a designated place. The person who picked up the key was to go to the motel room and find copies of the letters tucked under a blanket on the bed. Rather than send Murray to do the job, Richardson dispatched Lloyd ("Emmy") Emerson, a veteran reporter on the district attorney's beat. Within hours, Emerson delivered a thick envelope to Richardson. The graphic nature of the letters, most from Gollum, even embarrassed Richardson. Overell's letters were more innocent, pledging her love and loyalty to Gollum.

Richardson decided to write the story himself. Ray Van Ettisch gave him a private room, a single copy editor, and assigned one Linotype operator to set the type. When Richardson was done, he wrote a lengthy story that took up most of the front page. To ensure that the *Times* didn't replace its late morning editions with the letters story, Richardson set up a decoy press run. It was common for the *Times* to station a man just outside the pressroom of the *Examiner*, as the *Examiner* did the same at the *Times* plant. The *Times* man would grab an early copy of the *Examiner* as it rolled off the press and rush it back to the *Times* newsroom. The rival newspaper's rewrite desk would then crib the competition's story for their editions. Richardson had a couple hundred dummy copies of the *Examiner* run off the press until he was sure the *Times* representative got his copy and left the building. He then had the pressroom replace the front page with his story. The opposition papers were stunned, not to mention extremely angry, when the story broke. Murray had no clue that Richardson had the letters until reading about it in his own paper. He had served as Richardson's unwitting smokescreen. Immediately, rival reporters dropped their coverage at the Newport Beach police station and at the courthouse to follow Murray around. His notes were stolen. A reporter was found under his motel bed. Strange clicks were heard on his telephone. Howser, who could be a master showman when necessary, held an impromptu press conference the day the *Examiner* broke the story and announced that the "*Examiner* reporter" must have rifled the safe belonging to the Attorney General's office. From then on rival reporters regarded Murray as their most serious threat. He also was regarded as Los Angeles' newest Richard Harding Davis.

The afternoon papers had been outgunned and outclassed by the *Examiner*. The *Herald & Express* rarely came to obtain any significant news. At times, in fact, the *Herald & Express* appeared more infatuated with its mobile radio communication system than with the young couple charged with murder. The week the story broke, radios were installed in the newspaper's cars. For two days, the paper gave breathless accounts of how reporters could now transmit their stories from the field directly to the city desk. When Aggie Underwood sent writer Caroline Walker to Santa Ana to write a color piece on the two lovers, she radioed in her story. Her story appeared under the dateline "ABOARD HERALD-EXPRESS MOBILE RADIOPHONE CAR, SANTA ANA" as if she was reporting from the South Pacific. For some time each story that was dictated over the radiophone was identified with a reverse bar "BY RADIOPHONE" followed with the long dateline. When Underwood scooped the competition with her jailhouse interview with Overell, she rushed out of the jail to the *Herald & Express* station wagon to phone in her notes, only to find the radio didn't work. She drove around Santa Ana frantically looking for a pay telephone to make deadline. She finally found one and made deadline with only minutes to spare. The *Daily News* was more dignified in its coverage, but offered hardly anything spectacular to its readers.

It did have Pat O'Hara, who could be amazingly resourceful when backed into a corner. O'Hara was an eccentric who addressed everyone as "Dahling" and carried himself as if he were a British officer out of uniform. He spoke with such eloquence that fellow reporters in the pressroom at the Federal Building loved to just hear him talk. Jim Murray recalled being mesmerized by his stories and elaborate use of the English language, only to be disappointed when he read his rather pedestrian copy in the *Daily News*.

O'Hara was a heavy drinker who chased his bourbon with Farmer's Mix, an odd concoction of alfalfa juice purchased at a health food bar. He firmly believed the juice would counteract the damage done to his body by the bourbon. He had begun his journalism career in 1922 when he joined the Chicago *American*. He had just married and had followed his wife to Chicago. He had no newspaper experience, but a friend encouraged him to apply for a job after another man was fired for drunkenness. The friend drew him a map of the city room to point him to the city desk. He got the job right away and never thought about another profession again. He later returned to New York and landed a job at the *Daily News*. He rarely felt guilty about lying or identifying himself as a police officer to get a story. When his marriage broke up he moved to California, taking a job with the Los Angeles *Daily News*.

O'Hara was all the *Daily News* could muster for the trial. He dutifully phoned in his story in time for the afternoon editions, then joined the judge for a drink in chambers or found a bar to drink away the night. When the verdicts were ready to be announced, fellow staffer Lee Goodman was sent to the courthouse with a photographer to help with the final stories. There would be an extraordinary crush of newsmen and women, and Goodman's job was to pass along information while O'Hara snagged a phone. When Goodman arrived, O'Hara was there to greet him and took him into the judge's chambers during a break for a drink.

The trial of Gollum and Overell lasted nineteen weeks. The prosecution amassed considerable evidence against the couple. Gollum had signed for a large quantity of dynamite at a desert store, using a phony name. But a handwriting expert testified it was the young man's signature (Gollum claimed he had bought the dynamite for Walter Overell). The jury also had been tainted. Murray broke a story in which a woman juror had claimed friends of the defendant beat her up. However, it was later revealed that she had been beaten by her boyfriend and tried to cover it up with a phony story. The jury heard testimony from 120 witnesses (the 100 sexually explicit letters between the couple were ruled inadmissible as evidence), but took only two days to deliberate. When the jury foreman read the verdict "Not Guilty" for Overell, reporters scrambled for the telephone banks in the courthouse hallway. Thousands of people standing outside the courthouse erupted into cheers. The jury blamed Walter Overell for his careless handling of the dynamite, dismissing evidence that he was beaten to death before the yacht was blasted.

Amid the pandemonium, O'Hara elbowed his way to one of the eight telephones and got the *Daily News* city desk on the line. He had completely forgotten about Goodman. Not knowing exactly what O'Hara wanted, Goodman stayed behind to listen for Bud Gollum's verdict. Minutes later another "Not Guilty" verdict was announced. Goodman recorded the details and briefly interviewed the lawyers before finding O'Hara still on the phone. But O'Hara never needed Goodman's notes. Between sentences fed to the rewrite desk, O'Hara paused and eavesdropped on other reporters' reports to their own city desks. He then calmly pirated their information, smoothly dictating to his own rewrite desk. Goodman returned to the courtroom to interview the jurors. But O'Hara was done for the day. He left with Gollum, Overell, and their attorneys to attend a victory party.

The Gollum-Overell case was a closing chapter for both Murray and O'Hara. Murray would soon leave daily beat reporting, taking a job with *Time* magazine in February 1948. Five years later, he was assigned to help establish *Sports Illustrated*. In 1961, he returned to news papering as a sports columnist for the Los Angeles *Times*. His hard-news beat reporting days were long behind him.

O'Hara never covered another big story. When the *Daily News* sank in a financial morass in 1954, O'Hara couldn't muster the enthusiasm to look for another one. At fifty-five, he was a beaten man. He seemed to have taken the death of his newspaper personally. He moved to the Oceano area and rattled around in a little shack. He poached deer and dug clams to feed himself but did little else. He disappeared one day. His body was found a month later, hanging from a tree.

Chapter Nine

Gangsters and Cops

I.

On a cool autumn morning in 1947, two husky well-dressed men in wide-brimmed hats moved through the lobby of Queen of Angels Hospital dragging a huge, floral wreath. They moved quickly past the information desk, struggled into the elevator, and rode to the sixth floor. After moving past a trio of steely-eyed nurses and a startled orderly, the two men found Room 604. Inside was a young mother sleeping soundly. She had just given birth two days before to a boy and she was dead tired. The men rested the wreath against the wall opposite the mother's bed and slipped away. Printed in bright lettering on a ribbon stretched across the wreath was "To My Pals, Sparky and Helen. Much Success. Your Pal, Mickey."

Mickey's pal was Sparky Saldana, the popular, mild-tempered night city editor of the *Daily News*. And Mickey was Mickey Cohen, the city's most notorious and most publicized gangster since the Chicago papers gave virtually edition-by-edition coverage of mobster Al Capone.

Mickey Cohen loved Los Angeles newspapermen and he especially loved the *Daily News*. And the feeling was mutual. Newsmen and women generally were on a first-name basis with the diminutive clotheshorse and killer. Every reporter who covered the cops and courts after World War II through 1960 had Mickey Cohen tales to tell. And most of them were true. Cohen believed that reporters could print anything they liked about him as long as his name was spelled right. The relationship between Cohen and his henchmen with newspaper reporters were just as incestuous as it was between the reporters and police officers.

The youngest child of four boys and two girls, Cohen was born in the Brownsville section of Brooklyn, New York, to Russian immigrant parents, Sam and Fannie. Sam died when Mickey was just a baby, and his mother moved the family to a rented house on North Breed Street in Boyle Heights in 1915 when Mickey was just a toddler. The family was close-knit and the children excelled in school. Only Mickey had a troubled school history, often being tardy or absent from school, and was audaciously defiant for a scrawny five-year-old. He learned the value of money quickly and was extraordinarily impatient to earn it. By the time he reached the age of ten, he was hustling daily for every dollar he made. He sold the *Evening Record* at Soto Street and Brooklyn Avenue and defended his territory from interlopers with his fists. When he wanted another street corner that was more lucrative, he would use violence—typical in those rough days when boys would hawk up to ten editions a day on the street—to get a better location. Eventually he won the prized corner at Seventh and Spring streets. Whenever extras were published, Cohen would bolt from the classroom and run down to the *Record* building and would fight for the first copies off the press because it meant a bigger payoff to be first on the street. When he wasn't hawking papers, he ran a craps game behind the *Record* building.

As a teenager, Cohen idolized the fighters at the Main Street gym, taking informal lessons from Fiedel La Barba and Newsboy Brown. When he was fifteen, he ran away to Cleveland to live with his brother, Harry, who had left California to start a family and manage a chain of drugstores. Cohen was hoping to establish himself as a featherweight prizefighter. In the late 1920s and early '30s he toured New York, Philadelphia, Chicago, Pittsburgh, San Francisco, and Los Angeles, fighting in the flyweight and featherweight classes. He mostly lost and was rarely invited for return matches. By 1933, after little more than four years in the ring, his fighting career was over and he found himself back in Los Angeles. That year also recorded his first arrest, in July, when he was taken into custody on suspicion of robbery. The charge was dropped and he was rebooked on a vagrancy charge. But the incident sparked a string of arrests for Cohen on a variety of felony and vagrancy charges. In 1934, he was given a two-year suspended sentence on an embezzlement charge out of Cleveland.

Details of Cohen's mob activity during much of the 1930s and early '40s are murky. But he rose steadily through the ranks, working as an enforcer to protect West Coast interests. By the late 1930s, his name started appearing regularly in the Los Angeles press because of his bookmaking operation. Between 1940 and 1946, he was arrested sixteen times on charges ranging from bookmaking to assault with a deadly weapon. The charges would be either dropped or he would be fined or serve brief stints in the county jail.

He was suspected of trying to murder bookie Bennie ("The Meatball") Gamson. He had been involved in a gunfight in his own office, in which mobster Max Shaman was shot to death. Cohen was charged with murder, but the shooting was ruled self-defense. Cohen's star rose dramatically in 1947, when Benjamin ("Bugsy") Siegel was killed in a hail of gunfire in the living room of his girlfriend's Beverly Hills mansion. Siegel's death couldn't have been timelier or more fortuitous for the publicity-hungry Cohen. Siegel was snide, churlish, and deadly. Reporters preferred to cover him from a distance. The dapper, five-foot, five-inch, 145-pound Cohen—who listed his occupation variously as pugilist, salesman, cafe owner, and bartender—was colorful, cooperative with reporters, and accessible.

Even when rival gangsters mounted a campaign to liquidate Cohen after Siegel's death, Cohen remained available to the press. In 1948, Jimmy ("The Weasel") Frattiano and two other gunmen burst into Cohen's Sunset Boulevard haberdashery, which was a front for his bookmaking operation, spraying bullets. They killed Cohen's henchman, Hookie Rothman, but Cohen, a compulsive hand-washer, was in the restroom washing up and escaped the attack.

Not long after the shooting, Jack Jones, then a journalism student at USC, approached Cohen for an interview for a fashion story for returning war veterans. Arriving at the haberdashery unannounced in his '34 Plymouth, Jones was confronted on the sidewalk in front of the business by a group of bodyguards dressed smartly in wide-brimmed hats and long narrow ties, the uniform of the day for gangsters. Jones yanked from his pocket a copy of the university's *Daily Trojan* and asked for an interview. The bodyguards ushered him into Cohen's business. Cohen asked Jones if he wanted a shot of bourbon and Jones, nervous and tongue-tied, replied that a drink would be fine. He took the glass in a shaking hand and gulped the bourbon down in a single take. Cohen then gave Jones a tour of his shop, displaying $20 shirts and neckties and $400 diamond cufflinks. Mike Howard, Cohen's business manager, insisted on seeing a copy of the story before it was published. Jones refused, and Cohen waved off Howard's demand. After the interview, Jones drove to the *Daily News* building and asked sports writer Cleve Hermann for a file photo from the newspaper's morgue. Hermann pulled a photo of an unshaven Cohen, who had just been released from jail. The story was published. A few weeks later, Jones returned to the haberdashery and showed the article to Cohen. The gangster looked at it briefly, didn't look particularly impressed, and said, "Yeah, kid, that's fine."

If anything the article showed that Cohen was human. It wasn't something any reporter would attempt with Siegel. Cohen further gained valuable publicity when the *Daily News* ran a nine-part series of articles on Cohen in July and August 1949. Authored by Saldana and John Clarke, the series purported to give an in-depth look at the mobster's life since childhood. Saldana capitalized on his cozy relationship with Cohen and the fact that he had written several *True Detective* magazine articles about him. The series was relatively soft on Cohen, tracing his life from his turbulent history in Boyle Heights to his prize-fighting career and petty criminal activity to his star status as Hollywood's most glamorous mobster. The series was light on sourcing, although it painted a rather colorful portrait of his Cleveland boxing days. Clarke and Saldana attempted to psychoanalyze Cohen about his need for attention and propensity to embellish his boxing career and status in the criminal underworld. The reporters went so far as to dig up his Cleveland boxing records to disprove Cohen's boast that he had participated in a bantamweight title bout. Yet the series glossed over Cohen's role in a series of gangland murders that had paved the way for his rise to power on the West Coast.

Investigating mob murders was never a strength among Los Angeles newspapers. But Cohen's public displays of strong-arm tactics and tantrums provided newsmen with a steady diet of sensational pictures, even accidentally, much to the joy of Cliff Dektar, who was working the graveyard shift for the *Mirror* as a cop reporter.

Dektar was making a routine stop at Hollywood Receiving Hospital when he heard a call on the police radio at 4:30 a.m. that a sergeant was needed at Hollywood and Vine. Dektar and a photographer raced to the intersection where they found Cohen with his hat in his hand waving at a police officer. Patrolman Tommy Hutton had cited Cohen for failure to go on a green light. Cohen had stopped at a newsstand to pick up a paper and didn't move his car fast enough. Cohen was in the middle of the street challenging Hutton to take off his badge and fight, and then offered his car and wife to him if Hutton won. The *Mirror* photographer snapped four pictures of the incident and rushed back to the newsroom in time for the 9 a.m. edition. The *Herald & Express*, which thrived on such sensational pictures, was left with nothing.

Since Siegel's death, Cohen's monthly income was estimated at $800,000. When the East Coast mob offered to "protect" Cohen for a cut of his profits, Cohen refused. It touched off the so-called "Sunset Wars" and ultimately Cohen was branded by the press as "Public Nuisance No. 1." Hookie Rothman was killed and the assassination attempt on Cohen was made outside Sherry's nightclub in July 1949 (when Florabel Muir was wounded in the buttocks). And Cohen's attorney, Samuel L. Rummel, was gunned down outside his Laurel Canyon home. A more spectacular attempt on Cohen's life occurred when thirty sticks of dynamite had exploded under his spacious home on Moreno Avenue, near the Brentwood Country Club. Cohen miraculously escaped unharmed but the blast left a crater twenty feet wide and every window on the block shattered. Still, he persevered, much to the delight of headline writers and reporters who sought $100 loans from him.

Where the police and rival gangsters failed, the federal government succeeded. In June 1951, Cohen was convicted of tax evasion and was sentenced to three years in prison. The day Cohen was to surrender, Paul Weeks, then with the *Daily News*, went out to the gangster's home and rode with Cohen in the back of a limousine into downtown Los Angeles to begin his stint in prison. Cohen told stories and joked a bit, feeling as comfortable with Weeks as with any of his confederates.

In September 1954, the Brentwood home went on the auction block to pay for back taxes. Weeks, who seemed to be on the Cohen beat for the moment, wrote a eulogy of the domicile in typical *Daily News* mawkish sarcasm:

"Ghosts of the Little Mobster's henchmen, Neddie Herbert and maybe Davey Ogul and Frank Niccoli, must have stirred forlornly in their desolate old haunts hereabouts last night.

"For on the bulletin board of the Federal Building for all to see was the notice that the beautiful house at 513 Moreno Ave. in Brentwood that Mickey Cohen built out of the profits of haberdashing and hoodlumism will go under the auctioneer's hammer at 11 a.m. tomorrow.

"The last vestige of reality with the Mickey Cohen legend will soon be absorbed into the respectable community.

"This was the house that the Mick built after he rose to the kingship of the Los Angeles underworld following the sudden departure from this vale of Bugsy Siegel one humid night in June of 1947. Bugsy had too much lead in his head to get up off a couch that night."

Cohen shrugged off such purple prose and his friendship always remained intact with reporters. But he often would complain about the treatment his friends received from the press. "If I see a guy a couple of times or go out socially with him, all of a sudden he becomes my 'henchman.' What the hell is a henchman, anyway?"

The press wrote off Cohen after the tax-evasion conviction. Weeks all but penned his obituary, noting that the "little racketeer" had been "fading away" for some time under the onslaught of attempted assassinations and police investigations, but the federal government "stopped him cold" with the tax charges. But Cohen survived and was released in 1955, returning to the media spotlight. His prison sentence, however, had slowed him down a bit. He still wore the wide snap-brimmed hats, although they were going out of style by the late 1950s, and dressed impeccably. He looked older, a little wearier, than when he was at the height of his power.

The Hearst press treated him as little more than a carnival sideshow. When a bookie was slain in a San Fernando Valley restaurant in 1959, Cohen was there eating linguini with his dog, Mickey Jr. The gangster was taken into custody on suspicion of murder. The *Examiner* allowed him to "tell his own story" about the shooting, in which he described with humor (he wasn't properly dressed for a murder and Mickey Jr. was wearing a bib to eat Linguini) his role as an innocent bystander. Cohen was never charged with the crime.

When the state Assembly rackets subcommittee issued a report that labeled Cohen a "mass killer," the gangster vehemently denied it to the *Herald & Express*. Coverage of Cohen never went beyond speculation that he was involved in gang killings. The press, particularly the *Examiner*, preferred to speculate about Cohen's love life. They chronicled his long line of girlfriends, from strippers Candy Barr and Beverly Hills to actress Liz Renay and model Sandra Hagen. At one point in 1959, Cohen was to star with Renay in a low-budget film about his life. It was never made.

In 1960, a federal grand jury indicted Cohen on thirteen counts of income tax evasion. He was convicted and the following year began serving an eleven-year prison sentence. He was released in 1972 and died four years later of stomach cancer.

II.

The coverage of Mickey Cohen during the late 1940s and through most of the '50s was a prelude to one of the most sensational slayings in modern Los Angeles history. Johnny Stompanato had been a bodyguard for Cohen off and on for the better part of a decade. The son of a small town barber, Stompanato was thirty-three years old in 1958, dark and handsome, standing five-foot, eleven inches tall and weighing 180 pounds. He loved breeding birds and had operated a pet shop at one time. He also sold cars and furniture. But Stompanato preferred to prey on wealthy women. When he wasn't involved in the mob, he made his living as a gigolo. He had a violent temper and when potential paramours rebuffed him, the unpredictable and temperamental playboy could be dangerous.

Stompanato had been dating actress Lana Turner for several months when their relationship began to deteriorate in late March 1958. Stompanato had followed Turner to England where she was filming a movie. Turner then met Stompanato in Acapulco where they vacationed together before returning to Los Angeles on 19 March. Stompanato, whose temper began to frighten Turner, lobbied heavily for the two of them to marry. He also appealed to Turner's fourteen-year-old daughter, Cheryl Crane, by taking her shopping and stopping at soda fountains for ice cream. He tried to present to Cheryl that he was an ideal candidate to be husband to Turner and father to Cheryl. But Stompanato's mood began to sour and arguments between him and Turner escalated after she refused to have him escort her to the Academy Awards presentation in March.

During one of their many arguments on the night of 4 April, Turner demanded that Stompanato leave her Beverly Hills home. He refused, following her into her bedroom. Crane had followed them, but her mother told her to go to her own bedroom. But Crane could still hear the couple arguing as Stompanato became more and more belligerent. Crane heard Stompanato tell Turner, "I'll get you if it takes a day, a week, or a year. I'll cut your face up. I'll stomp you. And if I can't do it myself, I'll find somebody who will." Then Stompanato promised Turner that he would "get Steve (Crane, Turner's second husband and father of Cheryl), Cheryl and you."

Frightened, Crane went downstairs to the kitchen and retrieved an eight-inch boning knife and walked up to her mother's bedroom. "You don't have to take that, mother," Crane said. Stompanato walked toward the girl as she raised the knife and plunged it into his abdomen. Stompanato crumpled to the floor and died almost instantly.

It was 9:25 p.m. Five minutes later Cheryl called her father, Stephen Crane, at his restaurant, the Luau, and begged him to come to the house. Turner called her mother. Stephen Crane arrived at the house at 9:45 and celebrity criminal defense attorney Jerry Giesler was called just before 10. It wasn't until 10:33 that police and an ambulance were summoned. At 2 a.m. Crane was booked on suspicion of murder.

The press got wind of the slaying almost as soon as the police and descended on the house. Rather than assign one of its veteran crime reporters to write the lead story, the *Examiner's* city desk had gossip columnist Louella Parsons lead the writing chores. Parsons often dictated her columns to the rewrite desk, and given her habit of dictating such stories when she had been drinking, it's unlikely that Parsons was able to gather the details of the slaying and write a lengthy detailed report. But what Parsons did know was the intimate details of the Stompanato-Turner relationship and how to obtain information from sources on a moment's notice. Her byline, in a startling comprehensive report, appeared in the lead story. It would be her story, whether or not she actually did the legwork and writing herself.

The elements of the slaying made for a perfect story for the Hearst press: A top-ranked Hollywood film star witnesses her teenage daughter stab to death a notorious mobster in her own bedroom. Crane was taken into custody and Turner was emotional and often hysterical in public—at least according to the papers. The *Examiner* focused on virtually every aspect of Turner's personal and professional career, and labored endlessly about Crane's troubled background, dating back to her birth when she needed blood transfusions to treat anemia. There was a tendency during coverage to treat Crane as a spoiled rich girl, but generally coverage of her ordeal was restrained. Stompanato's status as a victim almost seemed inconsequential. He was portrayed as a dangerous, unstable hoodlum, much to the dismay of his family. Carmine Stompanato complained to the *Examiner* that the press, which had failed to treat him with respect, was maligning his brother.

Mickey Cohen also was troubled with the way the press depicted his one-time bodyguard. Press reports of Stompanato's chasing Turner from London to Acapulco to Los Angeles and threatening her along the way disturbed Cohen. He didn't believe that Turner was as innocent as Parsons and the rest of the press had reported. Four days after Stompanato's death, Cohen released to the *Herald & Express* a batch of love letters from Turner to Stompanato that clearly showed that Turner was deeply infatuated with the mobster.

While Turner was in England filming "Another Time, Another Place," she wrote to her lover, who was still in California.

"I need to touch you—to feel your tenderness and your strength!" she wrote. "To hold you in my arms, so, so close—to cuddle you sweetly—and then to be completely smothered in your arms and kisses, oh so many kisses!"

The letters were not lewd or obscene, but clearly painted a different portrait of the relationship between Turner and the victim. The police, however, were less concerned about the contents of the letters or even that Cohen leaked them. Rather, they launched an investigation to determine how the letters were burglarized from Stompanato's apartment and whether any other items were taken. Police never determined whether evidence was stolen from the apartment. Beverly Hills police chief Clinton H. Anderson said the letters didn't change the facts of the case.

"No matter how many letters were found or what they contain, it doesn't alter the fact that the girl, Cheryl Crane, stabbed Stompanato. After all, the girl was unaware of the existence of these letters and she has told us that she learned of her mother's fear of death at Stompanato's hands and has told us that she stabbed Stompanato to protect her mother."

Unlike the Black Dahlia case, which remains unsolved, and the Overell murder case, which lasted nine months and continued to develop right up to its sensational acquittal, the press in the Turner-Crane-Stompanato case was deprived of a continuing story. The facts of the Stompanato killing became available almost immediately and remained almost unchanged with the exception of the release of Turner's love letters.

A coroner's inquest was held a week after the slaying and few fresh facts emerged, although Turner's testimony made for riveting reading in the papers. In the end, the killing was ruled justifiable homicide and Crane was released from custody.

III.

While the press thrived in its love affair with mobsters, its relationship with the Los Angeles Police Department had soured.

Reporters were loath to bite the hand that fed them. As previously noted, Prohibition brought police officers and reporters together. They shared alcohol, women, and loot from raids. Reporters were paid handsomely for their silence, and in many cases the payoffs kept them quiet about criminal activity, either by gangsters or police officers. Some reporters were part of the same criminal conspiracy. Once they accepted a bribe, they often were forever tied to the criminal underworld.

There were exceptions to this unwritten code of silence. The Los Angeles press had vigorously covered the cases of seven police officers charged with bribery and extortion of a bootlegger in 1929, but coverage in the 1930s of corrupt police officers was almost non-existent except for the routine crusades against municipal corruption—including the police department—by the *Evening Record*. Over two years, starting in 1930, there were more than seventy gang-related murders in the city, but the general public never knew the reporters' inside knowledge, if not complicity. The *Times* and the *Examiner* were so thrilled that the police department's Red Squad was controlling the city's radical fringe that the two papers ignored annoying instances of corruption and brutality.

City historians regard the infamous "Bloody Christmas" case of 1951, in which eight Los Angeles police officers were indicted on charges of beating seven young men, as the turning point in relations between police and press. The press coverage of the indictments and subsequent trials signaled an adversarial relationship that had gotten so ugly that it led to the formation of the police department's press relations department in 1956.

The foundation for the changed police-press relationship began as early as 1938, when the newly elected Mayor Fletcher Bowron cleaned house by retiring police department's top-ranking officials and hiring a new chief. Reporters still often turned a blind eye to corruption since many newsmen benefited from it in the form of favors and gifts. Roughing up prisoners was still a standard interrogating technique by police. Even some newsmen, schooled in police reporting from the Prohibition era, conducted their interviews with prisoners in the same fashion. Whether police misconduct was reported in the papers depended on whether an incident occurred in a public place and whether a law-enforcement agency or the grand jury conducted a probe. Reporting misconduct also depended on gravity of the offense, such as the death of prisoner.

The *Examiner* reported such a story in 1942 when a suspected drunk driver died as the result of a police beating at the Central station. Stanley H. Beebe was taken into custody on drunken driving charges on 19 December. During booking, police officer Compton Dixon had beat and kicked Beebe, who died ten days later of peritonitis caused by a ruptured gall bladder. A second suspected drunk driver, Thomas Coleman, also was beaten that night, but he survived.

A month later, after police brass and patrolmen had refused to cooperate with an inquiry, district attorney John Dockweiler urged a state legislative committee to investigate. An internal investigation followed in February, and Dixon was charged with murder and four other police officers charged with perjury stemming from their criminal grand jury testimony.

High-toned gangster Benjamin ("Bugsy") Siegel is slain in the Beverly Hills mansion of his girlfriend, Virginia Hill, in 1947. Reporter Paul Weeks, then new to Los Angeles journalism, was appalled as *Herald & Express* and *Examiner* reporters pawed through the mobster's belongings inside the home while police investigated. (*Herald Examiner* Collection/Los Angeles Public Library)

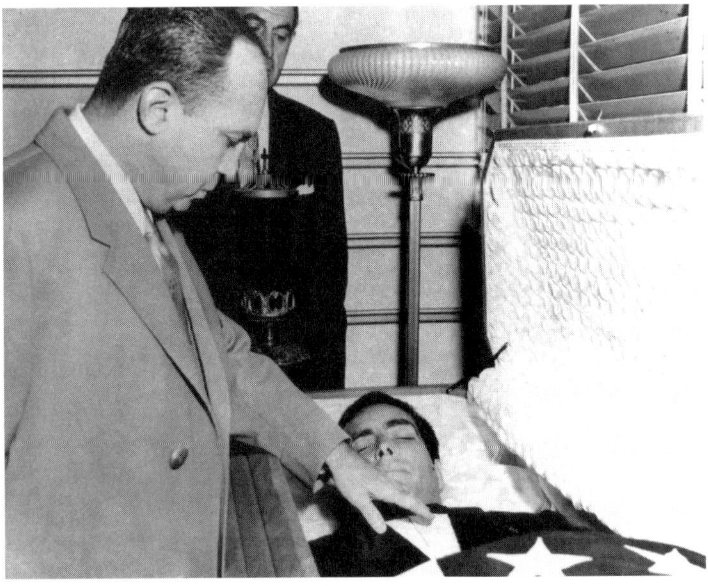

Gangster Mickey Cohen views the body of Johnny Stompanato at the funeral home of Godeau & Martinoni in 1958. Standing behind Cohen is funeral director Frank R. Palmieri. (*Herald Examiner* Collection/Los Angeles Public Library)

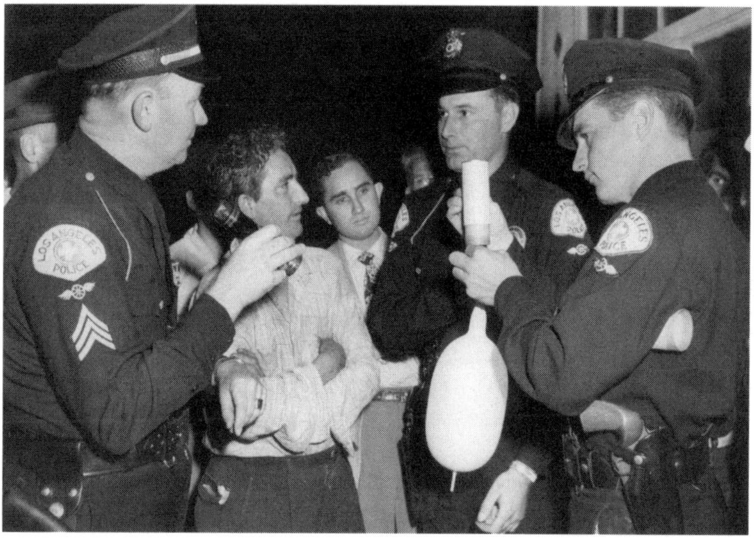

Los Angeles *Mirror* reporter Cliff Dektar, center, in March 1951, arrives on the scene of a drunk driving incident where police officers demonstrate a new device for measuring alcohol content of the driver, second from left. It was a era where police and reporters were close, if not very friendly, when working together. (courtesy Cliff Dektar)

The early 1950s marked a time when police officers and reporters worked hand-in-hand to sometimes get a dirty job done. Here reporters help law authorites retrieve a body from a ravine. Los Angeles *Times* reporter Art Wilcox is at right holding a flashlight. (courtesy Cliff Dektar)

Los Angeles *Examiner* city editor James H. Richardson holds court at the *Examiner* city desk at the height of his power in local journalism. Branded as the "last of the terrrible men," he was a newsman who inspired both fear and awe in his competitors and subordinates. (courtesy Margaret Richardson Kaplan)

James H. Richardson at the city desk in the *Examiner* newsroom in the early 1950s. (Courtesy Margaret Richardson Kaplan)

Dixon escaped conviction, but the incident at least heightened reporters' awareness of brutality cases. A similar incident made the front pages of the *Examiner* two years after the Beebe incident—on V-J Day—when two patrolmen pulled over an *Examiner* circulation employee for failing to yield to an ambulance. One of the patrolmen demanded the employee's draft card. When the employee said he burned the card when he heard that Japan had surrendered, the two officers beat him. They were charged with battery but never convicted. The Beebe and *Examiner* employee case, however, illustrated how reporters were selective about the brutality cases they covered. Police officers were not held accountable for beatings of minority Angelenos. And attacks on child killers and molesters also were ignored, as photographer Harry Watson learned.

Watson, a photographer for the *Daily News*, was summoned one night to the Hall of Justice to cover a story in which a suspected child molester would be available for photographs. Harry Hanson, a big ruddy-faced police sergeant, told newsmen they could come into a small conference room to photograph the suspect. As Watson entered the room, he saw a man sitting at a table with his face in his hands, saying over and over, "I know my rights, I know my rights." Suddenly, Hanson reached out and punched the man in the face, knocking him to the floor. He picked up the suspect and roughly pushed him back in his seat. News photographers began shooting as the man sat in the chair with blood dribbling down his chin. Back at the *Daily News*, an artist touched up the photograph to remove the blood from the man's chin. It never occurred to editors that it was inappropriate to "doctor" the photo.

Even if newsmen believed that the suspected child molester was entitled to his constitutional rights, none dared to cross Hanson. The sergeant once bragged to Watson of how he obtained "Third Street Bridge confessions." Whenever a suspect in a crime refused to cooperate with detectives, he would be taken to the Third Street Bridge and dangled over the edge to extract a confession. If the suspect still refused to cooperate, he was dropped to the concrete below.

Graft and corruption, on the other hand, were easier to report if a large number of police officers or high-profile criminals were involved. In April 1949, Hollywood vice officers raided a house of prostitution operated by the notorious madam Brenda Allen. As officers shut down the operation, Allen telephoned a sergeant of the vice squad, urging him to stop his men. But the raiding officers refused to talk with the sergeant and shut down the operation. The incident touched off one of the police department's biggest scandals since the Harry Raymond bombing. The scandal was exacerbated when some vice officers squabbled over who should collect Allen's bribe money to keep her business unmolested by police. In addition, the *Daily News* reported that wire recordings had been made of telephone conversations between a vice sergeant and Allen revealing a shakedown of Mickey Cohen for $5,000 to $25,000.

The city's five newspapers covered the Brenda Allen scandal almost daily after the county grand jury began its investigation in June, calling more than a dozen police officers, including Hollywood station brass. Police chief Clemence B. Horrall, Cohen, and a string of call girls also were placed on the grand jury's witness list. It was a story worthy of a Raymond Chandler yarn. Allen alleged she was "double-crossed" by Hollywood vice officers when she was arrested for attempted pandering after she tried to lure a female police officer into a prostitution ring. The vice officers who had raided Allen's home in April, suddenly found themselves suspended from duty on charges they used excessive force in a jailhouse beating the previous Christmas Eve. And two days after the start of the probe, a Baldwin Park garage was burglarized—while under guard by a district attorney's investigator—of six wire recordings of phone conversations between Allen and vice officers.

The press began to investigate the relationship between all the players, and found that Allen was once in a patrol car with a vice sergeant two years earlier when the officer gunned down an armed small-time hood during a robbery attempt. By mid-June Chief Horrall had been dragged into the picture. He told the grand jury that his office was already investigating Allen and the vice squad when the grand jury started its investigation. He alleged that Allen, Cohen, and "political enemies" of Fletcher Bowron "inspired" the probe in an attempt to discredit the police department. He was indicted by the grand jury for perjury, but was acquitted by a Superior Court judge following a trial in September.

The biggest blow came with an *Examiner* editorial published on 20 June. In typical *Examiner* fashion of using bold-face type and capital letters to drive home a point, it characterized the police department as a "super government" that operates "UNDER ITS OWN LAWS, ACTS AS ITS OWN JUDGE and generally is BEYOND THE READY OF ANY CONTROL short of prosecution in criminal courts."

The *Examiner* further alleged that Horrall had known for fourteen months about the wire recordings between Allen and vice officers, and that his office had failed to conclude an investigation of a state Crime Commission's charge that three police officers were involved in bookie payoffs. The newspaper also chided Horrall for operating a "kangaroo court" in which charges of misconduct against police officers by citizens were deemed secret and "not the public's interest." (The *Daily News* had reported that Hollywood vice officers conducted "back seat trials" in prowl cars for homosexuals, shaking them down for $50 before allowing them to go free.)

Horrall, his career in ruins, retired as police chief seven days after the *Examiner* editorial was published. He had served as the city's chief for eight years. Ultimately, four police officers were fired for their roles in the scandal.

While the Hollywood station struggled under the bad press, complaints of police brutality among Mexican Americans on the east side were growing louder. Horrall's replacement was W.A. Worton. He responded quickly to allegations that his officers were routinely beating youths during traffic stops. After less than a week on the job, Worton held a community meeting with social workers and civic leaders at the Hollenbeck station. Perhaps more out of curiosity of how the new police chief would conduct himself rather than genuine concern over excessive force, the press covered the meeting.

The *Examiner* reported that Worton promised to investigate all police-brutality claims. One resident told Worton that he needed to ride in her car instead of a prowl car to see the nightly instances of harassment. Worton replied that he would ride in an unmarked car to ferret out misconduct. After the meeting, Worton swung over to the Hollywood station in a show of support for the besieged officers.

Worton's promises were short-lived. By 1951, he was out of office and replaced by William H. Parker, a hard-drinking no-nonsense cop determined to end graft and to establish an aggressive police department that would stop crime before it happened. But Parker got off to a bad start with the press. *Daily News* editors found him insufferable and hated his excessive drinking (this coming from a newspaper management that allowed its librarians to sell drinks at 15 cents a glass out of a library file cabinet to editorial staffers).

But Parker quickly proved that he could take aggressive action against bad cops. On Christmas Eve 1951, two police officers, Julius L. Trojanowsky and Nelson L. Brownson tried to break up a raucous party at Max Kohn's Riverside Drive bar. When patrons refused to cooperate, a brawl broke out in the parking lot. One patrolman got a black eye and the other needed stitches for a cut on his forehead. A few hours later police swept through East Los Angeles and arrested seven young men. By the time they arrived at the Central station, about 100 police officers were having an rollicking Christmas party of their own. Word also leaked that one of the officers involved in the parking lot fight was going to lose an eye, which was untrue.

Leo Rodella, Manuel Hernandez, Edward Nora, Ray Marquez, and brothers Jack and Billie Wilson were booked at the jail, then lined up against a wall with Trojanowsky and Brownson for newspaper photographers. Daniel Rodella, however, was taken from his home to Elysian Park and beaten. He suffered a broken nose and other broken bones.

News photographers were unaware that Daniel Rodella had been taken to the park as they shot pictures of the remaining six men. In published photographs the next day, Trojanowsky and Brownson appeared to have been beaten. The six suspects had hardly a mark on them. *Daily News* photographer Harry Watson recalled that the men didn't look any different from when they had arrived at the station. After taking his shot, he stayed at the station watching police officers enjoy the party. Later in another room, he heard loud noises but couldn't tell whether people were being beaten or if someone was moving furniture. It was later revealed that the six men were being beaten over a 95-minute period. When the police were finished, blood covered the floor and walls.

Watson was subpoenaed to appear before the grand jury but could only testify of hearing noises from a room. He also testified that he saw police officers drinking from cups but couldn't be certain if it was alcohol. Watson never saw the victims after the beating. *Herald & Express* reporter Nieson Himmel did see the beatings, but he wasn't talking. He had seen enough police brutality and graft in his seven years on the cop beat to know that if he said anything about Bloody Christmas he could get hurt. When the grand jury subpoenaed him, Himmel was desperate for advice. He asked his city editor, Aggie Underwood, what to do, but she ignored him. Faced with the potential wrath of police officers he covered daily and expecting no support from his editor, Himmel lied to the grand jury about what he saw that night. He testified that he saw nothing

For all the publicity the incident garnered during the grand jury hearings and subsequent criminal trials, the media were extraordinarily slow to pick up the story. The next day, the press gave only the police version. "2 policemen beaten in bar brawl," reported the *Daily News*. "Gang Beating: 2 Officers Mauled by Youths in Bar," the *Herald & Express* reported. "Cops Gather 6 Who Fled After Ruckus," printed the *Mirror*. The *Times* reported, "Officers Beaten in Bar Brawl; Seven Men Jailed."

There was no coverage in the following days of the brutality. When the story finally broke weeks later, Parker was livid. He initially denied that his officers were guilty of wrongdoing. In a near identical repeat of statements made by Chief Horrall during the Brenda Allen scandal, Parker, too, accused critics of trying to discredit the police department. But this time he launched an investigation that involved interviews of more than 400 witnesses.

On 22 April 1952, eight police officers were indicted on felony assault charges. Parker immediately suspended Lieutenant Harry Fremont and officers Charles E. Minter, Robert Sanchez, William T. Bennett, Loren P. Colwell, Roy Lantz, William C. McCaffrey, and Charles D. Heinzelman.

Following trials during the summer, five officers—Lantz, Minter, McCaffrey, Heinzelman, and Colwell—were convicted of either felony or misdemeanor assault. The sentences ranged from one or two years in the county jail to a one-to-ten-year sentence in state prison for Minter, who had walked from jail cell to jail cell, beating each of the six victims. Fremont, Sanchez, and Bennett were acquitted. Fremont had been off-duty but was drunk. None of the victims identified him as striking them.

In all, Parker transferred fifty-four police officers to other assignments and suspended thirty-nine other men for their roles in the beatings. It was an impressive display of action to clean up the department that no doubt was in reaction to the negative press. But as shown so often in the past, the press failed to take the initiative and expose corruption and police brutality through its own investigation. Reporters relied on the department's own probe of Bloody Christmas and the subsequent grand jury investigation to tell the story.

The intense coverage of Bloody Christmas was simply another example of the new approach the local media were taking toward the department. It was increasingly clear that reporters, while still unwilling or unable to conduct true investigations of graft, corruption, and brutality, were not about to allow wrongdoing to go unnoticed. The *Daily News*, still burning to embarrass Parker in any way possible, had an unexpected gift present itself on one occasion. The paper decided that the days of touching up photographs of bloodied faces and sharing the booty of a raid were over. *Daily News* photographer Cliff Wesselman would help put an end to the coziness between the police and the press.

Wesselman was the newspaper's star veteran photographer. He was single and lived in a cluttered apartment. He lived for the paper and spent most of his nights, not at home, but cruising the streets listening to police chatter on the radio. One night, he heard of a call of shots fired in an alley. He arrived within minutes. Wesselman had developed a technique with his Speed Graphic probably taught to him by Sid Mautner, the top shooter for the old *Illustrated Daily News* in the 1920s. Wesselman often used a wide-angle lens. He shot from the hip in tight spots or when he wanted to be inconspicuous. He resisted the typical approach of shooting by lifting the camera to the eye so as not to draw attention to him. When he arrived at the alley, he spotted a man laying dead face down. He walked up to the scene and took a single shot from the hip, then turned around and left. No one was in the alley except two police officers that were too busy to notice him. A short while later, a Code Twenty was called, summoning the media to the crime scene. Wesselman turned his car around and returned. This time the alley was crawling with news photographers and police. Wesselman told no one that he had already shot the dead man, but simply took a second photo then left again.

When Wesselman developed his pictures at the *Daily News* plant, he was surprised to find the dead man clutching a gun in the second photo he took. The victim was unarmed in the first photo. Police officers had clearly planted the gun in the man's hand. *Daily News* editors ran both photos side by side on the front page. It was now open war between the police and the *Daily News*. A few days later, while Harry Watson was on assignment at the Highland Park police station, a police officer walked over to him and tried to move him into a remote area of the building. Watson braced himself for a beating but a reporter from a rival newspaper stepped in and rescued him. For many months, *Daily News* reporters and photographers sidestepped police officers whenever they found themselves alone with them.

The death of the *Daily News* did nothing to alter the worsening relationship. Press-police relations came to a head on 23 January 1956, when a Santa Fe Railway commuter train headed for San Diego hit a 15 mph curve at 70 mph and derailed just twelve minutes out of Union Station at the Los Angeles River.

The wreck was California's worst train accident. Thirty people had died, many of them ejected through car windows and smashed when the car rolled on top of them, and 131 were injured. The crash was horrific. Television crews scurried down embankments to the site. Film studios donated floodlights to help rescuers locate survivors. The Red Cross, the Salvation Army, and doctors and nurses assisted the living while deputy coroners sorted out the dead. One reporter arrived on the scene and explored the wreck alone. As he went from one side of the overturned car to the other, he was shocked to see rows and rows of sheet-covered bodies, some obviously children, stretched out alongside the tracks. A father and his seven-year old son, a young mother with a toddler son, and the young bride of a Marine were among the dead.

The old warhorse Marjorie Driscoll, still with the *Examiner*, pounded out in workman fashion on the rewrite desk the heartbreaking story of six-year-old Tommy Ferguson and his three-year-old sister, Cindy, who survived the crash but were orphaned when their parents were killed instantly.

Mirror reporter Ronnie Strobel wrote a first-person account of his experiences at the scene: "At first I saw no dead. Then I walked to the rear of the train, which lay on its side. There I stopped. They were human, but I had to look twice to be sure. The blood convinced me.

"Ten to 20 persons—women, children, men—had been thrown out of the shattered windows and ground into the ties and dirt of the right of way by the skidding cars."

The disaster was too massive for the police department to handle effectively. Chief Parker arrived on the scene, but he was too drunk to supervise and had to be held up by two aides. Looky-loos jammed Washington Boulevard, causing bumper-to-bumper jams. The swarms of newsmen, railway workers, civilians, rescue volunteers, and police hampered operations. Part of the problem was that there were too many reporters, photographers, and television cameramen. Los Angeles in 1956 was a four-newspaper town. Television reporters and cameramen were not much of a factor in day-to-day coverage but their numbers were increasing. Since World War II, press the police department and the Los Angeles County Sheriff's office had issued credentials. But it was an informal process in which anybody could apply for, and receive, a credential. In addition, most newsmen and women didn't bother displaying their credentials because everyone knew each other. The problem at the train wreck was there were too many people, very few of who were displaying credentials.

In such instances the coroner's office is in charge of the scene. Coroner's deputies had arrived late, but they immediately ordered all news reporters and photographers out of the area. Police officers lined up, and with their batons stretched horizontally in front of them, moved swiftly forward pushing back the press and spectators and rolling over anyone who fell down. One veteran officer spotted Harry Watson and joked that his brother, Coy, shooting for another news agency, "must be getting old because he didn't move as quickly as in the old days." Police lashed one reporter to a tree. Officers attacked a *Times* photographer, broke his camera, and then ejected him.

The next day, the managing editors of the four newspapers sent a stern warning to Parker: Never let it happen again or there would be a new police chief. The *Times* attacked Parker's handling of the disaster in an editorial. The City Council demanded an investigation.

It was a watershed event between the press and the police department. Parker conceded that his department was ill-equipped to control such disasters. In March, he appointed police Inspector Ed Walker, a nineteen-year veteran and trusted aide, to establish the department's press-relations office. According to the *Examiner*, the office would be "devoted to aiding harmonious relations between the Police Department and the press." Walker ordered changes in the Police Training Manual to "acquaint recruits with the activities of newspaper reporters." Joining the office later would be Lieutenant Dan Cooke, who would become the department's most visible officer to the public and most popular cop among newsmen until his retirement in 1988.

Chief Parker would emerge as the city's most progressive police chief. He stopped drinking and eliminated most of the corruption within the ranks of his department. His zeal to clean his department, however, did little to stem complaints from ethnic minorities, particularly African Americans, who harbored deep resentment and hatred of what they viewed as bigoted police officers. Parker had been so preoccupied with cleaning up his department that its relationship with the people it was supposed to protect suffered enormously. Prosecuting the officers involved in the Bloody Christmas incident, for example, was not followed up on the streets to improve community relations. Similarly, the press was not a vigilant watchdog to ensure brutality would be exposed. While the department earned a reputation for being the most honest police agency in the country, Parker's failure to also focus on mistreatment by his officers on Los Angeles residents would be the root of the department's ills for decades to come.

Chapter Ten

The Times' Bad Little Brother

I.

Since 1935, the *Times* had wanted to break into the afternoon field. Dummy papers had been created along with the strategy to break the tight grip of the *Herald & Express*, and, to some extent, of the *Daily News*.

World War II had put plans on hold, but Norman Chandler, who had taken over the *Times* upon the death of his father, Harry, in 1944, was eager to expand the empire. Whereas it was said that Harry had ruled Los Angeles like a king, Norman wanted to make his paper an institution.

The time seemed ripe after the war. Though at its strongest, the *Herald & Express* remained sensational and bawdy. The *Daily News* was showing signs of weakening, suffering from erratic management and thin resources. Manchester Boddy appeared more interested in other business ventures than running his newspaper. Associate publisher Robert Smith was bottom-line-oriented and less willing to champion liberal causes. The *Times* was not interested in capturing the Democratic audience but saw itself offering a product that stood between the *Daily News* and the *Herald & Express*.

But what made Los Angeles a good candidate for a new newspaper was its new image. Los Angeles of 1948 was a different city than the Los Angeles of 1935. The West Coast remained the Mecca for westward migration. Its population soared by forty-two percent since 1940. In 1948, the city ranked first in retail growth. Its major industries and employment centers—aircraft, automobile, apparel manufacturing, oil and petroleum production, motion pictures, food processing, rubber goods, and furniture and woodworking—guaranteed prosperity for the next two decades and beyond. Tourism meant $500 million a year in business and another $800 million was invested in new industrial plants. The city also ranked first in home construction.

J. Walter Thompson Co., a leading advertising agency hired by the *Times* to analyze the Los Angeles market, also noted demographics not found in other major population cities. Los Angeles possessed a young population. Young families and young single adults were potential readers. Even older families were relatively young compared to families in Chicago, New York, and St. Louis. There were few second or third generation native Angelenos. J. Walter Thompson also found that according to regional planning commission figures, 808,811 families lived within Los Angeles city limits. An estimated 315,449 of those families subscribed to the *Herald & Express* while 191,148 families purchased the evening editions of the *Daily News*. That left 302,214 families without an evening newspaper. Since 1935, four daily newspapers served the city. In 1948, their combined circulation was 984,114 to serve 1.9 million residents. By contrast New York boasted eight dailies to serve 3 million, while Boston had seven daily newspapers for 1.9 million residents. Chicago had four dailies for 3.4 million people. Given these impressive statistics, the *Times* saw a need for a new daily that would be designed to serve readers between the ages of fifteen and forty-five years old. It was to be a newspaper that was young, dynamic, and courageous.

In September 1946, construction of a ten-story, 150-foot building began at Second and Springs streets, adjoining the existing *Times* building. *Times* management leaked a rumor that the building was to house a television station. A little more than a year later, typography, design, price, the masthead, and even stationary, were implemented for the new publication. The tabloid was to be called the *Mirror,* in honor of a publication put out by Harry Chandler in the 19th century.

While the design of the *Mirror* was being polished and its various departments established, Norman Chandler named veteran United Press correspondent Virgil Pinkley as editor and publisher. Pinkley was an odd choice for the job. In fact, his selection would create some bumps in the road for the fledgling newspaper. He had virtually no metropolitan newspaper experience. It was rumored among staff that he had heavily lobbied Norman Chandler for the job when Chandler visited England in 1945. Chandler had studied the wildly popular English tabloids and wondered if a tabloid would work in his hometown. Pinkley was assigned to London at the time of his meeting with Chandler as UP's war correspondent.

Impressed with Pinkley's credentials and enthusiasm, Chandler kept the newsman in mind when it came time to select someone to helm the operation. A native of Nashville, Tennessee, Pinkley earned a journalism degree at USC before serving a brief stint on the San Bernardino *Sun and Telegram*. In 1929, he joined the UP. During the 1930s he shuttled between London, Rome, and Los Angeles in a variety of mostly management jobs. He was UP's European manager in 1943 and vice president in 1944. He established several bureaus in Europe before and during the war, covering such stories as the abdication of Edward VIII and the coronation of King George VI. He also scooped the other wire services with the only wartime exclusive interview with General Dwight D. Eisenhower.

Early in the war he had accompanied the Royal Air Force on seven bombing raids and was wounded in December 1941 in North Africa.

Pinkley arrived in Los Angeles in June 1948 at the age of forty-one, but the rumor mill was already churning. The Los Angeles-based *Fortnight* magazine had broken the news two months earlier. "Latest rumor to reach unbelieving *Times* ear (via the city room of the rival *Daily News*) was that a new afternoon paper would be forthcoming. *Times* men blandly let the rivals worry," the magazine reported. And to add a complication to Pinkley's duties there was talk of another new daily. The Los Angeles Independent Publishing Co., owned by Time-Life Inc., purchased seven weekly throwaway community newspapers in Santa Monica. Renamed the *Independent*, the papers had a combined circulation of about 90,000, although each paper would maintain its own identity in the community each paper covered. *Fortnight*, however, speculated that the company and its shareholders were planning to convert them into a daily. Their editorial staffing seemed too high-powered for a throwaway. James Parton, the executive editor, had been associated with *Fortune* magazine and had headed Time-Life's West Coast bureau before being assigned to the *Independent*. In addition, Charlie Judson, the *Daily News'* former city editor, was hired as managing editor. Hank Osborne, a former city editor with the Sacramento *Union*, also joined the staff.

The San Fernando Valley seemed to be the most promising territory for sales. The San Fernando *Valley Times*, had begun as a throwaway by Clinton McKinnon in the 1930s, then went daily in March 1946, serving North Hollywood, Van Nuys, Burbank, and San Fernando. Its circulation amounted to 35,000.

By early 1948, the "Valley" had become a hot market. The Valley's residents had spent $670 millions in 1947 and building permits for that year were valued at $100 million. Eight dailies and seven weeklies were trying to gain a foothold. The metropolitan dailies were selling about 75,000 copies a day there, and the Hollywood *Citizen-News* and *Valley Times* were selling 45,000 copies. The *Citizen-News* had bought the *Valley Journal*, and then killed it to create a zoned edition. The *Times* opened a bureau in May to serve the Burbank-Glendale area.

In August 1948, Norman Chandler finally announced that the *Mirror* would begin publishing in October. He released few details, saying only that the *Mirror's* editorial, business, advertising, and circulation departments would be housed in the new office building, but composing and presses would be shared with the *Times*.

The *Daily News* greeted the news with disinterest. Robert Smith told *Fortnight* that he was "not worried" about the new paper, though he acknowledged that his editorial writers were urged to become more liberal in their editorials. However, the paper dropped liberal Washington columnist Tom Stokes, who was promptly snatched by the *Mirror*. The *Daily News* was left with columnists Marquis Childs and Samuel Grafton.

J. Walter Thompson Co. initiated a billboard campaign in early September to create a buzz. Four weeks before publication, the teasers started with a woman presumably reading a newspaper (the billboard displays a woman with a startled look on her face with just a sliver of the top of newspaper in front of her) asking, "What will you SEE?" Another version displays a male reader. The following week the billboard answers, "You'll see pictures!" for the woman and "You'll see action!" for the man. The second week prior to publication, the teaser was heightened slightly to "Pictures galore!" and "Dynamic action!" to the couple, which at this point were almost giddy with anticipation. Finally, the last billboard erected just a week before the *Mirror's* appearance had friendly faces of the couple smiling down with the message "A new kind of newspaper." with the *Mirror* clearly visible in their hands.

Phone solicitors, meanwhile, called residents at random, offering a week's free subscription. Of about 20,000 people solicited, 8,000 were given the paper.

The *Mirror* was not a separate company from the *Times*. Rather, it was being funded by the sale of stocks and bonds and short-term loans. The building itself cost $5.8 million, and another $5 million was being used for payroll, equipment, and other related expenses. The *Mirror* occupied only the lower five floors of the ten-story building. The first floor consisted of the lobby, the classified advertising department, and, at the far side, a shipping concourse. In the front portion of the second floor was the mailroom. At the rear of the first and second floors was the pressroom. The third floor contained the editorial department, circulation offices on the fourth floor, and advertising and business offices on the fifth. There also were three underground levels for heating and air-conditioning equipment as well as storage and a carpenter and paint shop. The composing room was on the third floor and separated the editorial departments of the *Mirror* and the *Times*. On the top five floors were offices rented to the State of California. Some newspaper observers speculated that the *Times* had hoped to get an immediate partial return on its investment with tenants, and hedge against an untried newspaper that could indeed fail in less than five years.

In the beginning, the *Mirror* was a 5-column tabloid, which folded open into an 8-column front page, appearing every afternoon except Sunday. It sold for 5 cents a copy, compared to the 7 cents charged by its rivals, which had just raised their prices. Pictures would be accented with color. The stories would be terse, emphasizing the interests of women, youths, and sports fans. And, in defiance of the Los Angeles Publishers Association, it printed radio logs and features.

By late September, before the publication date was announced, advertisers had purchased a significant amount of space. Advertising had been bought strictly on the Times-Mirror Company's reputation since dummy pages were not available for review by local businesses. And no congratulatory advertising would be allowed. Pinkley told local retailers that he would rather wait a year and have "earned" the praise before accepting such ads.

The tabloid format raised eyebrows in a city that had little regard for mass transit. Harry Chandler was an aggressive advocate of the automobile, but son Norman ignored his father's vision of a sea of cars along vast highways throughout the region. Norman believed Los Angeles would grow like eastern cities. He had hoped to tap into the commuter market, but even the most oblivious resident could see that local commuters were a different animal than their counterparts in Chicago and New York where tabloids thrived. Los Angeles leaders had thrown their lot with the burgeoning freeway system. The Arroyo Seco Freeway was constructed in 1940 to connect Pasadena with downtown Los Angeles. The San Bernardino Freeway, or Interstate 10, would connect in six years the city with suburban areas east to Pomona, Ontario, and San Bernardino. The city's mass transit system, Pacific Electric's Red Cars, was in shaky condition. Pacific Electric generally operated at substantial losses. Between 1924 and 1941 it never made a profit, often recording losses of more than $2 million in a single year. Total annual passenger numbers dropped from a high of more than 109 million in 1924 to a low of 67 million in 1933. Ridership peaked at nearly 178 million in 1945, but it only recorded a profit of $356,264 for that year.

The industry press was heralding the *Mirror's* debut as a new newspaper war, closely watching the competitions' reaction. The *Daily News* began to tout its added features and the *Herald & Express* offered more photos. The week before the *Mirror* hit the streets; the *Herald & Express* published forty-five news pictures in a single edition, then forty-eight the following day. The *Daily News* averaged about thirty-two photos during the same period.

On Monday, 11 October 1948, at 8:21 a.m., as a television camera and five newsreel cameras were rolling, Pinkley pushed a red button and orange and black copies of the first issue started rolling off the press. About forty-five minutes later, the first issues hit downtown newsstands, quickly selling out. Trucks brought additional copies throughout the day, and the paper continued to sell at a quick pace.

At first-day ceremonies, Norman Chandler said, "Commencing tomorrow a new and differing newspaper will be published from these premises." Pinkley looked at Chandler and said, "Tomorrow he becomes my competitor." The ceremonies were typical Hollywood glitz. More than 500 people jammed into the *Times* auditorium to see Edgar Bergen and Charlie McCarthy perform. Actors Don Ameche and Marsha Hunt also attended along with Ray Noble's band, which played "Good News."

The 64-page newspaper was full of advertising. Major retailer I. Magnin & Co., had a two-column-by-ten-inch display ad on Page 5 and promised it would be there every Wednesday and Friday. The newspaper also carried full-page ads from Pontiac, Oldsmobile, Chevrolet, and Buick, all with full-page ads. Its front page was displayed horizontally for better display in the newsstands, but would be abandoned by December as readers resisted the awkward presentation.

The news content was breezy, if not brief and superficial. Its front-page lead asked: "How great is the danger of another war and how best can it be prevented?" It was addressed to such world leaders as Gov. Thomas E. Dewey, General Lucius Clay, and George Bernard Shaw among others. Inside, comics were spread throughout the paper (another irritant to readers who demanded and later received their comics clustered together). Use of color on the inside pages was extensive, but printing was poor due to inferior newsprint and the fact the presses had not been broken in. Classified advertising would not appear until five months after the paper was launched. And there were no complete stock reports.

Street and home sales hit 500,000 on that first day, but quickly settled down to about 100,000. The *Mirror* almost immediately found itself defending its operation. *Time* magazine reported that the *Mirror's* circulation had plummeted to below the 100,000 level guaranteed to advertisers. *Time* speculated that circulation had actually dropped to a low of between 35,000 and 75,000 (the story was incorrect, although circulation on Thanksgiving Day had dropped to 88,000). Pinkley reacted angrily, citing the report as "silly and farcical." He ordered an audit by Ernst & Ernst accounting firm, which reported the average daily circulation of the *Mirror* to be about 100,000 daily.

And two weeks after its first issue, its chief rival, the *Herald & Express*, ridiculed the *Mirror* over allegations of spying. It was a mean-spirited attack that illustrated the *Herald-Express'* anxiety over its new rival stealing readers. In its 25 October editions, the *Herald-Express* ran large photos of a *Mirror* copyboy picking up fresh copies of the Hearst paper in the *Herald & Express* pressroom. Over the photos were the headlines, "Photographs Bare Brazen Trick to Copy Herald News" and "Rough Stuff on *Mirror*phony." Standard procedure for any newspaper is to send staffers to competitors' pressrooms to take newspapers and phone in content and play to the city desk. In an era were scoops were measured in minutes and play often meant everything, this sort of tactic was part of the daily operation. But the *Herald & Express* claimed the *Mirror* copyboy was "sneaking" and "snatching" still-wet copies off their press, then stealing away at the nearby Hotel Georgia to phone in the details to the *Mirror* city desk. Apparently *Herald & Express* management had forgotten a similar ploy in 1930 when the old *Evening Express* made the same allegations of the then-*Herald* (a Hearst newspaper). In a story that probably was written by John Campbell, the *Herald & Express* labeled the *Mirror* as the "Charlie McCarthy of *Times* Square," and "the newborn infant that tries to walk like a man" was stealing news from its afternoon rival because it couldn't gather it on its own." Pinkley took the high road, thanking its

Les Wagner specialized in civil defense and smog issues for the Los Angeles *Mirror-News* in 1958. (courtesy author)

The Watson brothers were a pioneering brood of Los Angeles photojournalists. A Watson brother served stints on every Los Angeles daily newspaper from the 1920s into the 60s. From left: Coy Jr., Harry, Bill, Delmar, Garry, and Bobs. (courtesy Delmar Watson)

The Los Angeles *Times* building in 1935, on the southwest corner of First and Spring streets, before the addition of the *Mirror* annex. (Security Pacific Collection/ Los Angeles Public Library)

competitor for "devoting four-fifths of its front page to our new fast-on-its-feet newspaper."

Despite the brouhaha, the confrontation only served to spice up the circulation wars. Both papers benefited momentarily from increased street sales. But competitors were taking the new kid on the block seriously. They had made some changes in their operation, but it is difficult to tell whether these were modifications in response to the *Mirror* or simply standard upgrades. The *Examiner* by July 1949 completed construction of a new pressroom that included $4 million worth of new equipment. The *Herald & Express* redesigned its above-fold front page for better photo presentation.

The *Daily News* appeared to be at a loss on how to proceed. Manchester Boddy lamented competition not from his rivals but for readers' time. "Today there are many more components," Boddy told *Editor & Publisher*. "Picture magazines, night baseball and night football have entered the lists within the last few years. And now suppose you add an hour for television?" The *Times* was also feeling the glare of outside media. Managing editor L.D. Hotchkiss worried about accuracy and timeliness since radio provided accurate and instant news to Angelenos. Television, in particular, proved troublesome. Hotchkiss noted that watching political conventions through television was preferable than viewing it through the eyes of a print reporter.

II.

Editorially, the *Mirror* was far more liberal than the *Times*, although when political endorsements were announced the *Mirror* proved decidedly Republican. The *Times* political writer Kyle Palmer, who had been the newspaper's behind-the-scenes operator for more than thirty years, routinely influenced the *Mirror's* policies outlined on its editorial pages. Pinkley, however, took a more liberal approach in news content. "It must be warm, fair, accurate, impartial. It must give minorities a fair voice," he said. "In the *Mirror*, truth must dominate."

Pinkley wrote the paper's mission statement in his debut editorial:

1) Report news accurately, completely, fairly, and fast.
2) Tell both sides in covering political, economic and labor news, giving all the facts from which to judge.
3) Open the columns to give minority groups a fair hearing, regardless of religion or race or creed.
4) Keep the news columns free of editorial or personal opinion. News is facts, and must be dependable. Editorials are only opinion, which may be accepted or rejected.

In a city with a growing population of Jews, African Americans, Mexican Americans, and Asians, the *Mirror* kept its word and adhered to Los Angeles' working-class landscape. The paper, however, still struggled with credibility among liberal readers. It was a non-union paper trying to pass itself off as a publication for the blue-collar worker. And its political endorsements remained, for the most part; rigidly Republican up until it ceased publication.

Predictably, Pinkley chose managers who were United Press or USC alumni. J. Edward Murray, who would emerge as the single most important voice in the *Mirror*, was a veteran UP staffer. A graduate of the University of Nebraska, Murray joined the UP's Chicago bureau in 1938. Four years later he became one of the top war correspondents for the wire service, working out of London, Rome, and Paris. He was only thirty-three when he joined the *Mirror* as managing editor. Philip Ault, who was named assistant managing editor, had been the UP's London bureau chief. Clinton B. ("Pat") Conger, a former UP manager in Germany, was hired as sports editor. Les Wagner served nine years as a UP writer in Los Angeles and San Francisco. During the war he was a correspondent for the Office of War Information in India. He was at *Fortnight* a year before joining the *Mirror* staff. He first wrote the "*Mirror* Diary" column before specializing in rabies, civil defense, and smog issues.

From USC was sports writer Dean Cromwell, a USC track and field coach for nearly forty years. Not coincidentally, Ralph ("Casey") Shawhan became the *Mirror's* first city editor. Shawhan was a legendary distance runner at USC. He had worked as a police and general assignment reporter at the *Herald & Express* and *Examiner* before joining the *Mirror*. Rounding out the experienced staff were news editor Fred Shinney and chief photographer Andrew H. Arnott. *Times* political editor James Bassett also would join the staff as would Hank Osborne and *Times* man Bud Lewis, who would act as a troubleshooter for the Chandlers.

Joining these veterans were youngsters Kendis Rochlen, Charlie Erickson, Elaine St. Johns, Delmar Watson, novelist Jim Thompson, and Cliff Dektar who would write for the youth page. Dektar recalled a *Mirror* staff that was "very young and unfettered by tradition. Whereas the *Times* was stuffy, the *Mirror* was "more freewheeling." It was a staff that enjoyed wide latitude in enterprise reporting, generating a *esprit d' corps* not seen at the other papers.

Delmar Watson was the youngest member of the Watson brother's clan, which moved within press circles as news photographers. Delmar's uncle, George, had founded the Los Angeles Press Photographers Association. Delmar's brother Coy, as mentioned previously, had worked for the *Record* and the *Daily News*. Another brother, Billy, worked for the *Herald & Express*, and Harry, perhaps the most flamboyant of them all, worked for the *Daily News* and later pioneered television camera techniques for KTTV television. Delmar got his start working for Acme Newspictures in 1947, then moved to the *Mirror* when it was recruiting photographers. Even more so than the *Examiner* and the *Herald & Express*, photographers considered the *Mirror* a photographer's newspaper. *Mirror* management took to heart an Acme survey that determined the most popular photos published in American newspapers were in order (1) kids, (2) animals, and (3) kids and animals. Delmar Watson spent most of his time on the job shooting pictures of children sunbathing, playing ball, and then scouting out pet stores for puppy and kitten pictures. To Watson, nothing could attract readers more than weather shots of children playing in water.

For all of its photographic lightness and fluff, the *Mirror* was a serious-minded newspaper. Its aggressive coverage of issues startled even the most liberal *Times* staffers. It published a series on the life of Shaw, then would dive head first into issues facing Latinos and African Americans. The *Mirror* was a subscriber to New York *Post* editor James A. Wechsler's philosophy of selling news: Sex on page one, according to Wechsler, got the customer to buy the paper. Liberalism on the inside pages will make them buy it again. The *Mirror* loved to lace its pages with sex and scandal, but it refused to engage in partisan politics where it didn't belong. When Harry Truman fired General Douglas MacArthur during the Korean War, the *Times* and the *Herald & Express* were apoplectic, as if the firing was an affront to democracy. The *Mirror* played the story down the middle, never venturing or implying an opinion on its news pages. And it reveled in sensational stories that were nonetheless important to the working class. *Mirror* reporters investigated "B" girls, loan sharking, gambling, Communists on college campuses, black-market baby rackets, and even television repairmen who preyed on unsuspecting families by charging high prices to replace picture tubes that were in good working order.

Its biggest story would come early and it would take on one of the state's most powerful Republicans. William George Bonelli was larger than life in local politics. He manipulated the system so deftly that his opponents never knew what had hit them until long after he got what he wanted. Born in Kingman, Arizona, Bonelli long considered California his home state. He was an alumnus of USC and earned his law degree at Southwestern in 1924. Before he joined the faculty at Occidental College, he had lawyered in Los Angeles. He served on the Los Angeles City Council, then ran unsuccessfully for mayor in 1929, but was elected to the state Legislature in 1931. Seven years later Governor Frank Merriam named him to the powerful state Board of Equalization, which regulated state tax assessments and liquor licenses. Bonelli's district included all of Southern California. By 1953, he had been reelected four times, manipulating election laws by cross-filing and providing misinformation on his campaign statements. He also was the master of subtle smear campaigns. With the help of Kyle Palmer, Bonelli initiated a campaign against Ernest Debs during the 1950 general election that implied that Debs was a Socialist simply because his name was nearly identical to the controversial Socialist presidential candidate.

The *Times* continued to endorse him during every election, despite allegations that Bonelli had ties to organized crime. The Governor's Crime Commission in 1951 had failed to substantiate any of these charges but the rumors persisted.

Mirror reporter Art White had authored the "B" girl stories. During his investigation, he discovered that Bonelli was possibly receiving kickbacks while granting liquor licenses. He found a pattern of influence peddling in which liquor licenses were granted to shuttered businesses or fronts for known criminals, and then put on the black market to be sold at outrageous prices. White got permission from Murray to pursue the story. In a move that would portend of how Murray would run his newsroom, he decided not to tell Norman Chandler about the series.

The eight-part series began on 5 October 1953. It rocked local journalistic circles, which, up until the Bonelli piece, had an abysmal reputation as the city's watchdog. Not since the days of the *Evening Record* had a single newspaper gone out on a limb to expose corruption in high places. The *Mirror's* stories were all the more titillating because it was a newspaper owned by the old gray lady herself, the *Times*. The stories detailed the "bad trouble" brewing in Southern California. It cited a "sordid, sinister element operating within the confines of an otherwise legitimate business, the alcoholic beverages trade." By today's standards, the project was ripe with hyperbole, a fact that Chandler complained to Murray after the series ended. Yet it was a watershed moment for the young newspaper.

As expected, Bonelli was livid. But to Norman Chandler's credit, he refused to refute the series or discipline the editors involved. Even when the Board of Equalization later rejected an appeal a *Times'* on tax assessments of national advertising revenue, Chandler still refused to capitulate.

Bonelli sued the *Mirror* for $6 million, then recruited journalist Leo Katcher to ghost write a book on the Chandler family. Bonelli gave Katcher an unpublished manuscript on the *Times*, and then had Katcher fill in the holes. Ultimately, 20,000 copies of *Billion Dollar Blackjack*, mostly at Bonelli's expense, were published. Two years after the series was published, a criminal grand jury convened to indict Bonelli on violations of the state Election Code. But Bonelli had fled to Mexico. He never returned. In a twist of irony, a large park—Bonelli Regional Park—in San Dimas, in eastern Los Angeles County, had been named in his honor.

The series also resulted in some unexpected fallout. Just days after White's series was published, *Mirror* management found that Hollywood columnist Florabel Muir herself had sold a liquor license in much the same manner as Bonelli. Her exit from the newsroom was swift.

Murray enjoyed relative autonomy as managing editor during those early years, even with Bud Lewis shuttling between the *Times* and the *Mirror* to oversee operations and report back to Chandler. Lewis, however, was an editor not entirely respected by rank-and-file employees. He had his favorite reporters, whom he rewarded for their work, and punished the ones who didn't show him proper respect. What was important however was that Murray had the ear of Chandler. Lewis alternately praised and complained about what had become the *Times'* "bad little brother" as *Mirror* staffer Jim Bassett once called the paper. Lewis encouraged the paper's breezy style and suggested stunts to boost circulation. He introduced a contest to offer $5,000 to any reader who could solve any one of twenty unsolved murders. The competition was less imaginative. The *Herald & Express* had its $20,000 lucky names contest. The *Examiner* offered its "Who Am I" competition, and the *Daily News* provided readers a "Tic Tac Toe" game.

But Lewis occasionally complained to Chandler that it was *too* breezy, somewhat of an embarrassment to the *Times.* (*Time* magazine called it a "breezy, halter-and-shorts afternoon tabloid.") Lewis might have had a point. When actor Robert Mitchum was jailed on charges of possessing marijuana, the *Mirror* wrote a "confessional" that purported to be Mitchum's "own story" about the celebrated affair. The story, in fact, had been gleaned from routine reports in which Mitchum was interviewed by a probation officer. The *Mirror* defended its story, asserting that it never said the article was by Robert Mitchum. It boosted circulation by 10,000 for the day the story was published, but it also prompted snickers in newsrooms across town.

Murray and Pinkley worked together to iron out the kinks. It kept its fast and furious tone, never wavering from its mission to mix sex, scandal, and investigative pieces. It truly was an exciting paper when put alongside its competitors. In March 1949, just five months after its appearance, it recorded a circulation of 115,118, rising to 155,635 six months later. By September 1953, it reached 215,006, then 224,438 by the end of 1953. Ad lineage was healthy, too. The *Mirror* recorded 7,950,000 lines in its first full year of operation compared to the *Daily News,* which posted 10,261,000.

It was inevitable that the *Mirror* would sink into the red at first: an estimated $1.25 million during its first full year of operation. The Chicago *Sun*, by contrast, lost $6 million in 1948 and $2 million in 1949. This was after its merger with the tabloid *Times,* which lost $6 million in 1948 and $2 million in 1949. While not totally unexpected, some *Mirror* clerical staff hired to help with the extra work associated with a newspaper startup were laid off. Some editorial workers also lost their jobs. Thirty-five positions in the photography department were whittled down to fifteen after the first year.

The infant tabloid achieved better numbers than its competitors had expected, but not as well as *Times* management had hoped. The fact that management had to wait more than four years for the paper to break 200,000 circulation was frustrating.

Late in 1953, the *Mirror* conducted a poll about its appearance. Management found that while content ranked high on readers' list of appealing features, readers preferred in a 6-to-1 margin a broadsheet. In February 1954, the *Mirror* abandoned the tabloid and became an eight-column paper. The wishes of the reader were, in fact, only part of the reason for the dramatic change. Advertisers preferred a newspaper that allowed them to run full-size advertisements. The change boosted advertising revenue. Murray disliked the idea of a broadsheet, but *Times* management prevailed. Murray believed that by abandoning the tabloid—along with its brash style of journalism—it would make the *Mirror* nothing more than a junior version of the *Times*.

Changing the format also signaled Murray's waning autonomy. The whole operation had always made Norman Chandler nervous. *Times* reporter Carlton Williams, who had been an influential city hall reporter since 1938 and who had taken over the reins from the previous heavyweight *Times* reporter, Al Nathan, complained bitterly to Chandler about the *Mirror's* coverage of a controversial public-housing issue. Williams had a reputation for exerting immense influence on the Los Angeles City Council. His influence with Chandler was eroding by the mid-1950s, but for the time being, he still had the publisher's ear. Chandler began to question Murray about his coverage on public housing. Murray responded by gathering all of the *Mirror's* clippings on the issue. The clippings showed that the *Mirror* covered the story right down the middle. It was an example of objective journalism at its best, between the *Daily News'* pro-public housing position and the *Times'* stiff opposition.

There was a price to pay in the early 1950s for the *Mirror's* success. Newspaper circulation overall dropped by about 134,000, or 9 percent, since the *Mirror* first hit the streets. The *Daily News* was hit hard. At the end of *Mirror's* first full year, the *Daily News'* lost 42,265 readers. It was the beginning of a free-fall. In 1950 its circulation was 244,564, then dropped to 209,165 in 1951. In 1952, its daily circulation dropped below the 200,000 level at 189,181, despite starting a Sunday edition that garnered 220,000 readers. The consistently strong *Herald & Express* saw a startling decline that coincided with the *Mirror's* debut. Its circulation plummeted from 410,470 in 1948 to 358,921 the next year. It further dropped to 335,491 in 1950. It stabilized in 1951, and then fell like a rock in 1952 with 295,511 readers. The blame couldn't all be laid at the *Mirror's* feet. Skyrocketing newsprint ($100 in 1949; then a leap to $120.58 in 1952) meant a hike in advertising rates, not to mention the single copy sales hike, as already mentioned, in 1948 to 7 cents while the *Mirror* sold for 5 cents. The drop in circulation for the four dailies also probably supported Manchester Boddy's contention that the dailies were now not just competing for readers but for readers' time.

III.

Despite all these successes, the *Mirror's* leadership remained weak, as in the case of city editor Casey Shawhan who had impeccable credentials. His assistant city editor was Hank Osborne, who was brought over from the Los Angeles *Independent* when its metropolitan daily aspirations failed to materialize. Shawhan was immensely popular with his staff. But early in his tenure, the *Times* had given *Mirror* employees a survey on the operation of the paper. Editorial staffers were direct. Shawhan refused to take charge, and he couldn't say no to anyone.

What didn't appear on the survey was that Shawhan was also afraid of his assistant city editor. To some reporters, Osborne had fake credentials, a serious offense in any newsroom. Leo Batt recalled that Osborne had claimed to organize a team of reporters during his Chicago reporting days to handle a sensational child-murder case. The problem with fabricating war stories (and no newsman or woman was immune from the disease) is that there is usually someone in the newsroom that may be familiar with such stories. Not only did Batt make his bones in Chicago newspapering, he was intimate with crime reporting. He routinely covered gangland slayings in the 1930s, and once witnessed two police detectives dangle a gangster out of a second-story window to extract a confession. When Osborne boasted of his role in covering the child homicide, Batt checked with his former Chicago colleagues and found that Osborne had nothing to do with the story. The uncovered lie whipped through the *Mirror* newsroom and respect for Osborne in some quarters disappeared altogether. To add to the already tenuous relationship between Osborne and reporters, he was politicking with upper management. He also had a tendency to send several reporters to the same assignment, hoping that at least one will come back with a dynamite story.

On a June day one such newsgathering tactic to cover the news had tragic consequences. Osborne had decided to send a team of reporters to a train wreck that was about seventy miles east of Las Vegas near Tipton. Details of the derailment were sketchy but Osborne thought the accident included a coach train. The Associated Press sent a bulletin and advised a story would be forthcoming. The Las Vegas newspapers had pictures and were prepared to transmit them. A news editor suggested letting the wires handle the story, but Osborne insisted on sending a *Mirror* team. The team consisted of Batt, Earl Hazen, a *Mirror* reporter who had a pilot's license, photographer Bob Martin, and Harry Watson, the KTTV cameraman. It was 7 a.m. and the team was to have Hazen pilot his own airplane, a Cessna 170, to the crash site. Hazen had just finished a night shift on the cop beat and had worked twenty hours without sleep. At the Glendale airfield, Batt sat directly behind Hazen. Martin sat next to Batt in the rear. Watson sat in the front passenger seat. They flew to Bakersfield where they gassed up, then continued toward Las Vegas. During the flight Watson passed around a half-pint of whisky. Hazen refused but the other men drank some. Batt threw the empty bottle out of the plane over the desert, angering Hazen.

The story wasn't much. Batt immediately recognized from the air that the train had been carrying freight. But many residents of Tipton were watching the recovery operation from a short distance away. The plane landed and the team went to work. Watson shot about 600 feet of film. Batt decided to write a story about residents entertaining themselves by watching the action. When the four men got their story, they returned to the plane and took off heading east. Batt was sitting in the rear when he heard Watson say, "Earl, are we in trouble?" The plane hit a desert thermal—a vacuum—stalled and starting spinning toward the ground. Batt had no sensation because he could not see the horizon. Martin said "God, have mercy" moments before the craft slammed into the ground. Martin had curled up into a fetal position to help absorb the impact of the crash. Batt woke up to feel gasoline leaking onto his shoulder. Hazen was unconscious and bent over at the controls. Watson suffered four broken vertebrae and a double compound fracture of his left leg. Both ankles also were broken. Batt also had a broken vertebrae and a broken leg. Martin suffered severe torn muscles in his back, but walked three miles to find help. The men were moved to an ambulance. As Batt lay on a gurney, he turned to Hazen who was across from him on another gurney. Batt heard him take in his last breath before dying.

Watson, Martin, and Batt spent seventy-two days in the hospital, then an additional six months at home to recuperate. Howard Hughes, who always took a special interest in fliers, sent an orthopedic specialist to personally handle the trio's injuries on the condition that he receive no publicity for his kindness.

Watson, however, had had some tense history with Hughes. Just a few months before the crash, Watson was covering the county court beat when Hughes was scheduled to testify in a lawsuit. Hughes agreed to a brief photo opportunity with photographers, which lasted only a few seconds. Watson decided to stay behind and try to film Hughes when he entered the courtroom to begin his testimony. When Hughes entered, Watson fired up his lights and started the film rolling in his Bell & Howell camera. Hughes lost his temper and attacked Watson, wrestling the cameraman to the ground. The incident was captured on film. Later a Hughes aide tried to buy the film for $700, but Watson refused. KTTV staffers were ready to run the film on that evening's telecast, but Norman Chandler stepped in and demanded the film. The footage was never aired.

Watson told a Hughes aide shortly after the crash that Hughes should be told that although he was one of the crash victims, he also was the cameraman Hughes wrestled with just a few months prior. It didn't matter to Hughes, who only insisted that he received no publicity for offering the orthopedic surgeon or paying the medical bills.

The *Mirror* and KTTV honored his request.

By early 1954, upper management was losing confidence in Murray. Then, too, Pinkley, who rarely ventured into the newsroom, was being viewed by *Times* managers as an uninspired leader. Increasingly, Chandler, through Bud Lewis, was beginning to meddle in the newsgathering operations. In the end, this mixture of weakness and confusion would in the end damage, if not wreck, the *Mirror*.

Chapter Eleven

"So Long, Judas!"

I.

From the moment the *Mirror* hit the streets, speculation among newsmen was rampant that it was only a matter of time before the *Daily News* would die. Norman Chandler had denied from the onset that he intended to kill the Democratic paper with the *Mirror* as his weapon. And Robert Smith, associate publisher of the *Daily News* and later its editor and publisher, was outwardly indifferent to the *Mirror* encroaching on his readers.

Inevitably, both the *Daily News* and the *Herald & Express* saw their afternoon readers flock to the new *Mirror*. The *Daily News*, which as an independent paper never had the resources of the Hearst-owned *Herald & Express*, was indeed headed toward an agonizing death. After the paper folded on 18 December 1954, criticism was heaped on the Los Angeles Newspaper Guild for pushing owner Clinton McKinnon into a corner over a week's worth of back wages—about $16,000—held from the week of 14 March 1954 and due the week of 12 December.

The fact of the matter was that the *Daily News* had been in precarious financial condition since the day it began in 1923. The *Daily News* had made a profit in only thirteen years of its thirty-one-year life. The paper saw its first profit in 1929, under Manchester Boddy's management, then again in 1930. But it returned to the red next seven years. Between 1941 and 1948, the paper returned modest dividends to its stockholders. After the *Mirror* was in operation for one full year, the losses at the *Daily News* were staggering. In 1949, it lost $601,160. It was the beginning of the end. The bloodletting would continue for another five years.

II.

Manchester Boddy was beginning to lose his edge after World War II had ended. His acquisition of the *Post-Record*, the emergence of the *Evening News*, and the evolution of the twenty-four-hour operation had transformed Boddy's sick child into a strong voice in Los Angeles journalism.

As early as 1944, cracks in the foundation of the *Daily News* began to appear, signaling a ten-year slide into oblivion. Boddy had yearned for the fight. He tackled the bankrupt newspaper in 1926 because it was a challenge. He launched his crusades against vice and corruption and was threatened with arrest and jail. The economic disaster of the 1930s intrigued him on an intellectual level and he saw schemers and dreamers attempt to stamp out poverty with radical, if not hair-brained, solutions to create jobs. He had hoped that by giving news space to these odd economic plans, his readership would increase.

World War II solved the Depression. Corruption in the Los Angeles Police Department was minimized under the reformist mayor Fletcher Bowron. Boddy simply ran out of challenges. There was a time when he relished the idea of the city's establishment picking on his little paper. Now he was part of the establishment. He fully endorsed the New Deal. And although FDR often irritated him, he couldn't summon the energy to wage battles against an administration he threw his weight behind. And Smith had taken over the day-to-day operation, so internal struggles were largely left to someone else.

Midway through the war, Boddy began to stay away from the office. He had purchased 165 acres of wasteland in La Canada, a result of his days advocating the Land Chest movement in the early 1930s. He wanted to prove that with a modest beginning, one could make a living by working the land. The property was nothing more than live oaks and poison ivy. He cleared the poison ivy and planted camellias. In 1944, he tended to 650,000 camellia bushes in the semi-shade of the oak trees, now called the Descanso Gardens. He also produced meat, poultry, eggs, milk, vegetables, and fruits on the property. It was a commercial venture that earned him more income than his newspaper. But the result was he spent only two days a week, then one day a week, in his office at the *Daily News* building.

Despite Boddy's waning interest, Smith, in a promotional gambit for the paper, convinced Boddy to do radio spots twice a week commenting on the news and forecasting important events. Boddy hesitated, but finally agreed. By then, circulation started to climb again, hitting 217,000 in 1943.

Other events beyond the paper's control, however, conspired to weaken it. Newsprint rationing forced the paper to abandon classified advertising in April 1943, which resulted in a loss of more than $1 million a year even while newsprint prices were climbing after having remain static between 1940 and 1942, at $50 a ton. The cost of newsprint rose to $54.47 a ton in 1943, then to $60.25 at the end of the war.

When the war ended, mechanical problems with the presses prevented the paper from resuming classified advertising, although editorial and display advertising space increased. The *Daily News* didn't resume classified advertising until late 1949 when new Walter Scott press units and new Intertypes were installed in a pressroom annex opposite the plant. Newsprint shortages meanwhile plagued the *Daily News* throughout the late 1940s, prompting the paper at one point in May 1947 to refuse additional display advertising. The paper ran only sixteen pages during the week and twenty pages on Saturday so its readers would not have interrupted news service.

As the *Mirror* began to steal away *Daily News* readers by the hundreds, the situation worsened because of an alarming turnover rate in the newsroom. Chuck Chappell, James Felton, Charlie Judson, Sparky Saldana, and others moved in and out of the city desk spot at a dizzying pace. The paper, which often fired some employees plantwide in so-called "economy measures," brought out the ax again. This time fifty Los Angeles Newspaper Guild members were targeted. In January 1950, Smith announced that three morning editions would be discontinued effective 1 April. The decision, which would cost the paper 34,500 readers, abandoned the morning field to the *Times* and the *Examiner* and ended its prestigious position during the last ten years as a twenty-four-hour operation.

Publicly, the abandonment of the morning market was not an economy measure but a "long range" goal, according to Smith, to convert to a full-time afternoon operation and to attract larger advertisers who preferred the larger circulating *Times* and *Examiner*. He also wanted to intensify competition with the *Mirror* and the *Herald & Express*.

Privately, the morning editions were an expensive, money-losing operation. The morning editions had only 12,500 home subscribers and 22,000 in street sales. Smith pointed out with some pride that the *Daily News* had a circulation of 260,496 at the end of 1949, according to a survey conducted by the American Research Company. But the numbers were meaningless. An Audit Bureau of Circulations (ABC) review, the true barometer for circulation of daily newspapers, pegged circulation at 251,323, about 42,000 less readers than the previous year.

To accommodate the lost readers and the absence of the morning editions, Smith announced he was going to fire fifty Guildsmen, including several workers in the circulation department who had more than twenty years of service. Smith may have had some justification for trimming the staff. The *Daily News* had 117 editorial employees compared to 107 employed by the *Herald & Express*, which had about 108,000 more readers.

The Guild formed a strategy committee consisting of Ben Nathanson, Ralph Page, Lu Haas, and Lee Goodman to meet with executive editor Lee Payne and William Powell, the assistant general manager, in an attempt to ward off most of the layoffs. Smith refused to meet with the Guild committee. The Guild committee argued that by firing the fifty employees the workload would be shifted to other employees. Management wouldn't budge, and according to some committee members, Payne took on a patronizing and insulting tone by lecturing Guildsmen that he knew what was best to run the newspaper.

By the end of February, the Guild was pleading with Smith and Payne to postpone the layoffs until 29 April, to allow management to acquire some experience before gutting the staff. Guild members also wanted management to formulate a departmentwide seniority plan. Smith, instead, refused. He wanted a plantwide seniority agreement.

Meanwhile, *Fortnight* magazine reported that rising costs and diminishing returns had "plunged" the *Daily News* into debt of $600,000, which was borrowed from eastern investors to replace its "rickety" press, and that Boddy received an additional $100,000 from the Southern California Edison Company to remain afloat. The magazine also made much about the lost 34,500 readers when the morning editions were scraped. *Fortnight's* article led to bickering between Smith and Ben Nathanson. Smith had said his newspaper borrowed no money to purchase a high-speed Walter Scott press, but he also didn't say how the new press had been paid for. He also said that the *Daily News* decided not to end three morning editions but only two. And, in a stretch to put a positive spin on a dire situation, Smith claimed than an ABC audit showed a growth of more than 4,000 readers by 30 September 1949, minimizing the loss of morning readers. Smith made no mention of the serious losses in circulation since 1948. Smith also reminded *Fortnight* editors that fifty-three employees out of a total of 600 had been laid off while the Chicago *Sun-Times* dismissed 300 employees during the same month.

Smith's letter raised the hackles of Nathanson, who railed against Smith for not even participating in Guild meetings with management and overstating the number of total personnel employed the paper (there were 450 *Daily News* workers).

Petty squabbling between Smith and Nathanson did little to alter the paper's finances. And layoffs did not stem losses. For 1951, advertising revenue increased seven percent but circulation dropped twenty-four percent. In its income statement ending 31 December 1951, the *Daily News* showed a reduction in editorial and production expenses by nearly $458,000, including $27,000 in the editorial department and nearly $333,000 in cuts in newsprint and ink expenses. But the income from advertising and circulation sales fell by $543,000. In all, the *Daily News* recorded a net loss of $401,038. It was only slightly better than the $423,656 net loss from 1950.

The fallout from those revenue losses were efforts by Smith to trim expenses in 1951 by $225,000. That meant $175,000 in Guild departments and $50,000 in the executive payroll. The cuts resulted in the dismissal of thirty-three more employees.

Other Los Angeles newspapers also were suffering from rising production costs. The *Examiner* fired five editorial employees in September 1951 as part of an economy drive, while the *Herald & Express* slipped into the red for the first time. Their troubles were small compared to the *Daily News*, but it made for some jangled nerves in newsrooms across the city. The *Mirror*, of course, was still losing money but gaining circulation. The *Times* was the only paper to make money and keep its staff on the payroll because it had a lock on the city's major advertisers and its coffers were deep enough to sustain any losses for a short period of time.

III.

While Smith was battling with the Guild over layoffs, Boddy was preoccupied with different things. Boddy had always skirted the edge of active politics, priding himself on remaining aloof by observing political machinations at the state and national level from his "Views of the News" column.

In 1942, Los Angeles County Democratic leaders tried to draft him for chairman of the Democratic State Central Committee. Boddy refused. "I have never held political office and have consistently declined any major political appointment because I hold a firm conviction that politics, in the practical sense of the word, should be divorced as far as possible from the effort to produce a newspaper worthy of public confidence," Boddy said. Four years later he rejected pleas from Democratic Party leaders to run for U.S. Senate. But in 1950, Boddy's journalistic principles had changed. He was ready to run for the Senate.

Sheridan Downey, at the age of sixty-six, was a longtime liberal who had run for lieutenant government on Upton Sinclair's EPIC campaign ticket for governor. In 1938 he aligned himself with the controversial Ham 'N' Eggs movement and ran successfully for U.S. Senator. He was reelected in 1944, but antagonized liberal Democrats who were frustrated with his coziness with California oil companies and corporate farmers.

Congresswoman Helen Gahagan Douglas, a former stage actress who was highly popular in her largely African American district, decided to challenge Downey for his seat. But before the campaign got serious, Downey, who suffered from peptic ulcers, bowed out of the race. He tapped Boddy as his successor. In late March, with the primary scheduled just two months away, Boddy began his campaign.

Daily News editorial staffers regarded Boddy's bid for the Senate as heresy. Not only did Boddy appear to abandon his journalistic integrity, his campaign took on an increasingly conservative tone, which was contrary to the Democratic voice of the newspaper. Boddy, Douglas, and Republican congressman Richard M. Nixon cross-filed in the primary on both the Republican and Democratic tickets. Why Boddy decided to run for Senate was awkward to explain. Boddy himself never elaborated on his true feelings of running for public office other than to say it would be a "challenge" and he would meet interesting people. The *Daily News* had endorsed Douglas in past congressional elections. And she had supported Harry Truman's foreign policy and most of his domestic plans. Boddy's paper, too, stood solidly behind Truman and often lauded Douglas for her work.

Los Angeles newspaperman Robert C. Brownell observed in his profile of Boddy in *Frontier* magazine that the ultraconservative Democratic group who had controlled Downey distrusted Douglas and hoped to block her nomination on the Democratic ticket. The men who convinced Boddy to run against Douglas were state Democratic leaders Thomas Scully and John B. Elliott, wealthy oilman Edwin C. Pauley, Robert Smith, and Charlie Arnn, advertising director for the *Daily News*. Boddy received the endorsement of Fletcher Bowron, a Republican, but endorsements from labor groups were split. Douglas received strong support from CIO unions and some AFL locals, but Boddy won endorsements from the San Diego Central Labor Council and the AFL League for Political Education in San Diego. Perhaps his most important endorsements came from the McClatchy newspaper chain, which infuriated Douglas who had always received the chain's support.

It also was difficult for Douglas to lose the critical endorsement of the *Daily News*, but then to see her campaign virtually ignored on the news pages added insult. The *Times*, the *Examiner*, and the *Herald & Express* also ignored a much of her campaign. Only the *Mirror* seemed to be paying any attention to her.

Douglas had the edge, however, because Boddy entered the race late and his campaign was disorganized. It was soon evident that Boddy was all sizzle and no substance. Nearly sixty years old, Boddy was a handsome, if not debonair, man with his impeccable suits, silver hair, and an upright British-style mustache. He had an intellectual air about him and he was intrigued, as shown during the Depression, with economic issues and its effects on the workingman. He toured the state proposing public ownership of hydroelectric power plants and favored the controversial 160-acre limitations in the Central Valley. But he had no presence as a public speaker and his speeches often contained little depth. His charisma was minimal.

Times political editor Kyle Palmer thought of Boddy as a lightweight, writing, "Candidate Boddy is a late starter, but words flow from him easily, persuasively and endlessly. Ere long he will be in full cry and swing. He is a most agreeable gentleman and he will not run under some of the handicaps that Downey faced. Neither will he have many of the benefits and advantages which any incumbent enjoys."

In early May, Boddy suddenly switched tone, by giving Douglas the now-infamous label of the "Pink Lady." He implied that she was aligned with leftists, which was akin in 1950 to sleeping with Communists. Boddy then spoke of a group of "red hots" trying to gain control of the Democratic county committees. Other conservative Democrats picked up on the tone of Boddy's speeches. Soon

Douglas came to be linked to leftist congressman Vito Marcantonio who had voted against appropriations for the House on Un-American Activities Committee.

On 6 June, Douglas handily beat Boddy at the polls, winning a total of 889,000 votes from both tickets to Boddy's 532,000. Nixon tallied 1,060,000 votes. Boddy candidacy did exactly what party leaders feared. It split the Democratic Party and paved the way for Nixon to be California's newest U.S. Senator. The epithet "Pink Lady" dogged Douglas throughout her campaign. Nixon effectively used the smear after Douglas won in June. It was considered perhaps the single most important reason for her loss in the November election.

IV.

The election campaign only further distanced Boddy from the *Daily News* operation. He appeared bored with the paper, spending most all of his time either traveling or tending to his camellias. In February 1951, Boddy formalized what had been fact for so long. He had the board of directors name Robert Smith president of the *Daily News*. Boddy continued with the title of editor and publisher, and now chairman of the board. He owned eighty-nine percent of the stock in the Daily News Corporation, but he gave up his office to Smith and left for Descanso Gardens full-time.

The moves only paved the way for more dramatic, but inevitable changes. In August 1952, Boddy announced his retirement as publisher effective 1 September, almost exactly twenty-six years after he had taken over the moribund paper from Cornelius Vanderbilt's creditors. Smith was named publisher. Many longtime staffers were grief stricken over Boddy's absence and viewed Smith ascension to publisher as a bad sign. They had hoped Smith would find new financing for the paper, but it soon became apparent that none was forthcoming.

Looking for quick results, Smith made two moves within six months that revealed his impatience. In October he launched the *Sunday News* to compete against the Sunday editions published by the *Times* and the *Examiner*. The *Sunday News* replaced the money-losing Saturday edition (a bulldog edition of the *Sunday News* would appear on Saturday) and would sell for a dime. It would carry no colored comic sections, magazine supplements or advertising inserts. Rather, it contained "review and preview" of local, national, and international news for "serious minded readers who not only want the news but an interpretation of that news condensed for fast, easy reading."

The first issue totaled ninety-six pages and was crammed with advertising. Aaron Dudley was named Sunday editor, and Jack Jones and Jack Smith assisted him in editorial content. But the news hole was tiny, and the edition failed to deliver to readers what it promised. Nevertheless, a month after its appearance, Smith crowed about its success. In an advertisement published in *Fortnight*, Smith claimed the *Sunday News* had hit a circulation of 220,400 and management knew that it "had a hit" among readers. The Los Angeles *Guildsman* joined the *Daily News* in complimenting its new service to readers. It noted that the new edition was selling briskly, "a fact of some embarrassment to snipers recently sharp shooting in the *Sunday News'* direction."

But the Sunday edition never became profitable. In May 1953, Smith discontinued the *Sunday News*.

Meanwhile, the financial crisis of the paper worsened. Rumors surfaced almost weekly that the *Daily News* was ready to fold or that a buyer was poised to purchase it outright. Newsroom employees lived with the rumors, many refusing to speculate on the paper's future. It was as if a dear relative was dying in the next room, and no one in the family could bear to utter the words that death was imminent.

In February, while the *Sunday News* still had a chance to right the wobbly gait the *Daily News*, Smith hired William A. Townes, a noted newspaper "doctor" who had successfully revived several troubled daily newspapers. He was named to the newly created position of editor. Lee Payne remained as the executive editor.

The arrival of Townes only confirmed what *Daily News* competitors had been saying for nearly five years: the paper was in deep financial trouble. It also was a hopeful sign that Smith was serious about making the paper a viable operation.

Townes' reputation as a newspaper doctor was nationwide. He began his career at the age of fourteen on the Oklahoma (City) *News*, and then moved to the Cleveland *Press*, where he stayed for fifteen years. He served six years on the *Press'* city desk before moving to dailies in Seattle and Tacoma, shaking up newsrooms by banning gratuities and raising the bar of professionalism. Whatever paper he joined, circulation began to climb under his leadership. His biggest success came in 1948, when Ruth Finley, publisher of the Santa Rosa *Press Democrat* and its sister paper the *Evening Republican*, sought Townes to shake up her stagnate papers.

Townes, who had the manner of a Methodist minister, was barely thirty-eight years old at the time, but Finley was aware of the work he performed in Seattle and Tacoma. She gave her new general manager virtually complete control over the two newspapers. He gave the *Republican* a different makeup and renamed it the *Evening Press*. He pressured the executive editors of each paper to resign, and then fired the telegraph editor, who induced three fellow staffers walk out with him. Townes established an ambitious plan to create a regional evening newspaper to serve Mendocino, Lake, and Napa counties. A promotional campaign also was launched. In less than eighteen months the morning paper saw its circulation rise from 12,282 to nearly 16,000. The new *Evening Democrat's* success was even more impressive. Its circulation skyrocketed from 2,001 to 20,104.

With a record envied by every daily newspaper publisher in the country, Smith—through the urging of local Democratic leaders Ralph K. Davies and Samuel Mosher—lured Townes to Los Angeles to do for the *Daily News* what he had performed in Santa Rosa. Reporters were hoping Townes would help the paper return to Boddy's brand of personal journalism. He went to work at once, creating a horizontal layout, to make it tighter and easier to read. He dropped column rules on the inside pages and banned jumps. He adopted a folksy approach. His goal was to make the *Daily News* "a genuinely friendly paper, intimate with the people." He also launched an investigative series on drug addiction, and then demanded in editorials that police take action. When arrests followed, Townes congratulated his staffers. He was probably unaware, as a newcomer in town, that the *Mirror* had been publishing such stories for more than four years.

But Townes never had the opportunity to work his magic. After just twelve weeks on the job, Smith fired him. Townes posted a notice on the newsroom bulletin board that he was resigning due to a "difference in editorial policy" with Smith and Payne. Smith told the *Times* that Townes' resignation "was made in complete harmony after we talked over the situation."

Privately, however, Townes was frustrated with the second-guessing of Smith, Payne, and other managers. *Fortnight* reported that Townes had been hired to run the paper with a free hand, but quickly found that he "had a half-dozen bosses looking down his throat." Smith countered that he actually fired Townes but allowed him to resign gracefully. If anything, Townes' abrupt departure illustrated the hands-on management style of Smith, who unlike Boddy didn't necessary trust his editors to make the right decisions. Townes told *Newsweek* magazine that he felt he "was knocking my head against the wall. A newspaper must above all be a good product ... I soon found out that I could not make a good product out of the *News*." For one thing, he found the *Daily News* had many sacred cows. When Charlie Chaplin's "Limelight" had banned from U.S. theaters, management told him it wasn't news. Like with the *Sunday News*, Smith's new toy, William Townes, quickly bored him and Smith moved on to the next disaster.

Eight days after Townes' departure another ax fell on the paper. After consulting with Samuel Mosher, Smith switched the *Daily News* to a morning paper and cut fifty-five circulation employees from its roster of 145. Eight editorial employees, most of them newly hired, also were fired. By moving back to the morning field, the *Daily News* would publish fewer editions, deal with fewer traffic problems, and allow carriers more time to deliver the paper.

Meanwhile, Smith tried to drum up national advertising in the East. Smith, with Charlie Arnn and Hal Lindley flew to New York. The trio found accommodations at a four-star hotel, and then took out an advertisement in the New York *Times* and the *Herald-Tribune*, announcing they were calling on potential advertisers. They hit the luncheon circuit and attended every cocktail party possible. At a cocktail party at the Chatham Hotel, they presented a forty-five-minute promotional film on Los Angeles as a burgeoning market for New York advertisers. Spending money freely, if not lavishly, Smith, Arnn, and Lindley quickly drew the attention of advertising representatives. But the revenue never matched the initial enthusiasm.

V.

By the fall of 1953, the *Daily News* was losing $75,000 a month. Smith was desperate to find a buyer. New York *Post* Publisher Dorothy Schiff, James Roosevelt, Averell Harriman, and International Teamsters Union boss Dave Beck were all approached as potential buyers, but they each balked when they saw the books.

Smith finally found a buyer. Sheldon Fred Sackett was publisher of the Coos Bay (Oregon) *Times*, a 8,930-circulation newspaper that was netting Sackett $75,000 a year. An eccentric, Sackett had a reputation for moving through the Northwest buying up ailing newspapers and making them moneymakers. He also had a reputation for pie-in-the sky dreams that rattled his lawyers, who had quit representing him after thirteen tumultuous years. On 24 October, Smith and Sackett inked an agreement to buy the *Daily News* for $1,525,000. In hindsight, it was the best deal to come across Smith's desk.

The deal called for Sackett to pay $20,000 in cash, followed by a promissory note of $280,000, payable in thirty days with 4.5 percent interest. A note for $300,000 was payable on or before 31 December. A promissory note of $925,000 would be payable in thirty-six equal installments with the first installment due 1 February. To complete the agreement, Sackett was to deposit with Smith all the capital stock of his Oregon newspaper, valued at $1 million. To sweeten the pot, Sackett was to employ Smith as a part-time advisor for seven years at $25,000 a year.

But on 12 November, Smith canceled the contract, claiming that Sackett had failed to live up to its terms. Four days later, Sackett sued Smith for $5.6 million alleging breach of contract. Smith was never specific on what exactly Sackett had failed to deliver, but it appears he simply had changed his mind about the sale. He told *Time* magazine a week later "there is nothing wrong with the *Daily News* that more circulation wouldn't cure." Sackett told *Time*, "Mr. Smith accepted down payments, collateral and notes in the amount of $580,000, and secured by adequate collateral . . . Smith is now an employee of my corporation."

Sackett's posturing made little difference. Smith was already seeking another buyer. This time he hooked Clinton McKinnon, whose name would forever be linked to silencing the only liberal newspaper voice in Los Angeles. McKinnon was a bright young face in the eighty-first Congress. A Democrat, McKinnon enjoyed the full support of labor, joining the ranks of Helen Gahagan Douglas, Frank Havenner, and Chet Holifield, a potent California delegation. McKinnon favored public housing in San Diego, a hot topic in a city whose population had exploded because of the military and war-industry installations in the region. McKinnon also owned and published the San Diego *Journal*, which had experienced significant growth under the young congressman from a circulation of 34,869 in 1946 to 52,578 in 1950.

While Smith was embroiled in a spat with Sackett, state Democratic Party leaders and labor unionists lobbied McKinnon to take over the operation of the *Daily News*. Otherwise, McKinnon was told the paper would cease publication in December 1953. The creditors of the paper believed that from a tax standpoint it would be better for the paper to fold, but McKinnon hoped that it might remain alive for another six months while he secured additional financing.

McKinnon was well aware of the financial condition of the *Daily News*. At the time of his purchase on 24 December the paper was losing $125,000 a month, up $55,000 since October. But Smith assured McKinnon that he would receive the support of the business community. Smith even arranged a reception for McKinnon who was introduced to many of the city's powerbrokers and labor leaders. Smith also introduced McKinnon to the city's leading advertisers, who promised support.

McKinnon felt that he had been drafted for the job. No money exchanged hands with Smith. But the ailing child that passed from Boddy to Smith, and now from Smith to McKinnon, was in fact terminally ill, though Smith would make out reasonably well in the deal. He was to be paid $50,000 for services for the first year, then $25,000 each for the second and third years as an advisor. Smith, however, would act as an independent contractor and agreed under the terms of the contract to refrain from providing similar services to the other papers.

Using some of his own money, but mostly relying on unnamed investors in the East, McKinnon began pouring in cash, which ultimately amounted to $600,000, into the paper. In May, he devised a plan to keep the paper afloat by purchasing a profitable television station and making the publication a subsidiary. The station was earning $860,000 a year. McKinnon began arranging $2 million in financing to buy the station. He believed that by buying station he could save fifty-two percent in taxes. The savings would be diverted to the *Daily News*. The sale was approved on the condition that the station would not be obligated for any claims against the *Daily News*. The Los Angeles Newspaper Guild had $800,000 in claims in severance pay. McKinnon asked the Guild to give up the claim so he could buy the station. But Guild leaders hemmed and hawed over the request, stalling McKinnon. They didn't respond until October, when they rejected it. By then it was too late. The deal was rescinded and McKinnon was faced with finding financing through other means.

The *Daily News* was healthier under McKinnon than under Smith. McKinnon whittled the monthly losses down to about $20,000. Circulation climbed by about twenty percent, thanks to campaigns by local labor unions pushing subscriptions. Advertising revenue increased by about twenty-five percent. The lineage even surpassed the *Mirror*.

But McKinnon ran into the same brick wall as Smith. Prospective buyers took one look at the newspaper's books and shied away from any deal. A newspaper chain looked at the *Daily News* and immediately backed away. The *Times* was approached, but considered the $3 million price tag extravagant. McKinnon asked magazine publisher and radio station owner Robert Straus of New York to take out an option to buy the paper. But the deal failed when Straus couldn't find investors on the West Coast.

With Straus now out of the picture the noose around the *Daily News* began to tighten. On 10 December, George E. Hutchinson, administrative officer for the Los Angeles Newspaper Guild, sent a letter to McKinnon reminding him that a week's worth of pay deferred from 14 March was due the week of 12 December. McKinnon replied three days later that conditions beyond his control may prevent him from meeting the deadline. The next day McKinnon posted a notice in the city room announcing that he was unable to pay the deferred wages. That afternoon he called Albert Zugsmith, a newspaper broker, and pleaded with him to find a liberal who was willing to take over the paper.

Zugsmith was secretly representing the *Times'* interest, although Norman Chandler wasn't convinced that the *Daily News* was worth much money. McKinnon suspected that Zugsmith was representing either the *Times* or the Hearst chain and was not interested in selling to them. But he begged Zugsmith to find someone who would continue the *Daily News* tradition of an independent, liberal, and prolabor newspaper. Zugsmith was skeptical that any such buyer could be found. He later recalled that McKinnon had asked if "I have up my sleeve some new Dave Stern (publisher of the defunct Philadelphia *Record* and noted liberal) ... or some liberal fellow that was going to, in effect, subsidize the continued losses of this newspaper, and I was trying to explain to him that I had no such person up my sleeve."

McKinnon, it appeared to Zugsmith, was more interested in finding a liberal buyer than finding money to keep the newspaper afloat. When Zugsmith wouldn't give McKinnon the answer he was looking for, McKinnon immediately left for Washington, D.C., in a last-ditch effort to find a buyer. While McKinnon was looking for buyers, the Guild met and decided to hold a meeting to take a strike vote. The meeting was to be held on Monday, 21 December. A vote would be taken on whether or not to strike. But the Associated Press erroneously ran a bulletin that reported a strike vote had been taken. The dominoes began to fall. Union Bank & Trust Company of Los Angeles cut off credit to the *Daily News* immediately. It was a stunning blow, since the paper was now reduced to buying its newsprint for cash.

On Thursday, the sixteenth, McKinnon returned from Washington empty-handed. Zugsmith met with Norman Chandler and Norman's brother, Philip. Zugsmith suggested to the Chandlers that a corporation be formed to buy McKinnon's stock and certain notes worth $825,000 for $25,000 and buy other notes and stock worth $45,000 at face value. Times-Mirror would purchase from Stockholders Publishing Company, which owned the *Daily News*, $300,000 worth of notes for one-quarter their face value. The Chandlers rejected the plan, but authorized Zugsmith to tell McKinnon they were behind the negotiations. By Friday, the Chandlers had an offer for McKinnon: purchase the name, subscription lists, and goodwill of the *Daily News* for $165,000. The Chandlers were prepared to go higher if McKinnon put up a fuss. The hook was that the *Times* insisted that McKinnon would be required to join the *Mirror* as an advisor (at $25,000 a year under a five-year contract) if it bought the *Daily News*. Norman and Philip Chandler were uncomfortable with the politics of the *Daily News*, but they now wanted to attract liberal readers to the *Mirror*, a Republican paper.

At noon on Friday, McKinnon, John Shahan, his personal assistant and circulation manager, Arthur Desser, his lawyer; Zugsmith, his assistant Arthur Hogan, and the Chandler brothers met to negotiate the sale at Desser's office in Beverly Hills. McKinnon started the meeting complaining about his inability to find investors or a buyer. He also complained about his failed attempt to buy the television station that could help save the paper. The Chandlers listened, and then started discussing McKinnon's salary as soon as the *Mirror* and *Daily News* merged.

While McKinnon and the Chandlers were meeting, the Guild called an emergency meeting to form a committee to save the paper. Veteran political writer Les Claypool headed the special unit and asked McKinnon to attend. When McKinnon and the Chandlers broke for dinner, McKinnon returned to the newspaper plant and met with the committee. McKinnon, not divulging the details of his negotiations with the Chandlers, was not encouraging to Claypool. "The outlook is very dim unless we can find someone who can walk on water and perform miracles," McKinnon told Claypool.

Claypool offered to defer the payment of the retroactive salary and even defer part of the employees' wages. None of it meant cash in McKinnon's hand. "Unless I get money today or tomorrow, then we don't publish Monday."

It would take no less than $300,000 in cash to keep the paper alive. "Make me an offer," McKinnon said. "Come to me with a plan and I'll consider it." No such offer came.

McKinnon left the meeting to return to the negotiating table at Desser's office. Claypool suggested to the committee that the Guild, as a creditor, throw the paper into involuntary bankruptcy. The bankruptcy would allow the federal court to appoint a receiver and keep the paper going. But the suggestion went nowhere. Lu Haas urged Guild members to come to work over the weekend and put the paper out regardless of what McKinnon planned. As long as the newspaper was in operation, the thinking was that it could not fold. None of these ideas were carried out.

It was 10 p.m. when McKinnon met with the Chandlers for round two. McKinnon and Desser suggested a sale price of $400,000 that would include paying $181,000 withholding taxes, about $70,000 for payroll, and the rest for other debts. It was a stiff price. Zugsmith suggested $180,00 to $200,000, but the Chandlers finally settled for $275,000. It was early Saturday morning and McKinnon was crushed. He signed the sale agreement.

The terms of the agreement were simple. The *Times* would receive the library, name, goodwill, and circulation lists. The Jefferson Standard Life Insurance Company of North Carolina, which held the chattel mortgage on the Pico Boulevard and Los Angeles Street plant, would keep the physical assets. McKinnon would get his five-year contract and $25,000 annual salary. He would help *Daily News* readers make the transition to the *Mirror*. Initially, the merger would have the *Mirror* renamed the *Mirror & Daily News*, but it was quickly changed to the *Mirror-News*.

With the sales money and a $25,000 check given to him from the Times-Mirror Company as the first payment for working for the *Mirror*, McKinnon began paying off his debts. He immediately gave Smith his $25,000 to cover Smith's services in trying to have Robert Straus buy the paper. Arthur Desser received $10,000. Zugsmith received $19,166 for putting the *Daily News-Mirror* deal together. Two of Zugsmith's associates received a total of $18,292. The 450 employees of the *Daily News*, including 350 Guild members, would receive their one-week's severance pay a year later. McKinnon also paid the Internal Revenue Service $181,984 for unpaid withholding taxes, and $82,058 to Union Bank & Trust to free funds in accounts receivable. Smaller amounts went to the state Division of Labor Law Enforcement to pay for unemployment insurance, and to the Farmers & Merchants National Bank of Los Angeles to pay off some pledged accounts and free some accounts receivable.

On Saturday, McKinnon went down to the plant and posted a notice on the door: "NOTICE TO EMPLOYEES. Due to circumstances beyond my control, the *Daily News* suspends publication today."

On Saturday afternoon, Jack Cravens was attending a Christmas party sponsored by the Greater Los Angeles Press Club at the Ambassador Hotel. The children of newsmen and women were playing. Santa Claus was available to hear requests. Adults talked shop. One partygoer left the Ambassador to retrieve some presents at the *Daily News* plant. He returned with alarming news.

McKinnon's notice was posted on the door, and the plant was locked up tight and guarded by security officers. No one was allowed to enter. Some editorial employees managed to get in when the guard was absent from the door. They slipped up to the third floor and used rope to lower several typewriters and a photo enlarger from the third floor windows to the alley below. But most staffers were absent when McKinnon had posted the notice

Jack Kennett, the paper's assistant city editor, also was at the Press Club party, as was Lu Haas and his wife, Janet, when the news arrived.

Jack Jones was sitting at home when he got a telephone call from a friend who told him simply that he was out of a job.

Hal Lindley was working. At 9 a.m. sharp he was sitting in an advertiser's office, arranging to have ad plates sent to the plant. Two hours later, he found that those ad plates would not go anywhere, except perhaps, the *Mirror's* advertising department.

The news of its demise was shocking, a jolt that was followed by anger. Kennett, Lu and Janet Haas, and Jones arrived at the plant about the same time. This time a security guard allowed them on the third floor to collect their belongings. The paper's library had been boarded up to prevent reporters from raiding it for clips and photographs. Shiny black squares on desks were the only hint that typewriters had once been there. Nubbed pencils, half-used notebooks, and scrap paper littered the tables and floor. Overnight, the plant took on a ghostly appearance.

Kennett went straight to his desk and began cleaning it out. He was angry and upset. From the publisher's office, a light was shining. McKinnon could be seen at his desk working. After Kennett had cleaned out his desk, he tucked his belongings under his arm and headed for the elevator. McKinnon spotted him and jumped to his feet.

"Goodbye, Jack," McKinnon cried.

"So long, Judas!" Kennett replied

On Sunday night the Guild held a strategy meeting to find out if there was any chance to revive the *Daily News*, and if not, where to find jobs for its out-of-work members. The meeting quickly turned into a wake.

Pat O'Hara was somber. "It seemed like just a little while that the little man came into our lives and started turning out the lights," he said. "And now they're out for good."

Contrary to stories that circulated about the *Daily News* before its death, the newsroom operation had not been skeletonized. Though in late 1954 it possessed the smallest number of newsroom personnel of any of the five dailies, it still had a relatively healthy staff. Glenn R. Parson was the managing editor and Aaron Dudley had been promoted to assistant managing editor. The news editor was William Sanborn. Matt Weinstock and Tom Gwynne wrote local columns. Sara Boynoff wrote editorials and Les Claypool reported on politics. The copy desk consisted of a full nine-man crew, besides a wire editor, slot man, makeup editor, and editorial-page makeup editor. Chuck Chappell was the paper's last city editor. Under him were assistant city editors Kennett and Saldana, Lu Haas as picture editor and a full four-man staff in the art department under Alan Ferber. The rewrite battery had two open positions, but the specialty beats—schools, science, labor, and crime trends—were all filled. Seven of the ten reporting positions were filled and nine of the ten beats were filled. Only the county board of supervisors beat was open. Under Gib Brush, the photo department had eight of its nine positions filled. Sports, drama, business, and the radio/television departments were fully staffed, though the women's editor slot was unfilled. Even the library and copyboy desks were fully staffed.

Of course, the nature of the *Daily News* staff made it more difficult for other newspapers to absorb reporters. The *Times*, in particular, was reluctant to hire *Daily News* reporters because of their liberal leanings. Bud Lewis confided to Jack Smith that he "didn't want anyone from the *News* because they were all commies."

"Well, I'm from the *News* and I'm not a commie," Smith replied, who had joined the *Times* before the *Daily News* folded.

In the end, only Paul Weeks, Matt Weinstock, and Don Dwiggins went to the *Mirror-News*. Staffers Jack Jones, Ed Gamer, Lupi Saldana, John Beckler, and photographer Garry Watson went to the *Times*. Boynoff and Carol Phinney joined the *Examiner*. Not surprisingly, *Daily News* staffers did not go to the *Herald & Express*. Other newsmen left the business. Sparky Saldana and Roy Ringer went into public relations, although Ringer would later join the *Mirror-News*. Dudley edited trade publications before becoming a successful San Bernardino County businessman. Jack Cravens, who had been attending law school, joined the Los Angeles County District Attorney's office, first as an investigator and later as a prosecutor. Some reporters didn't make the transition to other papers well. Garry Watson soon left the *Times*. Beckler was bored to tears with his new job. *Times* editors would give him small assignments that required just a couple of paragraphs. He was afraid to get an early start on an assignment because he would be left with nothing to do for the rest of the day. Boynoff continued her remarkable career at the *Examiner* and later the *Herald-Examiner*, but Phinney lost her coveted science beat.

Local union leaders howled over the sale of the *Daily News* to Times-Mirror, believing that McKinnon had "betrayed" their members by surrendering to the anti-union *Times* and *Mirror*. William J. Bassett in the Los Angeles *Citizen* was perhaps the most vocal opponent of the sale. He complained that Times-Mirror had bought only certain intangible assets that allowed the company not to be liable for back wages, vacation, and severance pay. The Los Angeles Central Labor Council condemned the sale, putting the *Mirror-News* on the "We Do Not Patronize" list. It censured McKinnon and launched a campaign to keep McKinnon from transferring the *Daily News'* subscription lists to the Times-Mirror (not only did Times-Mirror obtain lists, but Hearst representatives scoured the city for former *Daily News'* delivery men and bribed them to turn over their lists as well). The council obtained many subscription lists from carriers and refused to hand them over to Times-Mirror. Other unions joining the *Mirror-News* boycott were the Building Services Employees International Union, the Machinist Union, Printing Specialties, Miscellaneous Restaurant Employees, and the Printing Trades Council.

Mirror-News publisher and editor Virgil Pinkley found himself besieged from both readers and unionists. Conservative readers didn't want the *Daily News'* liberal columnists and a liberal approach to news in the *Mirror-News*. *Daily News* subscribers demanded that the *Mirror-News* fill the void of Democratic newspapers.

On 20 December, Pinkley restated the *Mirror-News'* goals in a front-page editorial, assuring readers that he will continue its "liberal and progressive" policy to readers. But some confusion was inevitable. Many *Daily News* readers complained Monday afternoon that they had received no paper, including the *Mirror-News*. Advertisers wanted to know whether the *Mirror-News* was assuming the financial liabilities of the defunct paper. Pinkley promised that all *Daily News* readers would get the *Mirror-News*. He told advertisers that his paper was not responsible for the *Daily News'* debts.

On Christmas Day, Pinkley wrote another front-page editorial, this time responding to union complaints that Times-Mirror wasn't doing enough to find jobs for displaced workers. He also denied union allegations that Times-Mirror had a secret agenda and that it had forced the *Daily News* out of business. Rather, Pinkley pointed out, McKinnon had initially approached Times-Mirror about selling his paper.

Matt Weinstock looked at the death of the *Daily News* more objectively than others. In his first column for the *Mirror-News*, he wrote, "There must be enough circulation and advertising to afford the luxury of presenting a point of view, day in and day out. There simply weren't enough. To put it another way, not enough people cared. They were too busy with their own problems."

It was unfortunate that people only cared after the sickly child had died.

Chapter Twelve

A Two-Newspaper Town

I.

Examiner reporter Will Fowler remembers getting a glimpse of the future.

When the O'Conner Electroplating plant on East Pico Boulevard exploded in 1947, nearly destroying a city block, Fowler hurried from the *Examiner* building on Broadway to the scene. While interviewing a woman, he noticed a wagon parked next to a severely damaged building. Inside was character actor Dick Lane, who was setting up a remote television broadcasting station. It was television's early attempt at covering breaking news and it was broadcasting on the spot to a minuscule audience. Its impact on print journalism was negligible.

A little more than two years later, three-year-old Kathy Fiscus fell down a shaft while playing in an empty field in San Marino. By late Friday on 19 April, 200 spectators had shown up to observe fire and police try to rescue the toddler. Unlike the plant explosion, television news suddenly took top dog status during the rescue operations. Early Saturday KTLA established a remote crew in the field with cumbersome, heavy cameras, a tangle of thick heavy cables, and enough lights on tripods to illuminate Gilmore Stadium. Television newsmen Stan Chambers and Bill Welch arrived on the scene to provide a blow-by-blow account of the rescue. The *Examiner's* Margaret Scott and the *Mirror's* Kendis Rochlen stayed up most of the night covering the event. Whenever possible they slept in their cars before going back to the vacant lot. On early Saturday morning, Scott woke up, and surveyed the rescue efforts to find a television anchorman strolling across the field in riding boots and jodhpurs, as if he was parodying Cecil B. DeMille. But the news anchor was dead serious about his role as a journalist. The era of television news had arrived.

KTLA began televising the rescue operation nonstop thirty-six hours. Chambers and Welch wearily alternated reporting duties in front of the camera. Passersby stopped outside furniture stores to watch the rescue efforts live on television sets on display. Homes with televisions were crowded with neighbors who hung on every word from Chambers and Welch.

Initial rescue attempts of the young girl failed. A dwarf volunteered his service. Law-enforcement authorities considered using rail thin circus performers to help. An air hose was placed in the shaft. But hopes for a successful rescue were dimming. Kathy hadn't been heard from since shortly after she had fallen when she told a frantic neighbor almost immediately after she fell in that she was all right.

When rescuers determined that Kathy Fiscus was dead, they wept. It was Rochlen who broke the news to the girl's mother. But it was Welch who broke the news to the millions of television viewers. It was a giant leap for television news, although it would be many years in Los Angeles before it could capture the drama of moving images of a news event.

At first, print journalists didn't take the arrival of television news seriously. For one, television reporters rarely, if ever, showed up at a news event or press conference. A lone cameraman armed with a Bell & Howell would show up at a press conference, set his camera on a tripod, and shoot the event. The camera recorded the subject and the questions posed by print newsmen. Newspapermen and women found it annoying and frustrating. Television news directors found it convenient. Occasionally a soundman would show up with the cameraman, but neither were journalists. Whenever one would screw up the courage to ask a question, print reporters often shouted him down.

Print reporters in those early days did everything they could to ignore the intrusion from television. When Norman Chandler bought KTTV, a television news desk was set up in the corner of the *Times* newsroom. Harry Watson was the sole staffer to man the desk. *Times* city deskers were under orders from Chandler to pass along all breaking news to the KTTV desk. But often an editor would get a news tip, then walk back to the photo department to get a photographer to the scene. The photographers would slip out the back door unnoticed by Watson.

Once Watson glued to the wall next to his desk a photograph of George Putnam, then the top news anchor in Los Angeles, and wrote the caption, "Our Hero." Smoky Hale, whose newspaper career dated back to the 1920s, when he was a young police reporter, was incensed and ripped the photo from the wall. He took some paint and plaster with it. A maintenance crew tried to re-plaster and paint the portion of the wall, but the paint didn't match the rest of the newsroom. After a while, the entire newsroom was repainted. Even when Putnam wasn't underfoot of print reporters, he still had an annoying presence thanks to Hale and Watson.

Debates raged at Press Club meetings and in newsrooms that television news crews had no business piggy-backing off their press conferences. Some reporters resented asking all the questions but having news events televised as if it was television's news story. Senior print reporters began demanding that separate press conferences be held for print journalists and for television news crews.

But New York Governor Nelson Rockefeller put an end to it in two sentences. On a tour of California he stopped at Los Angeles. Newspaper reporters wanted their own press conference, effectively banning television cameramen from attending. When Rockefeller arrived at the press conference he sat at the table and surveyed the room full of newsmen and women. "I understand that the newspapers want a separate press conference from television. I'm telling you here and now that I'm only holding one press conference!"

The resentment among newspaper reporters didn't last. With brothers Coy and Harry Watson, who were old hands as newspaper photographers, taking on television camera duties, print reporters couldn't hold much of a grudge.

Still, there could be embarrassing moments for television newsmen as they struggled for acceptance during the 1950s. Harry Watson responded to a large brush fire in Azusa one afternoon and began filming firefighters battling the blaze. During a break in the action, one firefighter was relieving himself at the edge of the fire. One firefighter pointed his colleague out to Watson and suggested he film him putting out the fire. Watson obliged as a joke. Watson then returned to the KTTV newsroom. A short while later, Watson was watching the afternoon broadcast when George Putnam announced breathlessly on the air that KTTV had "unedited" footage of the Azusa fire filmed earlier in the afternoon. Within seconds, Watson's footage was broadcast clearly showing a firefighter urinating on the fire. An edict from television management followed within hours that no unedited film was to be broadcast again.

Perhaps television's worst moment—and the newspapers' most triumphant—during the decade's print/television news wars occurred in the spring of 1959. The Arechiga family of Chavez Ravine had become the darlings of local media when they battled eviction from their home by Los Angeles County sheriff's deputies to make way for Dodger Stadium and a proposed zoo.

The eviction process had been a long ordeal for both the Arechigas and the Los Angeles city officials. In 1951, the city Housing Authority had condemned the Arechiga property to build a low-rent apartment project. The superior court later determined the property was worth $10,050. Voters, however, rejected any proposed public housing plans and the city council agreed to buy the property. Two years later, the Arechigas sued the city to set aside the condemnation judgment, asserting that the public housing project had been abandoned. In 1957, the U.S. District Court of Appeals ruled in favor of the city. The $10,050 had been held in a trust for the Arechiga family, who had been living rent-free on the property since 1953. On 9 March 1959, the Arechigas, who had owned the property since the 1920s, were served with an eviction notice.

The evictions on 9 May were played out as high drama. Print and television reporters stood in front of two houses, one on Malvina Street and the other on nearby Davis Street, and watched sheriff's deputies negotiate with the Arechiga family on Malvina, and Ruth Rayford and Alice Martin, elderly occupants at the Davis home, to vacate. Deputies found Manuel Arechiga, who was seventy-three, in his yard, but he ignored them. The deputies then pounded on the front door. When there was no answer, they broke down the door and found Manuel Arechiga's wife, Avarana, sixty-two; and daughters Aurora Vargas, thirty-eight, and Victoria Angustain, twenty-nine. Five grandchildren also were in the house. Mrs. Arechiga and Angustain walked out of the house together with the crying children herded in front of them. But Vargas refused to move. She bit sheriff's deputy Gabrielle Johnston on the hand, and then was forcibly carried down the steps of the house as she screamed, "Murder! Murder!" She was quickly handcuffed and put in the back seat of a police cruiser.

A former Chavez Ravine resident, Miss Glen Walters, told the onlookers that the city and sheriff's deputies were abusing the Arechigas. "This is a fine justice you have when you drag people out of their own homes by the heals. This is a fine law. There is only one word for it. Murder! Murder! Murder!" When she rushed toward Mrs. Arechigas shouting, "Let me touch her!" she was wrestled away by deputies. She then slapped one deputy and was arrested for assault.

Meanwhile, Rayford, who was eighty-five, and Martin, seventy-three, brandished a cane and rolling pin to protect themselves from the deputies. But after a brief conversation with deputies, they willingly left their home. After both families were being removed from the homes, bulldozers moved in and demolished them.

The television footage broadcast early that evening was spellbinding. It was an emotional scene that made it appear that the Arechigas were being manhandled. Complaints from viewers flooded City Hall. Newspapers were besieged with letters to the editors. City Councilman Edward Roybal insisted the evictions were not legal and embodied "a complete disregard for human values." Another councilman compared the treatment of the Arechigas to Hitler's Germany.

The next day the Arechiga family returned to their wrecked home and set up a large tent, bringing food, cooking utensils, and bedding

Three days after the evictions, irate council members held a hearing to investigate the treatment of the family. Supporting the Sheriff's Department and the various city departments were Mayor Norris Poulson and Councilwoman Rosalind Wyman. Councilman Karl Rundberg led the attack against Poulson, showing the footage of the eviction. Emotions ran high when John Arechiga, son of the elder Arechigas, shouted insults at Wyman. "Mrs. Wyman is a black-hearted woman." Victoria Angustain joined Arechiga. "Mrs. Wyman is a mother and for her to vote for our eviction is awful," Angustain said as she burst into tears, prompting her three children to wail.

The pictures of the evictions were indeed riveting, but television had told the story in a vacuum. The traumatic struggle between the family and sheriff's deputies provided the drama for the moment. Lost in the television coverage was the back story. The Arechiga family had been living on the property rent-free for six years and had spurned numerous attempts by city officials to relocate to other housing. The appellate court had ruled in the city's favor.

From the onset, the city's four dailies had provided the background of the struggle. But they also agreed the sight of young mothers and children being tossed from their homes were an embarrassment to the city. "The public saw and heard over TV and radio only the horrible spectacle of officers pulling screaming women and children from their homes and then demolishing the houses," the *Examiner* noted on 12 May.

"It was a dramatic and altogether shocking portrayal of brutality and cruelty. This will give Los Angeles an undeserved reputation for ruthlessness in years to come; a reputation that could have been avoided by previously making the facts clear to all." The *Examiner* chided city officials for failing to present the facts of the eviction to television and radio audiences, giving the false impression that it was a thoughtless act.

On 13 May, the *Times* registered its disgust. "The television people were invited to the eviction and the cameras were a strong temptation to dramatics. The glosses of the commentators on the televised film made it appear as if somebody had wantonly pulled the hair of Our Lady of the Angeles.

"A councilman, warmed by the hot winds of the agitators, orated about the violations of individual rights, the Spanish Inquisition and Hitler's Germany, and all this eight years after the initial acts of condemnation, after rulings by two courts and two referendums to the people of Los Angeles, one rejecting the housing project, the other approving a Chavez Ravine baseball development."

Two days later, the *Times* commented: "The damage done by the television 'coverage' of the Chavez Ravine incident is hard to measure. How many people who look and listen but only read while they run will ever be cured of the opinion that the Arechiga clan was turned out of doors without decency or fair warning?"

The urge to dramatize an already unsettling event was confirmed when Ruth Rayford and Alice Martin told reporters, including Paul Weeks with the *Mirror-News*, that television newsmen, to display mock defiance, had coached them and had them posed for the cameras with their cane and rolling pin. "The television men told us to look fierce and I thought it would be fun, so I raised my cane and did the best I could," Rayford told the *Herald & Express*.

The lid blew off the story when the *Mirror-News* published on 13 May a report detailing every piece of property the Arechigas and their relatives owned: In all, the family owned eleven pieces of property that would have provided them a home following their eviction. It was a scoop of monumental proportions, since the press—both print and television—had been lulled into sympathizing with the victims. No matter how equitable the eviction proceedings were, it was difficult not to empathize with a family that had just lost its home.

But the *Mirror-News* reported that the Arechiga family was far from destitute, photographing each property and running profiles on the homes and their ownership history based on county tax records. The properties included rental homes owned by Manuel Arechiga on Glover Place and in City Terrace. The City Terrace home, valued at $9,500, was rented to a niece at $60 a month. Three homes were owned by son, John Arechiga and his wife. A daughter of the Arechigas, Nellie, owned another house in Santa Fe Springs. Aurora Vargas, who had bit a sheriff's deputy during the eviction, had a home on Simmons Avenue.

The day after the *Mirror-News'* report, the *Examiner* followed with its pictures and details of the home ownerships.

Mirror-News editors couldn't help but rub the noses of television newsmen in a story they missed.

"The residents of Chavez Ravine were willing 'stars' in the disgraceful dramatics directed by these civic obstructionists," the *Mirror-News* stated.

"Unhappily, a few television sensation mongers co-operated fully with the plotters who directed the scenario," the *Mirror-News* continued. "'They portrayed the far-from-homeless Arechigas as a destitute, tragic little family clinging in desperation to their humble cottage. Every shabby, tear-jerking trick in the book was employed to create a wholly false impression of the wicked driving the meek out into the cruel world with a blacksnake whip."

Feeling vindicated, Mayor Poulson gushed over the *Mirror-News'* coverage. "I think the *Mirror-News* deserves a Pulitzer Prize for its magnificent journalistic efforts. While a number of television actors—I won't call them newsmen—bled insincere tears up and down the picture tube without any effort to find out, or present, the true facts, the *Mirror-News* dug deeply into the story."

Within ten days, the Arechigas pulled down their tent and gave up the battle.

Print journalists may have won a morale victory in the Arechiga case, but television newsmen won viewers who got an early taste in reality TV.

II.

The effect of television news on the city's four daily newspapers is difficult to pinpoint. More and more Angelenos were tuning in to Clete Roberts, Bill Stout, and Stan Chambers, but city residents also were loyal to their newspapers. New- and used-car dealerships began diverting their advertising budgets to television because it could reach a reasonably broad audience at cheaper rates. While the popularity of television news in the late 1950s and early 1960s did not directly affect the health of the city's dailies, it certainly pushed it in a direction leading to the failure of two newspapers.

Though Norman Chandler would ultimately sink $20 million into the *Mirror-News,* its circulation, at least for the moment, was booming: to 308,000 by late 1955, within 22,000 of the *Herald & Express,* then still the largest afternoon daily west of the Mississippi River.

But readers weren't enough to keep the paper afloat. The complexion of downtown Los Angeles in the late 1950s was changing rapidly. In fact, downtown was dying. The city favored freeways over interurban and streetcar systems. Pacific Railway's Red Cars were losing hundreds of thousands of dollars each year. The city and Pacific Railway were unwilling to invest any more money. The system atrophied as lines to Orange County, San Bernardino County, Pasadena, Santa Monica, and San Pedro died out one by one.

Now relying on automobiles instead of transit systems, much of the public stopped reading newspapers, especially in the afternoon, when they returned home. Meanwhile, as the downtown faded away, so did retail sales: from 45 percent in 1950 to 18 percent by late 1961.

The metropolitan papers were also competing with about thirty suburban dailies and countless throwaway weeklies. Suburban shopping areas had grown by about fifty percent since the end of the war, but the advertising revenue was going to the outlying newspapers. The afternoon papers, both the *Herald & Express* and the *Mirror-News,* had difficulty in trucking papers in rush-hour traffic. The *Mirror-News* had relatively strong advertising lineage and circulation, but the costs of producing an afternoon paper was staggering. The price of newsprint alone had nearly doubled since the end of the war.

But even before then, staffers were noticing a lack of commitment from the Chandlers. Cliff Dektar, for example, had learned the ropes from the best newsmen in the city, but sensed the paper was beginning to founder. He quit in 1956.

Norman Chandler found his scapegoat in Virgil Pinkley. He considered him a weak leader, an outsider, a wire-service executive with little understanding of a daily newspaper. Chandler, always uncomfortable with the *Mirror-News'* slant toward crime, sex, scandal, and muckraking, remained frustrated with Pinkley's inability to right finances of the *Mirror-News*. He was fired in October 1957.

Bud Lewis was named editor to replace Pinkley. He would be given the added title of publisher in July 1958. Less than two weeks after Pinkley's departure, Lewis wrote an editorial restating the paper's Republican political philosophy and commitment to tackle such issues as transit, smog, and downtown improvements. The *Mirror-News* also introduced a "smartly styled" second front page of "broad family appeal" and "great array of hard news." The improvements, however, were superficial and did little to stem the hemorrhaging of red ink. National and regional advertisers, seeing no need to advertise in all four dailies became unwilling to put serious advertising dollars into the *Mirror-News*. The *Mirror-News* was expendable.

The *Mirror-News* moved along on automatic pilot. The meetings between *Times* management and the Times-Mirror board of directors were occupied by discussions of options for the newspaper. Otis Chandler, who supervised the company's newspaper division, suggested in a memo of combining the *Times* and *Mirror-News* into an all-day operation or continuing the *Mirror-News* as a thorn in the side of the *Herald & Express*. All were rejected at least for the moment.

In March 1960, Bud Lewis tried to shake up the news staff, a move that only alarmed reporters and editors, who were leaving the paper with sickening regularity. Arthur Laro, vice president and executive editor of the Houston *Post*, was named executive editor of the *Mirror-News*. It was a newly created position. Unlike Pinkley, Laro, who was forty-eight years old, had more than thirty years of newspaper experience under his belt. He was considered a *wunderkind* with his hard-driving news style. He was credited for boosting the *Post's* editorial content and circulation. He started his career when he was seventeen as a reporter and rewriteman on the San Antonio *Light*. In 1936, he joined the Houston *Press*, and then moved over to the *Post* two years later. He became the *Post's* city editor in 1946, then managing editor in 1950. Three months after Laro had joined the *Mirror-News*, he brought in Jack Donahue, another *Post* editor, as assistant managing editor. *Mirror-News* staffers began joking about "The Texans" and the "Texas Mafia" taking over the paper.

J. Edward Murray recognized Laro's hiring for what it was. His already diminishing authority under Lewis became further diluted with the addition of an executive editor. In July 1960, when Laro told Murray he couldn't effectively manage the paper while Murray was still around, Murray quit. It ended the paper's last hope for dynamic, freewheeling, and bold journalism. Laro quickly replaced Murray with Donahue. He named William Holzhauser, who had been with the *Mirror-News* from the beginning, as assistant managing editor, and F.E. ("Pete") White as news editor.

The *Mirror-News* began to inch closer to being a clone of the *Times*. Laro and Donahue during the paper's last eighteen months were simply plugging holes before *Times* management threw in the towel. Despite the *Mirror-News'* heavy losses, the *Times* wasn't suffering all that much. The Company achieved record profits of $5 million in 1959 with revenues of $97 million. Troubling, however, was the profit margin of five percent. The company was doing so well in fact that it acquired in November 1961 the Orange Coast Publishing Company, which published the Orange Coast *Daily Pilot*, the Costa Mesa *Globe-Herald Daily Pilot*, the Newport *Harbor Daily Pilot*, and the Huntington Beach *Daily Pilot*. Net paid circulation was 17,000. The *Mirror-News* could have gone on longer, but *Times* management was unwilling to sustain the losses. The broadsheet change in 1954 had diminished the paper's spunk and the succession of managers after the departure of Pinkley, and especially after Murray's resignation, left the ship rudderless.

But the Chandlers were not prepared to surrender the afternoon field to the Hearst chain without having Hearst give up one of its own. They started pressuring Hearst into killing one of the papers. It wasn't as unreasonable as it sounded. Hearst often folded community papers to periodically reorganize itself, and the corporation rarely displayed loyalty to the community it served. In addition, by the beginning of the 1960s, the corporation was considering closing down a number of its newspapers as cost-savings measures. Hearst papers nationwide were in financial trouble, losing $28 million between 1958 and 1962.

One offer made by the Chandlers was to buy the *Herald & Express* outright for $5 million, with the agreement that both the *Mirror* and *Examiner* would cease operations. It would leave the advertising-rich morning field to the *Times* and eliminate the stronger of the two Hearst papers. To the Chandlers, it was an attractive offer. Hearst balked because the corporation believed the *Times* would eventually kill off the weaker *Herald & Express,* leaving the entire Los Angeles market to the Chandlers.

In the end, the Chandlers needn't have worried. Hearst decided to shut down the *Examiner* on its own, claiming that for the past several years it had continued to rack up losses. It was a shocking decision. The *Examiner* was clearly the better of the two Hearst papers. The staff was better and the Sunday edition was one of the best in the country. It was mystifying how Hearst management could reason that the *Herald & Express* could survive in a shrinking afternoon market. *Examiner* circulation, by the end of 1961, had reached 381,037, up more than 56,000 from 1956 and making it the tenth best selling morning paper in the country. During the last decade, especially after the death of William Randolph Hearst in 1951, it toned down slightly its anti-Communist rhetoric, with its exhortations for "100 percent Americanism." Then, too, the retirement of the anachronistic city editor James Richardson in 1957 had led to a slight improvement in local coverage. His editorial position over twenty years was to give *Examiner* readers heavy doses of crime and sex. He lost touch with his readers, who had grown more sophisticated by the mid-50s. Sex and crime were good reading but not at the great lengths that the *Examiner* had gone to give it to them. Management also brought in William Townes, who had tried and failed to save the *Daily News*, as managing editor. Still, the Hearst chain, as Bruce Bliven pointed out in *The Reporter*, had "the same trouble that afflicts the entire chain—cumbersome, bureaucratic business-office control, a group of aging right-wing columnists with long-term contracts, and an old-fashioned tone, little changed over the years."

The *Herald & Express*, on the other hand, remained a shabby little product steeped in poor, superficial writing, loud headlines, and a continued reactionary attitude toward anything left of center. Yet, at the end of 1961, it had achieved a daily circulation of more than 390,000, outdistancing the *Mirror-News*, which had been slipping in circulation to 301,882.

Killing off the *Mirror-News* and the *Examiner* appeared to be a violation of antitrust laws and invited a federal government inquiry. The Chandlers and Hearst brass, however, both declared that their papers had been huge money-losing operations and should be shut down. Congressman Emanuel Celler, a New York Democrat who was chairman of the House Judiciary Committee, said his antitrust subcommittee would investigate whether collusion was involved. But in the end, the hearing resulted in nothing, as congressional leaders were reluctant to take to task two of the nation's most powerful publishing companies.

Rumors in both the *Mirror-News* and *Examiner* newsrooms quickly began flying. *Mirror-News* staffers were already jittery after the Saturday edition had been eliminated in November. They were waiting for more bad news. At the end of 1961, local radio and television commentators began to speculate that two of the city's dailies were about the fold. The local reports were amazingly accurate, pinpointing to the day when the papers would cease publication. On 3 January 1962 Townes and Jim Richardson went on KTLA television to deplore the "impending" loss of the *Examiner*. Townes lamented the loss of about 220 editorial jobs. Richardson complained that newspapers were at their best covering such big crime news at the Black Dahlia and the Overell murder cases. The same day, the Greater Los Angeles Press Club launched a drive to raise $250,000 to fund a plan to aid employees about to lose their jobs.

At 11 a.m., Friday, 5 January, Norman Chandler walked somberly into the *Mirror-News* newsroom and gathered the editorial staff. He announced that the *Mirror-News* was "consolidating" with the morning *Times*.

"I deeply regret that the consolidation required the loss of any persons," he said, his eyes brimming with tears. "I wish to express my deep appreciation for your service as Times-Mirror employees—and this includes those who have been loyal employees who will not continue with Times-Mirror Company. Thank you very much for your attention." Chandler's voice broke as he removed his glasses and wiped his eyes with a handkerchief. The room was silent as he left.

A few employees hung on to their jobs. Arthur Laro became the special assistant to Otis Chandler. *Times* editor Nick Williams and Otis Chandler had gone over the list of newsmen they wanted to keep and were already scrutinizing the *Examiner* list as well. They would hire only a handful from the *Examiner*. Of the 120 *Mirror-News* editorial employees, thirty were fired outright and forty were hired at the *Times*. Many over the age of fifty-five were retired and some were sent to other Times-Mirror properties, including the Costa Mesa papers.

The *Examiner's* management didn't care much for emotional farewells. Nat Honig, president of the Los Angeles Editorial Association, a federally charged union representing *Examiner* editorial employees, made his 11 a.m. announcement in a letter:

"It is with deep regret that the management of the Los Angeles *Examiner* hereby informs you that the publication of the *Examiner* is being discontinued beginning with the issue of Monday, Jan. 8, 1962.

"This will necessitate the termination of employment (effective as of the end of the last regularly scheduled work shift in the payroll week ending Sunday, Jan. 7, 1962) of all except a limited number of *Examiner* editorial department employees who will be offered employment in another division of the Hearst Publishing Company, Inc."

The entire *Examiner* staff—the best of the Hearst lot on the West Coast—was fired. Only the paper's name survived, for the new afternoon paper was now called the *Herald-Examiner*.

Knight Newspapers, the Detroit *Free Press*, and other newspaper companies immediately sent recruiters to Los Angeles. Hearst management at the *Examiner* plant on South Broadway, to help place the unemployed, established the Los Angeles *Examiner* Employees Placement Bureau.

The *Times* acted quickly to expand its turf, immediately delivering copies to former *Mirror-News* and *Examiner* subscribers. Readers from the two dead papers began flooding the *Times* switchboard—an estimated 1,800 calls an hour. The circulation of the *Times* soared to 757,000 on weekdays and 1,090,000 on Sundays. The newly created *Herald-Examiner*, by contrast, was left with little to show in new circulation, never achieving the numbers of the *Times*.

The effects of the Hearst blunder to stick with its afternoon paper became apparent in just a few years. A bitter strike hit the paper in 1967 just before Christmas, and lasted ten years. Not only did the strike cripple the newspaper's attempts to effectively cover the city, it still had to compete with television news audience. Readership and advertising revenue plummeted. Circulation dropped from a high of 730,000 to just 350,000 when the strike ended in 1977. By the time the *Herald-Examiner* closed its doors, on 2 November 1989, circulation was only 238,000.

The *Times,* with the morning field all to itself, flourished. *Times* editor Nick Williams had already been implementing policies at an incremental pace that would provide a broader, more fair and balanced, news coverage to its readers. The powerbroking days of Kyle Palmer, L.D. Hotchkiss, and Carlton Williams were over (when Sam Yorty defeated Norris Poulson for mayor in 1961, Williams' power vanished. He retired from the newspaper business soon after).

Williams' goal was to change the *Times'* performance from the "third worst newspaper in the country," as media surveys had announced, to the best in the country. In-depth, and above all, unbiased stories followed. Gene Blake wrote a series on the John Birch Society. It was an act of courage, given that Norman Chandler's brother and sister-in-law, Philip and Alberta Chandler, were staunch Birchers themselves. Although the *Times* continued to ignore the growing dissension in the African American community, it did a profound job of examining the causes of the Watts riots in 1965, earning itself a Pultizer Prize.

The *Times* stood out as the leading voice in journalism for decades to come, but the competitive nature of Los Angeles newspapering had died on 5 January 1962. The *Times* would expand its news policy to become a major player in national and international coverage. Local coverage took a back seat. Blow-by-blow accounts of scandal and local political wrongdoing had lost its edge. There was no one else competing for news. Soft leads and in-depth analysis had replaced the urgency of telling the news. Southern California dailies in the metropolitan markets have eschewed hard-hitting, just-the-facts-type of reporting for stories that provide more perspective. Today, journalism is better. It's fairer, more objective, and more accurate. Newsroom staffs are better educated and more diverse. Most newsrooms today strive for an equal gender balance and a minimum of twenty percent ethnic minority on staff to reflect the communities editors and reporters cover. The aggressive nature of print journalism was, in part, rooted when deadlines for up to ten editions a day demanded clear, concise writing.

The failures of the *Daily News*, the *Mirror-News,* and the *Examiner* were self-inflicted by their owners. The *Daily News* had often congratulated itself on his liberal editorial policy and embrace of Socialist and other leftist themes. But it frequently behaved cowardly when it was faced with political confrontations that threatened advertising revenue. The *Mirror-News* performed well by early postwar standards to serve the minority community and establish a presence in investigative journalism. But its owners also lacked courage by curtailing managing editor J. Edward Murray's vision and independence. Its last, great investigative story was the Arechiga eviction, but for nearly three years after, performed as the faint shadow of the *Times*. Hearst's top-heavy management structure, in which older supervisors mired in antiquated journalism filled its ranks, refused to recognize the needs of the reader of the 1960s, and paid dearly for it. The departure of editors such as Jim Richardson, John B.T. Campbell, and Agness Underwood came too late. The tastes of their readers and the needs of their advertisers had far exceeded what their newspapers could offer them. The public quickly forgot the deaths of these three newspapers. Only the men and women who worked in their newsrooms mourn them. The great newspaper wars of Los Angeles are now only a memory of the ghosts who haunts old newsrooms.

Who Was Who In Los Angeles Newspapers

A roster of selected editors, reporters, photographers, and artists, 1920-62

ADAMS, LESTER—He was appointed managing editor of *Illustrated Daily News* in an attempt to stabilize a besieged newsroom following a revolt by editorial staffers against publisher Cornelius Vanderbilt Jr. He broke into journalism at the Medford (Oregon) *Sun*. After serving a stint as telegraph editor at the Sacramento *Union*, he became makeup and copy editor of the San Francisco *Chronicle*. He also helped Vanderbilt launch the ill-fated San Francisco *Illustrated Daily Herald* and the Miami *Tab*.

AIKMAN, DUNCAN—He was considered one of the top liberal newsmen in the country. He worked for a variety of papers, including the New York *Evening Post* and as West Coast bureau chief for the Baltimore *Sun*. In 1932 he was hired as a special writer for the *Daily News*. He was promoted to managing editor in 1934, but conflicts with publisher Manchester Boddy hastened his resignation. He went on to help found the prestigious liberal newspaper, *PM*, in New York, in the 1940s.

ALLEN, HERB—He was part of the copy desk team at the *Evening Record*, later becoming a copy editor at the *Daily News* when the two newspapers merged.

ARNOTT, ANDREW H.—The first chief photographer for the *Mirror*.

ARRINGTON, JOHNNIE—Cubbed as a police reporter for the *Evening Record* before moving to the *Daily News*. He enjoyed a close relationship with the city's mobsters, including being on their payroll, from Prohibition well into the 1950s.

AULT, PHILIP—A veteran United Press staffer, Ault was the wire service's London bureau chief. He was named assistant managing editor when the *Mirror* was founded in October 1948. He went to the South Bend (Indiana) *Tribune* after leaving the *Mirror*.

BARNES, ELEANOR—She worked on the *Evening Record* as a general assignment reporter. Cornelius Vanderbilt Jr. offered her a job on the *Illustrated Daily News* where she wrote features. She survived the infamous purge of alleged disloyal editorial staffers of 1923 to become a longtime reporter on the *Daily News*.

BARR, WES—He was the managing editor of the *Evening Herald*. He is credited for recognizing the potential of a young Jim Richardson and named the young reporter city editor in 1924. Barr regretted his decision when he later fired Richardson because of alcoholism, but Richardson rebounded in later years.

BASSETT, JAMES—He was the widely read and respected political writer for the *Mirror* and later the *Times*.

BATT, LEO THOMAS—A veteran of the Chicago newspapers where he covered the gangland wars of the 1930s, he came to California after World War II to first work for the San Fernando *Valley Times*, then the *Mirror*. He helped eliminate the *Times'* influence of stories reporters covered by refusing to participate in story syndication.

BECKLER, JOHN—Longtime *Daily News* general assignment reporter. He joined the *Times* in 1954. He later was the correspondent for the Associated Press covering the House of Representatives. He also served as press secretary for the House Labor Committee, chaired by Rep. Gus Hawkins (D-Calif.).

BODDY, E. MANCHESTER—He rescued the *Illustrated Daily News* from bankruptcy in 1926 to develop the city's only true independently owned Democratic newspaper. He allowed his news staff freedom to pursue unconventional writing styles and approaches to daily coverage of the city. He became preoccupied with other business ventures in the late 1940s and allowed the paper to founder under the direction of Robert L. Smith. He retired as editor and publisher in 1952.

BOROUGH, REUBEN W.—As a fiery Socialist, he defined advocacy journalism while at the *Evening Record*. Considered the soul of the *Record*, he attacked the political machinations of city leaders thought untouchable by rival newspapers. He quit the newspaper in protest after its owners switched the paper's endorsement of U.S. senator from liberal William Gibbs McAdoo to the ultra-conservative the Rev Bob Shuler. After leaving the *Record*, he wrote for *Rob Wagner's Script* and edited Upton Sinclair's newsletter, the *EPIC News*. He also served as associate editor of the *League Bulletin of the Los Angeles Municipal League*.

BOYNOFF, SARA—Was a highly regarded reporter and rewrite staffer for the *Daily News*. When the *Daily News* folded in 1954, she went into radio, and then joined the *Examiner* where she wrote what was considered groundbreaking stories on minority affairs.

BRIGGS, HENRY B.R.—Editor of the *Evening Record*, he encouraged his reporters to engage in advocacy journalism and pursue Socialist causes. Under his leadership, the *Record* was the only newspaper engaged in investigative journalism of City Hall and the Los Angeles Police Department.

BRINK, RODNEY—He was managing editor of the *Evening Record*. In 1930 Brink, editor Gilbert Brown, and Henry B.R. Briggs were indicted by the county grand jury on contempt of court charges stemming from the paper's criticism of the court's handling of the C.C. Julian oil scandal. The charges were later dropped.

BROWN, GILBERT—Longtime reporter and later editor for the *Evening Record*. He wrote a series of articles on the *Record's* history when Manchester Boddy bought the paper. He, along with Rodney Brink and Henry B.R. Briggs, was indicted on contempt of court charges in the C.C. Julian case.

BRUSH, GIB—He was photo editor of the *Daily News*. He covered Japan's only attack on California in 1942. He specialized in postwar aviation photography.

BRUSH, HELEN—She was a pioneering woman news photographer for the *Daily News* and wife of photo editor Gib Brush. She trained many young photographers in lab work and guided cub reporters on their early assignments. She specialized in children, so-called women's stories, and features. She covered Harry S. Truman's presidential campaign through Los Angeles in 1948 among other national stories.

BURGER, JACK—An early city editor for the *Examiner* during the 1930s. He was fired when he ignored a fugitive murder suspect who walked into the newsroom to confess.

CAMPBELL, JOHN B.T.—A native of California and son of Judge Alexander Campbell, he was the colorful, conservative managing editor of the *Evening Herald & Express*. The Hearst-trained Campbell began his Los Angeles newspaper career on the *Evening Herald*. He was responsible for naming as city editor Agness Underwood, Los Angeles' only female city editor of a major metropolitan newspaper in the 1940s and '50s.

CARR, HARRY—Popular columnist and reporter for the *Times* during the first thirty-five years of the century. He began at the *Times* as a sports writer and editor. He was a combat correspondent during World War I, reporting from the German front. He authored a number of books, including *Old Mother Mexico* in 1931. His widely read series of articles, The New Smart Set, was published in 1929 and turned into a book the following year.

CATON, TOM—Largely considered a misogynist by female staffers, Caton was first a reporter, then an assistant city editor under Agness Underwood at the *Herald & Express*. He was noted for his encyclopedic mind and fast rewrites of reporters' copy.

CHAPPELL, CHARLES—He began his career in 1935 at the *Evening Record* before joining the *Daily News* following the merger of the two papers. He served as city editor of the *Daily News* during coverage of some of the most flamboyant and sensational crime cases in Los Angeles history. He also worked at the Compton *News-Tribune* before going to the *Daily News.*

CHURCHILL, DOUGLAS—A hotel beat reporter for the *Times*, he was lured to the *Illustrated Daily News* to become the paper's chief editorial writer and later assistant to publisher Cornelius Vanderbilt Jr.. He later became a Hollywood correspondent for the New York *Times* and *Redbook* magazine.

CLARKE, JOHN—A rewrite man for the *Daily News*, he penned with Sparky Saldana the life story of gangster Mickey Cohen in a nine-part series of articles in 1949.

CLAUSEN, CHRIS—He was primarily a rewrite man for the *Daily News*, before joining the *Examiner* in 1954 as a science writer.

CLAYPOOL, LESLIE—An active member of the Los Angeles Newspaper Guild, Claypool covered politics for the *Daily News*. He attempted at the eleventh hour to rescue the *Daily News* in 1954 by having employees become the newspaper's owners. The effort failed. He previously reported for the San Diego *Sun*, and then founded his own small weekly newspaper. In the late 1930s, he went to the *Examiner* before coming to the *Daily News* during World War II.

COHEE, JOHN—Identified as a Communist in the 1940s, Cohee was an active member of the Los Angeles Newspaper Guild. He wrote an analysis column on the United States' participation during World War II for the *Daily News*. He also worked the rewrite desk and was a reporter.

COLLINS, EDWIN R.—A veteran of the Spanish-American war, he worked variously for the Walla Walla (Washington) *Union*, the Oregon *Daily Journal*, the Boston *American*, and the Los Angeles *Examiner* before making the Los Angeles *Herald* his permanent home. He was named managing editor of the *Herald* in 1913. In 1924 he became editorial director of the Pacific Coast Division of the Hearst chain's afternoon dailies.

CONNELLY, PHILLIP—The blustery, confrontational negotiator for the Los Angeles Newspaper Guild. An editorial staffer for the *Herald & Express*, he personified the Guild's aggressive, if not crude, approach to contract negotiations with newspaper management. He was a prominent player in costly strikes at the Hollywood *Citizen-News* and the *Herald & Express*.

COONRADT, FRED—Picture editor of the *Daily News* and husband of Sara Boynoff. He also covered the Los Angeles journalism industry for *Editor & Publisher* magazine and was a professor of journalism at the University of Southern California.

COUGHLIN, GENE—He attended Medill School of Journalism and worked for Chicago newspapers before coming to Los Angeles to work for the *Illustrated Daily News*, first under Cornelius Vanderbilt and then for Manchester Boddy. He covered the court beat and evangelist Aimee Semple McPherson's disappearance in 1926. He continued working for the *Daily News* in a variety of jobs, including sports editor. He authored the unpublished biography of Boddy in 1953.

CRAVENS, JACK—Came to the *Daily News* in 1938, from Los Angeles City College. He worked as a copyboy and later a reporter. When the *Daily News* died, he joined the District Attorney's office first as an investigator and later a prosecutor. He was a co-founder of the Greater Los Angeles Press Club.

CROMWELL, DEAN—He wrote sports for the *Mirror*. A USC track and field coach for nearly forty years, he was one of several USC alumni to be hired at the *Mirror* by Ralph ("Casey") Shawhan.

CRONIN, NED—Longtime sports editor of the *Illustrated Daily News* and the *Daily News*.

DARSIE, DARSIE L.—Veteran golf writer and conservative editorial writer for the *Herald & Express*. He also wrote a book review column. He represented management during the lengthy Guild strike of 1946.

DEKTAR, CLIFF—He represented the new breed of young postwar reporters, joining the *Mirror* in 1948 to write for its youth page. He moved up to reporter, covering police and breaking news.

DENLINGER, H. SUTHERLAND—He was the *Illustrated Daily News'* first picture editor, supervising the paper's fourteen photographers. He was a veteran of World War I, serving with the French Foreign Legion.

DEVLIN, TOMMY—Police reporter for the *Examiner*, covering the Black Dahlia murder case, among dozens of other sensational crime stories of the 1940s.

DICKSON, EDWARD A.—Perhaps the West Coast's premier crusading reporter during the first decade of the century. He co-founded the Lincoln-Roosevelt League of Republican Clubs to help break the Southern Pacific Railroad's hold on the state Legislature. He helped make the *Evening Express* a formidable powerbroker in state politics. He served as the paper's Washington correspondent during 1911 and 1912. After serving as the paper's editor and publisher, he retired from the newspaper business in 1931.

DONAHUE, JACK—Part of the "Texas Mafia" that came to the *Mirror-News* in 1960, he was named managing editor after the abrupt resignation of J. Edward Murray.

DRISCOLL, MARJORIE—Perhaps the best rewrite staffer in Los Angeles over four decades for the *Examiner*, she could take a scrap of information from a reporter in the field and turn it into subtle prose. Her specialty was writing sob stories, but she was quick and accurate with breaking news. A graduate of Stanford University, she had also worked on the San Francisco *Chronicle* and San Francisco *Examiner* rewrite desks before coming to Los Angeles.

DUDLEY, AARON—A conservative among a sea of liberals while an editor at the *Daily News*, he began his career at the Huntington Park *Bulletin*. There, a Los Angeles Newspaper Guild strike divided the *Bulletin* staff with Dudley staying with management to put out the paper. His conservative views among leftist members of the Guild caused no rancor. A popular supervisor, he was a city editor of the *Daily News* and editor of the ill-fated *Sunday News*.

DURLING, E.V.—A columnist for the *Daily News*, he defected in the mid-1930s to the *Times*. He is perhaps best known today for paving the way for Matt Weinstock to become the city's voice.

DWIGGINS, DON—Although known more for his sensational, often manufactured stories, Dwiggins nonetheless was a colorful figure in 1940s and 1950s Los Angeles journalism. An avid flier, he authored numerous books and magazine articles on aviation.

ELDRIDGE, FRED—He was the dean of newspapermen in 1920s Los Angeles. Under William Randolph Hearst he was the managing editor of the New York *Evening Journal* and later the New York *American*. In New York he led an investigative team on the *American* to ferret out political corruption at the municipal and state levels of New York government. He was named managing editor of the Los Angeles *Examiner* in 1908. His son, Fred Eldridge, Jr., was a newspaper reporter in his own right. The younger Eldridge was a reporter on the *Examiner* and later owned his own newspaper in Corona, California.

ELLER, HARRY—A veteran Chicago newspaperman, he arrived in Los Angeles to become Boddy's managing editor of the *Daily News*. He supervised much of the *Daily News'* early crusading efforts to expose vice and corruption in 1920s Los Angeles.

EMERSON, LLOYD—A veteran court reporter for the *Examiner*, he helped obtain the infamous Overell letters in Orange County as the trial of two young lovers, accused of killing the girl's parents, was about to get underway.

ERICKSON, CHARLIE—He started his career in 1948 as a copyboy for the *Mirror*. As a reporter for the *Mirror* he covered issues in the Mexican American community. In later years he championed a number of Latino causes.

FELTON, JAMES—The son of Ray Felton, city editor of the Seattle *Star*, young Felton began his career at the *Star* before moving to the Seattle *Times*. He then became city editor of the Sacramento *Bee*. He also worked for the Santa Ana *Journal* and the San Diego *Sun*. An active Guild member, he was fired at the *Sun* for his union activities, but was rehired after a National Labor Relations Board hearing. He served as city editor of the *Daily News*. In 1947, he became editor of

Script magazine and helped boost its circulation from 817 to about 50,000. The magazine failed two years later.

FERGUSON, WILLIAM W.—His Los Angeles newspaper career started with the *Evening Record* as a general assignment and police reporter. He later joined the *Daily News* on the rewrite desk.

FOWLER, LARRY—He worked as part of the rewrite team on the *Daily News* copy desk. After the *Daily News* ceased publication, Fowler joined the San Fernando Valley *Daily News*.

FOWLER, PERRY—Was a staff photographer for many years with the *Herald & Express*. During the war he was a photographer for the U.S. Navy. He covered Harry S. Truman's swing through Los Angeles during the 1948 presidential campaign, among other stories.

FOWLER, WILL—The son of Gene Fowler, he joined the *Examiner* under the legendary city editor Jim Richardson. He quit the *Examiner* to work for the *Herald & Express*. In the 1950s he wrote for television, most notably for comedian Red Skelton.

FREDERICK, ALFRED HARDIN—He covered the hotel beat out of the Biltmore Hotel pressroom for many years for the *Examiner* until the paper folded in 1962.

FURILLO, BUD—A student at East Los Angeles Junior College, he joined the *Herald & Express* after the paper's four-month-old strike ended in December 1946. Furillo started as a copyboy then covered the police beat. In 1948, he moved to the sports department. He became executive sports editor at the *Herald-Examiner* in 1964.

GARRISON, PHIL—The managing editor of the *Daily News* during the 1940s and early 1950s. Self-described as a "flaming liberal" in his youth, he became increasingly conservative as he grew older. His changing politics figured prominently when he voted during a hearing to fire two reporters suspected of being Communists.

GODCHAUX, MAURY—A *Times* reporter during the late 1940s. He switched to the *Examiner* in late 1947, covering such stories as the Kathy Fiscus tragedy in 1949.

GREENBERG, CARL—A loyal Hearst-trained reporter for the *Examiner*, he was considered the paper's political powerbroker inside Los Angeles City Hall. He joined the *Times* after the *Examiner* folded in 1962 and continued his political coverage of the city.

HAAS, LUCIAN—A liberal and strong leader in the Los Angeles Newspaper Guild, he served as a shop steward for employees at the *Daily News*. He was part of a group of Guild members who attempted to rescue the dying newspaper during its last days. He worked as a copyboy, reporter, and photo editor. Stories he covered included the Kathy Fiscus accident in San Marino in 1949.

HALE, SMOKY—Longtime police reporter for the *Times*, he trained a legion of young newsmen on how to cover the police beat.

HANSON, CHESTER—Reporter for the *Times*.

HARVEY, RUTH—A *Daily News* reporter, she was initially scorned by male reporters because she was promoted from secretary of executive editor Lee Payne to a news beat. She proved, however, to be assertive as a newswoman and performed well in a variety of assignments.

HAYES, REED—A hardnosed San Francisco newspaperman who also was once the city editor of the *Evening Record*, Hayes was named the first managing editor of the *Illustrated Daily News*. He built the editorial staff of the *Daily News* from scratch, but was fired by Cornelius Vanderbilt Jr. following a newsroom revolt over the use of private detectives hired by Vanderbilt to spy on alleged disloyal employees.

HAZEN, EARL—An avid airplane pilot and reporter for the *Mirror*. He was killed in a plane accident near Las Vegas while on assignment for the paper.

HEBERT, BOB—He was a turf handicapper for the sports sections of four Los Angeles area daily newspapers during his thirty-five-year career. He signed on as sports editor of the Huntington Park *Signal* in 1930, and then moved to the *Post-Record*. In 1948 he became the *Mirror's* horseracing handicapper. At the *Mirror* he was acknowledged as the winningest handicapper in the history of Los Angeles horseracing. He became part of the *Times*' staff when the *Mirror* folded in 1962.

HERMANN, CLEVE—A popular sports writer for the *Herald & Express* and the *Daily News*. He also wrote for radio and television.

HIMMEL, NIESON—The quintessential police reporter of postwar Los Angeles. He worked briefly for City News Service and the *Daily News* before joining the *Herald & Express*. He was once arrested for trafficking narcotics across the U.S.-Mexico border while on assignment for a story under supervision of Agness Underwood. He was fined and released. He finished his career as a police reporter for the *Times*.

HOSTER, DAN—Was a *Daily News* photographer who often worked aviation and aerospace assignments.

HOLZHAUSER, WILLIAM—He began his newspaper career in Bisbee, Arizona. He joined the *Mirror* in 1948 and rose through the editing ranks. He was named assistant managing editor of the *Mirror-News* in 1960.

HOPPER, HEDDA—Powerful Hollywood gossip columnist for the *Times*.

HOTCHKISS, LOYAL DURANT—As the editor of the *Times* from 1934-58, Hotchkiss carried on the tradition of bland and gray journalism. Influential in Los Angeles politics, Hotchkiss often gave approval for promotions in the police department and worked as a liaison for reporters who may have had trouble with police. A native of Iowa, he began his career with the *Examiner*, then moved to the *Times* in 1922. He was named city editor in 1926 and remained in that spot until 1933 when he was named assistant managing editor.

HUGHES, SID—A police reporter for the *Examiner*, Hughes once served briefly as city editor on the *Mirror*.

JACOBY, NORMAN ("JAKE")—The dean of police reporters in the 1970s and '80s, he spent most of his career with the City News Service. He also worked as a police reporter for the *Herald & Express*. He was a co-founder of the Los Angeles Newspaper Guild and was part of the postwar effort to purge Communists from union ranks. He also edited *Alert*, an anti-Communist publication.

JONES, JACK—A graduate of USC, Jones began his career scoring an interview with mobster Mickey Cohen for an article in the *Daily Trojan*. He joined the *Daily News* in 1949, then later hired on at the *Times*. He was part of the Pulitzer Prize-winning team of reporters who wrote a series of articles in 1965 on the causes of the Watts Riots.

JOHNSON, ROGER C.—Liberal political editor of the Hollywood *Citizen-News*. He was a co-founder of the Los Angeles Newspaper Guild.

JORZ, MERRITT W. ("POP")—He served as a financial editor for the *Evening News* and at one time acted as liaison between *Daily News* management and Los Angeles merchants and businessmen. He was largely responsible for helping Manchester Boddy turn the newspaper into a liberal voice by supporting the policies and programs of President Franklin D. Roosevelt.

JUDSON, CHARLIE—One-time city editor of the *Daily News*, Judson was an ex-Communist who testified in a congressional hearing against Darr Smith and Vern Partlow. He was an editor of the short-lived Los Angeles *Independent* and senior editor at *Fortnight*. He finished his newspaper career at the San Luis Obispo *Telegram-Tribune*.

KENNETT, JACK—An assistant city editor of the *Daily News* in the early 1950s, Kennett also worked as a police reporter and rewrite man.

KEROPIAN, HAIG—He was a general assignment reporter for the Hollywood *Citizen-News*.

KERBY, PHIL—A veteran Los Angeles journalist, he frequently wrote critical essays on local journalism. He was editor of *Frontier* magazine. He eventually became an editorial writer for the *Times*.

KIRBY, DON—He started his career at the Huntington Park *Bulletin*. He later was hired at the *Daily News* to cover courts.

KNISELY, BURTON—A committed Socialist whose early career included stints on the Cleveland newspapers, Knisely was the managing editor of the *Evening Record*. Under Knisely and Henry B.R. Briggs, the newspaper did its best crusading journalism. Knisely founded the Pomegranates and Pemmican Club, an informal group of a half-dozen reporters who discussed and practiced literary journalism.

KNOX, WILLIAM BOARDMAN—He was the night city editor for the *Illustrated Daily News* under Vanderbilt. He later wrote a critical magazine article on Vanderbilt's early years as a publisher.

KRAUCH, ED—A *Herald & Express* sports writer who was involved in a scandal involving wrestling promoters paying off sports writers in the 1930s. Krauch was fired but returned as a caption writer. He later was promoted to photo editor. He was the brother of Herb Krauch, also on the editorial staff of the *Herald & Express*.

LANGLEY, HOWARD—A veteran sports writer for the *Illustrated Daily News*.

LARO, ARTHUR—A ringer brought in by Bud Lewis and the Chandler family in 1960 from the Houston *Post* to become executive editor of the troubled *Mirror-News*. He shook up the editorial department, but failed to help keep the paper alive.

LARSON, ARNOLD B.—He came to the *Evening Record* from Thermopolis, Wyoming, where he handled publicity for the local chamber of commerce. He covered general assignment for the *Record* during the 1920s.

LAVINE, MORRIS—Top reporter for the *Examiner* in the teens and 1920s. He was on the payroll of the C.C. Julian Petroleum Company in the mid and late 1920s. He was fired after attempting to extort $75,000 from mobster Charlie ("Gray Fox") Crawford in exchange for leaving Crawford's name out of a sensational series of articles on the C.C. Julian oil scandal.

LEE, WALT—He was an original artist for the *Illustrated Daily News*. He began his career sketching the Slim Jim comic strip before drawing Dudley Dudd panels for the *Daily News* from 1923 to 1939. In 1942, he joined the *Times* and remained there as a cartoonist until his retirement in 1953.

LEUNG, MAMIE—She often wrote stories from the so-called women's angle for breaking news for the *Daily News*. A rare minority female in the reporting ranks, Leung wrote features of such sensational criminal cases as the Paul Wright murder trial of 1938.

LEWIS, HUGH A. ("BUD")—A loyal *Times* editor, Lewis served as a liaison between the *Mirror* and *Times* management during the first years of the *Mirror*'s existence. He later would act as city editor. In 1957 he was named editor, then editor and publisher the following year. At the *Times* he was the city editor for more than twenty years. He retired in 1960.

LINDSEY, ESTELLE LAWTON—She was a sob sister for the *Evening Express* during the 1920s, covering such beats as the film industry, including the Roscoe ("Fatty") Arbuckle and William Desmond Taylor scandals.

LOCKWOOD, WAYNE—He wrote the pioneering series of articles on the African American history for the *Mirror* in the early 1950s. His series covered black history as well as profiles of African American community leaders.

MAAS, HERB—He was a veteran chief copy editor of the *Evening Record* and later the *Daily News*.

MAREK, CAPPY—He was city editor of the *Herald & Express* before Agness Underwood took over in the late 1940s. He kept the infamous "stooge list" of notable people who would say anything for print to further the Hearst press agenda, including inflammatory stories of minorities.

MARTIN, LANIE HAYNES—She wrote sob sister stories for the *Examiner* through the 1920s.

MAUTNER, SID—He was a veteran photographer of the Chicago newspapers before coming to L.A. to work for the *Illustrated Daily News*. He perfected the shoot-from-the-hip technique to capture pictures of unwilling subjects.

MEANS, BEVO—A reporter for the *Herald & Express*, Means covered the Black Dahlia case among other notorious crime stories. He was co-founder of the Greater Los Angeles Press Club.

MILES, MARVIN—A leading *Times* reporter for many years, Miles also was a co-founder of the Greater Los Angeles Press Club. Miles specialized in aviation issues.

MINGO, JOE—A staff photographer for the *Illustrated Daily News*, he specialized in aviation photography.

MONTEVERDE, AL—An *Examiner* photographer in the 1940s through the '50s. He covered many sensational cases, including the Overell murder trial of 1947.

MUIR, FLORABEL—A veteran New York reporter who covered Gotham's most sensational stories, including the execution of Ruth Snyder at Sing Sing prison. She owned City News Service briefly before joining the *Mirror* as a columnist. She was shot and wounded on the Sunset Strip during an assassination attempt on gangster Mickey Cohen.

MURRAY, J. EDWARD—Was the visionary managing editor of the *Mirror*, who often disregarded the *Times'* sacred cows to cover controversial issues. He authorized reporters to write an investigative series on influence peddling by the politically powerful William G. Bonnelli and supervised the coverage of numerous other politically charged stories.

MURRAY, JIM—He always acknowledged that he was a better writer than a beat reporter. His early years in Los Angeles were spent at the *Examiner* on the rewrite desk, although he was the lead reporter on the Overell murder case in Orange County through most of 1947. He left the *Examiner* to join *Time* magazine and help launch *Sports Illustrated*. He enjoyed an illustrious career as a sports columnist for the *Times*, ultimately winning the Pulitzer Prize.

NATHAN, AL—Was the *Times'* representative and political powerbroker inside City Hall from the 1920s to late 1930s. He made decisions for many city mayors and councilmen on behalf of Harry Chandler. He also gathered intelligence on Chandler's enemies from the Los Angeles Police Department's Red Squad.

NEWMAN, GUS—He was a reporter for the *Examiner* and co-founder of the Greater Los Angeles Press Club.

O'DONNELL, STEPHEN—A brash, young newsman, O'Donnell first worked in Los Angeles at the *Evening Record* under Henry B.R. Briggs. He later was hired at the *Daily News*. In 1930 Manchester Boddy named him editor and publisher of Boddy's Huntington Park *Signal*. He also served as editor of both the *Daily News* and *Post-Record* in the mid-1930s. While employed at the *Daily News*, O'Donnell also was on Mayor Frank Shaw's payroll to help him fend off a recall election in 1938.

O'HARA, PAT—A well-mannered, well-dressed court reporter for the *Daily News*. He was a heavy drinker but a health food advocate as well. When the *Daily News* folded in 1954, he retired to Pismo Beach where he committed suicide.

OLIVER, BILL—A drama writer and editor for the *Herald & Express*, he was a co-founder of the Los Angeles Newspaper Guild. He was a suspected Communist and generally worked in tandem with Phil Connelly in developing strategy for contract negotiations and potential strikes.

OLMO, FERDIE—Staff photographer of the *Examiner* during the 1940s and '50s.

OSBORNE, HANK—He was city editor of the Sacramento *Union* before coming to Los Angeles to help start the Los Angeles *Independent* as its managing editor. The newspaper failed after only a few months and he joined the *Mirror*, eventually becoming its city editor. He also served as city editor of the *Times* before becoming chief of the *Times'* zoned sections.

PAEGEL, FELIX—Star staff photographer for the *Examiner* during the 1940s and '50s. He was first photographer on the crime scene with Will Fowler in the Black Dahlia murder case. His clear shots of the corpse has been used widely in newspapers, magazines, and books over the decades.

PALMER, KYLE—Leading political writer for the *Times* in the 1920s, '30s, and '40s.

PARSONS, LOUELLA O.—Hollywood gossip columnist for the *Examiner*. Her byline appeared on many of the early stories of the Johnny Stompanato-Cheryl Crane homicide case.

PARTLOW, VERN—Folk singer and union activist, Partlow worked at newspapers in Milwaukee and San Francisco before coming to Los Angeles in 1940 as a part-time staffer. In 1944 he joined the *Daily News* staff full-time as a copy editor. He later wrote political columns and ghost wrote many of Manchester Boddy's columns. He wrote the folk song, "Old Man Atom," which garnered wide radio play. He was fired in 1952 when he refused to deny that he was a Communist.

PATRICK, SAM—He spent most of his career as an artist at the *Daily News*, from the Vanderbilt years to his retirement shortly before the paper folded.

PAYNE, LEE—He was executive editor of the *Daily News* in the late 1940s and early 1950s. He represented management during Guild contract negotiations. He was responsible for firing Vern Partlow and Darr Smith for their alleged Communist affiliations.

PAYNE, PAULINE—Sob sister for the *Evening Herald*. She often interviewed film celebrities during the 1920s.

PENDERGRAST, TED—General assignment reporter for the *Herald & Express*. Early in his career he was the Washington, D.C. correspondent for a Pittsburgh newspaper. He had the dubious distinction then of deciding not to break the Teapot Dome scandal because he had several friends involved.

PHINNEY, CAROL (TIEGS)—She helped blaze a trail for young women reporters covering specialty beats. She had worked for the San Francisco *Call-Bulletin*, then moved to the *Daily News* in the late 1930s where she covered the science beat. She moved to the *Examiner* when the *Daily News* folded. She died in 1956 of cancer.

PHINNEY, MILT—Husband of Carol Phinney and veteran rewrite man on the *Daily News*. He also was an active member of the Los Angeles Newspaper Guild. He once served as the paper's city editor shortly after World War II.

PIGUE, BILL—Assistant city editor in the 1950s for the *Herald & Express*.

PINKLEY, VIRGIL—Editor and publisher of the *Mirror*. He was a longtime United Press staffer, supervising several bureaus in Europe. Norman Chandler brought him to Los Angeles to launch the *Mirror* in 1948, bringing several UP editors with him.

PRICE, GERTRUDE—A society and women's page editor, she penned the popular "Cynthia Grey" columns in the 1920s and '30s at the *Evening Record*. She became part of the *Daily News* staff when the *Record* and *Daily News* merged.

PRICE, GUY—An *Evening Herald* general assignment reporter. His highly sensationalized stories of the Roscoe ("Fatty") Arbuckle scandal helped sway public opinion about the morals of the film community, putting movie studios on the defensive.

RAMLOW, JERRY—Police reporter for the *Daily News*. He was one of the last police reporters trained in prewar newsgathering where reporters often took on the role of police investigator when interviewing criminal suspects.

RAMSDELL, KERBY—Was a longtime conservative editor at the *Times*. He penned many of the *Times'* editorials in the 1950s.

RICHARDSON, JAMES H.—The legendary city editor of the *Examiner* who was once described by a media critic as "the last of the terrible men." A native of Canada, he was hired at the *Herald* where he quickly rose to city editor. Alcoholism threatened his career in the late 1920s and early '30s, but he proved that he could quit drinking and run an effective newsroom. He served brief stints at the *Post-Record* and *Daily News* before he was handed the city desk post at the *Examiner* in 1937. The *Examiner*'s strength during Richardson's reign was its in-depth and sensational coverage of crime news. He retired in 1957.

RICKMAN, JOEL—Was a flamboyant and hardnosed city editor of the *Illustrated Daily News* during the 1920s. He was arrested with publisher Manchester Boddy in 1928 for printing the entries on the Kentucky Derby race results, which was illegal under an obscure state law but a service performed for readers by the city's five daily newspapers. The effort by Los Angeles police was to stop Rickman and Boddy from uncovering police corruption. Charges were later dropped.

RINGER, ROY—His early newspaper career began in 1938 at the Huntington Park *Bulletin*. In 1945, after his discharge from the U.S. Coast Guard, he was hired at the *Daily News* as a copyboy. He later wrote for the sports and drama departments. In 1955 he wrote briefly for *Variety* before going into public relations. In 1958, he returned to the newspaper business, joining the *Mirror-News* where he remained for two years.

ROCHLEN, A.M.—Carl Greenburg's predecessor as the *Examiner*'s political insider at City Hall.

ROCHLEN, KENDIS—The daughter of A.M. Rocklen, she was dubbed the "Brenda Starr" of the *Mirror* newsroom. She was aggressive, politically savvy, and managed to scoop most of the rival male reporters on a regular basis.

ROGERS, FRANK—Was a city editor at the *Daily News* in 1946. He later was named Washington, D.C., correspondent for the *Daily News*. He left the newspaper business to work for California Gov. Edmund G. ("Pat") Brown.

ROWE, PETE—He's been described as the photo department's resident screwball at the *Illustrated Daily News*. He was hired in 1923 and specialized in photographing fires, usually beating the fire department to alarms.

RYAN, DON—He wrote a home front war column for the *Evening Herald & Express* and represented the newspaper at the Biltmore Hotel on the hotel beat.

SALDANA, JOSE ("SPARKY")—Was a popular reporter and night city editor of the *Daily News*. He handled a variety of tasks at the newspaper. He covered the police and harbor beats in the 1930s and early '40s. During World War II he supervised the Spanish-language division of the Office of War Information. He co-authored with John Clarke the life story of Mickey Cohen in 1949. For many years he was the highest-ranking Latino in Los Angeles journalism. He left the newspaper business when the *Daily News* folded in 1954 and went into public relations.

SALDANA, LUPI—He was the brother of Jose ("Sparky") Saldana and longtime sports writer for the *Daily News*. He wrote an outdoor column. When the *Daily News* folded in 1954, he joined the *Times* as an outdoor writer.

SANTLEY, JOE—Rewrite man for the *Examiner*.

SCOTT, MARGARET BOUTYETTE—A general assignment and features reporter for the *Examiner* from 1944 to the early 1950s. She covered the Kathy Fiscus story. She was once married to United Press reporter Vern Scott.

SHAMBRA, JIMMY—Police reporter for the *Herald & Express*. Like most reporters on the police beat during the era, he spent most of his time in police stations and phoning in his stories. He rarely wrote, but was considered the *Herald & Express'* top beat reporter in postwar Los Angeles.

SHAWHAN, RALPH ("CASEY") —He was the *Mirror*'s first city editor. He was a top distance runner while a student at USC. He worked primarily the police beat for the *Herald & Express* and the *Examiner* before joining the *Mirror*.

SHERMAN, GENE—He was co-founder of the Greater Los Angeles Press Cub and reporter for the *Times*. He specialized in smog issues among other topics. He also was a popular columnist for the *Times*.

SHIPPEY, LEE—Early columnist for the *Times*.

SHOREY, FREDERICK M.—He was an early managing editor for the *Illustrated Daily News* during the Vanderbilt years. He helped add credibility to the *Daily News* after its disastrous start under Vanderbilt.

SMITH, DARR—A drama writer for the *Daily News* for nearly a dozen years, he lost his job when former city editor Charlie Judson testified at a congressional hearing that he was a Communist. His career was ruined, never returning to metropolitan daily journalism.

SMITH, JACK—A combat war correspondent with the Marines in the Pacific Theater during World War II, he signed on with the *Daily News* when he returned home. From the *Daily News* he went to the short-lived Los Angeles *Independent*, then the *Herald & Express* before returning to the *Daily News* as a writer for the *Sunday News* edition. After leaving the *Daily News*, he worked briefly for the Carol Byoir public relations agency. He then joined the *Times*. Heavy drinking almost sidetracked his career, but he was given a column, which helped turn him around. He assumed the voice of Los Angeles from Matt Weinstock and was considered one of the most gifted newspaper columnists in the country.

SOUTHARD, JACK—Worked on the rewrite desk for the *Examiner*.

SPAFFORD, MARVIN –A staff photographer for the *Illustrated Daily News*, he specialized in dogs and animals. He had a special fondness for lions at Gay's Lion Farm in El Monte.

SPANGLER, COLIN A.—A reporter for the *Examiner* in the 1920s, he covered early Hollywood scandals, including Roscoe ("Fatty") Arbuckle manslaughter case. He helped lay the foundation for future scandal coverage of the Los Angeles press.

SPRAGUE, CHANDLER—An early reporter with the *Examiner*, he, like Colin Spangler covered many of the film industry's early scandals. In 1924 he wrote a positive series of articles on actress Mabel Normand in an effort to help rebuild her career and after she was romantically linked to film director William Desmond Taylor, who was murdered.

SPENCER, LYNN—Police reporter and later society editor for the *Examiner*.

SPENCER, HERBERT—He was a top police reporter and later city editor for the *Evening Express*. In 1931 he quit the newspaper to help launch the weekly magazine *Critic of Critics*. While on a visit to the offices of gangster Charlie ("Gray Fox") Crawford he was shot to death by former prosecutor and municipal court judge candidate Dave Clark. Crawford was wounded.

ST. JOHNS, ADELA ROGERS—She worked as a reporter for the *Evening Herald* from 1914-18, then left to join Hearst's International News Service. She often returned to Los Angeles to cover high profile stories involving sensational crimes and celebrity scandals.

ST. JOHNS, ELAINE—Daughter of William and Adela Rogers St. Johns, she was a reporter for the *Mirror*. She wrote a series of articles on East Los Angeles gang activity and the role the county probation department attempt to play to ease tensions between law-enforcement authorities and gang members. It was an early example of the *Mirror*'s aggressive coverage of minority affairs.

ST. JOHNS, WILLIAM IVAN("IKE")—A young, highly respected news editor for the old *Evening Herald* during much of the 1910s. He was married to Adela Rogers. The couple had a daughter, Elaine, who became a newswoman in her own right.

SUTHERLAND, HANK—A rewrite man for the *Examiner* in the 1940s and '50s.

SUTTON, WAIN—Legendary rewrite man for the *Examiner* through the 1940s and '50s. He broke the news to Phoebe Short, mother of Elizabeth Short, the Black Dahlia, that her daughter had been murdered.

teGROEN, WILLIAM—A World War I veteran who was wounded in combat, teGroen joined the *Evening Herald* in 1920. He spearheaded the movement among courthouse reporters to form a union. By 1936 the Los Angeles Newspaper Guild was founded. He also represented the Guild during the 1946 *Herald & Express* strike, although he had voted against it.

THOMAS, WILLIAM F.—Graduated from Northwestern University in 1951, Thomas began his career as a copy editor at the Buffalo *Evening News*. In California he was editor of the Sierra Madre *News* before joining the *Mirror* as a reporter in 1957. Following a stint on the copy desk, he was named assistant city editor of the *Mirror* in 1959, then city editor in 1961. After the *Mirror* folded, he was named metro editor of the *Times*. In 1971 he was promoted to executive editor. A year later he was named editor and executive vice president of the *Times*.

THOMPSON, TOMMY—Staff photographer for the *Daily News*, he was covering the county and federal court beats through most of the 1930s.

TRUEBLOOD, RALPH—Conservative editor for the *Times*. He established an anticrime commission Harry Chandler in the early 1920s to help stem the flow of organized crime into the city. But at the same time he endorsed as police chief James E. Davis, who allowed gambling and vice to flourish

TURNER, TIM—A reporter for the *Times*, Turner covered the hotel beat out of the Biltmore Hotel pressroom. As the senior reporter on the city's most influential newspaper, Turner decided which stories on the beat rival reporters should write. All stories under Turner's supervision would be syndicated, a regular practice until the 1950s.

TURPIN, DICK—Was a longtime staffer for the *Times*. He served as president of the Greater Los Angeles Press Club. He was the *Times*' education writer and editor from 1957-67, then moved to the real estate department where he assumed editing duties. He was a reporter and sports editor for the Burbank *Review* from 1946-48.

UNDERWOOD, AGNESS—She was the only woman city editor of a major metropolitan daily in Los Angeles during the height of the city's newspaper wars. She got her start in the business as a switchboard operator on the *Evening Record* then took a job as a general assignment reporter at the *Herald & Express*. Loved dearly by the male reporters but met with indifference by women staffers, she nonetheless became city editor in 1947. She remained on the job until the *Examiner* was folded into the *Herald & Express* to become the *Herald-Examiner*. At that time she was kicked upstairs to assistant managing editor, losing virtually all of her influence in the newsroom.

VANDERBILT, CORNELIUS—The hard luck founder, editor, and publisher of the troubled *Illustrated Daily News* from 1923-26. His prudish approach to journalism, misplaced faith in poor managers, and mismanagement of the paper's finances doomed his vision of a clean penny paper. It went bankrupt in 1926. He authored numerous books and free-lanced to many magazines and newspapers throughout his lengthy journalism career.

VOGDES, WALTER—Reporter for the *Examiner* during the 1920s. He scored many exclusive interviews with celebrities and crime suspects, becoming one of the few reporters of the era to earn bylines.

WAGNER, LEICESTER("LES")—He cubbed at the Santa Barbara *Morning Press*, then moved to the *Daily News* in 1929. He ultimately worked three separate stints at the *Daily News*, sandwiching in service at United Press in both the Los Angeles and San Francisco bureaus. During World War II, he served as a correspondent for the Office of War Information in India. After the war he returned to the *Daily News*, spent a year at *Fortnight* magazine, then signed on as a columnist at the *Mirror*. Later at the *Mirror* he specialized in rabies and smog issues. He was president of the Greater Los Angeles Press Club in 1950. He concluded his career at the Costa Mesa *Daily Pilot*.

WATSON JR., COY—He started his news career as a staff photographer at Acme Newspictures under the tutelage of his uncle, George Watson. He worked for the *Evening Record*, the *Daily News*, the *Times*, and the *Herald & Express*, covering virtually all of the city's most sensational crimes and scandals. He started Hollywood Reel, a television program, in 1949. He also was a television news cameraman for KTLA, KNXT, and KABC.

WATSON, DELMAR—Another member of the Watson clan, he began his career with Acme Newspictures. He joined the *Mirror* when it was founded in 1948 and stayed there until the paper folded in 1962. He is a frequent lecturer about photojournalism to various journalism and civic organizations.

WATSON, GARRY—He had worked as a staff photographer for the *Daily News* and the *Times* before becoming a free-lance photojournalist.

WATSON, GEORGE—As uncle of the pioneering Watson brothers, he became the *Times'* first staff photographer in 1917. He left the *Times* in 1929 to manage Acme Newspictures. He specialized in aviation photography, and was the first president of the Los Angeles Press Photographers Association in 1925. He retired in 1940, but briefly returned to the *Times* during World War II.

WATSON, HARRY—A leading staff photographer for the *Daily News* and probably the press corps' leading practical joker. He was a combat photographer in the South Pacific during World War II. He switched to television news in the early 1950s and became a pioneer in television camera work. He was severely injured in a plane crash that killed a *Mirror* reporter while on assignment near Las Vegas. He worked for KTTV television.

WEEKS, PAUL—A native of North Dakota, he began his career at 16 at the Albuquerque (N.M.) *Journal*. He joined the *Daily News* in 1946, working as a reporter and assistant city editor. After signing on at the *Mirror*, he helped pioneer coverage of the African American community, ultimately becoming one of the top civil rights reporters in the country. He also served a stint at the paper's Washington, D.C. bureau. He joined the *Times* when the *Mirror* folded in 1962. He later worked for the federal Office of Economic Opportunity and in public relations at the RAND Corp.

WEINSTOCK, HERB—Brother of Matt Weinstock, he was a financial reporter for the *Daily News*.

WEINSTOCK, MATT—Perhaps the single most important voice of Los Angeles during the prewar years through the mid-1950s. He served in various posts at the *Daily News* before becoming managing editor then a columnist. He was a student at UCLA writing sports copy for space rates at the *Examiner* when he was given a job at the *Daily News* in 1924.

WESSELMAN, CLIFF—He was a top photographer at the *Daily News* for many years. He covered the city's most sensational crimes. Some of his photographs helped expose police misconduct. His photographs are still published today in various books and publications depicting Los Angeles noir of the 1940s and '50s.

WHITE, ART—An investigative reporter for the *Mirror*, White was best known for penning a series of articles on influence peddling by William G. Bonnelli, a member of the state Board of Equalization.

WHITE, F.E. ("PETE") –He worked on several newspapers in the mid-west before coming to Los Angeles in 1945. He was an assistant news editor at the *Mirror-News*. He was promoted to news editor in 1960.

WILLIAMS, CARLTON—He succeeded Al Nathan as the *Times'* powerbroker in City Hall from about 1938 through the late '50s. While he was highly influential with both city council members and the Chandler family, his powered ebbed and all but disappeared when Nick Williams assumed the top post in the editorial department.

WILLIAMS, NICK B.—He started his journalism career with the Dallas *Morning News* as an office boy, then reported for the Fort Worth *Star Telegram* and the Nashville *Tennessean*. He began his lengthy tenure at the *Times* as a copy editor in 1931. He served variously as a telegraph editor, news editor, and picture editor among other jobs before replacing as editor L.D. Hotchkiss, who retired in 1958. Williams is credited for bringing about radical changes at the *Times* from a conservative, dull newspaper to a highly polished, professional one.

WILLIS, H.B.K. ("DOC")—An early staffer for the *Illustrated Daily News* under Cornelius Vanderbilt Jr. He was responsible for transporting the first pictures of the 1923 Tokyo earthquake to the *Daily News* offices.

WOOLARD, WARDEN—He was the assistant managing editor of the *Examiner*. He helped break the story of the Black Dahlia's identity by suggesting the dead woman's fingerprints be transmitted by the *Examiner*'s Soundphoto machine to the FBI in Washington, D.C. After two attempts, murder victim Elizabeth Short was identified.

YOUNG, LEWIS—He was the city editor of the *Herald & Express* in 1945-46.

ZELINKSY, BILL—Longtime police reporter for the *Examiner* during the 1940s and '50s

Notes & Sources

Abbreviations

AH	Alan Hensher
CP	California Publisher
E&P	Editor & Publisher
FE	Fourth Estate
FN	Fortnight
HC	Hollywood Citizen
HL CC	Honold Library, Claremont College
LAC	Los Angeles Citizen
LADN	Los Angeles *Daily News*
LAE	Los Angeles *Examiner*
LAEE	Los Angeles *Evening Express*
LAEH	Los Angeles *Evening Herald*
LAEHE	Los Angeles *Evening Herald & Express*
LAER	Los Angeles *Evening Record*
LAIDN	Los Angeles *Illustrated Daily News*
LAM	Los Angeles *Mirror*
LAMN	Los Angeles *Mirror*-News
LAPR	Los Angeles *Post-Record*
LAT	Los Angeles *Times*
RHC USC	Regional History Center, University of Southern California
RL UCR	Rivera Library, University of California, Riverside
RLW	author
SC UCLA	Special Collections, University of California, Los Angeles
TEBF	The Eight Ball Final
TGR	The Guild Reporter
TGM	The Guildsman

Introduction

Page 11, *It was the best* ... Weinstock, Matt, "Early Days of the *Daily News*," Leaves: From an Editor's Notebook, Vol. 1, No. 1, Pala, California, July 1963.

Page 11, *Los Angeles was* ... Henstell, Bruce, Sunshine and Wealth: Los Angeles in the Twenties and Thirties, San Francisco Chronicle Books, 1984.

Page 12, *The city couldn't* ... Starr, Kevin, Material Dreams: Southern California Through the 1920s, Oxford University Press, New York, 1989; E&P, June 5, 1920.

Page 12, *So other than* ... Murray, Jim, Jim Murray: An Autobiography, MacMillan Publishing Company, New York, 1993.

Page 15, *Chandler was born* ... Gottlieb, Robert and Wolt, Irene, Thinking Big: The Story of the Los Angeles *Times*, Its Publishers and Their Influence in Southern California, G.P. Putnam's Sons, New York, New York, 1977.

Page 15, *The tabloid* ... Bessie, Simon Michael, Jazz Journalism: The Story of Tabloid Newspapers, Russell & Russell, New York, 1938;

Page 18, *Los Angeles* ... American Newspaper Publishers Association, Average Annual Prices of Newsprint, 1923-1954, Pacific Coast Ports; "Wage Scales Paid by Newspapers in Chief American Cities," E&P International Yearbook Number, 1924 through 1937.

Page 19, *While Los Angeles* ... N.W. Auer and Son, American Newspaper Annual and Directory, 1924 through 1930.

Page 19, *Mimicking the* ... Bessie, Simon Michael, Jazz Journalism: The Story of Tabloid Newspapers, Russell & Russell, New York, 1938. Starr, Kevin, Material Dreams: Southern California Through the 1920s, Oxford University Press, 1990.

Page 22, *By the mid-1950s* ... Kerby, Phil, "No News is Bad News," *Frontier*, July 1956.

Chapter One

Page 25, *For Fred Eldridge* ... LAE, 10 September 1921; LAEH, 10 September 1921; LAEE, 10 September 1921; LAT, 10 September 1921; LAER, 10 September 1921.

Page 25, *No managing editor* ... LAE, 10 August 1937; LAE, 11 August 1937; LAE, 12 August 1937.

Page 26, *At Eldridge's side* ... LAE, 25 October 1951; LAT, 25 October 1951; LAE, 1 October 1940; LAE, 22 June 1943.

Page 26, *By the time* ... Siegel, Scott and Siegel, Barbara, The Encyclopedia of Hollywood, Avon Books, New York, New York, 1990.

Page 26, *Charlie Chaplin* ... Robinson, David, Chaplin: His Life and Art, McGraw-Hill Book Co., New York, New York, 1985.

Page 26, *In 1919, Chaplin* ... Monaco, James, The Encyclopedia of Film, Baseline II, Inc., New York, New York, 1991.

Page 27, *While Wall Street* ... LAE, 25 June 1918; LAE, 23 September 1918

Page 27, *A press-fueled scandal* ... Edmonds, Andy, Frame Up: The Untold Story of Roscoe "Fatty" Arbuckle, William Morrow & Co., Inc., New York, New York, 1991.

Page 28, *As Arbuckle prepared* ... LAE, 10 September 1921.

Page 29, *The Times* ... LAT 10 September 1921.

Page 29, *The night edition* ... LAH, 10 September 1921.

Page 29, *At first* ... LAE, 10 September 1921.

Page 29, *The Evening Record* ... LAER 10 September 1921; 16 September 1921

Page 30, *By 1921*... E&P, 27 March 1920, "Space-Buyers Chart and Market Survey of the State of California," E&P, 5 June1920; "Rates, Circulations and Executive Personnel of United States Daily Newspapers," E&P International Yearbook Number, 1923 through 1931; house ad, LAEH, 6 February, 1922; house ad, LAEE, 26 May 1926.

Page 30, *The Herald's offices* ... Pitt, Leonard and Dale, Los Angeles A to Z: An Encyclopedia of the City and County, University of California Press, Berkeley, California, 1997; Dash, Norman, Yesterday's Los Angeles, E.A. Seemann Publishing, Inc., Miami, Florida, 1976.

Page 30, *At the helm of* ... Who Was Who in Journalism, 1925-1928; LAE, 26 August 1936.

Page 31, *To serve as* ... Who Was Who in Journalism, 1925-1928; LAE, 11 September 1954; RLW interview with Will Fowler, 1 February 1997, Sherman Oaks, California; RLW interview with Nieson Himmel, 6 June 1998, Los Angeles, California; Fowler, Will, Reporters: Memoirs of a Young Newspaperman, Roundtable Publishing Company, Malibu, California, 1991.

Page 31, *Founded as a daily* ... E&P, 27 March 1920; LAT, 23 February, 1956; LAE 26 February 1956.

Page 32, *Since the afternoon* ... LAE, 11 September 1921.

Page 33, *As if statements* ... LAE, 11 September 1921.

Page 33, *But the Examiner* ... LAE, 12 September 1921.

Page 33, *The Times carried* ... LAT, 12 September 1921.

Page 33, *The Herald, though* ... LAEH, 12 September 1921.

Page 34, *The Evening Express'* ... LAEE, 12 September 1921.

Page 34, *As movie houses* ... LAEE, 13 September 1921.

Page 34, *That same day* ... LAEH, 13 September 1921.

Page 35, *James Hugh Richardson* ... Richardson, James H., For the Life of Me: Memoirs of a City Editor, G.P. Putnam's Sons, New York, 1959.

Page 35, *Richardson provided* ... LAEH, 15, September 1921.

Page 35, *Richardson's story was* ... LAE, 16 September 1921.

Page 38, *Richardson would come* ... LAEH, 16 September 1921

Page 39, *Arbuckle's first trial* ... Edmonds, Andy, Frame Up: The Untold Story of Roscoe "Fatty" Arbuckle, William Morrow & Co., Inc., New York, New York, 1991.

Page 40, *William Desmond Taylor* ... Giroux, Robert, The Deed of Death, Alfred A. Knopf, New York, 1990.

Page 40, *Normand was considered* ... Siegel, Scott and Siegel, Barbara, The Encyclopedia of Hollywood, Avon Books, New York, New York, 1990.

Page 41, *The Taylor story* ... LAEH, 2 February 1922.

Page 41, *Peavey discovered* ... LAEH, 2 February 1922.

Page 42, *The Examiner on* ... LAE, 3 February 1922.

Page 42, *Only the Record* ... LAER, 2 February 1922.

Page 43, *By 3 February* ... LAEH, 3 February 1922.

Page 43, *More alarming to* .. LAEE, 3 February 1922.

Page 43, *The Examiner's lead* ... LAE, 4 February 1922.

Page 44, *Curiously, the Examiner*, LAE, 11 February 1922.

Page 44, *While Normand may* .. LAE, 7 February 1922.

Page 44, *Writer and director* ... LAER, 13 February 1922.

Page 44, *English writer* ... LAE, 20 February 1922.

Page 46, *The coverage of* ... LAE, 17 February 1924.

Source material on the Arbuckle/Taylor scandals also were found in:

LAER, 12 September 1921; LAER, 13 September 1921; LAER, 14 September 1921;LAR, 15 September 1921; LAER, 16 September 1921; LAER, 17 September 1921; LAT, 11 September 1921; LAT, 13 September 1921; LAT, 14 September 1921; LAT, 15 September 1921; LAT, 16 September 1921; LAT, 17 September 1921; LAEE, 10 September 1921; LAEE 14 September 1921; LAEE, 15 September 1921; LAEH, 11 September 1921; LAEH, 14 September 1921; LAE, 11 September 1921; LAE, 12 September 1921; LAE, 13 September 1921; LAE, 14 September 1921; LAE, 15, September 1921; LAEH, 6 February 1922; LAEH, 3 February 1922; LAEH, 4 February 1922; LAEH, 5 February 1922; LAEH, 6 February 1922; LAEH, 7 February 1922;LAEH, 8 February 1922; LAEH, 9 February 1922; LAEH, 10 February 1922; LAEH, 11 February 1922; LAEH, 12 February 1922; LAEE, 2 February 1922; LAEE, 3 February 1922; LAEE, 4 February 1922; LAEE, 5 February 1922; LAEE, 6 February 1922; LAEE, 7 February 1922; LAEE, 8 February 1922; LAEE, 9 February 1922; LAE, 10 February 1922; LAE, 3 February 1922; LAE, 4 February 1922; LAE, 5 February 1922; LAE, 6 February 1922; LAE, 9 February 1922; LAE, 10 February 1922; LAE, 11 February 1922; LAE, 12 February 1922; LAE, 13 February 1922; LAE, 17 February 1924; LAE, 20 February 1922; HC, 17 February 1922; LAER, 2 February 1922; LAER 13 February 1922.

Chapter Two

Page 47, *Vanderbilt, full of* ... Knox, William Boardman, "The Collapse of the Vanderbilt Crusade," The Outlook, 26 May 1926.

Page 47, *Vanderbilt was perhaps* ... Hensher, Alan, "Penny Papers: The Vanderbilt Newspaper Crusade," California Historical Quarterly, Vol. LV, Summer 1972, No. 2, Selden, Charles A., "Young Vanderbilt's Crusade Against Filth," *The Ladies' Home Journal*, May 1924; "Cornelius Vanderbilt Jr., Newsman, Author, Dead," New York *Times*, 7 July 1974; Vanderbilt, Cornelius, Farwell to Fifth Avenue, Simon & Schuster, New York, New York, 1935; Vanderbilt, Cornelius, Man of the World: My Life on Five Continents, Crown Publishers, New York, New York, 1959.

Page 51, *In September* ... "How Vanderbilt Jr's Family Tried to Make Him A Snob," San Francisco *Examiner*, 20 February, 1927; Hensher, Alan, "Penny Papers: The Vanderbilt Newspaper Crusade," California Historical Quarterly, Vol. LV, Summer 1972, No. 2.

Page 51, *The Pacfic Coast* ... Selden, Charles A., "Young Vanderbilt's Crusade Against Filth," *The Ladies' Home Journal*, May 1924 Lang, Chas. J., Who's Who in Los Angeles, 1926-27, Los Angeles, California.

Page 51, *Believing that a true* ... New York *Times* 24 June 1923; San Francisco *Chronicle*, 24 June 1923; Vanderbilt, Cornelius, Prospectus of *Illustrated Daily News*, 1923.

Page 51, *Vanderbilt and Lewis* ... Vanderbilt, Cornelius, Prospectus of *Illustrated Daily News*, 1923.

Page 52, *Early indications* ... LAC, 29 June 1923; LAT, 4 July 1923; LAT, 6 July 1923; LAC, 6 July 1923 and FE, Vol. 30, 14 July 1923.

Page 52, *Vanderbilt resorted* ... Hensher, Alan, "Penny Papers: The Vanderbilt Newspaper Crusade," California Historical Quarterly, Vol. LV, Summer 1972, No. 2.

Page 52, *The buzz was* ... LAC, 6 July 1923.

Page 52, *What interested the* ... LAC, 11 January 1924.

Page 53, *Progress was rapid* ... LAC, 6 July 1923.

Page 53, *By mid-August* ... Hensher, Alan, unpublished manuscript on the History of the Los Angeles *Daily News*.

Page 56, *Hiring editorial staff* ... Weinstock, Matt, "Early Days of the *Daily News*," Leaves: From an Editor's Notebook, Vol. 1, No. 1, Pala, California, July 1963.

Page 56, *The first day* ... Selden, Charles A., "Young Vanderbilt's Crusade Against Filth," *The Ladies' Home Journal*, May 1924 and Knox, William Boardman, "The Collapse of the Vanderbilt Crusade," The *Outlook*, 26 May 1926.

Page 58, *On its editorial* ... LAIDN, 3 September 1923.

Page 58, *If circulation numbers* ... E&P, Vol. 56, 5 November 1923 and Western Advertising, Vol. 5, Page 49, September 1923.

Page 58, *While the Daily* ... Weinstock, Matt, "Early Days of the *Daily News*," Leaves: From an Editor's Notebook, Vol. 1, No. 1, Pala, California, July 1963; Weinstock's unpublished manuscript of the history of the early days of the *Daily News*, SC UCLA.

Page 59, *Vanderbilt later said* ... Knox, William Boardman, "The Collapse of the Vanderbilt Crusade," The *Outlook*, 26 May 1926.

Page 59, *Three weeks after* ... Matt Weinstock's unpublished manuscript of the history of the early days of the *Daily News*, SC UCLA.

Page 60, *For once, Vanderbilt* ... Letter from Lester Adams to Joel Rickman, undated (1925), Lester Adams scrapbooks, Ashland, Oregon, and letter from Lester Adams to Harvey Johnson of Vanderbilt Newspapers, Inc, Los Angeles, undated, Lester Adams scrapbooks, Ashland, Oregon.

Page 61, *If the Daily* ... Hensher, Alan, unpublished manuscript on the History of the Los Angeles *Daily News*.

Page 61, *Editorial staff did* ... Matt Weinstock's unpublished manuscript of the history of the early days of the *Daily News*, SC UCLA.

Page 62, *When the Daily* ... Knox, William Boardman, "The Collapse of the Vanderbilt Crusade," The *Outlook*, 26 May 1926.

Page 62, *The union trade* ... San Francisco *Labor Clarion*, Vol. 12, 28 September 1923.

Page 62, *By the end* ... FE, Vol. 30, 6 October 1923; LAC, 2 November 1923; LAC, 9 November 1923, LAC, 23 November 1923; San Francisco *Labor Clarion*, Vol. 22, 14 December 1923.

Page 64, *Unable to ignore* ... Hensher, Alan, unpublished manuscript on the History of the Los Angeles *Daily News*.

Page 64, *Former night city* ... Knox, William Boardman, "The Collapse of the Vanderbilt Crusade," *The Outlook*, 26 May 1926.

Page 65, *Vanderbilt again went* ... Hensher, Alan, unpublished manuscript on the History of the Los Angeles *Daily News*; LAT, 29 April, 1926; New York *Times*, 30 April, 1926; LAT, 30 April 1926; E&P, 1 May 1926; *Saturday Night*, 24 July 1926; E&P, 26 June 1926 and E&P, 24 July 1926.

Other source material on the Vanderbilt era are: LAT, 11 April 1924; LAIDN, 3 April 1924; LAE, 2 June 1932 and Pitt, Leonard and Dale, Los Angeles A to Z: An Encyclopedia of the City and County, University of California Press, Berkeley, California, 1997.

Chapter Three

Page 67, *Gene Coughlin was* ... Coughlin, Gene, unpublished manuscript of the history of the Los Angeles *Daily News* under E. Manchester Boddy's management, Los Angeles, 1953.

Page 68, *When Coughlin returned* ... LAE, 2 June 1932.

Page 68, *It was surprising* ... Rosenstone, Robert A, Manchester Boddy and the L.A. *Daily News*, California Historical Quarterly, Volume XLIX, No. 4, December 1970.

Page 69, *Boddy was born*... Coughlin, Gene, unpublished manuscript of the history of the Los Angeles *Daily News* under E. Manchester Boddy's management, Los Angeles, 1953.

Page 72, *Boddy's opportunity came* ... Rosenstone, Robert A, Manchester Boddy and the L.A. *Daily News*, California Historical Quarterly, Volume XLIX, No. 4, December 1970.

Page 72, *Chandler approved of* ... Carew, Harold D., "Good Aims for Bad Men," *Westways*, June 1934.

Page 73, *As vice continued to* ... Gottlieb, Robert and Wolt, Irene, Thinking Big: The Story of the Los Angeles *Times*, Its Publishers and Their Influence in Southern California, G.P. Putnam's Sons, New York, New York, 1977.

Page 73, *Police officers in* ... Arrington, Johnnie, "A Police Reporter's Memoirs," Seal Beach *Post & Wave*, 24 December 1942.

Page 74, *The repeated failures* ... Arrington, Johnnie, "A Police Reporter's Memoirs, Seal Beach *Post & Wave*, 12 March 1943 and 26 March 1943.

Page 76, *Manchester Boddy was* ... Coughlin, Gene, unpublished manuscript of the history of the Los Angeles *Daily News* under E. Manchester Boddy's management, Los Angeles, 1953.

Page 82, *As if local* ... Tygiel, Jules, The Great Los Angeles Swindle: Oil, Stocks, and Scandal During the Roaring Twenties, University of California Press, Berkeley, 1994.

Page 83, *Another, but more* ... E&P, 23 May 1931; Underwood, Agness, Newspaperwoman, Harpers & Brothers Publishers, New York, 1949; Pitt, Leonard and Dale, Los Angeles A to Z: An Encyclopedia of the City and County, University of California Press, Berkeley, California, 1997.

Page 84, *To a lesser degree* ... Arrington, Johnnie, "A Police Reporter's Memoirs," Seal Beach *Post & Wave*, 16 April 1943.

Page 85, *The end of* ... Coughlin, Gene, unpublished manuscript of the history of the Los Angeles *Daily News* under E. Manchester Boddy's management, Los Angeles, 1953.

Page 85, *The Daily News* ... E&P, Vol. 59, 27 November 1926.

Page 86, *A staunch Republican* ... AH interview with Merritt W. ("Pop") Jorz, 10 February 1970, Lodi, California; E&P, 30 June 1934, Vol. 67, p. 1.

Page 86, *While Boddy's endorsement* ... McWilliams, Carey, The Education of Carey McWilliams, Simon & Schuster, New York, New York, 1978; *New Decmocracy*, 15 December 1935, p 31.

Page 87, *More importantly to* ... LAIN, 30 November 1932 and 2 December 1932 and 14 Dember 1932.

Page 87, *Steeped in the traditions* ... Boulevard *Record*, 15 December 1932 and the Maywood *Journal*, 16 December 1932.

Page 88, *All of these* ... Mitchell, Greg, The Campaign of the Century: Upton Sinclair's Race for Governor of California and the Birth of Media Politics, Random House, New York, New York, 1992; Pitt, Leonard and Dale, Los Angeles A to Z: An Encyclopedia of the City and County, University of California Press, Berkeley, California, 1997; Rodriguez, Jose, "Script's Pulitzer Prize Candidate,", 21 January 1933, *Rob Wagner's Script*.

Page 88, *Sinclair lost the* ... Taylor, Frank J. "Man With a Borrowed Shoestring," The *Saturday Evening Post*, 2 December 1944.

Page 89, *Whatever his motives* ... AH interview with Robert E.G. Harris, 24 January 1966, Los Angeles, California.

Page 89, *The first prime* ... AH interview with Herb Weinstock, 9 September 1969, Hollywood, California; AH interview with Hal Lindley, 31 May 1968, Los Angeles, California; AH interview with Jack Kennett, 25 July 1969, Hollywood, California.

Page 89, *At almost the* ... AH interview with Merritt W. ("Pop") Jorz, 10 February 1970, Lodi, California; Milkman, Paul, PM: A New Deal in Journalism, 1940-1948, Rutgers University Press, New Brunswick, New Jersey, 1997; E&P, 30 June 1934; LADN, 7 July 1934; *Western Advertising*, January 1940.

Page 91, *If Boddy was* ... AH interview with Herb Weinstock, 9 September 1969, Hollywood, California.

Page 91, *Hal Lindley joined* ... AH interview with Hal Lindley, 31 May 1968, Los Angeles, California; AH interview with Jack Kennett, 25 July 1969, Hollywood, California.

Other source material on Boddy's crusades and management of the *Daily News* are:

CP, June 1932; Memo from Jack Thompson to Lee F. Payne, 23 June 1952, AH collection; LAIDN, 25 May, 1933; *Time*, 23 November 1942; Hensher, Alan, "No News Today: How Los Angeles Lost a Daily," Journalism Quarterly, 1970; LAIDN, 24 August 1926; Los Angeles Commerical and Financial Digest, Vol. 4, 10 January 1927 LAT, 17 January 1927; LAIDN, 6 August 1926; LAT, 7 August 1926; LAIDN, 9 August 1926; RLW interview with Norman ("Jake") Jacoby, 28 February 1998, Montrose, California; RLW interview with Leo Thomas Batt, 18 April 1998, Sun City, California; Arrington, Johnnie, "A Police Reporter's Memoirs," Seal Beach *Post & Wave*, 11 June 1943; LAEE, 12 June 1926; LAEE, 9 August 1926; LAE, 27 February 1938; Helmer, William and Mattix, Rick, Public Enemies: America's Criminal Past,1919-1940, Checkmark Books, New York, New York, 1998; LAE,

22 May 1928; LAE, 23 May 1928; *Los Angeles Commercial and Financial Digest*, 10 January 1927.

Chapter Four

Page 93, *It was Dickson's* ... "October linage from 1929", E&P, 29 November 1930 and "December linage from 1930", E&P, 24 January 1931; "Annual Tabulation of Newspaper Linage," E&P, 14 March 1931.

Page 93, *The Express had* ... "Los Angeles *Express* Sold to Paul Block", E&P, 14 February 1931.

Page 93, *At fifty-two, Dickson* ... LAT, 23 February, 1956; LAE 26 February 1956.

Page 94, *Earl and Dickson* ... LAT, 26 February 1931; LAT, 10 February 1931; LAT, 11 February 1931; LAER, 12 February 1931; LAE, 12 February 1931; LAE, 12 February 1931.

Page 95, *The Times howled* ... LAT, 11 February 1931.

Page 95, *On 10 February* ... LAT, 11 February 1931 and LADN, 11 February 1931; LAE, 17 February 1931.

Page 95, *Despite Block's indignant* ... LAT, 26 February 1931.

Page 96, *Bock and Hearst* ... LAH, 10 December 1931; LAT, 10 December 1931; LAR, 9 December 1931; LAT, 10 December 1931.

Page 96, *The Times couldn't* ... LAT, 11 December 1931.

Page 97, *The Record, one* ... AH interview with Reuben Borough, 24 May 1968, Los Angeles, California; Notes of the history of the Los Angeles *Daily News* (and Los Angeles *Evening Record*), Matt Weinstock papers, Collection 700, box 4, folder 4, UCLA Department of Special Collections, Research Library; Borough, Reuben W., "The Suicide of a Newspaper," *Frontier*, February 1965; "Reuben W. Borough and California Reform Movements," Oral History Program manuscript completed at UCLA, 1968.

Page 99, *When illness forced* ... EF, Vol. 31, page 22, 28 February 1925; LAT 28 September 1936.

Page 105, *As the election* ... Matt Weinstock papers, Collection 700, box 4, folder 4, UCLA Department of Special Collections, Research Library; Borough, Reuben W., "The Suicide of a Newspaper," *Frontier*, February 1965.

Page 106, *The Evening Herald* ... LAHE, 7 November 1932; LAT, 31 October 1932; LAR, 2 November 1932.

Page 106, *The next day* ... LAER, 8 November 1932.

Page 107, *On 31 October* ... LAER, 1 November 1933; LAR, 2 November 1933.

Page 107, *Sanders, who had* ... LAER, 2 November 1933.

Page 107, *Quietly, Sanders began* ... Hensher, Alan, unpublished manuscript on the History of the Los Angeles *Daily News*, "The Depression Years II: Consolidation and Expansion."

Page 108, *If Reuben Borough* ... LAT 28 September 1936.

Page 108, *On 7 January* ... LADN, 8 January 1935; Hensher, Alan, unpublished manuscript on the History of the Los Angeles *Daily News*, "The Depression Years II: Consolidation and Expansion."

Page 108, *O'Donnell, a brash* ... "O'Donnell is Editor of L.A. *Post-Record*", E&P, Vol. 57, 19 January 1935; RLW interview (telephone) with Coy Watson, 12 October 1997; RLW interview (telephone) with Coy Watson, 27 October 1997.

Page 109, *It was Hearst* ... Richardson, James H., For the Life of Me: Memoirs of a City Editor, G.P. Putnam's Sons, New York, 1959; RLW interview (telephone) with Coy Watson, 12 October 1997

Page 110, *The Post-Record* ... RLW interview (telephone) with Coy Watson, 12 October 1997; RLW interview (telephone) with Coy Watson, 27 October 1997; RLW interview with Delmar Watson, 13 September 1997, Hollywood, California.

Page 111, *The employees of* ... Chappell, Charles R., "All About the Forebear of the *Daily News* ... And That's No Bull!" TEBF, 1974.

Page 111, *Although not directly* ... Smith, Jack, "A Bit of L.A. Itself Left with Matt," LAT, 12 January 1970; Weaver, John D., By the Byline, *Westways*, Febrtuary 1976; AH interview with Matt Weinstock, 29 July 1969, Los Angeles, California; Matt Weinstock Certitificate of Death, Los Angeles County, 12 January 1970; LAT, 9 January 1970; RLW interview with Aaron Dudley, 17 November 1996, Chino, California

Page 113, *For Boddy, the* ... LAPR, 1 February 1936; LAT, 3 March 1934; Hensher, Alan, unpublished manuscript on the History of the Los Angeles *Daily News*, "The Depression Years II: Consolidation and Expansion."

Other source material used on the *Herald & Express* merger and the demise of the *Record* are:

LAT, 31 October 1931; LAHE, 16 October 1934; LAT, 1 April 1932; LAER, 27 May 1932; *The Nation*, Vol. 134, 29 June 1932; LAT, 18 January 1968; E&P, 4 November 1933.

Chapter Five

Page 115, *On a rainswept* ... Richardson, James H., For the Life of Me: Memoirs of a City Editor, G.P. Putnam's Sons, New York, 1959.

Page 115, *Across town at* ... Arrington, Johnnie, "A Police Reporter's Memoirs," The Seal Beach *Post & Wave*, 26 March 1943

Page 116, *Raymond had joined* ... LAE, 11 May 1938; LAE, 9 June 1938; Starr, Kevin, The Dream Endures: California Enters the 1940s, Oxford University Press, New York, 1997; Henstell, Bruce, "When the Lid Blew Off Los Angeles," *Westways*, Vol. 69, November 1977; Coughlin, Gene, unpublished manuscript of the History of the Los Angeles *Daily News* under E. Manchester Boddy's management, Los Angeles, 1953.

Page 117, *The city of* ... Starr, Kevin, The Dream Endures: California Enters the 1940s, Oxford University Press, New York, 1997.

Page 117, *Born in Canada* ... Sitton, Thomas Joseph, Urban Politics and Reform in New Deal Los Angeles: the Recall of Mayor Frak L. Shaw, a dissertation submitted in partial fulfillment of elements for the degree of Doctor of philosophy in history, June 1983, RL UCR.

Page 119, *The squad broke* ... LAE, 1 December 1931: Sitton, Thomas Joseph, Urban Politics and Reform in New Deal Los Angeles: the Recall of Mayor Frak L. Shaw, a dissertation submitted in partial fulfillment of elements for the degree of Doctor of philosophy in history, June 1983, RL UCR.

Page 119, *Seven years after* ... LAT 18 May 1952.

Page 120, *In February 1931* ... LAE, 10 February 1931; 19 February 1931.

Page 120, *Rioting at the* ... LAER, 26 November 1931.

Page 120, *The Evening Record* ... LAER, 30 November 1931; "Open letter: To the Editor of the Los Angeles Angeles *Record*" from William F. Hynes, acting captain of Detectives, LAPD, command Intelligence Bureau, 30 November 1931, RC USC.

Page 120, *The Record only* ... LAER, 2 December 1931.

Page 121, *Still, the strong-arm* ... RLW interview with Norman ("Jake") Jacoby, 28 February 1998, Montrose, California.

Page 121, *The confrontation with* ... LAER, 13 February 1933; LADN, 13 February 1933; LAE, 13 February 1933; LAE, 16 February 1933; LAE, 18 July 1933.

Page 122, *In June 1933* ... LAE, 29 June 1933, LAE, 8 January 1934.

Page 122, *The Squad began* ... LAE, 28 April 1938; LAE, 9 August 1938; LAE, 27 August 1938; LAE, 16 August 1938; LAE, 4 August 1938;LAE, 13 August 1938; LAE, 17 June 1938; LAE, 5 August 1938; LAE, 2 August 1938, LAE. 1 December 1938.

Page 122, *To compound the* ... Longstreet, Stephen, All Star Cast: An Anecdotal history of Los Angeles, Thomas Y. Crowell Co., New York, 1977.

Page 123, *The Times praised* ... LAT, 14 February 1936; Starr, Kevin, Endangered Dreams: The Great Depression, Oxford University Press, New York, 1995.

Page 123, *Bob Gans became* ... Arrington, Johnnie, "A Police Reporter's Memoirs," The Seal Beach *Post & Wave*, 26 March 1943.

Page 124, *Typically, the city's* ... Sitton, Thomas Joseph, Urban Politics and Reform in New Deal Los Angeles: the Recall of Mayor Frak L. Shaw, a dissertation submitted in partial fulfillment of elements for the degree of Doctor of philosophy in history, June 1983, RL UCR; Boynoff, Sara, "In Memoriam," TEBF, 1974.

Page 125, *In 1931, the* ... Henstell, Bruce, "When the Lid Blew Off Los Angeles," *Westways*, Vol. 69, November 1977; Starr, Kevin, Endangered Dreams: The Great Depression, Oxford University Press, New York, 1995.

Page 127, *Shortly before 10 a.m.* ... LAEHE, 14 January 1938.

Page 128, *The Times danced* ... LAT, 15 January 1938.

Page 128, *The Daily News* ... LADN, 15 January 1938.

Page 128, *The Times and* ... LADN, 15 January 1938; LAT, 15 January 1938.

Page 131, *The trial began* ... Underwood, Agness, Newspaperwoman, Harpers & Brothers Publishers, New York,1949.

Page 132, *Seven years after* ... Letter from Harry J. Raymond to California Governor Earl Warren, 23 November 1945, RHC USC; Letter from Harry J. Raymond to California Governor

Earl Warren, 29 November 1945, RHC USC; Letter from Harry J. Raymond to California Governor Earl Warren, 20 January 1948, RHC USC.

Page 133, *In his autobiography* ... Richardson, James H., For the Life of Me: Memoirs of a City Editor, G.P. Putnam's Sons, New York, 1959.

The unfolding events of the Harry Raymond bombing and the subsequent trial of Earl Kynette and Roy Allen were chronicled almost daily by the press. Source material for this segment are:

LAE, 15 January 1938; LAEHE, 15 January 1938; LAT, 16 January 1938; LADN, 16 January 1938;LAE, 16 January 1938;LAEHE, 17 January 1938; LAT, 17 January 1938;LADN, 17 January 1938; LAE, 17 January 1938; LAEHE, 18 January 1938; LAT, 18 January 1938; LADN, 18 January 1938; LAE, 19 January 1938; LAEHE, 19 January 1938; LAT, 19 January 1938; LADN, 19 January 1938; LAE, 20 January 1938; LAEHE 14 January 1938;LAT, 20 January 1938; LADN, 20 January 1938; LAE, 20 January 1938; LAEHE, 20 January 1938; LAT, 21 January 1938; LADN, 21 January 1938; LAE, 21 January 1938; LAEHE, 21 January 1938; LAT, 22 January 1938; LADN 22 January 1938; LAE, 22 January 1938; LAEHE, 22 January 1938; LAT, 25 January 1938;LADN, 25 January 1938; LAE, 25 January 1938; LAEHE, 25 January 1938; LAT, 26 January 1938; LADN, 26 January 1938; LAE, 26January 1938; LAEHE, 26 January 1938; LAT, 27 January 1938; LADN, 27 January 1938; LAE, 27 January 1938; LAEHE, 27 January 1938; LAT 28 January 1938; LADN, 28 January 1938; LAE 28January 1938; LADN, 4 February 1938; LADN, 10 February 1938; LAEHE, 28 February 1938; LAT, 19 February 1938; LADN, 19 February 1938; LAE, 19 February 1938.

Chapter Six

Page 135, *While Agness* ... Underwood, Agness, Newspaperwoman, Harpers & Brothers Publishers, New York,1949; Carlova, John, Lady Editor – the story of "Auggie" Underwood, publication and date unknown.

Page 135, *Across town at* .. RLW interview with Norman ("Jake") Jacoby, 28 February 1998, Montrose, California; RLW interview (telephone) with Jacoby, 4 March 1998; Wentz, Walter B., The Los Angeles Newspaper Guild, A thesis presented to the general faculty of the Claremont Graduate School in partial fulfillment of the requirements for the degree of Master of Arts, HL CC, 1956.

Page 135, *Artist Sam Patrick* ... Patrick Sam, "Cub Reporter's Column," LADN, 28 August 1939.

Page 136, T*he newspapermen and* ... Underwood, Agness, Newspaperwoman, Harpers & Brothers Publishers, New York,1949; RLW interview with Norman ("Jake") Jacoby, 28 February 1998, Montrose, California.

Page 137, *Although Underwood moved* ... RLW interview with Aaron Dudley, 15 November 1996, Chino, California; RLW interview (telephone) with Roy Ringer, 28 March 1998; RLW interview (telephone) with Coy Watson, 27 October 1997; Richardson, James H., For the Life of Me: Memoirs of a City Editor, G.P. Putnam's Sons, New York, 1959.

Page 138, *Even so, the* ... Wentz, Walter B., The Los Angeles Newspaper Guild, A thesis presented to the general faculty of the Claremont Graduate School in partial fulfillment of the requirements for the degree of Master of Arts, HL CC, 1956.

Page 138, *The effort by* ... *ibid.*

Page 139, *By the time* ... Chappell, Charles R., "All About the Forebear of the *Daily News* ... And That's No Bull!" TEBF, 1974.

Page 139, *Spurred by the* ... Wentz, Walter B., The Los Angeles Newspaper Guild, A thesis presented to the general faculty of the Claremont Graduate School in partial fulfillment of the requirements for the degree of Master of Arts, HL CC, 1956; Pitt, Leonard and Dale, Los Angeles A to Z: An Encyclopedia of the City and County, University of California Press, Berkeley, California, 1997; RLW interview with Norman ("Jake") Jacoby, 28 February 1998, Montrose, California; RLW interview (telephone) with Jacoby, 4 March 1998.

Page 140, *Though all were dedicated* ... RLW interview with Norman ("Jake") Jacoby, 28 February 1998; RLW interview (telephone) with Aaron Dudley, 1 June 1998; RLW interview with Nieson Himmel, 6 June 1998, Los Angeles, California; TGM, 3 May 1946; TGM, 1 June 1946 (convention issue).

Page 140, *Jacoby was born* ... RLW interview with Norman ("Jake") Jacoby, 28 February 1998, Montrose, California; RLW interview (telephone) with Jacoby, 4 March 1998.

Page 140, *But for the* ... RLW interviews with Jacoby; AH interview with Charles Judson, 27 January 1967, San Luis Obispo, California.

Page 141, *The Communist influences ... ibid.*

Page 141, *For the most part* ... Walter Wentz thesis.

Page 143, *In the Guild's* ... Los Angeles Newspaper Guild contract with the Los Angeles *Daily News*, 1939-1940, 1940-1941, 1941-1942, 1942-1943, 1943-1944, 1944-1945, 1945-1946.

Page 143, *While the Guild* ... RLW interview with Norman ("Jake") Jacoby, 28 February 1998, Montrose, California.

Page 144, *At first, all* ... Keropian, Haig, "Former C-N Staffers are Almost "Everywhere," TEBF, 1972; E&P, Vol. 64, page 8, 7 November 1931.

Page 144, *Hope for an* .. Walter Wentz thesis and Jacoby interviews.

Page 146, *As if LANG* ... RLW interview (telephone) with Roy Ringer, 28 March 1998; RLW interview with Aaron Dudley, 11 February 1999, Chino, California; RLW interview with Dudley, 16 February 1999, Chino, California.

Page 146, *The strike also* ... Roy Ringer correspondence to RLW, 28 March 1998.

Page 147, *As editor, Dudley* ... RLW interview (telephone) with Aaron Dudley, 1 June 1998.

Page 147, *Eleven months and* ... Roy Ringer correspondence to RLW, 28 March 1998.

Page 147, *Dudley was dumbstruck* ... RLW interview with Aaron Dudley, 11 February 1999, Chino, California.

Page 151, *The strike against* ... Walter Wentz thesis; LAE, 5 September 1946; LAE, 6 September 1946; LAE, 13 September 1946.

Page 151, *As now customary* ... LAE,11 September 1946; LAE, 27 September 1946; LAE, 5 November 1946; LAE, 12 November 1946; LAE, 14 November 1946.

Page 151, *By dawn on* ... TGM, 4 October 1946; Walter Wentz thesis.

Page 153, *LANG members received* ... TGM, 2 December 1946; Walter Wentz thesis.

Page 153, *By the seventh* ... RLW interview with Aaron Dudley, 11 February 1999, Chino, California; Los Angeles Newspaper Guild, Local 69, "*Herald & Express* Strike Fund" assessment receipt, 18 October 1946.

Page 153, *On 26 November, LANG* ... LAE, 27 November 1946.

Page 154, *Guild members from* ... RLW interview with Roy Ringer (telephone), 28 March 1998.

Page 154, *The union had* ... Walter Wentz thesis.

Page 154, *Despite modest gains* ... TGM, 3 May 1946.

Page 154, *Much had changed* ... RLW interview with Paul Weeks, 8 February 1997, Oceanside, California; RLW interview (telephone) with Paul Weeks, 12 May 1997.

Page 155, *City editor Charlie* ... AH interview with Charles Judson, 27 January 1967, San Luis Obispo, California.

Page 155, *Opinions of Judson* ... RLW interview with Paul Weeks, 8 February 1997, Oceanside, California; RLW interview with Aaron Dudley, 16 February 1999, Chino, California; "Charles Judson, newsman, dies," San Luis Obispo *Telegram-Tribune*, 1 February 1972.

Page 155, *Debates of abstract* ... AH interview with Phil Garrison, 13 June 1966, Lancaster, California; AH interview with Vern Partlow, 24 July 1969, Los Angeles, California; Bureau of National Affairs (Washington), Decisions of the National Labor Relations Board, Vol. 19, pages 39-40, 1952.

Page 156, *Editorial employees were* ... RLW interview with Aaron Dudley, 16 February 1999, Chino, California.

Page 156, *Partlow was another* ... AH interview with Vern Partlow, 24 July 1969, Los Angeles, California; Inside News (*Daily News* in-house publication), 1 May 1944; TGM, 1 June 1946; TGM, 4 August 1946; LAT, 4 March 1987; RLW interview with Paul Weeks, 8 February 1997, Oceanside, California.

Page 157, *The firings of* ... Rosswurm, Steve (ed.), The CIO's Left-Led Unions, Rutgers University Press, New Brunswick, New Jersey, 1992; RLW interview with Norman ("Jake") Jacoby, 28 February 1998, Montrose, California.

Page 157, *Editorial employee Lucian* ... RLW interview (telephone) with Lucian Haas, 11 May 1997; Bureau of National Affairs (Washington), Decisions of the National Labor Relations Board, Vol. 19, pages 39-40, 1952.

Page 158, *Before the panel* ... Bureau of National Affairs (Washington), Decisions of the National Labor Relations Board, Vol. 19, pages 39-40, 1952; CP, Vol. 31, page 10, September 1952; E&P Vol. 85, page 12, 12 July 1952; E&P, Vol. 85, page 9, 16 August 1952 CP, September 1952.

Page 159, *Time magazine was* ... *Time*, 1 September 1952.

Page 159, *Partlow rebounded from* ... RLW interview (telephone) with Lucian Haas, 11 May 1997; RLW interview with Norman ("Jake") Jacoby, 28 February 1998, Montrose, California; AH interview with Vern Partlow, 24 July 1969, Los Angeles, California.

Page 159, *Partlow, too, continued* ... RLW interview with Jack Jones, 10 April 1999, Carlsbad, California.

Source material for much of the information on the early efforts to form the Los Angeles Newspaper Guild and subsequent strikes at the *Hollywood Citizen-News*, the Huntington Park *Bulletin*, the *Herald & Express* came from Walter Wentz's master thesis on the Guild and interviews or correspondence with Aaron Dudley, Roy Ringer, and Norman ("Jake") Jacoby. Other sources consulted were: E&P, Vol. 72, page 16, 19 August 1939; TGR (New York), pages 1 and 6, 1 January 1937; E&P, pages 10 and 44, 4 December 1937.

Chapter Seven

Page 161, *The United Press* ... RLW interview with Jack Cravens, 1 February 1997, West Covina, California; LADN, 24 February 1942; LADN, 25 February 1942; LAT, 19 January 1998.

Page 161, *The city's air* ... RLW interview (telephone) with Coy Watson, 12 October 1997; RLW interview (telephone) with Coy Watson, 27 October 1997.

Page 162, *Los Angeles residents* ... LAT, 26 April 1943.

Page 162, *The Daily News* ... RLW interview with Paul Weeks, 8 February 1997, Oceanside, California.

Page 163, *In its 8* ... LAE, 8 December 1941; LAE, 9 December 1941; LAE, 14 December 1941.

Page 164, *Any pretense of* ... LAE, 19 December 1941.

Page 164, *The paper continued* ... LAE, 20 December 1941.

Page 164, *In April 1942* ... LAE, 13 April 1942; LAE, 14 April 1942; LAE, 18 April 1942.

Page 165, *The Hearst press* ... LAE, 25 January 1943; LAE, 23 March 1943.

Page 165, *In his 1944* ... McWilliams, Carey, Prejudice – Japanese-Americans: Symbol of Racial Intolerance, Little, Brown & Company, Boston, MA, 1944.

Page 165, *The Examiner's Washington* ... LAE, 13 June 1943; LAE, 14 June 1943; LAE, 15 June 1943; McWilliams, Carey, Prejudice Japanese Americans: Symbol of Racial Intolerance, Little, Brown & Company, Boston, MA, 1944..

Page 166, *The coverage by* ... Memo from James E. Lewis, reporter, to James Richardson, 1 May 1943, RHC USC.

Page 166, *Lewis couldn't confirm* ... Ration list from Colorado River War Relocation Project, Poston, Arizona, 13 January 1943, RHC USC.

Page 166, *A 1 May* ... Memo from James E. Lewis, reporter, to James Richardson, 1 May 1943, RHC USC.

Page 166, *The stories, coupled* ... McWilliams, Carey, Prejudice – Japanese-Americans: Symbol of Racial Intolerance, Little, Brown & Company, Boston, MA, 1944; LAEHE, 13 May 1943; 19 May 1943.

Page 167, *When Costello's subcommittee* ... LAT, 7 June 1943; LAE, 8 June 1943; LADN, 10 June 1943; LAE, 10 June 1943; LAEHE, 10 June 1943; LAE, 11 June 1943; LADN 11 June 1943; LAT 11 June 1943; LADN, 9 June 1943.

Page 168, *Less than a week* ... LAE, 13 June 1943; LAE, 15 June 1943.

Page 168, *Five days later* ... LAE, 20 June 1943.

Page 169, *But what did* ... McWilliams, Carey, Prejudice – Japanese-Americans: Symbol of Racial Intolerance, Little, Brown & Company, Boston, MA, 1944; Carr, Harry, Los Angeles: City of Dreams, Appleton-Century Co., New York, New York, 1935.

Page 169, *Other rank-and-file* ... Wagner, Leicester, "Presenting: The Dies Committee," *Rob Wagner's Script*, Vol. 24, No. 658, 10 July 1943; Wagner, Leicester, " 'Neighborliness' ... Begins at Home," *Rob Wagner's Script*, Vol. 24, No. 645, 9 January 1943.

Page 170, *Born in 1904* ... Pasadena *Star-News*, 23 November 1965; TEBF, 1965 annual.

Page 170, *Wagner complained in* ... Wagner, Leicester, "Presenting: The Dies Committee," *Rob Wagner's Script*, Vol. 24, No. 658, 10 July 1943.

Page 171, *Once again, the* ... Endore, Guy, The Sleepy Lagoon Mystery, The Sleepy Lagoon Defense Committee, Los Angeles, California, 1944; LAE, 5 August 1942; LAE, 7 August 1942.

Page 172, *Until 1942, the* ... LAE, 19 October 1931; LAE, 29 October 1931; LAE, 30 October 1931; LAE, 15 August 1931; LAE, 18 August 1931; LAE, 26 February 1932; LAE, 2 March 1932.

Page 172, *In a 30 October* ... LAE, 30 October 1931.

Page 172, *Guy Endore claimed* ... Endore, Guy, The Sleepy Lagoon Mystery, The Sleepy Lagoon Defense Committee, Los Angeles, California, 1944.

Page 173, *Unlike the plight ... ibid.*

Page 174, *In turn, city* ... LAE, 10 June 1943; LAEHE, 10 June 1943; LAE, 11 June 1943; LADN 11 June 1943; LAT 11 June 1943; LADN, 9 June 1943; LADN, 24 June 1943.

Page 174, In January 1944 ... LAE, 2 February 1943; LAE, 11 August 1943; LAE, 13 January 1943; LAE, 16 January 1943; LAE, 6 October 1944.

Page 174, *The Eastside ... Eastside Journal*, 20 January 1943.

Page 174, *Wartime Los Angeles* ... Mazon, Maurico,The Zoot-Suit Riots: The Psychology of Symbolic Annihilation, University of Texas Press, Austin, Texas, 1984.

Page 175, *Curiously, frequent violent ... ibid.*

Page 175, *Not surprisingly, the* ... LAE, 5 June 1943.

Page 175, *By contrast, the* ... LAEHE, 5 June 1943.

Page 176, *The Daily News* ... LADN, 6 June 1943.

Page 176, *By 8 June* ... LADN, 8 June 1943.

Page 176, *The Herald & Express* ... LAEHE, 5 June 1943; LAEHE, 9 June 1943; LAEHE, 10 June 1943.

Page 176, *In an upbeat* ... LAEHE, 7 June 1943.

Page 177, *The next day's* ... LAEHE, 8 June 1943.

Page 177, *By then Los ... Time*, 21 June 1943.

Page 177, *In the Examiner* ... LAE, 9 June 1943

Page 177, *The Herald & Express*, LAE, 10 June 1943.

Page 177, *To show that* ... LAEHE, 15 June 1943; LAE, 12 June 1943.

Page 179, *Daily News reporter* ... LADN, 9 June 1943.

Page 179, *Two days later* ... LAT, 11 June 1943.

Page 179, *In his 11 June* ... LADN, 11 June 1943.

Page 179, *Les Wagner, in* ... Wagner, Leicester, "Our Chickens Come Home," *Rob Wagner's Script*, Vol. 24, No. 657, 26 June 1943.

Page 180, *In early 1949* ... LAM, 27-28 March 1949.

Page 180, *By 1954, Mirror* ... LAMN, 7 February 1954

Page 181, *Erickson's series provided* ... McWilliams, Carey, "Nervous Los Angeles" The Nation, 10 June 1950.

Page 181, *In 1950 there* ... LAE, 22 October 1950.

Page 182, *Though ignored by* ... Prince, Virginia Ann, A Sociological Analysis of the Negro Press in Los Angeles, A Thesis Presented to the Faculty of the Department of Sociology Univeristy of Southern California, June 1946.

Page 182, *Until World War II* ... de Graaf, Lawrence Brooks, Negro Migration to Los Angeles, 1930 to 1950, a Dissertation, UCLA, 1962; Collins, Keith E., Black Los Angeles: The Maturing of the Ghetto, 1940-1950, Century Twenty One Publishing, Saratoga, California, 1980.

Page 182, *Up until the* ... Starr, Kevin, Endangered Dreams: The Great Depression in California, Oxford University Press, New York, 1997.

Page 183, *Times Columnist Harry* ... Carr, Harry, Los Angeles: City of Dreams, Appleton-Century Co., New York, New York, 1935.

Page 183, *But for a* ... LAEE, 7 June 1923; LAEE, 2 August1923; LAEE, 4 August 1923; LAEE, 11 June 1923; LAEE, 7 June 1923; LAEE, 9 August 1926.

Page 184, *In June 1926* ... LAEE, 12 June 1926.

Page 184, *Though this type*, LAEE, 7 June 1926.

Page, 184, *Other newspapers were* ... LAT, 14 January 1923.

Page 184, *By contrast, the* ... California *Eagle*, 18 January 1923.

Page 185, *Given the indifference* ... The *Link*: News Magazine of the Los Angeles Police Historical Society, Vol. 5, No. 1, February 1998; RLW interview with Los Angeles police Sgt. John Thomas, 30 July 1998, Parker Center, Los Angeles, California.

Page 185, *The Klan enjoyed ... ibid.*

Page 185, *Daily News reporter* ... RLW interview with Roy Ringer (telephone), 28 March 1998.

Page 185, *Coverage of the* ... RLW interview with Aaron Dudley, 15 November 1996, Chino, California; RLW interview with Roy Ringer (telephone), 28 March 1998.

Page 186, *The single exception* ... LeBerthon, Ted, Night Court, The *Los Angeles Daily News & Evening News*, date unknown; Boynoff, Sara, "In Memoriam," TEBF, 1974.

Page 187, *On its news* ... LADN, 17 March 1947.

Page 187, *In 1953, the* ... LAM, 9-13 February 1953.

Page 187, *The Mirror's competitors* ... RLW interview with Margaret Boutyette Scott, 24 January 1998, North Hollywood, California.

Page 187, *There were attempts* ... TGM, 1 June 1946.

Page 188, *Blacks and other* ... TGM, 5 August, 1946.

Page 188, *The Daily News* ... RLW interview with Paul Weeks, 8 February 1997, Oceanside, California; RLW interview with Jack Jones, 10 April 1999, Carlsbad, California.

Page 188, *White reporters performing* ... RLW interview with Paul Weeks, 8 February 1997, Oceanside, California.

Page 189, *The lure of* ... Los Angeles *Herald-Dispatch*, 29 March 1956.

Page 189, *The Times had* ... RLW interview with Jack Jones, 10 April 1999, Carlsbad, California.

Page 190, *The coverage of* ... LAE,, 13 May 1955; LAE, 10 June 1955; LAE, 13 May 1955; LAE, 21 June 1954; LAE, 22 June 1954; LAE, 9 October 1953; LAE, 28 October1955; LAE,, 11 March 1955; LAE, 1 July 1955; LAE, 18 Novbember 1955; LAE, 12 May 1955; LAE, 1 November 1955.

Page 190, *The Herald & Express* ... LAEHE, 2 February 1956.

Further source material on press coverage of Japanese Americans during World War II include:

LADN, 6 February 1942; LADN, 7 February 1942; LADN, 9 February 1942; LADN, 10 February 1942; LADN, 11 February 1942; LADN, 23 February 1942; LAE, 28 December 1942; LADN, 5 June 1943; LAEHE, 5 June 1943; LADN, 6 June 1943; Letter to J.M. Hill, Parker, Arizona, from Arizona Governor Sidney R. Osborn, 22 April 1943, RHC USC

Further source material on press coverage of the Zoot Suit riots include:

LADN 4 June 1943; LAE, 20 June 1943; LAE, 22 June 1943; LAE, 24 June 1943; LAE, 25 June 1943; LAE, 27 June 1943; LAE, 29 June 1943; LAE, 30 June 1943; LAE, 2 July 1943; LAT, 11 June 1943; LADN, 2 July 1943; LAE, 13 August 1943; LAEHE, 16 June 1943; LAE, 12 June 1943; LADN, 24 June 1943; LAE, 23 June 1943; LADN, 1 July1943; LADN, 25 June 1943; LAEHE, 14 June 1943; LAE, 14 June 1943; LAT 8 June 1943; LAT, 10 June 1943; LADN, 12 June 1943; LAE, 9 June 1943; LAE, 22 June 1943; LAEHE, 12 June 1943; Acuna, Rodolf F., A Community Uner Siege: A Chronicle of Chicanos East of the Los Angeles River, 1945-1975, Chicano Studies Research Center Publications, UCLA, 1984.

Further source material on press coverage of the African American community include:

LAE, 21 October 1944; LAEHE 2 February 1956; LAE,, 21 February 1960; LAE, 22 February 1960; LAE, 23 February 1960; LAE, 24 February 1960; LAE, 26 February 1960; AH interview with Charles Judson, 27 January 1967, San Luis Obispo, California; RLW interview with Will Fowler, 1 February 1997, Sherman Oaks, California; E&P, Vol. 82, Page 30, 30 July 1949; LAMN, 21 December 1954; LAMN, 11 February 1953; LAMN, 12 February 1953; LAMN, 13 February 1953; Fresno *Bee*, 1 February 1960.

Chapter Eight

Page 193, *Second-generation Mexican* ... Pitt, Leonard and Dale, Los Angeles A to Z: An Encyclopedia of the City and County, University of California Press, Berkeley, California, 1997.

Page 193, *Some publishers were* ... *Business Week*, 10 October 1942, Pages 64 and 66.

Page 194, *Mainstream newspapers also* ... LAEHE, 11 June 1943; LAEHE, 12 June 1943.

Page 194, *By 1943, thirty* ... Hensher, Alan, unpublished manuscript of the History of the Los Angeles *Daily News*.

Page 194, *The circulation of* ... "Rate, Circulations, and Executive Personnel of United States *Daily News*papers," Editor & Publisher, 1923-1954.

Page 194, *But such prosperity* ... "Wage Scales Paid by Newspapers in Chief American Cities," Editor & Publisher International Year Book Number, 1939-1946; "Average Annual Prices of Newsprint: 1923-1954," U.S. Federal Trade Commission and the American Newspaper Publishers Association, 11 October 1966.

Page 194, D*espite these increased* ... "*Daily News* Negotiations on Discontinuing A.M. 1950" drawer 6A 1905 82486, office of the Los Angeles Newspaper Guild; Hensher, Alan, unpublished manuscript of the History of the Los Angeles *Daily News*.

Page 195, *One such young* ... RLW interview with Paul Weeks, 8 February 1997, Oceanside, California.

Page 195, *Born in 1920 ... ibid.*

Page 195, *When Weeks arrived* ... RLW interview (telephone) with Jim Murray, 18 July 1998; Murray, Jim, Jim Murray: An Autobiography, MacMillan Publishing Company, New York, 1993.

Page 196, *Joining Murray at* ... RLW interview with Will Fowler, 1 February 1997, Sherman Oaks, California; Fowler, Will, Reporters: Memoirs of a Young Newspaperman , Roundtable Publishing Company, Malibu, California, 1991, Fowler, Will, Will Fowler Biography (unpublished), November 1991.

Page 196, *Fowler graduated from ... ibid.*

Page 196, *Also arriving in* ... RLW interview with Nieson Himmel, 6 June 1998, Los Angeles, California.

Page 197, *Moving to Los* ... Smith, Jack, "A Bit of L.A. Itself Left with Matt," LAT, 12 January 1970; Weaver, John D., By the Byline, *Westways*, Febrtuary 1976.

Page 197, *Smith succeeded Weinstock* ... RLW interview with Jack Jones, 10 April 1999, Carlsbad, California; Pitt, Leonard and Dale, Los Angeles A to Z: An Encyclopedia of the City and County, University of California Press, Berkeley, California, 1997.

Page 197, *When the Times* ... RLW interview with Jack Jones, 10 April 1999, Carlsbad, California.

Page 198, *There were other* ... RLW interview with Paul Weeks, 8 February 1997, Oceanside, California.

Page 198, *Some young reporters* ... RLW interview with Aaron Dudley, 17 November 1996, Chino, California; Saldana, Joseph, "Readers Waited for Copies Hot off Press," TEBF, 1974.

Page 199, *The postwar newsman* ... RLW interview (telephone) with Roy Ringer, 28 March 1998; RLW interview with Leo Thomas Batt, 18 April 1998, Sun City, California.

Page 199, *Nor did the* ... RLW interview with Paul Weeks, 8 February 1997, Oceanside, California.

Page 200, *But Dwiggins never let* ... Dwiggins, Don, "And That's The Way It Was," TEBF, 1974; Dwiggins, Don, "Investigative Reporting – So, What Else Is New," TEBF, 1979; RLW interview with Jack Jones, 10 April 1999, Carlsbad, California; RLW interview (telephone) with Aaron Dudley, 1 June 1998.

Page 200, *When an electroplating* ... Dwiggins, Don, "And That's The Way It Was," TEBF, 1974.

Page 200, *Dwiggins became so* ... Dwiggins, Don, "Investigative Reporting – So, What Else Is New," TEBF, 1979; RLW interview with Jack Jones, 10 April 1999, Carlsbad, California.

Page 201, *In 1946, some* ... RLW interview with Jack Cravens, 1 February 1997, West Covina, California; Caswell, Don, "Cupids in the Elevator," TEBF, 1972; Means, Bevo and Sherman, Gene, "Our L.A. Press Club," TEBF, 1957.

Page 201, *In what Will* ... RLW interview with Will Fowler, 1 February 1997, Sherman Oaks, California; Fowler, Will, Reporters: Memoirs of a Young Newspaperman , Roundtable Publishing Company, Malibu, California, 1991.

Page 202, *The role of queen* ... RLW interview with Aaron Dudley, 17 November 1996, Chino, California; RLW interview with Paul Weeks, 8 February 1997, Oceanside, California; RLW interview with Kendis Rochlen (telephone), 8 September 1997; RLW interview with Nieson Himmel, 6 June 1998, Los Angeles, California.

Page 202, *No less colorful* ... RLW interview with Will Fowler, 1 February 1997, Sherman Oaks, California.

Page 203, *For every Florabel* ... RLW interview with Margaret Boutyette Scott, 24 January 1998, North Hollywood, California

Page 203, *Scott benefited from* ... *ibid.*

Page 204, *Scott had little* ... Letter from Jim Richardson to Margaret Scott, 15 December 1951 (courtesy Margaret Scott).

Page 204, *Some women, though* ... RLW interview with Kendis Rochlen (telephone), 30 September 1997.

Page 205, *Her timid reaction* ... RLW interview with Kendis Rochlen (telephone), 30 September 1997; RLW interview with Leo Thomas Batt, Sun City, California, 18 April 1998.

Page 205, *To Batt, Rochlen* ... RLW interview with Leo Thomas Batt, Sun City, California, 18 April 1998; RLW interview with Will Fowler, 1 February 1997, Sherman Oaks, California.

Page 205, *Until the 1960s* ... RLW interview (telephone) with Paul Weeks, 3 May 1999; RLW interview (telephone) with Aaron Dudley, 1 June 1998; Boynoff, Sara, "In Memoriam," TEBF, 1974.

Page 206, *When the Daily* ... LAT, 25 August 1956; LAE, 25 August 1956.

Page 206, *This group of* ... RLW interview with Will Fowler, 1 February 1997, Sherman Oaks, California.

Page 206, *It was a* ... RLW interview with Will Fowler, 1 February 1997, Sherman Oaks, California; Fowler, Will, Reporters: Memoirs of a Young Newspaperman, Roundtable Publishing Company, Malibu, California, 1991; LAT, 6 January 1997.

Page 207, *Right after Paegel* ... Richardson, James H., For the Life of Me: Memoirs of a City Editor, G.P. Putnam's Sons, New York, 1959.

Page 208, *The Examiner had* ... RLW interview with Will Fowler, 1 February 1997, Sherman Oaks, California; "One reporter's life in 1940s Los Angeles," "Under the Dome," Los Angeles *Herald-Examiner* staff newsletter, 1988; LAEHE, 15 January 1947; LAE, 15 January 1947.

Page 208, *Fowler, Hughes, Zelinsky* ... LAE, 16 January 1947; Richardson, James H., For the Life of Me: Memoirs of a City Editor, G.P. Putnam's Sons, New York, 1959.

Page 208, *By late afternoon* ... Richardson, James H., For the Life of Me: Memoirs of a City Editor, G.P. Putnam's Sons, New York, 1959.

Page 209, *The competition was* ... LAEHE, 16 January 1947.

Page 209, *The Times didn't* ... Gottlieb, Robert and Wolt, Irene, Thinking Big: The Story of the Los Angeles *Times*, Its Publishers and Their Influence in Southern California, G.P. Putnam's Sons, New York, New York, 1977.

Page 209, *By the afternoon* ... RLW interview with Will Fowler, 1 February 1997, Sherman Oaks, California; Fowler, Will, Reporters: Memoirs of a Young Newspaperman , Roundtable Publishing Company, Malibu, California, 1991; RLW interview (telephone) with Jim Murray, 18 July 1998.

Page 214, *It was a major* ... Richardson, James H., For the Life of Me: Memoirs of a City Editor, G.P. Putnam's Sons, New York, 1959; LAE 18 January 1947.

Page 214, *The other scoop* ... RLW interview with Will Fowler, 1 February 1997, Sherman Oaks, California; LAEHE, 17 January 1947; LAEHE, 20 January 1947.

Page 215, *Most reporters from* ... RLW interview with Nieson Himmel, 6 June 1998, Los Angeles, California; RLW interview with Aaron Dudley, 11 February 1999, Chino, California.

Page 215, *Benzedrine, the 1940s* ... RLW interview with Nieson Himmel, 6 June 1998, Los Angeles, California.

Page 215, *The Daily News* ... RLW interview (telephone) with Roy Ringer, 28 March 1998.

Page 216, *It was no wonder* ... Richardson, James H., For the Life of Me: Memoirs of a City Editor, G.P. Putnam's Sons, New York, 1959; RLW interview with Will Fowler, 1 February 1997, Sherman Oaks, California.

Page 216, *"Late on the ..."* LAE, 20 January 1947.

Page 218, *By 25 January* ... LAEHE, 25 January 1947; LAE, 26 January 1947; Richardson, James H., For the Life of Me: Memoirs of a City Editor, G.P. Putnam's Sons, New York, 1959.

Page 218, *Two days later ... ibid.*

Page 219, *George ("Bud") Gollum* ... LAE, 24 March 1947; LADN, 24 March 1947; Murray, Jim, "Remembering Makes Me Wish I Could Forget!" TEBF, date unknown; Richardson,

James H., For the Life of Me: Memoirs of a City Editor, G.P. Putnam's Sons, New York, 1959.

Page 219, *Just before midnight* ... LAT, 17 March 1947; LAE, 17 March 1947.

Page 219, *On Monday morning* ... RLW interview with Will Fowler, 1 February 1997, Sherman Oaks, California; RLW interview (telephone) with Jim Murray, 18 July 1998.

Page 221, *As with any* ... Richardson, James H., For the Life of Me: Memoirs of a City Editor, G.P. Putnam's Sons, New York, 1959; RLW interview (telephone) with Jim Murray, 18 July 1998; Murray, Jim, "Remembering Makes Me Wish I Could Forget!" TEBF, date unknown.

Page 222, *Richardson decided to* ... Richardson, James H., For the Life of Me: Memoirs of a City Editor, G.P. Putnam's Sons, New York, 1959.

Page 222, *The afternoon papers* ... LAEHE, 18 March 1947.

Page 223, I*t did have* ... Jones, Jack, "No Man is an Island," TEBF, 1957; RLW interview (telephone) with Jim Murray, 18 July 1998.

Page 223, *The trial of* ... RLW interview (telephone) with Jim Murray, 18 July 1998.

Page 224, *The Gollum-Overell* ... RLW interview (telephone) with Jim Murray, 18 July 1998.

Page 224, O'*Hara never covered* ... Jones, Jack, "No Man is an Island," TEBF, 1957.

Source material on the daily coverage of the Black Dahalia case include:

LAEHE, 20 January 1947; LAEHE, 25 January 1947; LAE, 18 January 1947; LAE, 19 January 1947; LAE, 20 January 1947 LAE, 22 January 1947 LAE, 23 January 1947; LAE, 25 January 1947; LAE, 26 January 1947; LADN, 15 January 1947; LADN, 16 January 1947; LADN, 17 January 1947; LADN, 18 January 1947; LADN, 19 January 1947; LADN, 20 January 1947; LADN, 25 January 1947; LADN, 26 January 1947; LADN, 27 January 1947; LADN, 28 January 1947.

Source material for daily coverage of the Gollum-Overell murder trial include:

LAEHE, 22 March 1947; LAE, 17 March 1947; LADN, 17 March 1947; LAEHE, 17 March 1947; LAE, 20 March 1947; LAE, 22 March 1947; LAE, 24 March 1947; LAT, 24 March 1947; LAT, 17 March 1947; LAT, 21 March 1947; LAEHE, 18 March 1947; LAEHE, 19 March 1947.

Source material on reporter recollections and events in the early postwar era also include: Underwood, Agness, Newspaperwoman, Harpers & Brothers Publishers, New York,1949; Chappell, Charles R., "All About the Forebear of the *Daily News* ... And That's No Bull!"TEBF, 1974; Parsons, Louelle O., "Louella Says: 'The Richardson Legend Will Live On and On,' "TEBF, October 1957; Sutherland, Henry, "One of Our S-O-Bs are Missing, but He's Remembered Kindly," TEBF, 1957; Saldana, Joseph, "Readers Waited for Copies Hot off Press,"TEBF, 1974; RLW interview (telephone) with Paul Weeks, 12 May 1997; LAT, 27 November 1991; LAT, 14 March 1999.

Chapter Nine

Page 225, *On a cool* ... Levy, Hank, "Remembering a Legend," TEBF, 1979.

Page 225, *The youngest child* ... Clarke, John and Saldana, Joseph, "Life story of Mickey Cohen," LADN, 25 July 1949.

Page 225, *The family was* ... Clarke, John and Saldana, Joseph, "Cohen began as spoiled brat," LADN, 26 July 1949.

Page 226, *As a teenager* ... Clarke, John and Saldana, Joseph, "Mickey Cohen sought riches in ring," LADN, 27 July 1949; Clarke, John and Saldana, Joseph, "Cohen's career in prize ring," LADN, 28 July 1949.

Page 226, *Details of Cohen's* ... "Who's Mickey?" FN, 10 September 1948.

Page 226, *He was suspected* ... LAE memo for city desk: "Police file on Mickey Cohen up to 30 January 1946," RC USC.

Page 227, *Not long after* ... RLW interview with Jack Jones, 10 April 1999, Carlsbad, California.

Page 228, *Investigating mob murders* ... RLW interview with Cliff Dektar, 29 January 1997, Los Angeles, California.

Page 228, *Since Siegel's death* ... Rasmussen, Cecilia, "The Debonair Gangster of Brentwood," LAT, 8 April 1996.

Page 228, *Where the police* ... RLW interview with Paul Weeks, 8 February 1997, Oceanside, California.

Page 229, *In September 1954* ... LADN, 9 September 1954.

Page 229, *The Hearst press* .. LAE, 16 June 1959.

Page 229, *When the State* ... LAE, 4 December 1959.

Page 230, *The coverage of* ... LAE, 6 April 1958; LAE, 6 April 1958; LAE, 9 April 1958; LAE, 10 April 1958.

Page 231, *The press got* ... LAE, 6 April 1958.

Page 231, *Mickey Cohen also* ... LAHE, 9 April 1958.

Page 233, *There were exceptions* ... LAE, 5 October 1929.

Page 233, *The Examiner reported* ... LAE, 29 May 1943; LAE, 27 June 1943.

Page 237, *Dixon escaped conviction* ... LAE, 26 September 1945.

Page 237, *Watson, a photographer* ... RLW interview with Harry Watson, 14 June 1999, Tujunga, California.

Page 237, *Graft and corruption* ... LADN, 2 June 1949; LADN, 4 June 1949; LADN, 14 June 1949; LAE, 25 June 1949.

Page 237, *The Press began* ... LAE, 2 July 1949; LAE, 5 October 1960.

Page 238, *The biggest blow* ... LAE, 20 June 1949.

Page 238, *Horrall, his career* ... LAE, 2 July 1949.

Page 239, *Worton's promises were* ... RLW interview with Harry Watson, 14 June 1999, Tujunga, California.

Page 239, *But Parker quickly* ... RLW interview with Harry Watson, 14 June 1999, Tujunga, California; LADN, 25 December 1951; LAHE, 25 December 1951; LAM, 25 December 1951; Rasmussen, Cecilia, "The 'Bloody Christmas' of 1951," LAT, 21 December 1997.

Page 239, *News photographers were* ... RLW interview with Harry Watson, 14 June 1999, Tujunga, California.

Page 240, Watson was subpoenaed ... RLW interview with Harry Watson, 14 June 1999, Tujunga, California; RLW interview with Nieson Himmel, 6 June 1998, Los Angeles, California.

Page 240, *For all the* ... LADN, 25 December 1951; LAHE, 25 December 1951; LAM, 25 December 1951.

Page 240, *On 22 April* ... LAE, 23 April 1952; LAE, 20 May 1952.

Page 241, *In all, Parker* ... Rasmussen, Cecilia, "The 'Bloody Christmas' of 1951," LAT, 21 December 1997; Shaw, David, "Onetime Allies: Press and LAPD," LAT, 24 May 1992; Shaw, David, "Chief Parker Molded LAPD Image," LAT, 25 May 1992.

Page 241, *The intense coverage* ... RLW interview with Harry Watson, 14 June 1999, Tujunga, California.

Page 242, *The wreck was* ... Rasmussen, Cecilia, "A Tragedy's Legacy for LAPD, Media," LAT, 8 February 1998; Strobel, Ronnie, "Horrible Rail Carnage Described by Reporter," LAMN, 23 January 1956; LAMN, 24 January 1956; LAE, 23 January 1956; LAE, 24 January 1956; LAT, 23 January 1956.

Page 242, *The old warhorse* ... LAE, 24 January 1956.

Page 242, *Mirror reporter Ronnie* ... Strobel, Ronnie, "Horrible Rail Carnage Described by Reporter," LAMN, 23 January 1956.

Page 242, *The disaster was* ... RLW interview (telephone) with Coy Watson, 12 October 1997; RLW interview with Harry Watson, 14 June 1999, Tujunga, California; RLW interview with Cliff Dektar (telephone), 3 May 1999.

Page 242, *It was a* ... LAE, 13 March 1956; Rasmussen, Cecilia, "A Tragedy's Legacy for LAPD, Media," LAT, 8 February 1998.

Other source material on Mickey Cohen include:

Clarke, John, "How Cohen got into gambling," LADN, 29 July 1949; Clarke, John, "Mickey's Chicago flight told," LADN, 30 July 1949; Clarke, John, "Time running out for Cohen," LADN, 3 August 1949; memo to *Daily News* city desk, 15 August 1947, SC UCLA; LAT, 20 March 1958; LAE, 27 November 1959; LAE, 4 December 1959; LAHE, 16 June 1959; LA, 2 October 1959; LAHE, 1 October 1959; LAE, 18 July 1959; LAE, 23 June 1960; LAHE, 28 March 1960.

Additional source material on the Turner/Crane/Stompanato case include:

LAE, 5 April 1958; LAE, 6 April 1958

Addtional source material on the "Bloody Christmas" scandal include:

LAE, 5 August 1952; LAT, 16 September 1952; LAE, 21 October 1952; LAE, 17 December 1952.

Chapter Ten

Page 245, *Since 1935, the* ... Adler, Donald H., "Management Aspects of Estalishing and Operating a Recently Organized Daily City Newspaper in Los Angeles," A Thesis Presented to the Faculty of the Department of Managment The University of Southern California, USC, June 1950; Gotlieb, Robert and Wolt, Irene, Thinking Big: The Story of the Los Angeles *Times*, Its Publishers and Their Influence in Southern California, G.P. Putnam's Sons, New York, New York, 1977.

Page 245, *But what made* ... Adler, Donald H., "Management Aspects of Estalishing and Operating a Recently Organized Daily City Newspaper in Los Angeles," A Thesis Presented to the Faculty of the Department of Managment The University of Southern California, USC, June 1950.

Page 247, *Pinkley arrived in* ...FN 23 April 1948, Vol. 4, p. 21; FN, 4 June 1948, Vol. 4, pp. 10-11; Watson, Campbell, "Parton Fumes at Talk of Revolutionary Daily," E&P, 12 June 1948, Vol. 81, p. 16.

Page 247, *The San Fernando* ... Watson, Campbell, "L.A.'s Five Dailies Battle for Circulation," E&P, 16 July 1949, Vol. 82, p. 26.

Page 247, *The Daily News* ... *ibid.*

Page 248, *J. Walter Thompson* ... Donald Adler thesis.

Page 248, *In the beginning* ... E&P, 16 October, 1948, Vol. 81, p. 8; Printers' Ink, 15 October 1948, Vol. 225, p. 93; "Tabloid Outlook," Business Week, 22 October 1949; Watson, Campbell, "*Mirror*'s Bow on Oct. 11 Opens 'Battle of L.A.,' "E&P, 9 October 1948, Vol. 81, p. 13.

Page 249, *On Monday, 11* ... *ibid.*

Page 250, *And two weeks* ... "Hearst vs. L.A. *Mirror*" *Newsweek*, 8 November 1948, Vol. 32, pp. 56, 58.

Page 253, *Despite the brouhaha* ... FN, 24 September 1948, Vol. 5, p. 20.

Page 253, *Editorially, the Mirror* ... LAM, 11 October 1948.

Page 254, *Predictably, Pinkley chose* ... RLW interview with Cliff Dektar, 29 January 1997, Los Angeles, California; RLW interview with Kendis Rochlen (telephone), 20 September 1997; Gotlieb, Robert and Wolt, Irene, Thinking Big: The Story of the Los Angeles *Times*, Its Publishers and Their Influence in Southern California, G.P. Putnam's Sons, New York, New York, 1977.

Page 254, *Joining these veterans* ... .. RLW interview with Cliff Dektar, 29 January 1997, Los Angeles, California; Goldstein, Patrick, "The Resurrection of Jim Thompson" LAT, 11 March 1990.

Page 254, *Delmar Watson was* ... RLW interview with Delmar Watson, 13 September 1997, Hollywood, California.

Page 255, *For all of its* ... Stocker, Joseph, "Sex, Slaughter, and Liberalism," *American Mercury*, January 1953.

Page 255, *Its biggest story* ... Gotlieb, Robert and Wolt, Irene, Thinking Big: The Story of the Los Angeles *Times*, Its Publishers and Their Influence in Southern California, G.P. Putnam's Sons, New York, New York, 1977.

Page 257, *Murray enjoyed relative* ... *ibid; Time*, 15 July 1957, pp. 20-31; Cameron, Tom, "How's the L.A. *Mirror* Doing?" E&P, 21 May 1949, Vol. 82, p. 9.

Page 257, *Murray and Pinkley* ... "Personnel, Circulation, Rates, Services of U.S. *Daily* Newspapers," E&P International yearbook Number 1949, Vol. 83, pp. 25-26; "Personnel, Circulation, Rates, Services of U.S. *Daily* Newspapers," E&P International Yearbook Number 1950, Vol. 84, p. 25.

Page 258, *There was a* ... "Personnel, Circulation, Rates, Services of U.S. Daily Newspapers," E&P International Yearbook Number 1951, Vol. 85, p. 26; "Personnel, Circulation, Rates, Services of U.S. Daily Newspapers," E&P International Yearbook Number 1952, Vol. 86, p. 26; "Personnel, Circulation, Rates, Services of U.S. Daily *News*papers," Editor & Publisher International Yearbook Number 1953, Vol. 87, p. 28.

Page 259, *Despite all these* ... RLW interview with Cliff Dektar, 29 January 1997, Los Angeles, California; RLW interview with Leo Thomas Batt, 18 April 1998, Sun City, California.

Page 260, *On a June day* ... *ibid*; RLW interview with Harry Watson, 14 June 1999, Tujunga, California.

Other source material on the *Mirror* include:

Cameron, Tom "Los Angeles *Mirror* Thirves on Confidence," E&P, 15 October 1949, Vol. 82, p. 26; LAT, 13 February 1990; E&P, 25 December 1948, Vol. 81, p. 13; Watson, Campbell, "L.A.'s Five Dailies Battle for Circulation," E&P, 16 July 1949, Vol. 82, p. 26; CP, October 1948, Vol. 18, p. 48; *Sales Management*, 10 November 1948, Vol. 61, p. 168; E&P, 22 January 1949, Vol. 82, p. 41; E&P, 15 May 1949, Vol. 81, p. 62; CP, July 1949, Vol. 18, p. 10; *Business Week*, 13 November 1948; E&P, 16 July 1949, Vol. 82, p. 26; *Time*, 18 January 1954, p. 51; "Average Annual Prices of Newsprint: 1923-1954," U.S. Federal Trade Commission and the America Newspaper Publishers Association, 11 October 1966; *Mirror* house ad on circulation, LAM, 26 December 1951; "Personnel, Circulation, Rates, Services of U.S. Daily Newspapers," E&P International Yearbook Number 1948, Vol. 82, p. 26; "Personnel, Circulation, Rates, Services of U.S. Daily Newspapers," E&P Yearbook Number 1954, Vol. 88, p. 30.

Chapter Eleven

Page 263, *The fact of* ... Annual listing of *Daily News* debts and revenues, 1926-1952.

Page 264, *Midway through the* ... Taylor, Frank J. "Man With a Borrowed Shoestring," The *Saturday Evening Post*, 2 December 1944.

Page 264, *Other events beyond* ... *ibid*.

Page 265, *As the Mirror* ... RLW interview with Jack Cravens, 1 February 1997, West Covina, California; RLW interview (telephone) with Aaron Dudley, 1 June 1998; New York *Times*, 2 April 1950.

Page 265, *To accommodate the* ... "*Daily News* Negotiations on Discontinuing A.M. 1950" drawer 6A 1905 82486, office of the Los Angeles Newspaper Guild; "Comparison of *Daily News* and *Herald & Express* Editorial Departments, January 20, 1950," drawer 6A 1905 82486, office of the Los Angeles Newspaper Guild."

Page 266, *By the end* ... CP, May 1950; LAT, 2 April 1950; FN, 28 April 1950, Vol. 8, pp. 1-3; FN, 26 May 1950, Vol. 8, pp. 1-3; TGM, 28 February 1950; TGM, 31 January 1950.

Page 266, *Petty squabbling between* ... "Stockholders Publishing Co., Inc. auditor's report," 31 December 1950; "Stockholders Publishing Co., Inc. auditor's report," 31 December

1951; "Robert L. Smith letter to businessmen and advertisers," drawer 6A 1905 82486, office of the Los Angeles Newspaper Guild.

Page 267, *In 1942, Los* ... Brownell, Robert C., "The Who, What, Where, When and Why of Manchester Boddy," *Frontier*, 15 May 1950.

Page 267, *Daily News editorial* ... RLW interview with Aaron Dudley, 11 February 1999, Chino, California; RLW interview with Dudley, 16 February 1999, Chino, California; RLW interview with Paul Weeks, 8 February 1997, Oceanside, California.

Page 268, *Los Angeles newspaperman* ... Brownell, Robert C., "The Who, What, Where, When and Why of Manchester Boddy," *Frontier*, 15 May 1950; New York *Times*, 30 May 1950; *Newsweek*, 5 June 1950; *Time*, 10 April 1950; Sacramento *Bee*, 29 March 1950; New York *Times*, 1 April 1950.

Page 268, *Douglas had an* ... Sacramento *Bee*, 11 April 1950.

Page 268, *Times political editor* ... LAT, 2 April 1950.

Page 268, *In early May* ... Scobie, Ingrid Winther, Center Stage: Helen Gahagan Douglas, A Life, Rutgers University Press, New Brunswick, New Jersey, 1995; Scobie, Ingrid Winther, "Helen Gahagan Douglas: Broadway Star as California Politician," California History, December 1987.

Page 269, *The election campaign* ... LADN, 28 August 1952; *Newsweek*, 15 September 1952.

Page 269, *Looking for quick* ... LADN, 29 September 1952; CP, October 1952, Vol. 32, p. 17; *Newsweek*, 20 October 1952; FN, 10 November 1952, Vol. 13, pp. 32-33; TGM, 10 December 1952; FN, 13 October 1952, Vol. 13, p. 22.

Page 270, *But the Sunday* ... LAT, 16 April 1953; TGR, 24 April 1953, p. 1; *Time*, 27 April 1953.

Page 270, *Meanwhile, the financial* ... RLW interview (telephone) with Aaron Dudley, 1 June 1998.

Page 270, *In February, while* ... LADN, 1 February 1953; E&P, 7 February, 1953, Vol. 86, p. 11; *Newsweek*, 23 February 1953; FN, 16 February 2953; CP, March 1953.

Page 270, *Townes' reputation as* ... *Time*, 16 February 1948; FN, 4 June, 1948; CP, July 1949; CP, December 1949.

Page 271, *But Townes never* ... LAT, 16 April 1953; CP, May 1953; *Time*, 27 April 1953; RLW interview with Jack Cravens, 1 February 1997, West Covina, California.

Page 271, *Eight days after* ... FN, 11 May 1953, Vol. 14, pp. 22-23

Page 272, *By the fall* ... Hensher, Alan, unpublished manuscript on the History of the Los Angeles *Daily News*, "The Final Six Days."

Page 272, *Smith finally found* ... *Time*, 16 November 1953; LAT, 14 November 1953; Hensher, Alan, unpublished manuscript on the History of the Los Angeles *Daily News*, "The Final Six Days."

Page 273, *While Smith was* ... *New Republic*, 3 January 1949; Time, 16 November 1953; Reporter's transcripts of testimony of Clinton D. McKinnon and Albert Zugsmith at Los Angeles *Daily News* bankruptcy proceedings, 25 April and 10 May 1955.

Page 273, *Using some of ... New Republic*, 10 January 1955; "Coonradt, Frederic, "McKinnon Tells Difficulty in Getting Financial Help," E&P, 25 December 1954.

Page 273, *With Straus now* ... Reporter's transcripts of testimony of Clinton D. McKinnon and Albert Zugsmith at Los Angeles *Daily News* bankruptcy proceedings, 25 April and 10 May 1955.

Page 275, *At noon on* ... Hensher, Alan, unpublished manuscript on the History of the Los Angeles *Daily News*, "The Final Six Days."

Page 275, *While McKinnon and ... ibid.*

Page 276, *With the sales ... ibid.*

Page 277, *On Saturday afternoon* ... RLW interview with Jack Cravens, 1 February 1997, West Covina, California.

Page 277, *The news of its* ... RLW interview with Jack Jones, 10 April 1999, Carlsbad, California; RLW interview with Harry Watson, 14 June 1999, Tujunga, California.

Page 277, *On Sunday night ... ibid.*

Page 278, *Contrary to stories* ... RLW interview ("telephone") with Aaron Dudley, 20 August 1999; Los Angeles *Daily News* organizational chart, December 1954(courtesy Aaron Dudley).

Page 278, *In the end* ... RLW interview (telephone) with Aaron Dudley, 6 March 1999.

Page 279, *Local union leaders* ... Bassett, W.J., "Bassett Says," LAC, 24 December 1954; LAC, 24 December 1954; Bassett, W.J., "Basset Says: Open Letter to Virgil Pinkley, editor the *Mirror-Daily News*," LAC, 31 December 1954.

Page 279, *Mirror-News publisher* ... Pinkley, Virgil, "An Editorial," LAMN, 20 December 1954; Pinkley, Virgil "Some Facts About *Mirror-Daily News*," LAMN, 21 December 1954; Pinkley, Virgil, "For Your Information: All About the *Daily News*, Our Policy and Why," LAMN, 25 December 1954.

Page 279, *Matt Weinstock looked* ... Weinstock, Matt, "A Newspaper Dies Hard," Matt Weinstock column, 21 December1954, LAMN.

Other source material on the final years of the *Daily News* include:

E&P, 12 February 1951; E&P, 15 September 1951; FN, 4 June 1948, Vol. 4, pp. 11-12; *Time*, 24 September 1951; E&P, 21 November 1953, Vol. 86, p. 12; CP, June 1955; E&P, 25 December 1954; E&P International Year Book Number, 1949, 1950, 1951, 1952; LAT, 31 December 1957; AH interview with Robert E.G. Harris, 24 January 1966, Los Angeles, California; *Time*, 16 November 1953; LAT, 17 November 1953 Carpenter, Bill, "Los Angeles: The Death of the News," *New Republic*, 10 January 1955.

Chapter Twelve

Page 281, *Examiner reporter Will* ... RLW interview with Will Fowler, 1 February 1997, Sherman Oaks, California; Fowler, Will, Reporters: Memoirs of a Young Newspaperman , Roundtable Publishing Company, Malibu, California, 1991.

Page 281, *A little more* ... RLW interview with Margaret Boutyette Scott, 24 January 1998, North Hollywood, California; RLW interview (telephone) with Kendis Rochlen, 30 August 1997.

Page 282, *When rescuers determined* ... RLW interview (telephone) with Kendis Rochlen, 30 August 1997.

Page 282, *Print reporters in*... RLW interview with Harry Watson, 14 June 1999, Tujunga, California.

Page 283, *But Governor Nelson* ... *ibid.*

Page 283, *The eviction process* .. LAMN, 15 May 1959; LAE, 9 May 1959; LAE, 16 May 1959; LAE, 14 May 1959; LAMN, 13 May 1959; LAE, 14 May, 1959; LAHE, 15 May 1959; LAT, 13 May 1959; LAT, 15 May 1959; LAE, 19 May 1959; LAE, 12 May 1959; LAE, 9 May 1959; LAT, 21 April 1959.

Page 284, *The urge to* ... RLW interview (telephone) with Paul Weeks, 3 May 1999.

Page 287, *Though Norman Chandler* ... Gottlieb, Robert and Wolt, Irene, Thinking Big: The Story of the Los Angeles *Times*, Its Publishers and Their Influence in Southern California, G.P. Putnam's Sons, New York, New York, 1977.

Page 287, *Now relying on* ... Bagdikian, Ben, "Why Dailies Die," *New Republic*, 16 April 1962; Bliven, Bruce, "Two Newspapers in Search of a City," *The Reporter*, 26 April 1962.

Page 287, *But even before* ... RLW interview with Cliff Dektar (telephone), 3 May 1999.

Page 287, *Norman Chandler found* ... Gottlieb, Robert and Wolt, Irene, Thinking Big: The Story of the Los Angeles *Times*, Its Publishers and Their Influence in Southern California, G.P. Putnam's Sons, New York, New York, 1977.

Page 288, *In March 1960* ... LAMN, 23 March 1960.

Page 288, J. Edward Murray ... LAMN, 8 July 1960; LAMN, 2 August 1960; LAMN, 5 August 1960; Gottlieb, Robert and Wolt, Irene, Thinking Big: The Story of the Los Angeles *Times*, Its Publishers and Their Influence in Southern California, G.P. Putnam's Sons, New York, New York, 1977.

Page 288, *The Mirror-News* ... LAT, 19 November 1961.

Page 289, *In the end* ... Gewecke, Clifford G., "The World As Seen Through Los Angeles Editorials, 1939-40 and 1954-55," a thesis presented to the faculty of the Graduate School of USC, January 1956.

Page 290, *Rumors in both* ... LAT, 1 March 1961; E&P, 6 January 1962; E&P, 13 January 1962; Gottlieb, Robert and Wolt, Irene, Thinking Big: The Story of the Los Angeles *Times*, Its Publishers and Their Influence in Southern California, G.P. Putnam's Sons, New York, New York, 1977.

Page 291, *The effects of* ... Pitt, Leonard and Dale, Los Angeles A to Z: An Encyclopedia of the City and County, University of California Press, Berkeley, California, 1997.

Other source material on the final years of the *Mirror*-News include:

"*Mirror-News* Now over 308,000 Circulation," house advertisement, 2 November 1955; LAMN, 11 November 1957.

Index

The Author

Rob Leicester Wagner began his journalism career in 1974 at his hometown newspaper in Sierra Madre, California. He has worked as a reporter, city editor, night editor, and managing editor for daily newspapers in Los Angeles, Riverside, San Bernardino, and San Diego counties. He also authored fifteen books on regional, film and automotive history. Mr. Wagner's grandfather, Les Wagner, was a newspaperman for more than forty years. His great-grandfather, Rob Wagner, was editor and publisher of *Rob Wagner's Script*, a literary film magazine. Mr. Wagner lives in Riverside, California, with his wife, Deniece, and their three children — Nicholas, Selena, and Danielle.